The Handicapped in Literature

A Psychosocial Perspective

Edited by Eli M. Bower
University of California, Berkeley

LOVE PUBLISHING COMPANY
Denver · London

All rights reserved. No part of this publication may be reproduced, stored in a retrieval system or transmitted, in any form or by any means, electronic, mechanical, recording or otherwise, without the prior written permission of the publisher.

Copyright © 1980 Love Publishing Company
Printed in the U.S.A.
ISBN 0-89108-098-8
Library of Congress Catalog Card Number 79-57278
10   9   8   7   6   5   4   3   2   1

To Phyllis

Foreword

The student says that what is taught as psychology is common sense made erudite by verbiage. A nationally known child development expert declares that the fate of psychology is to know more and more about less and less. Perhaps these are only testament of adult failure. Perhaps the state of psychological ignorance need not remain. Children demonstrate that psychological awareness is not foreign to the human species until we make an academic mess of it. Mischel, Mischel, and Walter, in an article in the *American Psychologist,* reported that youngsters understood much of the basic psychological knowledge that we teach as academic courses.[1] They learned about human nature by studying the behavior of people around them. What happened to insight we once possessed as children when we become adults? How best can we get that insight back again? Children develop meaningful understanding of human behavior both because such knowledge is necessary to negotiate their lives and because they use a laboratory setting wherein they observe how people behave in real life. They deal first in persons, not in theoretical abstractions. Most children do quite well in recognizing and accepting individual differences, too. For the young child human variation is a fact of life, even when it comes to handicapped children.

Adult survival, just as with children, is more and more dependent upon our understanding and accepting humankind in all of its varieties. We read of persons with views that diverge from those we hold. We make tragic mistakes in appreciating what makes people behave the way they do. We cannot better understand, empathize, and accept another without a corollary of our own self-awareness and self-acceptance. Interestingly, adults make almost as many mistakes in relating to those we know best — even those with whom we live intimately — as we do with those on the other side of the globe. Psychological ignorance knows no geography. There must be a better way to cultivate

---

[1] "On the Interface of Cognition and Personality," *American Psychologist* 34, 9 (1979):740-754.

understanding and empathy than the traditional psychology textbook!

It is hardly news that able writers, dramatists, and poets tell us more about mankind and ourselves than the psychological textbooks. In fact, it has been held that Freud's hold on psychology is based more on his dramatic sense of the human dilemma than on his specific notions.[2] He touched off our awareness of the struggles in us and in others. He dealt with actual people and the drama of the inner lives they lived.

In depicting the human dilemma, a literary account is often more vivid than even our everyday experiences because essentials are winnowed from the ephemeral and highlighted. We are left with the human essence, which carries the meaning far richer and more poignant than one sees in the helter skelter of fortuitous observation. The artistic gift is the revelation of psychological meaning in context. If this is correct, the way to human understanding is to be found in creative literary writing.

Right now there is no segment of humanity more in need of such humanistic understanding than the focus of this book — the handicapped. The law of the land says that such persons, young or old, must not suffer discrimination in either schools or community. All citizens, and particularly regular and special teachers, are affected by these sanctions. Special education, travesty though it may be, has largely left out the *person*. Special services are currently possessed by a cohort of demons: the testing demon, the manipulate others demon, the vapid IEP demon, the target behavior demon, the artificial classification demon, advocating demon, simple-minded curricula demon, and token giving demon. Special education stands at the top of all the teaching fields where the helper should know both one's own life and the lives of those to be given assistance. The way to understand the nature of the special education task is to *know* the children and youth. One excellent way to know them is to experience their lives, drawn taut by the sensitivity and insight of the literary masters. That is the "why" of this book. It does not stop with information; it arouses and activates empathic feelings for handicapped.

That Eli Bower should produce such a volume is natural and fitting. In the first place, his humanistic identification with special education is long. It covers activity in many settings ranging

---

[2] See Jerome S. Bruner, "Freud and the Image of Man," *American Psychologist* 11 (1956):463-466.

from "hands on" to national policy determination. He has seen various movements explode like sky rockets, into sparks and darkness. He knows how slow is accomplishment and how painful is progress. He is not mesmerized into believing the job is done by laws and new procedures. Because he has always been a humanist, his focus has remained on the human experience in special education.

That would explain Bower's motivation, but there is also the matter of competency. An omnivorous reader and constant literary observer, he has always been sensitive to literature as a source of real psychological understanding. His writings have always contained such references. His conversation is counterpoint psychology and literature. The study of modern and classic drama, one step bolder in depicting personality, constitutes one of his preoccupations. Because he is an iconoclastic psychologist and special educator in addition to being well read, he is the one to compile this book.

The ten selections — each by a writer of renown — cover a great many conditions. There are two ways to use these selections. One is the direct experience one gets from joining another life — reading is in itself rewarding. The other way to use the book is by adding to one's own experience the wisdom of a senior scholar in the field of special education. Bower has given us valuable insights and reflections in the introductory and concluding commentary accompanying each selection. Ordinarily, one would expect a set of questions on such material to somehow jar the experience out of phase. Ordinary questions would. But the questions Bower has posed are seminar "think" type questions, provocative questions. It is next best to having an evening discussion with him.

William C. Morse
University of Michigan

Preface

A preface offers one the opportunity to apologize for one's sins before the reader is fully aware of them. When I first started working on this collection of readings, I had no clear idea of what I was trying to do. As explained more fully in the introduction, I finally selected the ten works used in this book and examined them and myself carefully to determine how I and they had come together.

Let me say at the outset (who's to stop me?) that none of the selections came to mind as an illustration, an example, or a clinical fable of this or that kind of handicap. Rather, they were — as I look back — the most interesting and mind-stretching of the lot, to me. Each story and its people orbited around what we in Western Culture, circa 1980, call a handicapped person. In some of the stories, the handicapped person was quite normal under normal circumstances but handicapped by other factors. With the exception of two nonfiction pieces, all the stories were products of lively and creative imaginations. In some ways the two true stories seem more unreal than the fiction — calling to mind Mark Twain's observation that the difference between truth and fiction is that fiction has to be sensible.

What I had in mind in my selections, commentary, and discussion questions were specific themes related to the handicapped and nonhandicapped. These were:

* A person's potential to fully realize his or her human capacities is shaped by that person's biological, psychological, and cultural integrity. Loss of or significant reduction of such integrity changes the person, associated persons, and the ensuing relationships.

* Sensory, motor, intellectual, and emotional losses of integrity in a person can lead to significant and predictable outcomes to self and others. Such predictable outcomes are played out in unpredictable ways.

* Cultures and societies act to enhance, penalize, and in some cases define persons with handicaps. In the Country of the Blind, the culture looks upon the one-eyed man as a blithering idiot!

* Sensory, motor, intellectual, and emotional losses of integrity in a person can be serious in themselves. But, generally, the

emotional, inter- and intra-personal consequences are more crucial to self and others.

    * All cultures (i.e., social prescribers of values and behavior) bestow varying degrees of acceptance and support upon those handicapped by the culture's own norms. Literature can help widen the norms and reduce the standard deviations.

    Some among us will see John Singer's deafness, Stevie Verloc's retardation, Scott Moss' aphasia, Dale Maple's scholarly brilliance, and many of the others as case or class examples of this or that kind of handicap. This is not intended to be so, nor is it so. The handicapped persons and others in the stories are part of a time, place, and set of circumstances in which events are played out interestingly — not always happily, but with a pressing theme: If this "handicapped" person had not existed at this time in this setting, what then? For example, in Joseph Conrad's *The Secret Agent* fifteen-year-old Stevie is retarded and is seen as needing care and supervision by his sister, Winnie Verloc. She, in turn, cajoles and goads her husband to accept the boy as his son. Stevie's mother sacrifices her home with the Verlocs in an attempt to help Stevie gain acceptance in that household. All of these human forces meet at a strange and tragic crossroad. Stevie inadvertently becomes the hub around which these lives circle and crash. Might they have spun to the same destiny if Stevie had not been handicapped?

    None of the writers represented in this volume deemed themselves experts on the handicapped. All of the protagonists save two are realities of the human mind. When Carson McCullers was writing *The Heart is a Lonely Hunter,* which is about two deaf persons, her husband suggested that she might wish to attend a convention of the "deaf and dumb" being held in a nearby city, to check out her fictionalized characters. Carson declined, pointing out that her people had reality and authenticity in her mind — which was real enough for her.

    What you learn from what you read is up to you. Keep in mind that what you are about to read are stories. They are intended to be interesting and provocative. Transcending the possible learning and interest in subject, the reading is intended to be enjoyable. As an old Scot noted, "It's a dry tale that doesna end in a drink."

Eli M. Bower
January 1980

x

Contents

Introduction

Somewhere along the evolutionary trail our present-day readers and writers became symbol inventors and users. For those who need reasons for this interesting occurrence, it might have been an attempt to bridge the gap between our inner world of dreams and our outer realities. In any case, groups of people all over the earth developed structures called language, by which we were able to express fears, hopes, and dreams, and at the same time describe the objects and forces facing us in the outer world. In time we learned to look at ourselves as objects although, as Freud pointed out, we were and are highly resistant to such investigations.

Although languages were in general made up of similar structures and had some translatability from one to another, it became apparent that the utility of language was compromised by its degrees of meaning. From the basic realization of language, however, we were able to discover and explore new kinds of language that enabled us to share new kinds of knowing. Literature was one way of knowing; science (derived from mathematical language) became another. Each of these languages functions within its own conceptual and metaphorical constraints. Occasionally they meet at strange crossroads. Such a crossroad is the handicapped person.

The crossroad meetings do not in any way destroy or subvert the goals and premises of the respective languages. Science is concerned with what is empirical, observable, replicable, and generalizable; literature is concerned with the creation of human, empathic identities grasping at all the cognitive-emotional insides of readers. Each seeks truth in its own fashion. One seeks data; the other seeks clear images.

Several years ago a psychologist interviewing the playwright Arthur Miller asked him how he figured out the psychological connections between the characters in his plays. Miller unashamedly confessed that he didn't figure out anything — he just imagined it. Well, then, asked the psychologist, on the basis of what psychological theory had he imagined the relationships — Jungian, Freudian, Watsonian, Piagetian, or what? Miller had to

1

remind the psychologist that Oedipus, before he became a complex, was a character in a Greek play, and that Shakespeare was writing plays with Freudian or Jungian themes before either of these psychologists had been born.[1] Science has a way of confirming what some men have known in unscientific ways.

There is another facet to the processes of "knowing" that makes the crossroads meeting of science and literature significant: Science and scientists "do their thing" in cognitive domains. Good writers are, of course, highly cognitive craftsmen, but their major task is to help us *feel* and *experience*. Research psychiatrists and psychologists may marshal all that is known about a psychotic episode and describe such a phenomenon exactly and completely. This is one kind of knowing. Another is to read Conrad Aiken's "Silent Snow, Secret Snow," and to experience and feel with Paul, a twelve-year-old:

> The darkness was coming in long white waves. A prolonged sibilance filled the night — a great seamless seethe of wild influence went abruptly across it — a cold low humming shook the windows . . . The bare black floor was like a little raft tossed in waves of snow, almost overwhelmed, washed under whitely, up again, smothered in curled billows of feather. The snow was laughing; it spoke from all sides at once; it pressed closer to him as he ran and jumped exulting into bed.[2]

Can sibilances fill the night? What indeed is a "seamless seethe" or a "cold humming?" What do such wild fancies have in common with scientific descriptions such as: (1) tends to lose contact with reality; (2) often hears voices; (3) withdraws from relationships? Is Paul a scientifically accurate example of a psychotic episode? Is the previous question useful, heuristic, or answerable?

A junior high school student was discussing her English assignment with her father. The assignment was to read certain short stories and explain the title and meaning of each. This she could do except for one story by Dorothy Parker called, "Clothe the Naked." She asked her father (the fount of knowledge and

---

[1] Arthur Miller, "The Writer as Independent Spirit," *Saturday Review*, 4 June, 1966.

[2] Conrad Aiken, "Silent Snow, Secret Snow," *Collected Short Stories* (New York: World Publishing Co., 1922), p. 6.

funds) to read the story and share his meaning with her. . . How does one do justice to Big Lannie and Raymond, her blind grandson? What can one say about a child who is beaten by laughter? Under usual conditions blind children do not walk about with their head up high. But Raymond does. Furthermore, the reader comes to *know* Big Lannie and Raymond. . . All the father could say to his daughter was that the story is about what made the people in it feel good and bad. "But what does it mean?" the girl persisted. "I don't know what it means to you," the father replied, "but it gives me a sense of horror coupled with an overriding sense of the dignity of people even under inhuman conditions." She looked at him. "What do I tell my teacher?" The father continued on somewhat haltingly with vague references to listening to music, emotional responses citing Spinoza, Freud, and Rogers. "Well," concluded the daughter, "I guess you don't know what the story means either."

In much the same vein I recall attending one of the opening performances of Samuel Beckett's play *Waiting for Godot* at the Marines Memorial Theatre in San Francisco. Eavesdropping in the lobby during intermission, I was struck by the anger and frustration of most of the patrons. A character in the play, Estragon, had lamented, "Nothing happens, nobody comes, nobody goes — it's awful" — a sentiment apparently shared by most of the audience. Some weeks later the cast was invited to perform the play at San Quentin, a residential institution for men (the invitation having been tendered because members of the cast were all males). The actors were somewhat concerned about audience reaction — especially when considering the limitations on walking out or being refunded. Not to worry — the San Quentin audience was enthralled and excited. They *knew* what the play was about — waiting or, as this audience knew it, "serving time." The meaning of Beckett's play was as immediately "known" to them as it was highly mystical to the San Francisco audience.

Good literature has the capacity to contribute to one's knowledge, a knowing that in some ways is like knowing a culture after living in it as opposed to reading about it — yet, not quite. While one feels completely taken over by good literature and the people one meets therein, one still needs to be free to enter into imagination and experience. As a scientist, I could on occasion fault Dorothy Parker for misleading me on this or that detail; but no matter — everything about her story was *real*.

Occasionally, someone like Lindauer suggests that one kind of knowing (science) should investigate the other kind of knowing.

Literature, he says in his introduction to the *Psychological Study of Literature*, should be looked at from a scientific point of view in which the main focus will be "the systematic and objective collection of empirical data, the reliance on facts which can be measured, counted and statistically described and analyzed . . ."[3] I suppose one can subject literature to scientific analyses as one can art, music, or religion — or even God. It is easy to understand God — if we just don't try to explain her or him!

Literature is about people and so is science. Art is I; science is we. Creative imagination is indeed open to creative investigation. Dorothy Parker's blind Raymond may not have fit the scientific picture of blind children, but it did fit Raymond. One cannot impose one kind of conceptual framework upon another having different assumptions and goals without the danger of destroying both, or, as Crews suggests, the result may be much like the "uninvited guest whose muddy boots will smudge the figure on the carpet."[4]

One can, if one wishes, subject Joseph Conrad's creation of a retarded boy, Stevie Verloc, to scientific study. Some of my colleagues suggest that Conrad may not have known much about mental retardation. Indeed, little was known or understood about this condition early in the twentieth century. Yet, Stevie is there, an "I" who speaks in his own way to the "we" of others like him. Of more recent vintage is Algernon Pendleton, whose secret life might be regarded as somewhat schizophrenic. Here again, some of my clinical colleagues beat their empirical heads against soft walls in their scientific scrutiny of Algernon's behavior. Others are appalled by the author's light or frivolous approach to some of life's serious problems. Is Algernon for real? He is to me.

THE RATIONALE

The field of exceptional children is presently awash with stately and comprehensive textbooks, research monographs, and other learned treatises. Most are informative and helpful to students, pre-professionals, and professionals. They present what

---

[3] M. S. Lindauer, *The Psychological Study of Literature: Limitations, Possibilities and Accomplishments* (Chicago: Nelson Hall, 1974), p. IX.

[4] F. Crews, "Literature and Psychology," *Relations of Literary Study*, ed. James Thorpe (New York: Modern Language Assn., 1967).

we know scientifically about sensory, motor, intellectual, and emotional handicaps. The narratives in these books are consistent with their purpose to present what is scientifically known. When necessary, I can follow the straight and true pathways of these books and hold on to the data for quite some time. But when I can add to this the passion and wholeness I felt when reading Helen Keller's recounting of her first experience with language or seeing it happen in *The Miracle Worker,* all my "knowings" seem satisfied.

We need and search for a balance between these kinds of knowing — the artistic/literary and the empirical/scientific. To some degree this volume is an effort to keep the seesaw on an even keel and add weight to Walt Whitman's notion of a book: "Books are to be call'd for and supplied on the assumption that the process of reading is not a half sleep but in the highest sense an exercise, a gymnast's struggle; that the reader is to do something for himself."[5]

It doesn't take long to discover that reading stories is generally preferable to reading textbooks or misty, dusty research reports. But not all stories are enjoyable and, conversely, some research reports can indeed be thrilling. So when I set out to put this group of readings together, my major goal was to select what was, in my judgment, the best writing and reading about handicapped persons. I did allow a few less significant goals to temper my enthusiasm. I did not want selections to be repetitive or to concentrate too heavily on one or another handicapping condition. I wanted all readers — be they interested parents, students, or professionals — to be "grabbed" by the selections. Overall, I sought a collection that offered an integrative and empathetic opportunity for readers interested in this field personally, professionally, or intellectually.

Enjoyment as a goal is an arrogant assertion that you will enjoy what I enjoy. For me to tell you that I have read and enjoyed all these selections as literature is easy enough. The stories have set me to thinking and feeling about certain handicapped children and adults I have known personally and professionally. In some instances the stories have produced a "gymnast's struggle" to work something out for myself. Some of these struggles are still going on.

---

[5] Walt Whitman, "Democratic Vistas 1870," in *A New Dictionary of Quotations,* ed. H. L. Mencken (New York: Knopf, 1962), p. 118.

THE SEARCH

When I first planned an introductory course on the psychology and education of handicapped persons, I was convinced that the usual this-is-what-you-need-to-know about the physically handicapped, the blind, the speech impaired, or mentally retarded would not fill the bill. My students at Berkeley, like many undergraduates in the 'sixties and 'seventies, thirsted for intellectual stimulation, an opportunity for commitment, and a chance to taste or bite into a field or proposed career. Most of the texts covered and uncovered the data comprehensively but, true to their purpose and goals, without punch or passion. My first attempt to supplement this deficiency was to find ways of having each student work with a handicapped child or adult in a school, community agency, or hospital. It became mandatory for students enrolled in the course to serve from three to as many volunteer hours as possible (with commensurate credit, of course) helping the handicapped. Students who worked with children or adults having somewhat similar handicaps met together and with me to crystallize and integrate their experiences. Most importantly, class members had the chance to share and exchange doubt and meaning arising from their experiences.

The standard texts provided the facts, and the volunteer service offered the experience. But this was not enough. There was a need for more integrative glue, the mystery and search for "the still sad music of humanity" that could make students feel and experience as the San Quentin residents did in *Waiting for Godot*. One year I decided to use the Long, Morse, Newman book *Conflict in the Classroom* for sections of the course dealing with emotionally handicapped children.[6] In the evaluation of their course experience, student comments on the book were unanimous on how helpful the first part of the book had been — the part made up of selections from literature about persons with mental and emotional disorders. One boy described the power and insight he had gained about the imperious nature of psychosis through Conrad Aiken's "Silent Snow, Secret Snow"; another related the relationship of a physical handicap to feelings of inadequacy through reading the selection from *Of Human Bondage*. Then there was Dickens' delightful portrait of David Copperfield's mildly retarded first wife, Dora, who most sagaciously

---

[6] Nicholas J. Long, William C. Morse, Ruth G. Newman, *Conflict in the Classroom*, 3rd ed. (Belmont, CA: Wadsworth Publishing Co., 1976).

informs David when he tries to change her, "It's better for me to be stupid than uncomfortable." The students were quite convincing in their praise of this kind of reading.

A substantial amount of such literature is available. The problem, for me, was to identify which was suitable, usable, honest, heuristic, and compassionate. Thus, I launched a search for the best and the most appropriate literature on the handicapped to assign undergraduates in a beginning course on handicapped children and adults. I sought help from my colleagues, principally faculty members in the Departments of English, Literature, and Comparative Literature (including Mid-East, Slavic, Scandanavian, Hispanic, and others). I directed the following written communication to them:

Since 1968 I have been involved in teaching and research on the psychology, development, and education of handicapped children and youth. In the process of developing such programs, I have been struck by the positive response of students to literature (novels, plays, poems, autobiographies, biographies, and letters) describing the world and experience of handicapped persons. For example, instead of delineating a host of studies on the impact of an orthopedic handicap, one reads:

But meanwhile he had grown horribly sensitive. He never ran if he could help it because he knew it made his limp more conspicuous and he adopted a peculiar walk. . . . Because he could not join in the games which other boys played, their life remained strange to him; he only interested himself from the outside in their doings; and it seemed to him that there was a barrier between them and him.

So Somerset Maugham goes on to describe Philip in *Of Human Bondage:*

But he had grown very self-conscious. The newborn child does not realise that his body is more a part of himself than surrounding objects and will play with his toes without any feeling that they belong to him more than a rattle by his side; and it is only by degrees, through pain, that he understands the fact of the body.

(What follows the above is an excellent description of the inner world of Philip and his experiences at school as a "club-footed blockhead".)

I would like to put together readings like these and others that would help undergraduate and graduate students empathize as well as cognitize the problems and processes of handicapped individuals in our culture. By the term "handicapped" I include the following:

Sensory handicaps

Blind and partially seeing
Deaf and hard of hearing
Stroke victims who are affected by hearing, sight, speech, or
   orthopedic loss

Motor handicaps

Speech and articulation problems including stuttering
Ambulatory problems including plastic, paraplegic, quadri-
   plegic, and palsied conditions
Touching, feeling, or grasping problems as a result of ampu-
   tation, neurological impairment, or injury

Mental or emotional handicaps

Mental retardation of all types
Emotional disorders (behavior problems, neuroses, psychoses)
Hereditary conditions relating to mental retardation or mental
   disorder such as Huntington's chorea (as in Eugene
   O'Neill's *Strange Interlude*)

Social handicaps

Cultural deviancies that may dispose children toward handicaps
Maladaptive problems including juvenile delinquency
Gifted and talented children who have unusual difficulties.

I am hoping that you or someone you might know can help me identify specific works of literature that address themselves in part or in whole to the topic areas outlined above. We are, of course, doing a library search ourselves but, as you might guess, this kind of information is not the kind one readily obtains in indices or abstracts.

Please feel free to share this request with friends and colleagues who you think might be helpful.

I was also fortunate in obtaining the interest and help of a graduate student, Mrs. Judy Lepire, who sank her teeth into the problem and began to separate and identify the digestible, assimilatable possibilities. We compiled and read novels, short stories, plays, poems, essays, biographies, and autobiographies. We ate popcorn and watched films. The challenge we had raised to faculty and other friends, students, and relatives was met graciously and handsomely. Many responded by offering to assist through the teaching and discussion of a particular short story or novel. Almost all were intrigued and interested in the possibilities of such encounters.

At the end of the first year, Judy Lepire and I had compiled and categorized more than 300 good prospects for such a reader. At this point I departed on a Fulbright Fellowship to search for more material in the bazaars and bistros of Istanbul and Boğaziçi University. How culture-bound were some of the "great" works? Would students of other cultures respond in the same cognitive and affective manner as those at Berkeley, Illinois, Georgia, or Colorado? Could a southern story like *The Heart is a Lonely Hunter* or the Vonnegut fantasy "Harrison Bergeron" be compassionately and insightfully read by culturally different students? The answer was most emphatically, yes — with requests for more. So I proceeded.

Profitable and promising books of this kind have served other fields — for example, the volume edited by Landau, Epstein, and Stone, *Child Development Through Literature*,[7] and *The Abnormal Personality Through Literature,* edited by Alan and Sue Stone.[8] Apparently the editing Stones come from different rock formations. In any case, both volumes are targeted and comprehensive selections from excellent literature — books that I had not encountered heretofore, and now only because of a sudden common interest.

Both *Child Development Through Literature* and *The Abnormal Personality Through Literature* began with the set notion

---

[7] Elliott Landau, Sherrie Epstein, and Ann Stone, eds., *Child Development through Literature* (Englewood Cliffs, NJ: Prentice-Hall, 1972).

[8] Alan Stone and Susan Stone, eds., *The Abnormal Personality Through Literature* (Englewood Cliffs, NJ: Prentice-Hall, 1966).

of illustrating specific concepts in child development or abnormal psychology. For example, the Stones in *The Abnormal Personality Through Literature* assigned themselves the comprehensive task of finding illustrations in literature for psychoses, neuroses, character disorders, struggles with impulse, schizophrenia, affective psychoses, senility, hallucinations, paranoid jealousy, autism, idio savants, hysteria, phobias, and so forth, and finally the psychotherapeutic process and psychiatry and the law. *Child Development Through Literature* is divided into three selections or excerpts for "Early Development," four for "Personality Development," seven for "Emotional Development," four for "Intellectual Development," two for "Communication," three for the "Meaning of Play," three for the "Handicapped Child," and so on.

THE SELECTIONS

This volume was not created out of a need or desire to cover an entire field or to offer readings to illustrate this or that educational or psychological theorem about handicapped children, adolescents, or adults. The persons that come alive in the following selections can in no way be said to be representatives of any handicapped population or group. They are here simply because they catch and hold one. All are known and real creations for interested and empathetic minds.

Each selection is introduced briefly and topped off at its conclusion by what many might consider useless commentary. The introduction merely tells why the piece is there and little more. The epilogue is my own reaction to the reading, to be shared with the reader as a friend might share a good movie or a hot fudge sundae. I can well remember one of my idolized professors of English Literature reading and explaining line by line the sonnet by Keats that begins, "When I have fears that I may cease to be" and Shelley's "Ozymandias." My professor's precise interpretation, enthusiasm, and sensuous sparkle added to the printed message, but as I became more confident in responding to my own thinking, I learned to listen to him differently. Similarly, the instructor and reader may take or leave the transition sections here. The introductions to each piece may be read in safety since these are mostly of an historical slant and provide a setting or stage. Actually, one probably would benefit from reading the introductions to those selections wrested from novels. Although it appears to me that these excerpts can pretty well go on their own, it might prove helpful to be filled in on significant narrative gaps.

On what bases were the final selections made? First, I wanted a combination of selections that would result in an interesting, economically sized volume of the best readings available to students and other interested readers. Selected for inclusion, then, were the pieces that I enjoyed most and that moved me the most. These were pieces with intellectual substance, thunderous and enlightening in their impact, the best literature I could find. There were sufficient excellent selections to be categorized, as follows, for those persons requiring categorization.

Severely and multiply handicapped	*Johnny Got His Gun*
Blind	"The Country of the Blind"
Deaf	*The Heart is a Lonely Hunter*
Mentally retarded	*The Secret Agent*
Emotionally Disturbed - Psychotic	*The Secret Life of Algernon Pendleton*
Dyslexic	"The Verger"
Speech impaired	*Recovery with Aphasia*
Orthopedically handicapped	*People Will Always Be Kind*
Gifted and talented, and culturally deviant	"The Philologist" *Harrison Bergeron*

All of the selections are fiction except "Recovery with Aphasia" and "The Philologist." The former is written by a clinical psychologist and his wife in a unique literary style. The latter, E. J. Kahn's true story of a gifted, creative, and troubled young man, is, to my way of thinking, a literary gem. Another selection bears special comment: I have labeled Somerset Maugham's story, "The Verger," as being about a dyslexic, but it is really a story about a man who cannot read and what happens to him. Now it is true that not much good comes to those who cannot read, be they dyslexic, reading disabled, visually handicapped, or illiterate.[9] Yet, Maugham

---

[9] For example, there is Eunice Parchman in Ruth Rendell's excellent portrayal of the tragedy of illiteracy in *A Judgement in Stone* (New York: Bantam, 1979).

11

chose to look at the bright side of things and have fun with our realities. Why not? He is not writing a scientific treatise on the subject.

Other questions I posed to myself were: (1) Why "butcher" some of these superb novels and extract the materials relevant to my subject? Why not indicate to students that they should get the books, the short stories, and read them *in toto*; (2) How much, where, and how should I lead or direct readers? Should I precede each selection with my reactions, other reactions, and ensure that all popular and unpopular interpretations are exposed? How deep should I delve into character or plot analysis?

In my reply to my first question, tracking down some of these readings proved troublesome, laborious, and at times almost impossible. Some are out of print. Many can be obtained only in large libraries, and then after extensive pursuit. If intended for use by a class or study group, only a few of these readings can be found in sufficient numbers. "Butchering" the lengthy novels irked me, but I decided that perhaps tasty morsels might lead to tastier meals.

On the other questions — I decided to tread carefully in my commentary before and after each selection without dirtying anyone's carpets or boots. My major challenge was to share with readers my own gymnastic leaps without at the same time suggesting that this is the only way to go. I firmly hold to Whitman's principle that readers ought to be encouraged to do as much for themselves as they can and wish. If you get a little lazy (as I do from time to time) some of the additional readings and discussion questions may help out. But be encouraged to try a few gymnastic leaps in your own thinking. After all, the opportunities are not that abundant.

The handicap of handicaps . . .

1

Johnny Got His Gun

Dalton Trumbo

1

Starting this volume with excerpts from Dalton Trumbo's classic anti-war novel is not exactly easing one gently into the subject matter of the handicapped, but why not plunge right in? The writing of this novel has itself an almost storybook quality to it, as does its subsequent publishing history. It was written during the fiercely anti-pacifist years of the late 1930s as a reaction to the macabre romanticism of World War I — the war "to make the world safe for democracy." Ironically, the book was first published on September 3, 1939, two days after World War II erupted. It was supposedly banned during that war, but copies were available in libraries, including Armed Forces facilities. Interestingly enough, Trumbo noted that if it had been totally banned during World War II, he would not have protested too loudly.

When the book went out of print (as it has done repeatedly) during World War II, this became a civil liberties issue with extreme rightist groups that felt the book was being suppressed by Jews, Communists, and international bankers so that Americans would not demand an immediate negotiated peace with Hitler and Mussolini. When the war ended, the book became a leftist favorite but went out of print again during the Korean War.

Where Trumbo's imagination obtained the insight and data to create Johnny Bonham is anyone's guess. Although Johnny exemplifies the horror of war, he is at the same time a moving and penetrating example of the human spirit.

All you need to know to read these excerpts is that Johnny Bonham is lying in a hospital bed, thinking.

JOHNNY GOT HIS GUN

Dalton Trumbo

He was a sick man. He was a sick man and he was remembering things. Like coming out of ether. But you'd think the telephone would stop ringing sometime. It couldn't just go on forever. He couldn't go over and over the same business of answering it and hearing his father was dead and then going home through a rainy night. He'd catch cold if he did that much more. Besides his father could only die once.

The telephone bell was just part of a dream. It had sounded different from any other telephone bell or any other sound because it had meant death. After all that bell was a particular kind of thing a very particular kind of thing as old Prof Eldridge used to say in Senior English. And a particular kind of thing sticks with you but there's no use of it sticking too close. That bell and its message and everything about it was way back in time and he was finished with it.

The bell was ringing again. Way far off as it echoing through a lot of shutters in his mind he could hear it. He felt as if he were tied down and couldn't answer it yet he felt as if he had to answer it. The bell sounded as lonesome as Christ ringing out in the bottom of his mind waiting for an answer. And they couldn't make connections. With each ring it seemed to get lonesomer. With each ring he got more scared.

He drifted again. He was hurt. He was bad hurt. The bell was fading. He was dreaming. He wasn't dreaming. He was awake even though he couldn't see. He was awake even though he couldn't hear a thing except a telephone that really wasn't ringing. He was mighty scared.

Selected excerpts from *Johnny Got His Gun,* by Dalton Trumbo. Copyright © 1959 by Dalton Trumbo. Published by arrangement with Lyle Stuart, Inc., New York.

He remembered how when he was a kid he read The Last Days of Pompeii and awakened in the middle of a dark night crying in terror with his face suffocating in the pillow and thinking that the top of one of his Colorado mountains had blown off and that the covers were lava and that he was entombed while yet alive and that he would lie there dying forever. He had that same gasping feeling now. He had that same cowardly griping in his bowels. He was unchristly scared so he gathered his strength and made like a man buried in loose earth clawing out with his hands toward air.

Then he sickened and choked and fainted half away and was dragged back by pain. It was all over his body like electricity. It seemed to shake him hard and then throw him back against the bed exhausted and completely quiet. He lay there feeling the sweat pour out of his skin. Then he felt something else. He felt hot damp skin all over him and the dampness enabled him to feel his bandages. He was wrapped in them from top to bottom. Even his head.

He really was hurt then.

The shock caused his heart to smash against his ribs. He grew prickly all over. His heart was pounding away in his chest but he couldn't hear the pulse in his ear.

Oh god then he was deaf. Where did they get that stuff about bombproof dugouts when a man in one of them could be hit so hard that the whole complicated business of his ears could be blown away leaving him deaf so deaf he couldn't hear his own heart beat? He had been hit and he had been hit bad and now he was deaf. Not just a little deaf. Not just halfway deaf. He was stone deaf.

He lay there for a while with the pain ebbing and thinking this will give me something to chew on all right all right. What about the rest of the guys? Maybe they didn't come out so lucky. There were some good boys down in that hole. How'll it seem being deaf and shouting at people? You write things on paper. No that's wrong they write things on paper to you. It isn't anything to kick up your heels and dance about but it might be worse. Only when you're deaf you're lonesome. You're godforsaken.

So he'd never hear again. Well there were a hell of a lot of things he didn't want to hear again. He never wanted to hear the biting little castanet sound of a machine gun or the high whistle of a .75 coming down fast or the slow thunder as it hit or the whine of an airplane overhead or the yells of a guy trying to explain to somebody that he's got a bullet in his belly and that his breakfast is coming out through the front of him and why won't somebody stop going forward and give him a hand only nobody can hear him they're so scared themselves. The hell with it.

Things were going in and out of focus. It was like looking into one of those magnified shaving mirrors and then moving it toward you and away from you. He was sick and probably out of his head and he was badly hurt and he was lonesome deaf but he was also alive and he could still hear far away and sharp the sound of a telephone bell.

* * *

He shot up through cool waters wondering whether he'd ever make the surface or not. That was a lot of guff about people sinking three times and then drowning. He'd been rising and sinking for days weeks months who could tell? But he hadn't drowned. As he came to the surface each time he fainted into reality and as he went down again he fainted into nothingness. Long slow faints all of them while he struggled for air and life. He was fighting too hard and he knew it. A man can't fight always. If he's drowning or suffocating he's got to be smart and hold back some of his strength for the last the final the death struggle.

He lay back quietly because he was no fool. If you lie back you can float. He used to float a lot when he was a kid. He knew how to do it. His last strength going into that fight when all he had to do was float. What a fool.

They were working on him. It took him a little while to understand this because he couldn't hear them. Then he remembered that he was deaf. It was funny to lie there and have people in the room who were touching you watching you doctoring you and yet not within hearing distance. The bandages were still all over his head so he couldn't see them either. He only knew that way out there in the darkness beyond the reach of his ears people were working over him and trying to help him.

They were taking part of his bandages off. He could feel the coolness the sudden drying of sweat on his left side. They were working on his arm. He felt the pinch of a sharp little instrument grabbing something and getting a bit of his skin with each grab. He didn't jump. He simply lay there because he had to save his strength. He tried to figure out why they were pinching him. After each pinch there was a little pull in the flesh of his upper arm and an unpleasant point of heat like friction. The pulling kept on in short little jerks with his skin getting hot each time. It hurt. He wished they'd stop. It itched. He wished they'd scratch him.

He froze all over stiff and rigid like a dead cat. There was something wrong about this pricking and pulling and friction heat. He could feel the things they were doing to his arm and yet he couldn't rightly feel his arm at all. It was like he felt inside his arm. It was like he felt through the end of his arm. The nearest thing he could think of to the end of his arm was the heel of his hand. But the heel of his hand the end of his arm was high high high as his shoulder.

Oh Jesus Christ they'd cut his left arm off.

They'd cut it right off at the shoulder he could feel it plain now.

Oh my god why did they do a thing like that to him?

They couldn't do it the dirty bastards they couldn't do it. They had to have a paper signed or something. It was the law. You can't just go out and cut a man's arm off without asking him without getting permission because a man's arm is his own and he needs it. Oh Jesus I have to work with that arm why did you cut it off? Why did you cut my arm off answer me why did you cut my arm off? Why did you why did you why did you?

He went down into the water again and fought and fought and then came up with his belly jumping and his throat aching. And all the time that he was under the water fighting with only one arm to get back he was having conversation with himself about how this thing couldn't possibly happen to him only it had.

So they cut my arm off. How am I going to work now? They don't think of that. They don't think of anything but doing it their own way. Just another guy with a hole in his arm let's cut it off what do you say boys? Sure cut the guy's arm off. It takes a lot of work and a lot of money to fix up a guy's arm.

This is a war and war is hell and what the hell and so to hell with it. Come on boys watch this. Pretty slick hey? He's down in bed and can't say anything and it's his tough luck and we're tired and this is a stinking war anyhow so let's cut the damn thing off and be done with it.

My arm. My arm they've cut my arm off. See that stump there? That used to be my arm. Oh sure I had an arm I was born with one I was normal just like you and I could hear and I had a left arm like anybody. But what do you think of those lazy bastards cutting it off?

How's that?

I can't hear either. I can't hear. Write it down. Put it on a piece of paper. I can read all right. But I can't hear. Put it down on a piece of paper and hand the paper to my right arm because I have no left arm.

My left arm. I wonder what they've done with it. When you cut a man's arm off you have to do something with it. You can't just leave it lying around. Do you send it to hospitals so guys can pick it to pieces and see how an arm works? Do you wrap it up in an old newspaper and throw it onto the junk heap? Do you bury it? After all it's part of a man a very important part of a man and it should be treated respectfully. Do you take it out and bury it and say a little prayer? You should because it's human flesh and it died young and it deserves a good sendoff.

My ring.

There was a ring on my hand. What have you done with it? Kareen gave it to me and I want it back. I can wear it on the other hand. I've got to have it because it means something it's important. If you've stolen it I'll turn you in as soon as I get these bandages off you thieving bastards you. If you've stolen it you're grave robbers because my arm that is gone is dead and you've taken the ring from it and you've robbed the dead that's what you've done. Where is my ring Kareen's ring before I go under again? I want the ring. You've got the arm isn't that enough where's my ring Kareen's ring our ring please where is it? The hand it was on is dead and it wasn't meant to be on rotten flesh. It was meant always to be on my living finger on my living hand because it meant life.

"My mother gave it to me. It's a real moonstone. You can wear it."

* * *

He thought well kid you're deaf as a post but there isn't the pain. You've got no arms but you don't hurt. You'll never burn your hand or cut your finger or smash a nail you lucky stiff. You're alive and you don't hurt and that's much better than being alive and hurting. There are lots of things a deaf guy without arms can do if he doesn't hurt so much he goes crazy from pain. He can get hooks or something for arms and he can learn to read lips and while that doesn't exactly put him on top of the world still he's not drowned in the bottom of a river with pain tearing his brain to pieces. He's still got air and he's not struggling and he's got willow trees and he can think and he's not in pain.

He couldn't understand why the nurses or whoever had charge of him wouldn't lay him out level. The lower half of him was light as a feather while his head and chest were dead weights. That was why he had thought he was drowning. His head was too low. If he could move whatever was under his legs and bring his body to an even level he'd feel better. He wouldn't have that drowning dream any more.

He started to kick out with his feet to move what was under his legs. He only started because he didn't have any legs to kick with. Somewhere just below his hip joints they had cut both of his legs off.

No legs.

No more running walking crawling if you have no legs. No more working.

No legs you see.

Never again to wiggle your toes. What a hell of a thing what a wonderful beautiful thing to wiggle your toes.

No no.

If he could only think of real things he would destroy this dream of having no legs. Steamships loaves of bread girls Kareen machine guns books chewing gum pieces of wood Kareen but thinking of real things didn't help because it wasn't a dream.

It was the truth.

That was why his head had seemed lower than his legs. Because he had no legs. Naturally they seemed light. Air is light too. Even a toenail is heavy compared to air.

He had no arms and no legs.

He threw back his head and started to yell from fright. But he only started because he had no mouth to yell with. He was so surprised at not yelling when he tried that he began to work his jaws like a man who has found something interesting and wants to test it. He was so sure the idea of no mouth was a dream that he could investigate it calmly. He tried to work his jaws and he had no jaws. He tried to run his tongue around the inside of his teeth and over the roof of his mouth as if he were chasing a raspberry seed. But he didn't have any tongue and he hadn't any teeth. There was no roof to his mouth and there was no mouth. He tried to swallow but he couldn't because he had no palate and there weren't any muscles left to swallow with.

He began to smother and pant. It was as if someone had pushed a mattress over his face and was holding it there. He was breathing hard and fast now but he wasn't really breathing because there wasn't any air passing through his nose. He didn't have a nose. He could feel his chest rise and fall and quiver but not a breath of air was passing through the place where his nose used to be.

He got a wild panicky eagerness to die to kill himself. He tried to calm his breathing to stop breathing entirely so he would suffocate. He could feel the muscles at the bottom of his throat close tight against the air but the breathing in his chest kept right on. There wasn't any air in his throat to be stopped. His lungs were sucking it in somewhere below his throat.

He knew now that he was surely dying but he was curious. He didn't want to die until he had found out everything. If a man has no nose and no mouth and no palate and no tongue why it stands to reason he might be shy a few other parts as well. But that was nonsense because a man in that shape would be dead. You couldn't lose that much of yourself and still keep on living. Yet if you knew you had lost them and were thinking about it why then you must be alive because dead men don't think. Dead men aren't curious and he was sick with curiosity so he must not be dead yet.

He began to reach out with the nerves of his face. He began to strain to feel the nothingness that was there. Where his mouth and nose had been there must now be nothing but a hole covered with bandages. He was trying to find out how far up that hole went. He was trying to feel the edges of the hole. He was grasping with the nerves and pores of his face to follow the borders of that hole and see how far up they extended.

It was like staring into complete darkness with your eyes popping out of your head. It was a process of feeling with his skin of exploring with something that couldn't move where his mind told it to. The nerves and muscles of his face were crawling like snakes toward his forehead.

The hole began at the base of his throat just below where his jaw should be and went upward in a widening circle. He could feel his skin creeping around the rim of the circle. The hole was getting bigger and bigger. It widened out almost to the base of his ears if he had any and then narrowed again. It ended somewhere above the top of what used to be his nose.

The hole went too high to have any eyes in it.

He was blind.

It was funny how calm he was. He was quiet just like a storekeeper taking spring inventory and saying to himself I see I have no eyes better put that down in the order book. He had no legs and no arms and no eyes and no ears and no nose and no mouth and no tongue. What a hell of a dream. It must be a dream. Of course sweet god it's a dream. He'd have to wake up or he'd go nuts. Nobody could live like that. A person in that condition would be dead and he wasn't dead so he wasn't in that condition. Just dreaming.

But it wasn't a dream.

He could want it to be a dream forever and that wouldn't change things. Because he was alive alive. He was nothing but a piece of meat like the chunks of cartilage old Prof Vogel used to have in biology. Chunks of cartilage that didn't have anything except life so they grew on chemicals. But he was one up on the cartilage. He had a mind and it was thinking. That's more than Prof Vogel could ever say of his cartilages. He was thinking and he was just a thing.

Oh no. No no no.

He couldn't live like this because he would go crazy. But he couldn't die because he couldn't kill himself. If he could only breathe he could die. That was funny but it was true. He could hold his breath and kill himself. That was the only way left. Except that he wasn't breathing. His lungs were pumping air but he couldn't stop them from doing it. He couldn't live and he couldn't die.

No no no that can't be right.

No no.

Mother.

Mother where are you?

Hurry mother hurry hurry hurry and wake me up. I'm having a nightmare mother where are you? Hurry mother. I'm down here. Here mother. Here in the darkness. Pick me up. Rockabye baby. Now I lay me down to sleep. Oh mother hurry because I can't wake up. Over here mother. When the wind blows the cradle will rock. Hold me up high high.

Mother you've gone away and forgotten me. Here I am. I can't wake up mother. Wake me up. I can't move. Hold me. I'm scared. Oh mother mother sing to me and rub me and bathe me and comb my hair and wash out my ears and play with my toes and clap my hands together and blow my nose and kiss my eyes and mouth like I've seen you do with Elizabeth like you must have done with me. Then I'll wake up and I'll be with you and I'll never leave or be afraid or dream again.

Oh no.

I can't. I can't stand it. Scream. Move. Shake something. Make a noise any noise. I can't stand it. Oh no no no.

Please I can't. Please no. Somebody come. Help me. I can't lie here forever like this until maybe years from now I die. I can't. Nobody can. It isn't possible.

I can't breathe but I'm breathing. I'm so scared I can't think but I'm thinking. Oh please please no. No no. It isn't me. Help me. It can't be me. Not me. No no no.

Oh please oh oh please. No no no please no. Please.

Not me.

* * *

He would be in this womb forever and ever and ever. He must remember that. He must never expect or hope for anything different. This was his life from now on every day and every hour and every minute of it. He would never again be able to say hello how are you I love you. He would never again be able

25

to hear music or the whisper of the wind through trees or the chuckle of running water. He would never again breathe in the smell of a steak frying in his mother's kitchen or the dampness of spring in the air or the wonderful fragrance of sagebrush carried on the wind across a wide open plain. He would never again be able to see the faces of people who made you glad just to look at them of people like Kareen. He would never again be able to see sunlight or the stars or the little grasses that grow on a Colorado hillside.

He would never walk with his legs on the ground. He would never run or jump or stretch out when he was tired. He would never be tired.

If the place in which he lay were burning he would simply stay there and let it burn. He would burn up with it and not be able to make a move. If he should feel an insect crawling over the stump of body that remained he could not move one finger to destroy it. If it stung him he could do nothing to ease the itch except maybe to writhe a little against his covers. And this life wouldn't last only today or tomorrow or until the end of next week. He was in his womb forever. It wasn't any dream. It was real.

He wondered how he could have come through it alive. You heard about somebody scratching his thumb and the next thing you knew he was dead. The mountain climber fell off the front stoop and fractured his skull and died by Thursday. Your best friend went to the hospital to have his appendix taken out and four or five days later you were standing beside his grave. A little germ like influenza carried off five maybe ten million people in a single winter. Then how could a guy lose his arms and legs and ears and eyes and nose and mouth and still be alive? How did you make any sense out of it?

Still there were plenty of people who had lost just their legs or just their arms and were living. So maybe it was reasonable to think that a man could live all right if he lost both his legs and his arms. If one was possible probably both were possible. The doctors were getting pretty smart especially now that they had had three or four years in the army with plenty of raw material to experiment on. If they got to you quickly enough so you didn't bleed to death they could save you from almost any kind of injury. Evidently they had got to him quickly enough.

It was fairly reasonable when you thought of it. Plenty guys had their hearing smashed from concussion. Nothing unusual about that. Lots of guys had been blinded. You even read in the papers once in a while about somebody trying to put a bullet through his temple and ending up healthy except he was blind. So his blindness made sense too. There were plenty guys in hospitals back of the lines who were breathing through tubes and plenty without chins and plenty without noses. The whole thing made sense. Only he had combined them all. The shell had simply scooped out his whole face and the doctors had got to him soon enough to keep him from bleeding to death. Just a nice clean slice of the shell that somehow missed his jugular vein and his spine.

Things had been pretty quiet for a while just before he got his. That meant the doctors in back of the lines had more time to play with him than during an offensive when guys were being brought in by the truckload. That must be it. They had picked him up quickly and hauled him back to a base hospital and all of them had rolled up their sleeves and rubbed their hands together and said well boys here's a very interesting problem let's see what we can do. After all they'd only carved up ten thousand guys back there learning how. Now they had come upon something that was a challenge and they had plenty of time so they fixed him up and tucked him back into the womb.

But why hadn't he bled to death? You'd think that with the stumps of two arms and two legs spouting blood a man could at least die. There were some mighty big veins in your legs and arms. He'd seen guys bleed to death from losing just an arm. It didn't seem reasonable the doctors could work fast enough to stop all four flows at once before a man died. Then he thought maybe I was only wounded in them just wounded a little and they were cut off later maybe to save trouble or maybe because they were infected. He remembered stories of gangrene and of soldiers found with their wounds filled with maggots. That was a very good sign. If you had a bullet in your stomach and the hole was squirming alive with maggots then you were all right because the maggots ate away the pus and kept the wound clean. But if you had the same hole and no maggots you simply festered for a while and then you had gangrene.

* * *

But there weren't many like him. There weren't many guys the doctors could point to and say here is the last word here is our triumph here is the greatest thing we ever did and we did plenty. Here is a man without legs or arms or ears or eyes or nose or mouth who breathes and eats and is just as alive as you or me. The war had been a wonderful thing for the doctors and he was the lucky guy who had profited by everything they learned. But there was one thing they couldn't do. They might be perfectly able to put a guy back into the womb but they couldn't get him out again. He was there for good. All the parts that were gone from him were gone forever. That was the thing he must remember. That was the thing he must try to believe. When that sank in he could calm down and think.

It was like reading in the paper that someone has won a lottery and saying to yourself there's a guy who won a million to one shot. You never quite believed that a man could win against such odds yet you knew he had. Certainly you never expected to win yourself even if you bought a ticket. Now he was just the reverse. He had lost a million to one shot. Yet if he read about himself in a newspaper he wouldn't be able to believe it even though he knew it was true. And he would never expect it to happen to him. Nobody expected it. But he could believe anything from now on out. A million to one ten million to one there was always the one. And he was it. He was the guy who had lost.

He was beginning to quiet down now. His thoughts were coming through a little clearer a little more connectedly. He could lie here against his sheet and put things together. He could figure out the small things that were wrong with him in addition to the great. Down somewhere near the base of his throat there was a scab that was sticking to something. By tossing his head slightly to the right and then to the left he could feel the pull of the scab. He could also feel a little tug at his forehead as if a cord had been tied around there halfway between his eye sockets and his hairline. He began to puzzle about the cord and why it pulled when he tossed his head to get the feel of the scab near his neck. In the hole which was the middle of his face he could feel nothing so it made a nice little problem. He lay there tossing to the right tossing to the left feeling the pressure and feeling the scab pull. Then he got it.

They had put a mask over his face and it was tied at the top around his forehead. The mask was evidently some sort of soft cloth and the lower part of it had stuck to the raw mucus of his face wound. That explained the whole thing. The mask was just a square of cloth tied securely and pulled down toward his throat so that the nurse in her comings and goings wouldn't vomit at the sight of her patient. It was a very thoughtful arrangement.

Now that he understood the purpose and mechanics of the mask the scab became an irritation instead of merely a curious thing. Even when he was a kid he could never let a scab quite heal over. He was always picking at it. Now he was picking at this scab by tossing his head and drawing the mask tight. But he couldn't dislodge the mask or start the scab to peeling. The task became a kind of mania with him. The place where the cloth stuck to the scab didn't hurt. It wasn't that. But the whole thing was an annoyance and a challenge and an issue of strength. If he could dislodge the mask then he was not completely helpless.

He tried to stretch his neck so he could rip the cloth from the flesh. But he couldn't stretch far enough. He found himself concentrating all his energy and all his mind on that tiny point of irritation. And then tug by tug he realized he would never be able to dislodge it. Just so small a thing as a piece of cloth stuck to his skin yet all the muscles of his body and all the power of his brain couldn't budge it. That was worse than being in the womb. Babies sometimes kicked. They sometimes turned over in their dark silent watery resting places. But he had no legs to kick with and no arms to thrash with and he couldn't turn over because he had no leverage in his body to start him rolling. He tried to shift his weight from side to side but the muscles in what was left of his thighs wouldn't flex properly and his shoulders were cut down so narrowly that they weren't any good either.

He abandoned the scab and the mask and began to scheme about turning over. He could produce a faint rocking motion but nothing more. Perhaps with practice he might increase the strength of his back and thighs and shoulders. Perhaps after one or five or twenty years he could develop such strength that the circle of his rocking would become wider and wider and wider. And then one day flipflop and he'd be turned over. If he could do this he might be able to kill himself because if the tubes which fed his lungs and stomach were of metal the weight of his body might plunge the metal into some vital organ. Or if they were soft like rubber his weight would shut them off and he would suffocate.

But all he could get out of his most violent efforts was that faint rocking motion and even to produce that made him wet with sweat and dizzy from pain. He was twenty years old and he couldn't even summon enough strength to turn over in bed. He had never been sick a day in his life. He had always been strong. He had been able to lift a box packed with sixty loaves of bread with each loaf weighing a pound and a half. He had been able to throw such a box over his shoulder and on top of a seven foot route bin without even thinking of it. He had been able to do this not only once but hundreds of times each night until his shoulders and biceps were hard as iron. And now he could only flex his thighs weakly and make a little rolling motion like a child rocking itself to sleep.

Suddenly he was very tired. He lay back quietly and thought about that other that minor injury he had begun to notice. There was a hole in his side. It was just a small hole but evidently it wouldn't heal. His legs and arms were healed and that took a lot of time. But during all that time of healing during all those weeks or months when he had been fainting in and out of things the hole in his side had remained open. He had been noticing it little by little for a long while and now he could feel it plainly. It was a patch of moisture inside a bandage and from it moisture was slipping down his left side in a slick little trail.

He remembered the time he visited Jim Tift at the military hospital in Lille. Jim had been put in a ward where there were a lot of guys who had holes here and there that wouldn't heal. Some of them had been lying there draining and stinking for months. The smell of that ward when you hit it was like the smell of a corpse you stumble over on patrol duty like the smell of a rich ripe corpse that falls open at the touch of a boot and sends up a stench of dead flesh like a cloud of gas.

Maybe he was lucky his nose was shot off. It would be pretty bad to have to lie and smell the perfume of your own body as it rotted away. Maybe he was a lucky guy after all because with a smell like that constantly in your nose you wouldn't have much of an appetite. But then that wouldn't bother him anyhow. He ate regular. He could feel them sliding stuff into his belly and he knew he was eating all right. Flavor didn't matter to him.

* * *

When you're completely unconscious there is no such thing as time it goes like the snap of your finger you're awake and zip you're awake again with no idea of how long a time passed between. Then when you're fainting in and out time must still seem shorter than to a normal person because you're really half crazy and half awake and time bunches up on you. They said his mother was in labor three days when she had him and yet when it was all over she figured she had been in labor for about ten hours. Even with pain and everything time had seemed shorter to her than it really was. Now if all this was true he probably had lost more time than he suspected. He might even have lost a year two years. The idea gave him a funny prickling feeling. It was a kind of fear yet not like any ordinary fear. It was more of a panic it was the panicky dread of losing yourself even from yourself. It made him a little sick at his stomach.

The whole idea had been taking form in his head for a long while the idea of trapping time and getting himself back into the world but he hadn't been able to concentrate on it. He had drifted off into dreams or he had found himself suddenly in the middle of thinking of something entirely different. Once he thought he had the problem solved by the visits of the nurse. He didn't know how many times she came into his room every twenty-four hours but she must have a schedule. All he had to do was to count the seconds then the minutes then the hours between each visit she made until he had twenty-four hours counted and after that he would be able to figure the days simply by counting her visits. There would be no danger of a slip-up because the vibration of her footsteps always awakened him. Then just in case the spacing of her visits might be changed sometime he could figure out things like the number of his bowel movements each day and he could also figure out the other things which happened maybe only two or three or four times a week like his baths and the changing of his bed clothes and mask. Then if any of these things changed he could check up on it by the others.

It took a long time to make his mind stick on the idea long enough to figure out this formula because he wasn't used to thinking but in the end he thought it through and started putting it into effect. The instant the nurse left him he began to count. He counted to sixty which meant a minute as nearly as he would ever be able to figure it. Then in one side of his mind he checked up the minute he had measured and began counting from one to sixty again. The first time he tried it he got up to eleven minutes before his mind slipped off the track and his figures were lost. It happened like this. He was counting along on the seconds when all of a sudden he thought maybe you're counting too fast and then he thought remember it seems to take a sprinter an awful long time to run a hundred yards yet he does it in only ten seconds. Then he slowed down his counting while he watched an imaginary sprinter step off a hundred yards and then he was in the middle of a high school track meet Shale City against Montrose watching Ted Smith run the hundred yard dash and win it with his head high lunging for the tape and all the kids from Shale City yelling their heads off and then he had lost count.

That meant he had to wait all over again for the nurse because she was his starting point. It seemed like hundreds maybe thousands of times that he got started out and then lost track and had to sink back angrily into the darkness of his mind and wait for the vibration of her feet and the feel of her hands on him again so he could start anew. Once he got up to a hundred and fourteen minutes and thought I wonder how long a hundred and fourteen minutes is in hours and stopped in spite of himself to figure it out and discovered it was an hour and fifty-four minutes and then he remembered a phrase fifty-four forty or fight and almost went crazy trying to recall where it came from and what it meant. He couldn't remember and when he got back to the counting he realized that he had lost a lot of minutes in thinking and so even though he had broken a record he was no farther along than when the idea of time first entered his mind.

On that day he realized he was tackling the thing from the wrong angle because to figure it out he would have to stay awake for twenty-four hours in a stretch counting steadily all the time without making a mistake. In the first place it was almost impossible for a normal person to stay awake counting that long much less a guy whose body was two-thirds asleep to begin with. And in the second place he couldn't help making a mistake because he couldn't keep the minute figures separate in his mind from the second figures. He would be counting along on the seconds when all of a sudden he would get panicky and think how many minutes was it I had? And even though he was almost positive it was twenty-two or thirty-seven or whatever it was the tinge of doubt that had first caused him to ask the question hung on and then he was sure he was wrong and by that time he had lost count again.

He never succeeded in counting the time from one visit to the next but he began to realize that even if he did he would then have to keep three sets of figures the seconds the minutes and the count of the nurse's visits until twenty-four hours were completed. Then he would have to stop sometime to reduce the minutes to hours because when the minute figures got too high he wouldn't be able to remember them at all. So with the hours he would have a fourth set of figures. In counting just the seconds and minutes which was as far as he ever got he tried to pretend that they were actual figures that he could see on a blackboard. He pretended he was in a room with a blackboard on the right side and another on the left. He would keep the minutes on the left hand blackboard and then they would be there when he needed to add another to them. But it didn't work. He couldn't remember. Each time he failed he could feel choking gasps in his chest and stomach and he knew that he was crying.

He decided to forget all about the counting and to check up on simpler things. It didn't take long to discover that he had a bowel movement about once in every three visits from the nurse although sometimes it took four visits. But that didn't tell him anything. He remembered that doctors used to say twice a day was healthy but the people doctors were talking about had normal food and they ate it with their mouths and swallowed it with their throats. The stuff he was fed might give him a much higher average than ordinary people. Then again just lying in his bed from one year to the next he might not need much food and so his score might be much less than ordinary people. He also discovered that his bath and change of bed clothes came about once in every twelve visits. It was thirteen once and another time only ten so he couldn't count on it absolutely but it was at least a figure. He was a little surprised to discover that where he had first thought of seconds and minutes he was now thinking of days and even series of days. That was how he got on the right track.

It came to him while he was lying and feeling with the skin of his neck the line that the covers made at his throat. He got to imagining them a mountain range snuggling down against his throat. He had one or two strangling dreams from them but he kept on thinking. He got to thinking that the only part of him that wasn't covered up that was free that was just as it should be was the skin on the sides of his neck which went from the cover-line to his ears and the half of his forehead above the mask. That skin and his hair. He said to himself maybe there is some way you could use those patches of skin they are free to the air and they are healthy and a guy with as few healthy things as you've got should put them to use. So he got to thinking of what a man did with skin and he realized that it was used to feel with. But that didn't seem enough. He thought about skin some more and then he remembered that you could also sweat with it and that when you started sweating you were hot but by the time the sweat covered your skin you were cool from the air drying the sweat. That was how he got the idea of heat and cold and that was how he came to wait for the sunrise.

The whole thing was so simple that his stomach grew hard with excitement just from thinking about it. All he had to do was to feel with his skin. When the temperature changed from cool to warm he would know it was sunrise and the beginning of a day. Then he would check right through counting the nurse's visits to the next sunrise and then he would have the number of her visits per day and he would forever afterward be able to tell time.

He started trying to stay awake until the change in temperature occurred but half a dozen times running he fell asleep before it happened. Other times he got confused thinking to himself is it hot now or is it cool what kind of a change am I waiting for maybe I am running a fever maybe I am too excited and am sweating from excitement and that would spoil the whole thing oh please god don't let me sweat don't let me run a temperature let me know whether I'm hot now or whether I'm cold. Give me some idea of when the sunrise is coming and then I'll be able to catch it. And then after a long long while with a lot of false starts he said to himself here sit down and think this thing over seriously. Right now you're panicky you're too anxious and you're blundering. Each time you make a mistake you've lost more time and that is one thing you can't afford to lose. Think what usually happens in the morning in a hospital and try to figure out what follows that. That's easy he said to himself in the mornings in a hospital nurses try to get their heavy work done. That meant that he was bathed and his bed clothes were probably changed in the morning. He would have to take that as his starting point. He would have to assume a few things and the first assumption would be that this was true. He already knew that the bath and change of bedding came on an average of once in every twelve visits.

Now he had to begin assuming again. You would think in a hospital like this that your bedding would be changed at least every other day. Maybe it was once a day but he didn't think so because at the rate of one change in every twelve visits that would make the nurse visit him every two hours and there was so little to do he couldn't see why her trips should be that often. So he would figure that every two days she bathed him and changed his bedclothes and that she did this in the morning. If this was true then she came into his room six times in a day and night. That would make it every four hours. The simplest schedule for her to follow would be to come in at eight twelve four eight twelve four and so on. She would probably change the bedding as early as possible in the morning so that would be at eight o'clock.

Now he said to himself what is it you want to try to check up on the sunrise first or the sunset? He decided it was the sunrise because when the sun sets the warmth of the day usually hangs on and the change is so slow that those two pieces of skin on his neck might not be able to catch it. But in the early dawn everything is cool and almost the first flash of sunlight should give some kind of heat. At least the change should be more complete in the morning than at night so he would catch the sunrise.

He had a panicky minute when he thought what if you are on the west side of the hospital and the setting sun comes in full on the bed and then you'll mistake that for sunrise? What if you're on the north or south side of the hospital and never get the direct sunlight at all? Maybe that would be simpler. Then he realized that even if he were on the west side and caught the heat of the setting sun he would still have the visits of the nurse to check on to tell him which was which because by now he was convinced she changed the bed clothes in the morning.

Now you damn fool he said to himself you're getting things so complicated you'll never come out if you don't stop. The first thing to do is to catch the sunrise. Next time the nurse comes into the room and bathes you and changes the bed clothes you are going to assume it is eight o'clock in the morning. Then you can think about anything you want to without worrying or you can even go to sleep because each time she comes in she awakens you. You will wait and count five more visits and that should make the fifth one somewhere around four o'clock in the morning. Four o'clock in the morning is just before sunrise so after the fifth visit from the nurse you will stay awake and concentrate every bit of your mind and skin on the job of catching the temperature change when it comes. Maybe it'll work and maybe it won't. If it does all you have to do is to wait six more trips and see if there is another sunrise and if there is you'll have the number of trips every twenty-four hours and that will give you a way of setting up a calendar around the nurse's visits. The important thing is to catch two sunrises in a row and then you have trapped time forever then you can begin to catch up with the world.

It was eight visits later before he felt the nurse's hands on him as she took off his nightshirt and began to sponge his stump with warm water. He felt his heart quicken and his blood send a warm glow of excitement to his skin because he was going to start out once more to trap time only now he was doing it smartly he was doing it wisely. He felt himself rolled over on his side and held there while the bed quivered from the nurse's work. Then he was rolled back between crisp cool sheets. The nurse thumped around at the foot of the bed for a minute. He felt the vibrations of her footsteps as she walked from place to place in the room. Then the vibrations receded and there was a sharp little tremor of the door closing and he knew he was alone.

Calm down he said to himself calm down because you haven't proved anything yet. You may have this thing doped out all wrong. Maybe the things you've assumed are all wrong. If they are then you've got to make a whole new set of assumptions so don't get so cocky. Just calm down and lie back and count five more visits. He dozed a little and he thought of a lot of things but always on the blackboard in his mind he kept the number two or three or whatever it was and finally the fifth visit came with the nurse's feet vibrating against the floor and her hands on him and on the bed. According to the things he had figured out it should now be four o'clock in the morning and in a little while depending on whether it was winter or summer or fall or spring the sun would rise.

When she left he began concentrating. He didn't dare fall asleep. He didn't dare permit his mind to wander for one minute. He didn't dare let the suffocating excitement that was all over him and inside of him interfere with his thinking and feeling as he lay there waiting for the sunrise. He had come on the trail of something so precious and so exciting that it was almost like being born all over again into the world. He lay there and thought in one hour three hours certainly in ten hours I will feel a change on my skin and then I will know whether it is day or night.

It seemed that time was standing perfectly still just to spite him. He got panicky little spasms when he felt sure the change had occurred without him catching it and with each little spasm he seemed to get sick at his stomach. Then there would be a clear period when he would very calmy feel with his skin and convince himself that he was sane that he hadn't fallen asleep and missed it that his mind hadn't wandered that the change was still ahead.

And then all of a sudden he realized it was coming. The muscles in his back and thighs and stomach stiffened because he knew it was coming. He could almost feel the sweat squeeze out of his body as he tried to hold his breath lest he miss it. The pieces of skin on each side of his neck and the half of his forehead seemed to tingle as if they had been paralyzed and now were getting a fresh supply of blood. It felt as if the pores of his neck were actually reaching out to grab at the change to suck it in.

The whole thing was so slow so gradual that it seemed impossible it was happening at all. There was no danger now of his mind wandering or of falling asleep. It would be like falling asleep in the middle of a first kiss. It would be like falling asleep in the middle of running a hundred yard dash and winning it. The only thing he could do was wait and feel out with his skin and catch every second of the change every slow movement of time and temperature as they offered him a return to life.

It seemed like he lay there stiff and expectant and excited for hours. There were times when he was sure that the nerves of his neck were not registering when it seemed they had suddenly gone numb and that the change might slip away from him. And then there were other times when it felt as if his nerves had jabbed through so near the surface of his skin that there was actual pain sharp and fine and penetrating as they groped to register the change.

And then the thing began to happen swiftly and more swiftly and although he knew he was in a sheltered hospital room as far removed as possible from changes in temperature it seemed to him when it came that it came in a blaze of heat. It felt like his neck was seared burned scorched from the heat of the rising sun. It had penetrated his room. He had recaptured time — he had won his fight. The muscles of his body relaxed. In his mind in his heart in whatever parts of him that were left he was singing singing singing.

It was dawn.

* * *

And then an astonishing thing happened. One day toward the middle of the year the nurse gave him a completely fresh change of bed linen when he had received a change only the day before. This had never happened before. Every third day he was changed no sooner and no later. Yet here everything was upset and for two days in a row he was getting the change. He felt all in a hub-bub. He felt like bustling around from room to room and chattering about how busy he was and what great things were going to happen. He felt all bright with expectation and excitement. He wondered if he would get a fresh change of linen every day from now on or whether they would return again to the old schedule. This was as important as if an ordinary man with legs and arms and other parts were suddenly confronted with the possibility of living in a new house every day. It would be something to look forward to from day to day throughout the years. It would be something to break up time to make it something a guy could stand without mulling over Matthew Mark Luke and John.

Then he noticed something else. In addition to giving him an unexpected bath the nurse was spraying him with something. He could feel the spray cool and misty against his skin. Then she put a clean nightshirt on him and folded the covers back at his throat. This was different too. He could feel her hand through the covers as it passed over the fold smoothing smoothing smoothing. He was given a fresh mask which the nurse arranged very fussily so that it fell to his throat and there was carefully tucked under the fold of the bedcovers. After that she combed his hair carefully and left. He could feel the vibrations of her footsteps as she went away and the little jar of the door closing behind her. Then he was alone.

He lay perfectly still because it was a very luxurious feeling to be so completely redone. His body glowed and his sheets were cool and crisp and even his scalp felt good. He was afraid to move for fear he would spoil the good feeling. There was only a moment of this and then he felt the vibrations of four maybe five people coming into his room. He lay tense trying to catch their vibrations and wondering why they were there. The vibrations got heavier and then they stopped and he knew that people were gathered around his bed more people than ever before had been in his room at the same time. It was like the first time he went to school and was embarrassed and bewildered with so many people around. Little tremors of expectation ran through his stomach. He was stiff with excitement. He had visitors.

The first thought that passed through his mind was that they might be his mother and sisters and Kareen. There was just a chance that Kareen forever lovely and young was standing by him was looking down at him was even this minute putting out her hand her soft and tiny hand her beautiful beautiful hand to touch his forehead.

And then just as he could almost feel the touch of her hand his delight turned suddenly to shame. He hoped more than anything else in the world that it was not his mother and sisters and Kareen who had come to visit him. He didn't want them to see him. He didn't want anybody he had ever known to see him. He knew now how foolish it had been to wish for them as sometimes in his loneliness he had. It was all right to think about having them near it was comforting it was warm and pleasant. But the idea that they might be beside his bed right now was too terrible to cope with. He jerked his head convulsively away from his visitors. He knew this dislodged his mask but he was beyond thinking of masks. He only wanted to hide his face to turn his blind sockets away from them to keep them from seeing the chewed up hole that used to be a nose and mouth that used to be a living human face. He got so frantic that he began to thrash from side to side like someone very sick with a high fever who can only monotonously repeat a motion or a word. He fell into his old rocking motion throwing his weight from one shoulder to the other back and forth back and forth back and forth.

A hand came to rest on his forehead. He quieted because it was the hand of a man heavy and warm. Part of it lay on the skin of his forehead and part of it he felt through the mask which cut across his forehead. He lay still again. Then another hand began to fold the covers back from his throat. One fold. One and a half folds. He grew very quiet very alert very curious. He thought very hard about who they might be.

Then he had it. They were doctors come to examine him. They were visiting firemen. He was probably a very famous guy by this time and the doctors were beginning to make pilgrimages. One doctor was probably saying to the others you see how we were able to do it? You see what a clever job we did? You see where the arm came off and you see the hole in his face and you see he still lives? Listen to his heart it's beating just like your heart or mine. Oh we did a fine job when we got him. It was a great piece of luck and we're all very proud. Stop by in my office on your way out and I'll give you one of his teeth for a souvenir. They take a wonderful polish he was young you see and his teeth were in good condition. Would you like a front one or would you prefer a good thick tusker from farther back? The thick ones look best on a watch chain.

Somebody was plucking at his nightshirt over his left breast. It was as if a forefinger and thumb were pinching up a portion of it. He lay very quiet now deathly quiet his mind jumping in a hundred different directions at once. He could sense that something important was about to happen. There was a little more fumbling with the pinch of nightshirt and then the cloth fell back against his chest once more. It was heavy now weighted down by something. He felt the sudden coolness of metal through his nightshirt against his chest over his heart. They had pinned something on him.

Suddenly he did a curious thing a thing he hadn't done for months. He started to reach with his right hand for the heavy thing they had pinned on him and it seemed that he almost clutched it in his fingers before he realized that he had no arm to reach with and no fingers for clutching.

Someone was kissing his temple. There was a slight tickling of hair as the kiss was given. He was being kissed by a man with a moustache. First his left temple and then his right one. Then he knew what they had done to him. They had come into his room and they had decorated him with a medal. He knew furthermore that he must be in France instead of England because French generals were the ones who always kissed you when they handed out medals. Still that might not be true. American generals and English generals shook your hand but since he had no hand to shake maybe this was an Englishman or an American who had decided to follow the French custom because there was no other way to do it. But still the chances now seemed even that he was in France.

When he snapped back from thinking of where he was and adjusting himself to the idea that it might be France he was a little surprised to find that he was getting mad. They had given him a medal. Three or four big guys famous guys who still had arms and legs and who could see and talk and smell and taste had come into his room and they had pinned a medal on him. They could afford to couldn't they the dirty bastards? That was all they ever had time to do just run around putting medals on guys and feeling important and smug about it. How many generals got killed in the war? There was Kitchener of course but that was an accident. How many others? Name them name any of the soft-living sons-ofbitches and you could have them. How many of them had got all shot up so they had to live wrapped in a sheet for the rest of their lives? They had a lot of guts coming around and giving medals.

When he had thought for an instant that his mother and his sisters and Kareen might be standing beside the bed he had wanted to hide. But now that he had generals and big guys he felt a sudden fierce surging desire for them to see him. Just as before he had started to reach for the medal without an arm to reach with so now he began to blow the mask off his face without having mouth and lips to blow with. He wanted them to get just one look at the hole in his head. He wanted them to get their fill of a face that began and ended with a forehead. He lay there blowing and then he realized that the air from his lungs was all escaping through his tube. He began to roll again from shoulder to shoulder hoping to dislodge the mask.

While he lay there rolling and puffing he felt a vibration way down in his throat a vibration that might be a voice. It was a short deep vibration and he knew that it was making a sound to their ears. Not a very big sound not a very intelligent sound but it must seem to them at least as interesting as the grunting of a pig. And if he could grunt like a pig why then he was accomplishing a great thing because before he had been completely silent. So he lay thrashing and puffing and grunting like a pig hoping that they would see damned well how much he appreciated their medal. While he was in the middle of this there was an indefinite churning of footsteps and then the departing vibrations of his guests. A moment later he was all alone in the blackness in the silence. He was all alone with his medal.

Suddenly he quieted. He was thinking about the vibrations of those footsteps. He had always carefully felt for vibrations. He had measured the size of his nurses and the dimensions of his room by them. But suddenly to feel the vibrations of four or five people tramping across the room made him think. It made him realize that vibrations were very important. He had thought of them up to this time only as vibrations coming to him. Now he began to consider that also there could be vibrations going from him. The vibrations which he received told him everything — height weight distance time. Why shouldn't he be able to tell something to the outside world by vibrations also?

In the back of his mind something began to glimmer. If he could in some way make use of vibrations he could communicate with these people. Then the glimmer became a great dazzling white light. It opened up such breathless prospects that he thought he might suffocate from sheer excitement. Vibrations were a very important part of communication. The fall of a foot on the floor is one kind of vibration. The tap of a telegraph key is simply another kind.

When he was a kid way back maybe four years ago or five he had a wireless set. He and Bill Harper used to telegraph each other. Dot dash dot dash dot. Particularly on rainy nights when their folks wouldn't let them go out and there was nothing to do and they just lounged around the house and got in everybody's way. On such nights he and Bill Harper used to dot and dash at each other and they had a hell of a good time. He still remembered the Morse code. All he had to do in order to break through to people in the outside world was to lie in his bed and dot dash to the nurse. Then he could talk. Then he would have smashed through his silence and blackness and helplessness. Then the stump of a man without lips would talk. He had captured time and he had tried to figure geography and now he would do the greatest thing of them all he would talk. He would give messages and receive messages and he would have made another step forward in his struggle to get back to people in his terrible lonely eagerness for the feel of people near him for the things that were in their minds for the thoughts they might give him his own thoughts were so puny so unfinished so incomplete. He would talk.

Tentatively he raised his head from the pillow and let it fall back again. Then he did it twice quickly. That would be a dash and two dots. The letter d. He tapped out SOS against his pillow. Dot-dot-dot dot dot dot-dot-dot. SOS. Help. If there was anybody in the whole world needed help he was the guy and now he was asking for it. He wished the nurse would hurry back. He began to tap out questions. What time is it? What's the date? Where am I? Is the sun shining or is it cloudy? Does anybody know who I am? Do my folks know I'm lying here? Don't tell them. Don't let them know anything about it. SOS. Help.

The door of the room jarred open and the nurse's footsteps came up to the bed. He began to tap out more frantically now. Here he was right on the brink of finding people of finding the world of finding a big part of life itself. Tap tap tap. He was waiting for her tap tap tap in response. A tap against his forehead or his chest. Even if she didn't know the code she could tap just to let him know she understood what he was doing. Then she could rush away for someone who could help her get what he was saying. SOS. SOS. SOS. Help.

He felt the nurse standing there looking down at him trying to figure out what he was doing. The mere possibility that she didn't understand after all he had gone through before discovering it himself shocked him into such excitement and fear that he began to grunt again. He lay grunting and tapping grunting and tapping until the muscles in the back of his neck ached until his head ached until he felt that his chest would burst from his eagerness to shout out to explain to her what he was trying to do. And still he felt her standing motionless beside his bed looking down and wondering.

Then he felt her hand against his forehead. For just a moment she held it there. He kept on tapping growing angry now and hopeless and feeling like he wanted to throw up. She began to stroke his forehead in slow gentle motions. She was stroking it in a way she had never done it before. He felt pity in the softness of her touch. Then her hand went from his forehead clear back through his hair and he remembered that Kareen used to do that sometimes. But he put Kareen out of his mind and kept right on tapping because this was such an important thing that he couldn't stop for pleasant sensations.

The pressure of the hand against his forehead was getting heavier. He realized that she was trying by the weight of her hand to make him tired so he'd quit tapping. He began to tap all the harder all the faster to show her that her plan wouldn't work. He could feel the vertebrae in the back of his neck crack and pop from the strain of this unexpected work. The nurse's hand grew heavier and heavier on his head. His neck grew tireder and tireder. It had been a terrible day a long day an exciting day. His tapping grew slower and her hand got still heavier and finally he lay back very quietly against the pillow while she brushed his forehead.

* * *

He had lost all track of time. All his work to trap it all his counting and calculation of it might just as well never have happened. He had lost track of everything except the tapping. The instant he awakened he began to tap and he continued until the moment when drowsiness overcame him. Even as he fell asleep the last portion of his energy and thought went into the tapping so that it seemed he dreamed of tapping. Because he tapped while he was awake and dreamed of tapping while he was asleep his old difficulty in distinguishing between wakefulness and sleep sprang up again. He was never quite positive that he was not dreaming when awake and tapping when asleep. He had lost time so utterly that he had no idea how long the tapping had been going on. Maybe only weeks maybe a month perhaps even a year. The one sense that remained to him out of the original five had been completely hypnotized by the tapping and as for thinking he didn't even pretend to any more. He didn't speculate about the new night nurses in their comings and goings. He didn't listen for vibrations against the floor. He didn't think of the past and he didn't consider the future. He only lay and tapped his message over and over again to people on the outside who didn't understand.

The day nurse tried hard to soothe him but she did it only as if she were trying to calm an irritable patient. She did it in such a way that he knew he would never break through as long as he had her. It never seemed to occur to her that there was a mind an intelligence working behind the rhythm of his head against the pillow. She was simply watching over an incurably sick patient trying to make his sickness as comfortable as possible. She never thought that to be dumb was a sickness and that he had found the cure for it that he was trying to tell her he was well he was not dumb any longer he was a man who could talk. She gave him hot baths. She shifted the position of his bed. She adjusted the pillow in back of his head now higher now lower. When she moved it higher the increased angle bent his head forward. After tapping for a short time in this position he could feel pain shooting all the way down his spine and across his back. But he kept right on tapping.

She got to massaging him and he liked that she had such a brisk gentle touch to her fingers but he kept on tapping. And then one day he felt a change in the touch of her fingers. They were not gentle and brisk any longer. He felt the change through the tips of her fingers through the tenderness of her touch he felt pity and hesitancy and a great gathering love that was neither him for her nor her for him but rather a kind of love that took in all living things and tried to make them a little more comfortable a little less unhappy a little more nearly like others of their kind.

He felt the change through the tips of her fingers and a sharp little twinge of disgust when through him but in spite of the disgust he was responding to the touch responding to the mercy in her heart that caused her to touch him so. Her hands sought out the far parts of his body. They inflamed his nerves with a kind of false passion that fled in little tremors along the surface of his skin. Even while he was thinking oh my god it's come to this here is the reason she thinks I'm tapping goddam her god bless her what shall I do? — even while he was thinking it he fell in with her rhythm he strained to her touch his heart pounded to a faster tempo and he forgot everything in the world except the motion and the sudden pumping of his blood . . .

* * *

He awakened as a man awakens out of a drunk — hazy-brained and foggy swimming slowly and painfully back toward reality. He awakened tapping with his head against his pillow. The tapping by now had become so much a part of awakening that the first glimmer of consciousness found him already tapping and later on when exhaustion overcame him and his mind began to grow dim and sleep crept over his body he was still tapping. He lay there not thinking of anything his brain aching and throbbing and his head tapping against the pillow. SOS. Help.

And then as his mind sharpened and began to think instead of only to feel he stopped his tapping and lay still. Something very important was happening. He had a new day nurse.

He could tell it the minute the door opened and she began to walk across the room. Her footsteps were light where those of his regular day nurse his old efficient fast-working day nurse were heavy. It took five steps to bring this new one to his bedside. That meant she was shorter than the regular nurse and probably younger too because the very vibration of her footsteps seemed gay and buoyant. It was the first time within his memory that the regular day nurse had not appeared to take care of him.

He lay very still very tense. This was like learning a new secret like opening a new world. Without a moment's hesitation the new nurse threw back his covers. And then like all of the others before her she stood quietly for a moment beside his bed. He knew she was staring down at him. He knew she must have been told what to expect. Yet the sight of him was probably so much worse than any description that she could do nothing for that first instant but stare. Then instead of hastily throwing the covers back over him as some of them did or running out of the room or standing and weeping and letting the tears fall against his chest she put her hand against his forehead. No one had ever done it before in just this way. Perhaps no one had been able to do it. It was like putting a hand near an open cancer something so terrible and sickening that no one could endure the thought much less the action. Yet this new nurse this nurse with the light happy step was not afraid.

She put her hand to his forehead and he felt that her hand was young and small and moist. She put her hand to his forehead and he tried to ripple his skin to show her how much he appreciated the way she had done it. It was like resting after a long long period of work. It was almost like sleep it was so lovely and soothing to have her hand against his head.

Then he began to think of the possibilities of this new nurse. For some reason the old one was gone. The old one had never understood what he was trying to do had never understood that he was trying with every ounce of his strength to talk to her. She had paid no attention at all to his tapping except to try to stop it. But she was gone and in her place he had a new nurse a young new nurse who was unafraid and gentle. How long he would have her no one could tell. She might leave the room and never come back again. But for the moment he had her and he knew that somehow she felt as he felt or she couldn't have put her hand so quickly to his forehead. If he could tap very firmly very clearly very plainly to her she might understand what no one else had considered worth trying to understand. She might understand that he was talking. The old nurse might return and he might never hear the footsteps of the new one again. If this new one went his last chance would go with her. He would go on through the rest of his life tapping tapping tapping with no one understanding that he was trying to work a miracle. The new nurse was his reprieve his one tiny opportunity in all the hours and weeks and years of his life.

He stiffened the muscles of his neck and prepared once more to start tapping his head against the pillow. But another strange thing was happening to arrest him. She had opened his nightshirt so that his breast was now naked to the air. She was moving the tip of her finger against the skin of his breast. For a moment he was merely puzzled unable to understand what she was doing. Then by concentrating all of his mind on the skin of his breast he began to understand that her finger was not traveling aimlessly. It was making a design against his skin. It was making the same design over and over again. He knew there was some purpose behind such repetition and he grew tense and alert to discover it. Like an eager dog spoken to by its master and trying very hard to be good and to understand he lay stiffly and concentrated on the design the nurse was making.

The first thing he noted about the design was that it had no curves. It was all straight lines and angles. It began with a straight line moving up and then it went down at an angle and then it came up again at an angle and then it went straight down and stopped. She repeated the design over and over now slowly now rapidly now slowly again. Sometimes she paused at the finish of the design and with the strange understanding that seemed to have sprung up between them he knew that her pauses were question marks that she was looking down at him and asking him if he understood and waiting for his response.

Each time she paused he shook his head and then she repeated the design once more and in the midst of this patient repetition the barrier between them suddenly broke down. With one quick rush of comprehension he understood what she was doing. She was tracing the letter M against the skin of his breast. He nodded quickly to tell her that he understood and she patted his forehead encouragingly as if to say you are remarkable you are wonderful how hard you try and how quickly you learn. Then she began to trace other letters.

The others came easier because he now understood what she was doing. He tightened the skin of his chest so that he could better receive the impression of her finger. Some of the letters she had to do only once he was so quick at getting them. He got the letter E and he nodded and the letter R and he nodded and again the R and then he got the letter Y and he nodded and there was a long pause. The rest of the letters tumbled into his mind in a perfect torrent. There was C and H and R and I and S and T and M and A and S and the whole thing spelled merry christmas.

Merry christmas merry christmas merry christmas.

Now he understood. The old nurse had left to spend the christmas holidays away from him and this new nurse this young lovely beautiful understanding new nurse was wishing him merry christmas. He nodded back at her frantically and his nod meant merry christmas to you merry christmas oh a merry merry christmas.

* * *

When he finally forced his mind away from thoughts of christmas of merry christmas he began to tap once more. Only this time he tapped firmly with vigor full of hope and confidence for he saw that this new nurse this lovely new nurse was thinking as hard as he was and of the same thing. He knew as plainly as if she had told him that she was determined to batter down the silence which stood between him as a dead man and him as a live man. Since she had already thought of a way to speak to him he knew that she would pay attention when he tried to speak to her. The others had been too busy or too tired or else not bright enough to see what he was doing. They had taken his tapping as a nervous habit as a disease as the whim of a child as a symptom of insanity as anything but what it really was as anything but a cry from the darkness a voice from the dead a wail in the silence for friendship and someone to talk to. But the new nurse would understand and help him.

He tapped very carefully very slowly to show her that he had a method in what he was doing. Just as she had repeated the design of the letter M on his chest over and over again so he now tapped his distress signal back to her. But slowly . . . so slowly. Dot dot dot   dot dot   dot dot dot. S O S. H e l p. Over and over again he repeated it. Once in a while he would stop at the completion of the signal. That was his question mark just as her pauses had been question marks. He would stop and try to make all that was visible of him — his hair and half his forehead above the mask — take on an air of expectancy. Then when he received no sign from her he would do it again. And all the while he tapped he was conscious of her near him watching and thinking.

After a long period of waiting and watching and thinking she began to do things. She did them very deliberately so deliberately that even her movements seemed thoughtful. First she slipped the urinal in under the covers touching it against his body so that he could recognize it. He shook his head. She took the urinal away and slipped the bed pan against him. He shook his head. She took the bed pan away. There was no hesitation between her movements now. It seemed that she had each move figured out before she finished the last one. She was working skillfully and intelligently to eliminate all possible causes for his tapping one by one with no pauses in between. He knew that during the time she had stood beside him watching and thinking she had made up her mind

49

to a plan and now was putting it into effect with as little nonsense as possible.

She took the blanket off him leaving him with only a sheet for covering. He shook his head. She put the blanket back and threw another one over it to give him more covers than before. He shook his head. He had stopped tapping now waiting alertly until she was through with her plan. She took the covers off him entirely and adjusted the position of the breathing tube in his throat. He shook his head. She patted the bandage over the hole in his side. He shook his head. He shook his head and marveled that he had the sense left to do it because he was so charged with excitement that he could scarcely think. She lifted the nightshirt that covered him and began gently to rub his body. He shook his head. She threw the covers over him again and moved toward the head of the bed. She rubbed his forehead soothingly. He shook his head. She smoothed his hair back and scratched his scalp and massaged it with her knuckles. He shook his head. She loosened the cord that held the mask over his face. He shook his head. She lifted the mask up and fanned it gently to let the air in and be sure it wasn't sticking. He shook his head. She replaced the bandage and stopped everything. He could feel her standing beside the head of the bed looking down at him attentively as alert and eager as he was himself. She had done everything she could think of and now she was standing there quietly as if to say it's your turn now please try hard to tell me and I will try hard to understand.

He began to tap again.

It seemed to him that he stopped breathing. It seemed that his heart stopped and the blood in his body turned solid. It seemed that the only living moving thing in the whole world was his head as it tapped tapped tapped against his pillow. He knew it was now or never. There was no good in fooling himself now. This minute this instant this very second everything was about to be decided. Never again would he have a nurse such as this one. She might turn and walk out of the room in five minutes and never return. When she walked away she would carry his life with her she would carry madness and loneliness and all his godforsaken silent screams and she would never know it she would never hear the screams. She would simply go and ever after he would be forgotten. She was loneliness and friendship she was life and death and she stood now waiting quietly for him to tell her what he wanted.

While he tapped he was praying in his heart. He had never paid much attention to praying before but now he was doing it saying oh please god make her understand what I'm trying to tell her. I've been alone so long god I've been here for years and years suffocating smothering dead while alive like a man who has been buried in a casket deep in the ground and awakens and screams I'm alive I'm alive I'm alive let me out open the lid dig away the dirt please merciful christ help me only there's no one to hear him and so he's dead. I know you're very busy god I know there are millions of people praying to you every minute every hour for something they need I know there are a lot of important people who are after you for big things that are all tied up with nations and continents and maybe even the whole world. I know all these things god and I don't blame you if you get behind on your orders nobody's perfect but what I want is such a little thing. If I were asking you for something big something like a million dollars or a private yacht or a skyscraper I could understand if I didn't get it because there are only so many dollars and so many yachts and so many skyscrapers. But I only want you should take a tiny little idea that is in my mind and put it into her mind two maybe three feet away. That's all I want god. The idea is so small so light that a humming bird could carry it a moth a mayfly the breath of air that comes from the mouth of a baby. It won't take any time and it means I can't tell you what to me. Honestly I wouldn't ask you god only this is such a little thing. It's such a little thing . . .

He felt her finger against his forehead.

He nodded.

He felt her finger tap four times against his forehead.

That is the letter H he thought only she doesn't know it she's got no idea she's just tapping there to test if that's what I want.

He nodded.

He nodded so hard his neck ached and his head seemed to whirl. He nodded so hard the whole bed shook.

Oh thank you god he thought she got it you put the idea where I asked you should thank you. Thank you thank you thank you.

He felt her hand pressed against his forehead reassuringly for just a minute. Then he got the rapidly receding vibrations of her footsteps going away. He knew she was running from the room to tell them. The door slammed behind her. The sound quivered against his bedsprings like an electric shock. She was gone.

He lay back surprised to find how exhausted he was. It was like he had worked three nights in a row at the bakery during the summer when he couldn't get any sleep in the daytime. The breath was gone out of him and his head throbbed and every muscle in his body was sore. Yet inside he was all confetti and high-flying flags and double-time band music that marched up and up straight into the face of the sun. He had done it he had succeeded the thing was accomplished and even though he lay perfectly still perfectly exhausted it seemed he could see the whole world lying below him. There was no telling it there was no thinking it there was no imagining it he was so happy.

It was as if all the people in the world the whole two billion of them had been against him pushing the lid of the coffin down on him tamping the dirt solid against the lid rearing great stones above the dirt to keep him in the earth. Yet he had risen. He had lifted the lid he had thrown away the dirt he had tossed the granite aside like a snowball and now he was above the surface he was standing in the air he was leaping with every step miles above the earth. He was like nobody else who had ever lived. He had done so much he was like god.

The doctors who brought their friends in to see him would no longer say here is a man who has lived without arms legs ears eyes nose mouth isn't it wonderful? They would say here is a man who can think here is a man who lay in his bed with only a cut of meat to hold him together and yet he thought of a way to talk. Listen to him speak. You see his mind is unaffected he speaks like you and me he is a person he has identity he is part of the world. And he is part of the world only because he all by himself with perhaps the aid of a prayer and a god figured out a way to speak. Look at him and then let us ask you if this isn't even more wonderful than all the splendid operations we have performed upon his stump?

He knew now that he had never been really happy in his whole life. There had been times when he had thought he was happy but none of them were like this. There was the time when all year long he had wanted an erector set and when at christmas time he got it. That was probably as happy as he had ever been while he was a kid. There was the time when Kareen told him she loved him and that was as happy as he had ever been up to the time the shell exploded and blew him out of the world. But this happiness this new wild frantic happiness was greater than anything he could conceive. It was a thing so absolute so towering so out of this world that it hit him almost like delirium. His legs that were smashed and gone got up and danced. His arms that were rotted these five six seven years swung fantastically free at his sides to keep time with the dance. The eyes they had taken from him looked up from whatever garbage heap they had been consigned to and saw all the beauties of the world. The ears that were shattered and full of silence rang suddenly with music. The mouth that had been hacked away from his face and now was filled with dust returned to sing. Because he had done it. He had accomplished the impossible. He had spoken to them like god out of a cloud out of a thick cloud and now he was floating on top of the cloud and he was a man again.

And the nurse . . .

He could imagine her running through the halls. He could hear her clattering like a noisy ghost through the halls of death. He could feel her running from ward to ward from the ward of the cripples to the ward of the deaf men to the ward of the blind men to the ward of the voiceless men summoning all the people of the hospital screaming out to them the news of the wonder that had happened. He could hear her voice as she told them that up in a little room far away from the rest of the hospital a lid had been lifted from a coffin a stone had been rolled away from a tomb and a dead man was tapping and talking. Never before in the world had the dead spoken never since Lazarus and Lazarus didn't say anything. Now he would tell them everything. He would speak from the dead. He would talk for the dead. He would tell all the secrets of the dead. And while he thought of what he would tell them the nurse was running running running through wards and corridors from floor to floor from basement to attic all through that great place from which so many dead had gone. She was trumpeting through the hospital like the angel Gabriel telling them to come and to listen to the voice of the dead.

While he waited for all the people she had summoned to come to him he could feel their presence as an actor must feel the presence of a thousand people in that moment before the curtain goes up. He could feel the vibrations of their footsteps dozens of them as they thronged into his room. He could feel his bed jostled back and forth as they pressed against it in their eagerness. The springs of his bed seemed to send up a constant low hum as his guests shifted for positions to get a better view of the dead man who was speaking. The temperature of the room became so much warmer that he could almost feel the heat of their massed bodies against the skin of his neck and the half of his forehead that was naked above the mask.

Then the door opened. He felt the vibration of a footstep a light one the nurse's footstep. He strained to feel the rest. Then came the vibrations of another footstep this one heavier belonging to a man. He waited for the rest he waited for the hum of his bedsprings. But everything was quiet. Everything was still. There was no one in the room for the great thing that was about to happen except him and his nurse and this heavy-footed stranger. No one at all but the three of them. He felt an odd pang of disappointment that they should consider such a great event so lightly. And then he remembered the thing that was even more important than crowds. He lay there stiff quiet more like a dead man than he had ever been before. He lay there waiting to receive his response.

A finger came out of the darkness a finger so enormous that it shattered against his forehead like the crash of a pile driver. It echoed inside his brain like thunder in a cave. The finger began to tap . . .

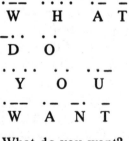

What do you want?

That any of us in professional work with handicapped persons will experience a real Johnny Bonham is highly improbable. Nevertheless, a person's imagination can soar far beyond reality and in its own way present realities that make us think and feel in new ways. So Trumbo has given us a "real" person — and a condition beyond the multiples of multiple handicaps. Johnny cannot see, hear, feel with his hands, walk with legs, smell, or taste. He can move his head, wrinkle his skin perhaps, and feel pressure on what is left of his body. He can think and feel, as he does when he becomes aware sequentially of his many handicaps. He senses his total inner imprisonment with some despair but with always an optimistic search for a little light at the end of an increasingly lengthy and dark tunnel.

He must escape. He must get out of his inner world and contact the others around him. The reader is reminded of the frustrations and despair of an autistic child who is somewhat similarly cut off from the outer world but having the mobility and strength to "escape." Persons who have suffered strokes or head injuries resulting in expressive or receptive aphasia often report this feeling of wanting to get out of an inner prison. This feeling also is delightfully recalled by Hellen Keller after a dining room battle with Anne Sullivan and the blind girl's forceful march to the water pump to get cleaned up. "The few signs I used," wrote Helen, "became less and less adequate and my failures to make myself understood were invariably followed by outbursts of passion. I felt as if invisible hands were holding me and I made frantic efforts to free myself — after awhile the need of some means of communication became so urgent that these outbursts occurred daily, sometimes hourly."[1]

Johnny can't walk, feel, see, or hear but what bothers him the most is his inability to tell anyone anything — especially how he feels about the whole thing. Young deaf children often exhibit the same frustrations, especially those who can think without language but cannot share these thoughts without speech. And persons overburdened by heavy loads of unexpressible emotion can feel similarly trapped.

Undoubtedly, handicaps that restrict or constrain communication exact the greatest mental health toll on an individual's resources. We've all seen the young child attempting to convey an idea or wish to a confused adult and finally exploding in

---

[1] Hellen Keller, *Story of My Life* (New York: Grosset & Dunlap, 1902), p. 17.

frustration at the adult's lack of understanding. Often, one needs to bring in another child as interpreter!

Whatever else Johnny is as a handicapped person, he is not retarded. He tries hard to escape his internal prison. He works out a way to reach the outer world. His mind and body, bereft of senses and mobility, struggle and succeed. Using his head figuratively and literally, he becomes a thinking social organism. He contacts the outside world. The outside world responds, "What do you want?"

Our excerpt ends at this point since the rest of the story is bitter tea for sensitive readers. In response to the question, "What do you want?" Johnny decides on the most realistic and practical possibility — to travel about as an educational exhibit. He taps out, "Take off my nightshirt and build a glass case for me and take me down to the places where people are having fun where they are on the lookout for freakish things . . . This will be the goddamest dime's worth a man ever had." Take me to your cities, farms, parliaments, congresses, schools, churches — let them see and talk to me, requests Johnny.

A finger taps a reply on his forehead: "What you ask is against regulations. Who are you?"

QUESTIONS FOR DISCUSSION

1. How does Johnny discover and evaluate the various clues that tell him about his condition?

2. Can you think of and conceptualize electronic aids that might be of some help to Johnny?

3. Why does Johnny want to communicate?

4. To what extent can you identify with Johnny as a living, real person?

5. What is your reaction to Johnny's decision on how he might best serve as a handicapped person?

6. Certain clinical insights and research data from investigations in sensory deprivation bear on Johnny's condition. What are some of these findings, and how relevant are they to Johnny Bonham?

7. Is the severity of Johnny's condition too unreal to be considered a real possibility? Do you know of any comparable situations?

8. What factors in Johnny's personality allow him to cope with the series of shocks that his mind and "flesh are heir to?"

9. How would you rewrite Johnny's story from the point of view of the nurse? a social worker? a rehabilitation worker? a newspaper reporter? a biographer?

10. Are there comparable instances in life where non-handicapped persons might have experiences similar to that of Johnny Bonham's?

11. If Johnny had not known Morse Code, what other systems of communication might he have used?

ADDITIONAL READINGS

- Fiedler, Leslie. *Freaks: Myths and Images of the Secret Self.* New York: Simon & Schuster, 1978.
- Goffman, Erving. *Stigma: Notes on the Management of Spoiled Identity.* Englewood Cliffs, NJ: Prentice-Hall, 1963.
- Zubek, John, ed. *Sensory Deprivation: Fifteen Years of Research.* New York: Century-Crofts, 1969.

Indeed, is the One-eyed Man King in the Country of the Blind?

2

The Country of the Blind

H. G. Wells

2

Blindness is generally thought to be the most tragic and insulting handicap to human beings, and especially to children. Nevertheless, early deafness may be even more debilitating to children who are cut off from many of their own thoughts and from communication with others. With some adjustments and assistance, blind children can grow up in relatively normal environments, learn at relatively high levels and, with electronic aids, do many things not previously possible. In any case, most parents react to blindness in a child as catastrophic and far worse than deafness. (The hypothetical choice is, of course, purely for discussion purposes — it is the kind of choice even Hobson would reject.)

Indeed, blindness has historically been the most terrorizing real and potential handicap. Psychologically, its association with guilt and punishment has embodied it with cultural overtones of sin, revenge, crime, and falsity. Laws and cultures still exist in which death and blindness are deemed comparable punishments. The Bible contains several examples of blinding as punishment. Freud incorporated the story of Oedipus (who put out his own eyes after learning that he had unknowingly married his mother) into a basic psychoanalytic concept.

Percentages have varied, but combined information indicates that about eighty percent of our information is processed through vision. Although comparing the eye to a camera is a typical analogy, some marked differences exist. The significant fact in vision is that what is seen is created — not passively focused on film or retina. As Gregory points out in his excellent book *Eye and Brain*,[1] light that enters the eye travels through layers of blood vessels, nerve fibers, and supporting cells before it gets to where the "film" would be — in this case, the rods and cones. Comparing this to a camera,

---

[1] R. L. Gregory, *Eye and Brain: The Psychology of Seeing* (New York: World University Library, McGraw Hill, 1966).

it would be as if one were to load the film inside out so that the light would hit the dark backing. In addition, the optic nerves in human eyes are not attached to the light receptors but form part of the brain.

Seeing, therefore, is a nervous system creation — a perception, if you wish. When we look down the length of tracks or a bridge and "see" parallel lines converging, this reality is our own construction. With vision we construct the concepts and percepts of vision. A blind person doesn't grow up as a person without sight but as a person who constructs a world by other means — hearing, smell, taste, and touch. A world so constructed is not easily given up or modified should circumstances provide vision in later life.

John Locke was asked: Suppose a man were born blind and taught by his touch to distinguish between a cube and sphere of the same metal. Now as an adult, if the blind man were suddenly able to see, could he differentiate the cube from the sphere? The answer is probably no.

Fortunately, the question does lend itself to empirical verification. In some documented cases, these people, blind during developmental stages with recovered vision later, could see little at first and were unable to name or distinguish objects or shapes. Many such persons have become depressed, finding the world uncomfortable, drab, and difficult.

All of this leads us to Nunez and his adventures in the Country of the Blind. The population of this strange country cannot be understood by comparing it to isolated individuals without vision. The population in the story lives in a dark world, in a culture of vast social, psychological, and value differences from those of a sighted world. In typical human self perception, vision has it all over nonvision — the one-eyed man *of course* would be king in the Country of the Blind. Or at least Nunez thinks so.

A word about Herbert George Wells for the younger, less literary minded folk. One might attribute his career as a scientist, historian, social rebel, and writer to two broken legs — one his and the other his father's. The elder Wells was a professional cricket player who broke his leg sliding into the equivalent of second base and reducing an already poor family to dire poverty. Early on, Herbert had to seek employment — jobs that bored him to distraction and encouraged an appreciation of intellectual and imaginative creations. When he was about seven, he was tossed in the air playfully by an older friend who somehow failed to catch him. The resulting broken leg curtailed Herbert's physical activity and turned him into a voracious reader.

In his *Experiment in Autobiography* (as befits a man of science, not only is his perception of his own experiences an experiment but is subtitled "Discoveries and Conclusions of a Very Ordinary Brain"), Wells comments, "My world began to expand very rapidly [after the broken leg] and when presently I could put my foot to the ground the reading habit had got me securely. Both my parents were doubtful of the healthiness of reading and did their best to discourage this poring over books as soon as my leg was better."[2]

As we know, his parents didn't succeed in that regard and H. G. went on to outline history, crystalize the invisible man, chronicle the war of the worlds, and invent a time machine. His later novels and stories reflected a greater interest in culture and deviance, of which "The Country of the Blind" is a good example.

[2] H. G. Wells, *Experiment in Authobiography* (New York: AMS Press, 1934), p. 54.

THE COUNTRY OF THE BLIND

H. G. Wells

Three hundred miles and more from Chimborazo, one hundred from the snows of Cotopaxi, in the wildest wastes of Ecuador's Andes, there lies that mysterious mountain valley, cut off from the world of men, the Country of the Blind. Long years ago that valley lay so far open to the world that men might come at last through frightful gorges and over an icy pass into its equable meadows; and thither indeed men came, a family or so of Peruvian half-breeds fleeing from the lust and tyranny of an evil Spanish ruler. Then came the stupendous outbreak of Mindobamba, when it was night in Quito for seventeen days, and the water was boiling at Yaguachi and all the fish floating dying even as far as Guayaquil; everywhere along the Pacific slopes there were land-slips and swift thawings and sudden floods, and one whole side of the old Arauca crest slipped and came down in thunder, and cut off the Country of the Blind for ever from the exploring feet of men. But one of these early settlers had chanced to be on the hither side of the gorges when the world had so terribly shaken itself, and he perforce had to forget his wife and his child and all the friends and possessions he had left up there, and start life over again in the lower world. He started it again but ill, blindness overtook him, and he died of punishment in the mines, but the story he told begot a legend that lingers along the length of the Cordilleras of the Andes to this day.

He told of his reason for venturing back from that fastness, into which he had first been carried lashed to a llama, beside a vast bale of gear, when he was a child. The valley, he said, had in it all that the heart of man could desire — sweet water, pasture, and even climate, slopes of rich brown soil with tangles of a shrub that bore an excellent fruit, and on one side great hanging forests

"The Country of the Blind," by H. G. Wells, was published by Strand in 1904.

of pine that held the avalanches high. Far overhead, on three sides, vast cliffs of grey-green rock were capped by cliffs of ice; but the glacier stream came not to them but flowed away by the farther slopes, and only now and then huge ice masses fell on the valley side. In this valley it neither rained nor snowed, but the abundant springs gave a rich green pasture, that irrigation would spread over all the valley space. The settlers did well indeed there. Their beasts did well and multiplied, and but one thing marred their happiness. Yet it was enough to mar it greatly. A strange disease had come upon them, and had made all the children born to them there — and indeed, several older children also — blind. It was to seek some charm or antidote against this plague of blindness that he had with fatigue and danger and difficulty returned down the gorge. In those days, in such cases, men did not think of germs and infections but of sins; and it seemed to him that the reason of this affliction must lie in the negligence of these priestless immigrants to set up a shrine so soon as they entered the valley. He wanted a shrine — a handsome, cheap, effectual shrine — to be erected in the valley; he wanted relics and such-like potent things of faith, blessed objects and mysterious medals and prayers. In his wallet he had a bar of native silver for which he would not account; he insisted there was none in the valley with something of the insistence of an inexpert liar. They had all clubbed their money and ornaments together, having little need for such treasure up there, he said, to buy them holy help against their ill. I figure this dim-eyed young mountaineer, sunburnt, gaunt, and anxious, hat-brim clutched feverishly, a man all unused to the ways of the lower world, telling this story to some keen-eyed, attentive priest before the great convulsion; I can picture him presently seeking to return with pious and infallible remedies against that trouble, and the infinite dismay with which he must have faced the tumbled vastness where the gorge had once come out. But the rest of his story of mischances is lost to me, save that I know of his evil death after several years. Poor stray from that remoteness! The stream that had once made the gorge now bursts from the mouth of a rocky cave, and the legend his poor, ill-told story set going developed into the legend of a race of blind men somewhere "over there" one may still hear to-day.

And amidst the little population of that now isolated and forgotten valley the disease ran its course. The old became groping and purblind, the young saw but dimly, and the children that were born to them saw never at all. But life was very easy in that snow-rimmed basin, lost to all the world, with neither thorns nor briars, with no evil insects nor any beasts save the gentle breed of llamas they had lugged and thrust and followed up the beds of the shrunken rivers in the gorges up which they had come. The seeing had become purblind so gradually that they scarcely noted their loss. They guided the sightless youngsters hither and thither until they knew the whole valley marvellously, and when at last sight died out among them the race lived on. They had even time to adapt themselves to the blind control of fire, which they made carefully in stoves of stone. They were a simple strain of people at the first, unlettered, only slightly touched with the Spanish civilisation, but with something of a tradition of the arts of old Peru and of its lost philosophy. Generation followed generation. They forgot many things; they devised many things. Their tradition of the greater world they came from became mythical in colour and uncertain. In all things save sight they were strong and able, and presently the chance of birth and heredity sent one who had an original mind and who could talk and persuade among them, and then afterwards another. These two passed, leaving their effects, and the little community grew in numbers and in understanding, and met and settled social and economic problems that arose. Generation followed generation. Generation followed generation. There came a time when a child was born who was fifteen generations from that ancestor who went out of the valley with a bar of silver to seek God's aid, and who never returned. Thereabouts it chanced that a man came into this community from the outer world. And this is the story of that man.

He was a mountaineer from the country near Quito, a man who had been down to the sea and had seen the world, a reader of books in an original way, an acute and enterprising man, and he was taken on by a party of Englishmen who had come out to Ecuador to climb mountains, to replace one of their three Swiss guides who had fallen ill. He climbed here and he climbed there, and then came the attempt on Parascotopetl, the Matterhorn of the Andes, in which he was lost to the outer world. The story of the accident has been written a dozen times. Pointer's narrative is the best. He tells how the little party worked their difficult and almost vertical way up to the very foot of the last and greatest precipice, and how they built a night shelter amidst the snow upon a little shelf of rock, and, with a touch of real dramatic power, how presently they found Nunez had gone from them. They shouted, and there was no reply; shouted and whistled, and for the rest of that night they slept no more.

As the morning broke they saw the traces of his fall. It seems impossible he could have uttered a sound. He had slipped eastward towards the unknown side of the mountain; far below he had struck a steep slope of snow, and ploughed his way down it in the midst of a snow avalanche. His track went straight to the edge of a frightful precipice, and beyond that everything was hidden. Far, far below, and hazy with distance, they could see trees rising out of a narrow, shut-in valley — the lost Country of the Blind. But they did not know it was the lost Country of the Blind, nor distinguish it in any way from any other narrow streak of upland valley. Unnerved by this disaster, they abandoned their attempt in the afternoon, and Pointer was called away to the war before he could make another attack. To this day Parascotopetl lifts an unconquered crest, and Pointer's shelter crumbles unvisited amidst the snows.

And the man who fell survived.

At the end of the slope he fell a thousand feet, and came down in the midst of a cloud of snow upon a snow slope even steeper than the one above. Down this he was whirled, stunned and insensible, but without a bone broken in his body; and then at last came to gentler slopes, and at last rolled out and lay still, buried amidst a softening heap of the white masses that had accompanied and saved him. He came to himself with a dim fancy that he was ill in bed; then realised his position with a mountaineer's intelligence, and worked himself loose and, after a rest or so, out until he saw the stars. He rested flat upon his chest for a space, wondering where he was and what had happened to him. He explored his limbs, and discovered that several of his buttons were gone and his coat turned over his head. His knife had gone from his pocket and his hat was lost, though he had tied it under his chin. He recalled that he had been looking for loose stones to raise his piece of the shelter wall. His ice-axe had disappeared.

He decided he must have fallen, and looked up to see, exaggerated by the ghastly light of the rising moon, the tremendous flight he had taken. For a while he lay, gazing blankly at that vast pale cliff towering above, rising moment by moment out of a subsiding tide of darkness. Its phantasmal, mysterious beauty held him for a space, and then he was seized with a paroxysm of sobbing laughter. . . .

After a great interval of time he became aware that he was near the lower edge of the snow. Below, down what was now a moonlit and practicable slope, he saw the dark and broken appearance of rock-strewn turf. He struggled to his feet, aching in every joint and limb, got down painfully from the heaped loose snow about him, went downward until he was on the turf, and there dropped rather than lay beside a boulder, drank deep from the flask in his inner pocket, and instantly fell asleep. . . .

He was awakened by the singing of birds in the trees far below.

He sat up and perceived he was on a little alp at the foot of a vast precipice, that was grooved by the gully down which he and his snow had come. Over against him another wall of rock reared itself against the sky. The gorge between these precipices ran east and west and was full of the morning sunlight, which lit to the westward the mass of fallen mountain that closed the descending gorge. Below him it seemed there was a precipice equally steep, but behind the snow in the gully he found a sort of chimney-cleft dripping with snow-water down which a desperate man might venture. He found it easier than it seemed, and came at last to another desolate alp, and then after a rock climb of no particular difficulty to a steep slope of trees. He took his bearings and turned his face up the gorge, for he saw it opened out above upon green meadows, among which he now glimpsed quite distinctly a cluster of stone huts of unfamiliar fashion. At times his progress was like clambering along the face of a wall, and after a time the rising sun ceased to strike along the gorge, the voices of the singing birds died away, and the air grew cold and dark about him. But the distant valley with its houses was all the brighter for that. He came presently to talus, and among the rocks he noted — for he was an observant man — an unfamiliar fern that seemed to clutch out of the crevices with intense green hands. He picked a frond or so and gnawed its stalk and found it helpful.

About midday he came at last out of the throat of the gorge into the plain and the sunlight. He was stiff and weary; he sat down in the shadow of a rock, filled up his flask with water from a spring and drank it down, and remained for a time resting before he went on to the houses.

They were very strange to his eyes, and indeed the whole aspect of that valley became, as he regarded it, queerer and more unfamiliar. The greater part of its surface was lush green meadow, starred with many beautiful flowers, irrigated with extraordinary care, and bearing evidence of systematic cropping piece by piece. High up and ringing the valley about was a wall, and what appeared to be a circumferential water-channel, from which the little trickles of water that fed the meadow plants came, and on the higher slopes above this flocks of llamas cropped the scanty herbage. Sheds, apparently shelters or feeding-places for the llamas, stood against the boundary wall here and there. The irrigation streams ran together into a main channel down the centre of the valley, and this was enclosed on either side by a wall breast high. This gave a singularly urban quality to this secluded place, a quality that was greatly enhanced by the fact that a number of paths paved with black and white stones, and each with a curious little kerb at the side, ran hither and thither in an orderly manner. The houses of the central village were quite unlike the casual and higgledy-piggledy agglomeration of the mountain villages he knew; they stood in a continuous row on either side of a central street of astonishing cleanness; here and there their parti-coloured facade was pierced by a door, and not a solitary window broke their even frontage. They were parti-coloured with extraordinary irregularity, smeared with a sort of plaster that was sometimes grey, sometimes drab, sometimes slate-coloured or dark brown; and it was the sight of this wild plastering first brought the word "blind" into the thoughts of the explorer. "The good man who did that," he thought, "must have been as blind as a bat."

He descended a steep place, and so came to the wall and channel that ran about the valley, near where the latter spouted out its surplus contents into the deeps of the gorge in a thin and wavering thread of cascade. He could now see a number of men and women resting on piled heaps of grass, as if taking a siesta, in the remoter part of the meadow, and nearer the village a number of recumbent children, and then nearer at hand three men carrying pails on yokes along a little path that ran from the encircling wall towards the houses. These latter were clad in garments of llama cloth and boots and belts of leather, and they wore caps of cloth with back and ear flaps. They followed one another in single file, walking slowly and yawning as they walked, like men who have been up all night. There was something so reassuringly prosperous and respectable in their bearing that after a moment's hesitation Nunez stood forward as conspicuously as possible upon his rock, and gave vent to a mighty shout that echoed round the valley.

The three men stopped, and moved their heads as though they were looking about them. They turned their faces this way and that, and Nunez gesticulated with freedom. But they did not appear to see him for all his gestures, and after a time, directing themselves towards the mountains far away to the right, they shouted as if in answer. Nunez bawled again, and then once more, and as he gestured ineffectually the word "blind" came up to the top of his thoughts. "The fools must be blind," he said.

When at last, after much shouting and wrath, Nunez crossed the stream by a little bridge, came through a gate in the wall, and approached them, he was sure that they were blind. He was sure that this was the Country of the Blind of which the legends told. Conviction had sprung upon him, and a sense of great and rather enviable adventure. The three stood side by side not looking at him, but with their ears directed towards him, judging him by his unfamiliar steps. They stood close together like men a little afraid, and he could see their eyelids closed and sunken, as though the very balls beneath had shrunk away. There was an expression near awe on their faces.

"A man," one said, in hardly recognisable Spanish — "a man it is — a man or a spirit — coming down from the rocks."

But Nunez advanced with the confident steps of a youth who enters upon life. All the old stories of the lost valley and the Country of the Blind had come back to his mind, and through his thoughts ran this old proverb, as if it were a refrain —

"In the Country of the Blind the One-eyed Man is King."

"In the Country of the Blind the One-eyed Man is King."

And very civilly he gave them greeting. He talked to them and used his eyes.

"Where does he come from, brother Pedro?" asked one.

"Down out of the rocks."

"Over the mountains I come," said Nunez, "out of the country beyond there — where men can see. From near Bogota, where there are a hundred thousands of people, and where the city passes out of sight."

"Sight?" muttered Pedro. "Sight?"

"He comes," said the second blind man, "out of the rocks."

The cloth of their coats Nunez saw was curiously fashioned, each with a different sort of stitching.

They startled him by a simultaneous movement towards him, each with a hand outstretched. He stepped back from the advance of these spread fingers.

"Come hither," said the third blind man, following his motion and clutching him neatly.

And they held Nunez and felt him over, saying no word further until they had done so.

"Carefully," he cried, with a finger in his eye, and found they thought that organ, with its fluttering lids, a queer thing in him. They went over it again.

"A strange creature, Correa," said the one called Pedro. "Feel the coarseness of his hair. Like a llama's hair."

"Rough he is as the rocks that begot him," said Correa, investigating Nunez's unshaven chin with a soft and slightly moist hand. "Perhaps he will grow finer." Nunez struggled a little under their examination, but they gripped him firm.

"Carefully," he said again.

"He speaks," said the third man. "Certainly he is a man."

"Ugh!" said Pedro, at the roughness of his coat.

"And you have come into the world?" asked Pedro.

"*Out* of the world. Over mountains and glaciers; right over above there, half-way to the sun. Out of the great big world that goes down, twelve days' journey to the sea."

They scarcely seemed to heed him. "Our fathers have told us men may be made by the forces of Nature," said Correa. "It is the warmth of things and moisture, and rottenness — rottenness."

"Let us lead him to the elders," said Pedro.

"Shout first," said Correa, "lest the children be afraid. This is a marvellous occasion."

So they shouted, and Pedro went first and took Nunez by the hand to lead him to the houses.

He drew his hand away. "I can see," he said.

"See?" said Correa.

"Yes, see," said Nunez, turning towards him, and stumbled against Pedro's pail.

"His senses are still imperfect," said the third blind man. "He stumbles, and talks unmeaning words. Lead him by the hand."

"As you will," said Nunez, and was led along, laughing.

It seemed they knew nothing of sight.

Well, all in good time he would teach them.

He heard people shouting, and saw a number of figures gathering together in the middle roadway of the village.

He found it tax his nerve and patience more than he had anticipated, that first encounter with the population of the Country of the Blind. The place seemed larger as he drew near to it, and the smeared plasterings queerer, and a crowd of children and men and women (the women and girls, he was pleased to note, had some of them quite sweet faces, for all that their eyes were shut and sunken) came about him, holding on to him, touching him with soft, sensitive hands, smelling at him, and listening at every word he spoke. Some of the maidens and children, however, kept aloof as if afraid, and indeed his voice seemed coarse and rude beside their softer notes. They mobbed him. His three guides kept close to him with an effect of proprietorship, and said again and again, "A wild man out of the rocks."

"Bogota," he said. "Bogota. Over the mountain crests."

"A wild man — using wild words," said Pedro. "Did you hear that — *Bogota?* His mind is hardly formed yet. He has only the beginnings of speech."

A little boy nipped his hand. "Bogota!" he said mockingly.

"Ay! A city to your village. I come from the great world — where men have eyes and see."

"His name's Bogota," they said.

"He stumbled," said Correa, "stumbled twice as we came hither."

"Bring him to the elders."

And they thrust him suddenly through a doorway into a room as black as pitch, save at the end there faintly glowed a fire. The crowd closed in behind him and shut out all but the faintest glimmer of day, and before he could arrest himself he had fallen headlong over the feet of a seated man. His arm, outflung, struck the face of some one else as he went down; he felt the soft impact of features and heard a cry of anger, and for a moment he struggled

73

against a number of hands that clutched him. It was a one-sided fight. An inkling of the situation came to him, and he lay quiet.

"I fell down," he said; "I couldn't see in this pitchy darkness."

There was a pause as if the unseen persons about him tried to understand his words. Then the voice of Correa said: "He is but newly formed. He stumbles as he walks and mingles words that mean nothing with his speech."

Others also said things about him that he heard or understood imperfectly.

"May I sit up?" he asked, in a pause. "I will not struggle against you again."

They consulted and let him rise.

The voice of an older man began to question him, and Nunez found himself trying to explain the great world out of which he had fallen, and the sky and mountains and sight and such-like marvels, to these elders who sat in darkness in the Country of the Blind. And they would believe and understand nothing whatever he told them, a thing quite outside his expectation. They would not even understand many of his words. For fourteen generations these people had been blind and cut off from all the seeing world; the names for all the things of sight had faded and changed; the story of the outer world was faded and changed to a child's story; and they had ceased to concern themselves with anything beyond the rocky slopes above their circling wall. Blind men of genius had arisen among them and questioned the shreds of belief and tradition they had brought with them from their seeing days, and had dismissed all these things as idle fancies, and replaced them with new and saner explanations. Much of their imagination had shrivelled with their eyes, and they had made for themselves new imaginations with their ever more sensitive ears and finger-tips. Slowly Nunez realised this; that his expectation of wonder and reverence at his origin and his gifts was not to be borne out; and after his poor attempt to explain sight to them had been set aside as the confused version of a new-made being describing the marvels of his incoherent sensations, he subsided, a little dashed, into listening to their instruction. And the eldest of the blind men explained to him life and philosophy and religion, how that the world (meaning their valley) had been first an empty hollow in the rocks, and then had come, first, inanimate things without the gift of touch, and llamas and a few other creatures that had little sense, and then men, and at last angels, whom one could hear singing and making fluttering sounds, but whom no one could touch at all, which puzzled Nunez greatly until he thought of the birds.

He went on to tell Nunez how this time had been divided into the warm and the cold, which are the blind equivalents of day and night, and how it was good to sleep in the warm and work during the cold, so that now, but for his advent, the whole town of the blind would have been asleep. He said Nunez must have been specially created to learn and serve the wisdom they had acquired, and that for all his mental incoherency and stumbling behaviour he must have courage and do his best to learn, and at that all the people in the doorway murmured encouragingly. He said the night — for the blind call their day night — was now far gone, and it behoved every one to go back to sleep. He asked Nunez if he knew how to sleep, and Nunez said he did, but that before sleep he wanted food.

They brought him food — llama's milk in a bowl, and rough salted bread — and led him into a lonely place to eat out of their hearing, and afterwards to slumber until the chill of the mountain evening roused them to begin their day again. But Nunez slumbered not at all.

Instead, he sat up in the place where they had left him, resting his limbs and turning the unanticipated circumstances of his arrival over and over in his mind.

Every now and then he laughed, sometimes with amusement, and sometimes with indignation.

"Unformed mind!" he said. "Got no senses yet! They little know they've been insulting their heaven-sent king and master. I see I must bring them to reason. Let me think — let me think."

He was still thinking when the sun set.

Nunez had an eye for all beautiful things, and it seemed to him that the glow upon the snowfields and glaciers that rose about the valley on every side was the most beautiful thing he had ever seen. His eyes went from that inaccessible glory to the village and irrigated fields, fast sinking into the twilight, and suddenly a wave of emotion took him, and he thanked God from the bottom of his heart that the power of sight had been given him.

He heard a voice calling to him from out of the village. "Ya ho there, Bogota! Come hither!"

At that he stood up smiling. He would show these people once and for all what sight would do for a man. They would seek him, but not find him.

"You move not, Bogota," said the voice.

He laughed noiselessly, and made two stealthy steps aside from the path.

"Trample not on the grass, Bogota; that is not allowed."

Nunez had scarcely heard the sound he made himself. He stopped amazed.

The owner of the voice came running up the piebald path towards him.

He stepped back into the pathway. "Here I am," he said.

"Why did you not come when I called you?" said the blind man. "Must you be led like a child? Cannot you hear the path as you walk?"

Nunez laughed. "I can see it," he said.

"There is no such word as *see*," said the blind man, after a pause. "Cease this folly, and follow the sound of my feet."

Nunez followed, a little annoyed.

"My time will come," he said.

"You'll learn," the blind man answered. "There is much to learn in the world."

"Has no one told you, 'In the Country of the Blind the One-eyed Man is King?' "

"What is blind?" asked the blind man carelessly over his shoulder.

Four days passed, and the fifth found the King of the Blind still incognito, as a clumsy and useless stranger among his subjects.

It was, he found, much more difficult to proclaim himself than he had supposed, and in the meantime, while he meditated his *coup d'état,* he did what he was told and learnt the manners and customs of the Country of the Blind. He found working and going about at night a particularly irksome thing, and he decided that that should be the first thing he would change.

They led a simple, laborious life, these people, with all the elements of virtue and happiness, as these things can be understood by men. They toiled, but not oppressively; they had food and clothing sufficient for their needs; they had days and seasons of rest; they made much of music and singing, and there was love among them, and little children.

It was marvellous with what confidence and precision they went about their ordered world. Everything, you see, had been made to fit their needs; each of the radiating paths of the valley area had a constant angle to the others, and was distinguished by a special notch upon its kerbing; all obstacles and irregularities of path or meadow had long since been cleared away; all their methods and procedure arose naturally from their special needs. Their senses had become marvellously acute; they could hear and judge the slightest gesture of a man a dozen paces away — could hear the very beating of his heart. Intonation had long replaced expression with them, and touches gesture, and their work with hoe and spade and fork was as free and confident as garden work can be. Their sense of smell was extraordinarily fine; they could distinguish individual differences as readily as a dog can, and they went about the tending of the llamas, who lived among the rocks above and came to the wall for food and shelter, with ease and confidence. It was only when at last Nunez sought to assert himself that he found how easy and confident their movements could be.

He rebelled only after he had tried persuasion.

He tried at first on several occasions to tell them of sight. "Look you here, you people," he said. "There are things you do not understand in me."

Once or twice one or two of them attended to him; they sat with faces downcast and ears turned intelligently towards him, and he did his best to tell them what it was to see. Among his hearers was a girl, with eyelids less red and sunken than the others, so that one could almost fancy she was hiding eyes, whom especially he hoped to persuade. He spoke of the beauties of sight, of watching the mountains, of the sky and the sunrise, and they heard him with amused incredulity that presently became condemnatory. They told him there were indeed no mountains at all, but that the end of the rocks where the llamas grazed was indeed the end of the world; thence sprang a cavernous roof of the universe, from which the dew and the avalanches fell; and when he maintained stoutly the world had neither end nor roof such as they supposed, they said his thoughts were wicked. So far as he could describe sky and clouds and stars to them it seemed to them a hideous void, a terrible blankness in the place of the smooth roof to things in which they believed — it was an article of faith with them that the cavern roof was exquisitely smooth to the touch. He saw that in some manner he shocked them, and gave up that aspect of the matter altogether, and tried to show them the practical value of sight. One morning he saw Pedro in the path called Seventeen and coming towards the central houses, but still too far off for hearing or scent, and he told them as much. "In a little while," he prophesied, "Pedro will be here." An old man remarked that Pedro had no business on path Seventeen, and then, as if in confirmation, that individual as he drew near turned and went transversely into path Ten, and so back with nimble paces towards the outer wall. They mocked Nunez when Pedro did not arrive, and afterwards, when he asked Pedro questions to clear his character, Pedro denied and outfaced him, and was afterwards hostile to him.

Then he induced them to let him go a long way up the sloping meadows towards the wall with one complacent individual, and to him he promised to describe all that happened among the houses. He noted certain goings and comings, but the things that really seemed to signify to these people happened inside of or behind the windowless houses — the only things they took note of to test him by — and of these he could see or tell nothing; and it was after the failure of this attempt, and the ridicule they could not repress, that he resorted to force. He thought of seizing a spade and suddenly smiting one or two of them to earth, and so in fair combat showing the advantage of eyes. He went so far with that resolution as to seize his spade, and then he discovered a new thing about himself, and that was that it was impossible for him to hit a blind man in cold blood.

He hesitated, and found them all aware that he had snatched up the spade. They stood alert, with their heads on one side, and bent ears towards him for what he would do next.

"Put that spade down," said one, and he felt a sort of helpless horror. He came near obedience.

Then he thrust one backwards against a house wall, and fled past him and out of the village.

He went athwart one of their meadows, leaving a track of trampled grass behind his feet, and presently sat down by the side of one of their ways. He felt something of the buoyancy that comes to all men in the beginning of a fight, but more perplexity. He began to realise that you cannot even fight happily with creatures who stand upon a different mental basis to yourself. Far away he saw a number of men carrying spades and sticks come out of the street of houses, and advance in a spreading line along the several paths towards him. They advanced slowly, speaking frequently to one another, and ever and again the whole cordon would halt and sniff the air and listen.

The first time they did this Nunez laughed. But afterwards he did not laugh.

One struck his trail in the meadow grass, and came stooping and feeling his way along it.

For five minutes he watched the slow extension of the cordon, and then his vague disposition to do something forthwith became frantic. He stood up, went a pace or so towards the circumferential wall, turned, and went back a little way. There they all stood in a crescent, still and listening.

He also stood still, gripping his spade very tightly in both hands. Should he charge them?

The pulse in his ears ran into the rhythm of "In the Country of the Blind the One-eyed Man is King!"

Should he charge them?

He looked back at the high and unclimbable wall behind — unclimbable because of its smooth plastering, but withal pierced with many little doors, and at the approaching line of seekers. Behind these others were now coming out of the street of houses.

Should he charge them?

"Bogota!" called one. "Bogota! Where are you?"

He gripped his spade still tighter, and advanced down the meadows towards the place of habitations, and directly he moved they converged upon him. "I'll hit them if they touch me," he swore; "by Heaven, I will. I'll hit." He called aloud, "Look here, I'm going to do what I like in this valley. Do you hear? I'm going to do what I like and go where I like!"

They were moving in upon him quickly, groping, yet moving rapidly. It was like playing blind man's buff, with every one blind-folded except one. "Get hold of him!" cried one. He found himself in the arc of a loose curve of pursuers. He felt suddenly he must be active and resolute.

"You don't understand," he cried in a voice that was meant to be great and resolute, and which broke. "You are blind, and I can see. Leave me alone!"

"Bogota! Put down that spade, and come off the grass!"

The last order, grotesque in its urban familiarity, produced a gust of anger.

"I'll hurt you," he said, sobbing with emotion. "By Heaven, I'll hurt you. Leave me alone!"

He began to run, not knowing clearly where to run. He ran from the nearest blind man, because it was a horror to hit him. He stopped, and then made a dash to escape from their closing ranks. He made for where a gap was wide, and the men on either side, with a quick perception of the approach of his paces, rushed in on one another. He sprang forward, and then saw he must be caught, and *swish!* the spade had struck. He felt the soft thud of hand and arm, and the man was down with a yell of pain, and he was through.

Through! And then he was close to the street of houses again, and blind men, whirling spades and stakes, were running with a sort of reasoned swiftness hither and thither.

He heard steps behind him just in time, and found a tall man rushing forward and swiping at the sound of him. He lost his nerve, hurled his spade a yard wide at his antagonist, and whirled about and fled, fairly yelling as he dodged another.

He was panic-stricken. He ran furiously to and fro, dodging when there was no need to dodge, and in his anxiety to see on every side of him at once, stumbling. For a moment he was down and they heard his fall. Far away in the circumferential wall a little doorway looked like heaven, and he set off in a wild rush for it. He did not even look round at his pursuers until it was gained, and he had stumbled across the bridge, clambered a little way among the rocks, to the surprise and dismay of a young llama, who went leaping out of sight, and lay down sobbing for breath.

And so his *coup d'état* came to an end.

He stayed outside the wall of the valley of the Blind for two nights and days without food or shelter, and meditated upon the unexpected. During these meditations he repeated very frequently and always with a profounder note of derision the exploded proverb: "In the Country of the Blind the One-eyed Man is King." He thought chiefly of ways of fighting and conquering these people, and it grew clear that for him no practicable way was possible. He had no weapons, and now it would be hard to get one.

The canker of civilisation had got to him even in Bogota, and he could not find it in himself to go down and assassinate a blind man. Of course, if he did that, he might then dictate terms on the threat of assassinating them all. But — sooner or later he must sleep! . . .

He tried also to find food among the pine trees, to be comfortable under pine boughs while the frost fell at night, and — with less confidence — to catch a llama by artifice in order to try to kill it — perhaps by hammering it with a stone — and so finally, perhaps, to eat some of it. But the llamas had a doubt of him and regarded him with distrustful brown eyes, and spat when he drew near. Fear came on him the second day and fits of shivering. Finally he crawled down to the wall of the Country of the Blind and tried to make terms. He crawled along by the stream, shouting, until two blind men came out to the gate and talked to him.

"I was mad," he said. "But I was only newly made."

They said that was better.

He told them he was wiser now, and repented of all he had done.

Then he wept without intention, for he was very weak and ill now, and they took that as a favourable sign.

They asked him if he still thought he could "*see*."

"No," he said. "That was folly. The word means nothing — less than nothing!"

They asked him what was overhead.

"About ten times ten the height of a man there is a roof above the world — of rock — and very, very smooth." . . . He burst again into hysterical tears. "Before you ask me any more, give me some food or I shall die."

He expected dire punishments, but these blind people were capable of toleration. They regarded his rebellion as but one more proof of his general idiocy and inferiority; and after they had whipped him they appointed him to do the simplest and heaviest work they had for any one to do, and he, seeing no other way of living, did submissively what he was told.

He was ill for some days, and they nursed him kindly. That refined his submission. But they insisted on his lying in the dark, and that was a great misery. And blind philosophers came and talked to him of the wicked levity of his mind, and reproved him so impressively for his doubts about the lid of rock that covered their cosmic casserole that he almost doubted whether indeed he was not the victim of hallucination in not seeing it overhead.

So Nunez became a citizen of the Country of the Blind, and these people ceased to be a generalised people and became individualities and familiar to him, while the world beyond the mountains became more and more remote and unreal. There was Yacob, his master, a kindly man when not annoyed; there was Pedro, Yacob's nephew; and there was Medina-saroté, who was the youngest daughter of Yacob. She was little esteemed in the world of the blind, because she had a clear-cut face, and lacked that satisfying, glossy smoothness that is the blind man's idea of feminine beauty; but Nunez thought her beautiful at first, and presently the most beautiful thing in the whole creation. Her closed eyelids were not sunken and red after the common way of the valley, but lay as though they might open again at any moment; and she had long eyelashes, which were considered a grave disfigurement. And her voice was strong, and did not satisfy the acute hearing of the valley swains. So that she had no lover.

There came a time when Nunez thought that, could he win her, he would be resigned to live in the valley for all the rest of his days.

He watched her; he sought opportunities of doing her little services, and presently he found that she observed him. Once at a rest-day gathering they sat side by side in the dim starlight, and the music was sweet. His hand came upon hers and he dared to clasp it. Then very tenderly she returned his pressure. And one day, as they were at their meal in the darkness, he felt her hand very softly seeking him, and as it chanced the fire leapt and he saw the tenderness of her face.

He sought to speak to her.

He went to her one day when she was sitting in the summer moonlight spinning. The light made her a thing of silver and mystery. He sat down at her feet and told her he loved her, and told her how beautiful she seemed to him. He had a lover's voice, he spoke with a tender reverence that came near to awe, and she had never before been touched by adoration. She made him no definite answer, but it was clear his words pleased her.

After that he talked to her whenever he could take an opportunity. The valley became the world for him, and the world beyond the mountains where men lived in sunlight seemed no more than a fairy tale he would some day pour into her ears. Very tentatively and timidly he spoke to her of sight.

Sight seemed to her the most poetical of fancies, and she listened to his description of the stars and the mountains and her own sweet white-lid beauty as though it was a guilty indulgence. She did not believe, she could only half understand, but she was mysteriously delighted, and it seemed to him that she completely understood.

His love lost its awe and took courage. Presently he was for demanding her of Yacob and the elders in marriage, but she became fearful and delayed. And it was one of her elder sisters who first told Yacob that Medina-saroté and Nunez were in love.

There was from the first very great opposition to the marriage of Nunez and Medina-saroté; not so much because they valued her as because they held him as a being apart, an idiot, incompetent thing below the permissible level of a man. Her sisters opposed it bitterly as bringing discredit on them all; and old Yacob, though he had formed a sort of liking for his clumsy, obedient serf, shook his head and said the thing could not be. The young men were all angry at the idea of corrupting the race, and one went so far as to revile and strike Nunez. He struck back. Then for the first time he found an advantage in seeing, even by twilight, and after that fight was over no one was disposed to raise a hand against him. But they still found his marriage impossible.

Old Yacob had a tenderness for his last little daughter, and was grieved to have her weep upon his shoulder.

"You see, my dear, he's an idiot. He has delusions; he can't do anything right."

"I know," wept Medina-saroté. "But he's better than he was. He's getting better. And he's strong, dear father, and kind — stronger and kinder than any other man in the world. And he loves me — and father, I love him."

Old Yacob was greatly distressed to find her inconsolable, and, besides — what made it more distressing — he liked Nunez for many things. So he went and sat in the windowless council-chamber with the other elders and watched the trend of the talk, and said, at the proper time, "He's better than he was. Very likely, some day, we shall find him as sane as ourselves."

Then afterwards one of the elders, who thought deeply, had an idea. He was the great doctor among these people, their medicine-man, and he had a very philosophical and inventive mind, and the idea of curing Nunez of his peculiarities appealed to him. One day when Yacob was present he returned to the topic of Nunez.

"I have examined Bogota," he said, "and the case is clearer to me. I think very probably he might be cured."

"That is what I have always hoped," said old Yacob.

"His brain is affected," said the blind doctor.

The elders murmured assent.

"Now, *what* affects it?"

"Ah!" said old Yacob.

"*This*," said the doctor, answering his own question. "Those queer things that are called the eyes, and which exist to make an agreeable soft depression in the face, are diseased, in the case of Bogota, in such a way as to affect his brain. They are greatly distended, he has eyelashes, and his eyelids move, and consequently his brain is in a state of constant irritation and distraction."

"Yes?" said old Yacob. "Yes?"

"And I think I may say with reasonable certainty that, in order to cure him completely, all that we need do is a simple and easy surgical operation — namely, to remove these irritant bodies."

"And then he will be sane?"

"Then he will be perfectly sane, and a quite admirable citizen."

"Thank Heaven for science!" said old Yacob, and went forth at once to tell Nunez of his happy hopes.

But Nunez's manner of receiving the good news struck him as being cold and disappointing.

"One might think," he said, "from the tone you take, that you did not care for my daughter."

It was Medina-saroté who persuaded Nunez to face the blind surgeons.

"*You* do not want me," he said, "to lose my gift of sight?"

She shook her head.

"My world is sight."

Her head drooped lower.

"There are the beautiful things, the beautiful little things — the flowers, the lichens among the rocks, the lightness and softness on a piece of fur, the far sky with its drifting down of clouds, the sunsets and the stars. And there is *you*. For you alone it is good to have sight, to see your sweet, serene face, your kindly lips, your dear, beautiful hands folded together. . . . It is these eyes of mine you won, these eyes that hold me to you, that these idiots seek. Instead, I must touch you, hear you, and never see you again. I must come under that roof of rock and stone and darkness, that horrible roof under which your imagination stoops. . . . No; you would not have me do that?"

A disagreeable doubt had arisen in him. He stopped, and left the thing a question.

"I wish," she said, "sometimes——" She paused.

"Yes," said he, a little apprehensively.

"I wish sometimes — you would not talk like that."

"Like what?"

"I know it's pretty — it's your imagination. I love it, but *now*——"

He felt cold. "*Now?*" he said faintly.

She sat quite still.

"You mean — you think — I should be better, better perhaps——"

He was realising things very swiftly. He felt anger, indeed, anger at the dull course of fate, but also sympathy for her lack of understanding — a sympathy near akin to pity.

"*Dear*," he said, and he could see by her whiteness how intensely her spirit pressed against the things she could not say. He put his arms about her, he kissed her ear, and they sat for a time in silence.

"If I were to consent to this?" he said at last, in a voice that was very gentle.

She flung her arms about him, weeping wildly. "Oh, if you would," she sobbed, "if only you would!"

For a week before the operation that was to raise him from his servitude and inferiority to the level of a blind citizen, Nunez knew nothing of sleep, and all through the warm sunlit hours, while the others slumbered happily, he sat brooding or wandered aimlessly, trying to bring his mind to bear on his dilemma. He had given his answer, he had given his consent, and still he was not sure. And at last work-time was over, the sun rose in splendour over the golden crests, and his last day of vision began for him. He had a few minutes with Medina-saroté before she went apart to sleep.

"To-morrow," he said, "I shall see no more."

"Dear heart!" she answered, and pressed his hands with all her strength.

"They will hurt you but little," she said; "and you are going through this pain — you are going through it, dear lover, for *me*. . . . Dear, if a woman's heart and life can do it, I will repay you. My dearest one, my dearest with the tender voice, I will repay."

He was drenched in pity for himself and her.

He held her in his arms, and pressed his lips to hers, and looked on her sweet face for the last time. "Good-bye!" he whispered at that dear sight, "good-bye!"

And then in silence he turned away from her.

She could hear his slow retreating footsteps, and something in the rhythm of them threw her into a passion of weeping.

He had fully meant to go to a lonely place where the meadows were beautiful with white narcissus, and there remain until the hour of his sacrifice should come, but as he went he lifted up his eyes and saw the morning, the morning like an angel in golden armour, marching down the steeps. . . .

It seemed to him that before this splendour he, and this blind world in the valley, and his love, and all, were no more than a pit of sin.

He did not turn aside as he had meant to do, but went on, and passed through the wall of the circumference and out upon the rocks, and his eyes were always upon the sunlit ice and snow.

He saw their infinite beauty, and his imagination soared over them to the things beyond he was now to resign for ever.

He thought of that great free world he was parted from, the world that was his own, and he had a vision of those further slopes, distance beyond distance, with Bogota, a place of multitudinous stirring beauty, a glory by day, a luminous mystery by night, a place of palaces and fountains and statues and white houses, lying beautifully in the middle distance. He thought how for a day or so one might come down through passes, drawing ever nearer and nearer to its busy streets, and ways. He thought of the river journey, day by day, from great Bogota to the still vaster world beyond, through towns and villages, forest and desert places, the rushing river day by day, until its banks receded and the big steamers came splashing by, and one had reached the sea — the limitless sea, with its thousand islands, its thousands of

islands, and its ships seen dimly far away in their incessant jour-
neyings round and about that greater world. And there, unpent
by mountains, one saw the sky — the sky, not such a disc as one
saw it here, but an arch of immeasurable blue, a deep of deeps in
which the circling stars were floating. . . .

His eyes scrutinised the great curtain of the mountains with
a keener inquiry.

For example, if one went so, up that gully and to that chimney
there, then one might come out high among those stunted pines
that ran round in a sort of shelf and rose still higher and higher
as it passed above the gorge. And then? That talus might be managed. Thence perhaps a climb might be found to take him up to
the precipice that came below the snow; and if that chimney failed,
then another farther to the east might serve his purpose better.
And then? Then one would be out upon the amber-lit snow there,
and half-way up to the crest of those beautiful desolations.

He glanced back at the village, then turned right round and
regarded it steadfastly.

He thought of Medina-saroté, and she had become small and
remote.

He turned again towards the mountain wall, down which the
day had come to him.

Then very circumspectly he began to climb.

When sunset came he was no longer climbing, but he was far
and high. He had been higher, but he was still very high. His
clothes were torn, his limbs were blood-stained, he was bruised
in many places, but he lay as if he were at his ease, and there was a
smile on his face.

From where he rested the valley seemed as if it were in a pit
and nearly a mile below. Already it was dim with haze and shadow,
though the mountain summits around him were things of light
and fire, and the little details of the rocks near at hand were
drenched with subtle beauty — a vein of green mineral piercing
the grey, the flash of crystal faces here and there, a minute,
minutely-beautiful orange lichen close beside his face. There were
deep mysterious shadows in the gorge, blue deepening into purple,
and purple into a luminous darkness, and overhead was the il-
limitable vastness of the sky. But he heeded these things no longer,

but lay quite inactive there, smiling as if he were satisfied merely to have escaped from the valley of the Blind in which he had thought to be King.

The glow of the sunset passed, and the night came, and still he lay peacefully contented under the cold clear stars.

Erasmus, according to H. G. Wells, was misinformed. In the Country of the Blind, not only is the sighted person not king but he turns out to be a frightened, blithering idiot. Nunez is sighted but handicapped. Medina-saroté is blind but normal.

Several significant concepts related to the field of the handicapped surface in the story. One is that of deviance and its counterpart, normality. Then there are concepts relating to culture, culture shock, and the behavior of persons who move from one cultural assumption to another.

In the strict orthodox interpretation of deviance, one confronts the notions of injury, disability, and handicap. For instance, if an individual suffers some structural damage to the physical self, like a broken leg, this may or may not be disabling. If the broken leg results in being hospitalized, missing school, cancelling several business appointments, or being unable to participate in a tennis tournament, the injury may be slightly, moderately, or markedly disabling. If the individual has played tennis only occasionally for relaxation, gets into a comfortable walking cast, and attends school or business as before, that person is injured but perhaps not disabled. The concept of disability suggests restrictions in behavioral response or functioning ability. And even though the injury may result in some behavioral restrictions, the condition can hardly be said to be disabling when the social, psychological, and behavioral consequences are minimal.

In contrast, an injury causing a condition or disability that impedes, hinders, or reduces behavioral freedom over a period of time can sometimes represent a real handicap. And in addition to physical or sensory injuries, there are social, psychological, and cultural injuries, disabilities, and handicaps. Certainly, Nunez has no biological injury or disability — yet his existence in the Country of the Blind is as a handicapped person. He is given an opportunity to become "normal" and marry his beloved, but in this case normality seems too high a price to pay.

From a behavioral, cultural, and statistical point of view, Nunez is deviant. From a biological, structural viewpoint, Nunez is normal and the citizens of the Country of the Blind are deviant. Not all values are culturally relativistic, nor are all deviances a matter of relative norms. Dental caries and colds, for example, are conditions of some prevalence in our population, yet one would hardly call them normal (i.e., healthy).

After Nunez discovers the unique nature of normality in the culture he has stumbled into, his assumption is that his deviance (sight) will be highly valued and desirable. His feelings can be compared to a highly bright child in a class of dullards or Jack Nicklaus playing golf with any Sunday hacker. These comparisons are clearly in the same conceptual ballpark separated by degrees of competency. In Nunez's case, his deviance turns out to be undesirable just as is hostile behavior, stealing cars, street fighting, and psychotic behavior. His deviance is unacceptable to the sightless culture and cannot be tolerated within its value system or borders. He can be normal in this place only if he is sightless.

Cultures and societies vary in their flexibilities to deal with deviance. One may move to or live in many societies, but culture is both prescriptive and imperious. Culture sticks to the person; it incorporates the personal values and perceptions of a group into the personality of the individual — not, of course, in the same way, quality, or style, but in some way nevertheless. And so, finally, to survive, Nunez accepts the assertion that he cannot "see" and that there is a roof above the world. The blind community comes to accept Nunez not as a king but as an idiot and an inferior being.

In this Country of the Blind, the sighted person suffers from culture shock and rejection. That biological advantage warrants rejections and whippings. He can be accepted if he will give up his "strange" behavior — seeing.

As a footnote, I asked a group of undergraduates what they would do if they were Nunez and were given the option of giving up their eyesight for the kind, loving, and desirable Medina-saroté. All indicated *nolo contendere* — no one would give up eyesight to live in the Country of the Blind. One young man did suggest though, that he might be tempted by a mythical combination of a younger Elizabeth Taylor and Eleanor Roosevelt — but that he could easily resist even that temptation!

QUESTIONS FOR DISCUSSION

1. Can you relate the initial thoughts and feelings of Nunez when he discovers that he is in the Country of the Blind to any of your own experiences? If not, can you think of an analogous situation?

2. The Country of the Blind is a society of blind persons, but it is also a culture of non-seeing persons. What is the difference?

3. The Country of the Blind has dealt with its cultural and biological needs in functional ways — through radiating pathways, preponderant angles, kerbing notches, windowless houses, day and night reversals to conserve

energy, etc. Considering all the advances in the knowledge of electronics, sociology, and psychology in the seventy-five years since the story was written, how would you construct a modern day country of the blind?

4. Consider what has happened technologically since Wells published the story in 1904. Would the story be any different if rewritten in 1980? If no, why not? If yes, how?

5. Does our society have any subcultures in which a modern day Nunez would indeed be "king" — or a blithering idiot? If so, how have they survived without the shelter of the Andes and the snows of Cotopaxi?

6. Suppose that instead of wandering into the Country of the Blind, Nunez had stumbled into the Country of the Deaf? Take a moment and create the country in your mind. How would it differ from the Country of the Blind? What physical features would be different or the same? Would the one-eared man be king?

7. Would the unsighted receive any advantages or disadvantages in learning about the sighted world? If Nunez had been accepted as a different person rather than a deviant person, what might the Country of the Blind have learned from him that would be helpful?

ADDITIONAL READINGS

- Bjarnhof, Karl. *The Star Grows Pale.* New York: Knopf, 1958.
- Gershe, Leonard. *Butterflies Are Free* (play). New York: School Book Service, 1973.
- Gregory, R. L. *Eye and Brain, The Psychology of Seeing.* New York: McGraw-Hill, 1966.
- Haddow, Alexander. "On a Possible Advantage Accompanying Blindness." *Perspectives in Biology and Medicine* 18 (Winter 1975): 208-11.
- Kipling, Rudyard. *The Light That Failed.* New York: Grosset & Dunlap, 1920.
- Lowenfeld, Berthold. *Our Blind Children.* 3d ed. Springfield, IL: Charles C Thomas, 1971.
- Scott, Robert A. *The Making of Blind Men.* New York: Russell Sage Foundation, 1969.
- Resnick, Rose. *Sun and Shadow.* New York: Atheneum, 1975.
- Trevor-Roper, P. *The World Through Blunted Sight.* London: Thames & Hudson, 1970.

Listening with a deaf ear . . .

3

The Heart is a Lonely Hunter

Carson McCullers

3

Whereas color, form, shadows, and movement may be considered the "primal sanities" of the seeing brain, language and communication are the human sanities of the hearing brain. You will be meeting Singer and Antonapoulos, two deaf adults, friends, roommates, and residents of a small southern town. Carson McCullers uses the term "deaf-mute" — an historically paired duo that has disappeared as muteness and deafness have become better understood. John Singer and Spiros Antonapoulos are unlike any two normal or handicapped persons. But their deafness is an integral part of their lives, their relationship, and their interaction with others.

Let us consider for a moment hearing and nonhearing as a sensory dimension and its relationship to personal functioning. Hearing responds to sound, which has more of a temporal quality than vision. For example, one cannot "freeze" music or words as easily as one can a painting or a scene. One cannot close one's ears as one can one's eyes. There is no defense against unsightly sound or noise except distance. One cannot avoid sounds as one can avoid sights.

Language is a sound wave phenomenon structured by a brain and auditory senses. Language is normally spoken and heard before it can be written or read. Therefore, loss of hearing in early life can be, and usually is, more isolating and depriving to a child than is loss of sight. Unfortunately, there are no sensory equivalents by which sound can be converted to sight so that deaf children can learn to speak by seeing or blind children to see by hearing. A child blind from birth cannot find conceptual equivalents for sky, red, lightning, or sunset. Or a child deaf from birth is not able to experience tones as structured in music, playing with words as in puns or jokes, or high level abstractions that require other high level abstractions for understanding.

Zuckerkandl suggests that the human organism creates his outer life by seeing.[1] He also suggests that in general the quietness, equanimity, and piety of the blind stand in some contrast to the irritability and suspicion often found in the deaf. Yet, one will note the utter calm and piety of John Singer — the deaf person who listens to everyone.

Although increasing amounts of research have been done on personality variables of deaf children and adults, what it all adds up to is still not clear. Undoubtedly, any significant auditory failure exacts an emotional toll but if found early and dealt with competently, the resultant toll is close to free passage. Early studies found the deaf to be more neurotic, introverted, less dominant, insecure, egocentric, impulsive, and suggestible than hearing people. Present studies, however, seem less confirmatory of these traits. Current investigators point out that instruments used with the deaf are adapted or maladapted from those used with hearing populations. An instrument such as the *Minnesota Multiphasic Personality Inventory* used with deaf adults seems inappropriate since the concepts used may be understood in highly idiosyncratic ways by deaf adults. In addition, any kind of testing or stressful relationship that involves language (written or spoken) is seen as threatening to many deaf persons.

Yet, hearing and vision have leading roles in "knowing" the environment, including self. When a distance sense like hearing is lost, the individual is forced into other types of dependencies and integrations. In some ways the deaf, especially those deaf from birth or early in life, seek to function in their own subculture if a choice is available.

Most research on deaf adults strongly supports the notion that these adults do well or, rather, do no less well than hearing adults in work, marriage, health status, and so on. That is interesting, suggests Furth, since deaf and hearing-impaired children often do not do well in school.[2] In any event, rarely does one find a deaf child/deaf adult who becomes a leader, executive, or shows outstanding creative ability in the arts and humanities. This is not surprising since everything in deaf children's lives moves them toward validating processes rather than creative or divergent ones.

---

[1] Victor Zuckerkandl, *Sound and Symbol* (Princeton: Princeton University Press, 1954).

[2] Hans G. Furth, *Deafness and Learning: A Psychosocial Approach* (Belmont, CA: Wadsworth Publishing, 1973).

One wouldn't exaggerate to the extreme in saying that about the only health disability Carson McCullers *didn't* have in her lifetime was deafness. At age fifteen she had a fever, incorrectly diagnosed as rheumatic fever, followed by pernicious anemia, pleurisy, and a series of strokes, all before she was thirty years old. For at least half her life, she was an invalid. Like H. G. Wells, books and her own lively imagination were her salvation. When asked as a preschooler what she would like for her birthday or for Christmas or for anything, she always chose books. She was a loner but seldom lonely. Her mother would often find her looking at a blank wall or staring out the window. "What are you doing, precious?" she would ask. "Thinking, Mama, thinking. That's fun," was the reply. When Carson was well into writing *The Heart is a Lonely Hunter* and developing the characters of John Singer and Spiros Antonapoulos, her husband informed her about a conference of deaf persons in a nearby city. Would she like to attend to authenticate her fiction? Carson declined, stating that John Singer was as real to her as anyone she might meet at the conference.

Carson was always physically frail but psychologically vigorous and creative. She was taller than her agemates, called weird and freaky by her schoolmates, disliked by her teachers, and admired by her professional colleagues. Her sensitivity to the handicapped and the downtrodden gave her imagination the necessary strength to live and create in an ailing body. When she was about four years old, growing up in the South of the 1920s as part of a genteel white family, Carson was sent to the store and asked to get some "niggertoes." She recalls not knowing what to do — whether to return home and ask her mother what they were or to ask the clerk. She finally decided to ask for a pound of "colored toes," but all she got from the clerk was a shrug of his shoulders. She went home empty-handed but soon returned to the store happy and beaming for a "pound of Brazil nuts, please."

THE HEART IS A LONELY HUNTER

Carson McCullers

In the town there were two mutes, and they were always together. Early every morning they would come out from the house where they lived and walk arm in arm down the street to work. The two friends were very different. The one who always steered the way was an obese and dreamy Greek. In the summer he would come out wearing a yellow or green polo shirt stuffed sloppily into his trousers in front and hanging loose behind. When it was colder he wore over this a shapeless gray sweater. His face was round and oily, with half-closed eyelids and lips that curved in a gentle, stupid smile. The other mute was tall. His eyes had a quick, intelligent expression. He was always immaculate and very soberly dressed.

Every morning the two friends walked silently together until they reached the main street of the town. Then when they came to a certain fruit and candy store they paused for a moment on the sidewalk outside. The Greek, Spiros Antonapoulos, worked for his cousin, who owned this fruit store. His job was to make candies and sweets, uncrate the fruits, and to keep the place clean. The thin mute, John Singer, nearly always put his hand on his friend's arm and looked for a second into his face before leaving him. Then after this good-bye Singer crossed the street and walked on alone to the jewelry store where he worked as a silverware engraver.

In the late afternoon the friends would meet again. Singer came back to the fruit store and waited until Antonapoulos was ready to go home. The Greek would be lazily unpacking a case of peaches or melons, or perhaps looking at the funny paper in the kitchen behind the store where he cooked. Before their departure

Excerpts from *The Heart is a Lonely Hunter,* by Carson McCullers. Copyright © 1967 by Carson McCullers. Reprinted by permission of Houghton Mifflin Co.

Antonapoulos always opened a paper sack he kept hidden during the day on one of the kitchen shelves. Inside were stored various bits of food he had collected — a piece of fruit, samples of candy, or the butt-end of a liverwurst. Usually before leaving Antonapoulos waddled gently to the glassed case in the front of the store where some meats and cheeses were kept. He glided open the back of the case and his fat hand groped lovingly for some particular dainty inside which he had wanted. Sometimes his cousin who owned the place did not see him. But if he noticed he stared at his cousin with a warning in his tight, pale face. Sadly Antonapoulos would shuffle the morsel from one corner of the case to the other. During these times Singer stood very straight with his hands in his pockets and looked in another direction. He did not like to watch this little scene between the two Greeks. For, excepting drinking and a certain solitary secret pleasure, Antonapoulos loved to eat more than anything else in the world.

In the dusk the two mutes walked slowly home together. At home Singer was always talking to Antonapoulos. His hands shaped the words in a swift series of designs. His face was eager and his gray-green eyes sparkled brightly. With his thin, strong hands he told Antonapoulos all that had happened during the day.

Antonapoulos sat back lazily and looked at Singer. It was seldom that he ever moved his hands to speak at all — and then it was to say that he wanted to eat or to sleep or to drink. These three things he always said with the same vague, fumbling signs. At night, if he were not too drunk, he would kneel down before his bed and pray awhile. Then his plump hands shaped the words "Holy Jesus," or "God," or "Darling Mary." These were the only words Antonapoulos ever said. Singer never knew just how much his friend understood of all the things he told him. But it did not matter.

They shared the upstairs of a small house near the business section of the town. There were two rooms. On the oil stove in the kitchen Antonapoulos cooked all of their meals. There were straight, plain kitchen chairs for Singer and an over-stuffed sofa for Antonapoulos. The bedroom was furnished mainly with a large double bed covered with an eiderdown comfort for the big Greek and a narrow iron cot for Singer.

Dinner always took a long time, because Antonapoulos loved food and he was very slow. After they had eaten, the big Greek would lie back on his sofa and slowly lick over each one of his teeth with his tongue, either from a certain delicacy or because he did not wish to lose the savor of the meal — while Singer washed the dishes.

Sometimes in the evening the mutes would play chess. Singer had always greatly enjoyed this game, and years before he had tried to teach it to Antonapoulos. At first his friend could not be interested in the reasons for moving the various pieces about on the board. Then Singer began to keep a bottle of something good under the table to be taken out after each lesson. The Greek never got on to the erratic movements of the knights and the sweeping mobility of the queens, but he learned to make a few set, opening moves. He preferred the white pieces and would not play if the black men were given him. After the first moves Singer worked out the game by himself while his friend looked on drowsily. If Singer made brilliant attacks on his own men so that in the end the black king was killed, Antonapoulos was always very proud and pleased.

The two mutes had no other friends, and except when they worked they were alone together. Each day was very much like any other day, because they were alone so much that nothing ever disturbed them. Once a week they would go to the library for Singer to withdraw a mystery book and on Friday night they attended a movie. Then on payday they always went to the ten-cent photograph shop above the Army and Navy Store so that Antonapoulos could have his picture taken. These were the only places where they made customary visits. There were many parts in the town that they had never even seen.

The town was in the middle of the deep South. The summers were long and the months of winter cold were very few. Nearly always the sky was a glassy, brilliant azure and the sun burned down riotously bright. Then the light, chill rains of November would come, and perhaps later there would be frost and some short months of cold. The winters were changeable, but the summers always were burning hot. The town was a fairly large one. On the main street there were several blocks of two- and three-story shops and business offices. But the largest buildings in the town were the factories, which employed a large percentage of the population. These cotton mills were big and flourishing and most of the workers in the town were very poor. Often in the faces along the streets there was the desperate look of hunger and of loneliness.

But the two mutes were not lonely at all. At home they were content to eat and drink, and Singer would talk with his hands eagerly to his friend about all that was in his mind. So the years passed in this quiet way until Singer reached the age of thirty-two and had been in the town with Antonapoulos for ten years.

Then one day the Greek became ill. He sat up in bed with his hands on his fat stomach and big, oily tears rolled down his cheeks. Singer went to see his friend's cousin who owned the fruit store, and also he arranged for leave from his own work. The doctor made out a diet for Antonapoulos and said that he could drink no more wine. Singer rigidly enforced the doctor's orders. All day he sat by his friend's bed and did what he could to make the time pass quickly, but Antonapoulos only looked at him angrily from the corners of his eyes and would not be amused.

The Greek was very fretful, and kept finding fault with the fruit drinks and food that Singer prepared for him. Constantly he made his friend help him out of bed so that he could pray. His huge buttocks would sag down over his plump little feet when he kneeled. He fumbled with his hands to say "Darling Mary" and then held to the small brass cross tied to his neck with a dirty string. His big eyes would wall up to the ceiling with a look of fear in them, and afterward he was very sulky and would not let his friend speak to him.

Singer was patient and did all that he could. He drew little pictures, and once he made a sketch of his friend to amuse him. This picture hurt the big Greek's feelings, and he refused to be reconciled until Singer had made his face very young and handsome and colored his hair bright yellow and his eyes china blue. And then he tried not to show his pleasure.

Singer nursed his friend so carefully that after a week Antonapoulos was able to return to his work. But from that time on there was a difference in their way of life. Trouble came to the two friends.

Antonapoulos was not ill any more, but a change had come in him. He was irritable and no longer content to spend the evenings quietly in their home. When he would wish to go out Singer followed along close behind him. Antonapoulos would go into a restaurant, and while they sat at the table he slyly put lumps of sugar, or a pepper-shaker, or pieces of silverware in his pocket. Singer always paid for what he took and there was no disturbance. At home he scolded Antonapoulos, but the big Greek only looked at him with a bland smile.

The months went on and these habits of Antonapoulos grew worse. One day at noon he walked calmly out of the fruit store of his cousin and urinated in public against the wall of the First National Bank Building across the street. At times he would meet people on the sidewalk whose faces did not please him, and he would bump into these persons and push at them with his elbows and stomach. He walked into a store one day and hauled out a floor lamp without paying for it, and another time he tried to take an electric train hè had seen in a showcase.

For Singer this was a time of great distress. He was continually marching Antonapoulos down to the courthouse during lunch hour to settle these infringements of the law. Singer became very familiar with the procedure of the courts and he was in a constant state of agitation. The money he had saved in the bank was spent for bail and fines. All of his efforts and money were used to keep his friend out of jail because of such charges as theft, committing public indecencies, and assault and battery.

The Greek cousin for whom Antonapoulos worked did not enter into these troubles at all. Charles Parker (for that was the name this cousin had taken) let Antonapoulos stay on at the store, but he watched him always with his pale, tight face and he made no effort to help him. Singer had a strange feeling about Charles Parker. He began to dislike him.

Singer lived in continual turmoil and worry. But Antonapoulos was always bland, and no matter what happened the gentle, flaccid smile was still on his face. In all the years before it had seemed to Singer that there was something very subtle and wise in this smile of his friend. He had never known just how much Antonapoulos understood and what he was thinking. Now in the big Greek's expression Singer thought that he could detect something sly and joking. He would shake his friend by the shoulders until he was very tired and explain things over and over with his hands. But nothing did any good.

All of Singer's money was gone and he had to borrow from the jeweler for whom he worked. On one occasion he was unable to pay bail for his friend and Antonapoulos spent the night in jail. When Singer came to get him out the next day he was very sulky. He did not want to leave. He had enjoyed his dinner of sowbelly and cornbread with syrup poured over it. And the new sleeping arrangements and his cellmates pleased him.

They had lived so much alone that Singer had no one to help him in his distress. Antonapoulos let nothing disturb him or cure him of his habits. At home he sometimes cooked the new dish he had eaten in the jail, and on the streets there was never any knowing just what he would do.

And then the final trouble came to Singer.

One afternoon he had come to meet Antonapoulos at the fruit store when Charles Parker handed him a letter. The letter explained that Charles Parker had made arrangements for his cousin to be taken to the state insane asylum two hundred miles away. Charles Parker had used his influence in the town and the details were already settled. Antonapoulos was to leave and to be admitted into the asylum the next week.

Singer read the letter several times, and for a while he could not think. Charles Parker was talking to him across the counter, but he did not even try to read his lips and understand. At last Singer wrote on the little pad he always carried in his pocket:

You cannot do this. Antonapoulos must stay with me.

Charles Parker shook his head excitedly. He did not know much American. "None of your business," he kept saying over and over.

Singer knew that everything was finished. The Greek was afraid that some day he might be responsible for his cousin. Charles Parker did not know much about the American language — but he understood the American dollar very well, and he had used his money and influence to admit his cousin to the asylum without delay.

There was nothing Singer could do.

The next week was full of feverish activity. He talked and talked. And although his hands never paused to rest he could not tell all that he had to say. He wanted to talk to Antonapoulos of all the thoughts that had ever been in his mind and heart, but there was not time. His gray eyes glittered and his quick, intelligent face expressed great strain. Antonapoulos watched him drowsily, and his friend did not know just what he really understood.

Then came the day when Antonapoulos must leave. Singer brought out his own suitcase and very carefully packed the best of their joint possessions. Antonapoulos made himself a lunch to eat during the journey. In the late afternoon they walked arm in arm down the street for the last time together. It was a chilly afternoon in late November, and little huffs of breath showed in the air before them.

Charles Parker was to travel with his cousin, but he stood apart from them at the station. Antonapoulos crowded into the bus and settled himself with elaborate preparations on one of the front seats. Singer watched him from the window and his hands began desperately to talk for the last time with his friend. But Antonapoulos was so busy checking over the various items in his lunch box that for a while he paid no attention. Just before the bus pulled away from the curb he turned to Singer and his smile was very bland and remote — as though already they were many miles apart.

The weeks that followed did not seem real at all. All day Singer worked over his bench in the back of the jewelry store, and then at night he returned to the house alone. More than anything he wanted to sleep. As soon as he came home from work he would lie on his cot and try to doze awhile. Dreams came to him when he lay there half-asleep. And in all of them Antonapoulos was there. His hands would jerk nervously, for in his dreams he was talking to his friend and Antonapoulos was watching him.

Singer tried to think of the time before he had ever known his friend. He tried to recount to himself certain things that had happened when he was young. But none of these things he tried to remember seemed real.

There was one particular fact that he remembered, but it was not at all important to him. Singer recalled that, although he had been deaf since he was an infant, he had not always been a real mute. He was left an orphan very young and placed in an institution for the deaf. He had learned to talk with his hands and to read. Before he was nine years old he could talk with one hand in the American way — and also could employ both of his hands after the method of Europeans. He had learned to follow the movements of people's lips and to understand what they said. Then finally he had been taught to speak.

At the school he was thought very intelligent. He learned the lessons before the rest of the pupils. But he could never become used to speaking with his lips. It was not natural to him, and his tongue felt like a whale in his mouth. From the blank expression on people's faces to whom he talked in this way he felt that his voice must be like the sound of some animal or that there was something disgusting in his speech. It was painful for him to try to talk with his mouth, but his hands were always ready to shape the words he wished to say. When he was twenty-two he had come South to this town from Chicago and he met Antonapoulos immediately. Since that time he had never spoken with his mouth again, because with his friend there was no need for this.

Nothing seemed real except the ten years with Antonapoulos. In his half-dreams he saw his friend very vividly, and when he awakened a great aching loneliness would be in him. Occasionally he would pack up a box for Antonapoulos, but he never received any reply. And so the months passed in this empty, dreaming way.

In the spring a change came over Singer. He could not sleep and his body was very restless. At evening he would walk monotonously around the room, unable to work off a new feeling of energy. If he rested at all it was only during a few hours before dawn — then he would drop bluntly into a sleep that lasted until the morning light struck suddenly beneath his opening eyelids like a scimitar.

He began spending his evenings walking around the town. He could no longer stand the rooms where Antonapoulos had lived, and he rented a place in a shambling boarding-house not far from the center of the town.

He ate his meals at a restaurant only two blocks away. This restaurant was at the very end of the long main street, and the name of the place was the New York Café. The first day he glanced over the menu quickly and wrote a short note and handed it to the proprietor.

Each morning for breakfast I want an egg, toast,
and coffee —   *$0.15*
Lunch I want soup (any kind), a meat sandwich,
and milk —   *$0.25*
Please bring me at dinner three vegetables (any kind
but cabbage), fish or meat, and a glass of
beer —   *$0.35*
                   Thank you.

The proprietor read the note and gave him an alert, tactful glance. He was a hard man of middle height, with a beard so dark and heavy that the lower part of his face looked as though it were molded of iron. He usually stood in the corner by the cash register, his arms folded over his chest, quietly observing all that went on around him. Singer came to know this man's face very well, for he ate at one of his tables three times a day.

Each evening the mute walked alone for hours in the street. Sometimes the nights were cold with the sharp, wet winds of March and it would be raining heavily. But to him this did not matter. His gait was agitated and he always kept his hands stuffed tight into the pockets of his trousers. Then as the weeks passed the days grew warm and languorous. His agitation gave way gradually to exhaustion and there was a look about him of deep calm. In his face there came to be a brooding peace that is seen most often in the faces of the very sorrowful or the very wise. But still he wandered through the streets of the town, always silent and alone.

* * *

By midsummer Singer had visitors more often than any other person in the house. From his room in the evening there was nearly always the sound of a voice. After dinner at the New York Café he bathed and dressed himself in one of his cool wash suits and as a rule did not go out again. The room was cool and pleasant. He had an icebox in the closet where he kept bottles of cold beer and fruit drinks. He was never busy or in a hurry. And always he met his guests at the door with a welcome smile.

Mick [a young girl] loved to go up to Mister Singer's room. Even if he was a deaf-and-dumb mute he understood every word she said to him. Talking with him was like a game. Only there was a whole lot more to it than any game. It was like finding out new things about music. She would tell him some of her plans that she would not tell anybody else. He let her meddle with his cute little chess men. Once when she was excited and caught her shirt-tail in the electric fan he acted in such a kindly way that she was not embarrassed at all. Except for her Dad, Mister Singer was the nicest man she knew.

. . .Doctor Copeland [the town's only black physician] went to the back of the house and sat with Portia [his daughter] awhile in the kitchen. Then he climbed the stairs to the white man's room. There was truly none of the quiet insolence about this man. They had a lemonade together and the mute wrote down the answer to the questions he wished to know. This man was different from any person of the white race whom Doctor Copeland had ever encountered. Afterward he pondered about this white man a long time. Then later, inasmuch as he had been invited in a cordial manner to return, he made another visit.

Jake Blount [patron of the New York Café] came every week. When he walked up to Singer's room the whole stairway shook. Usually he carried a paper sack of beers. Often his voice would come out loud and angry from the room. But before he left his voice gradually quieted. When he descended the stairs he did not carry the sack of beers any longer, and he walked away thoughtfully without seeming to notice where he was going.

Even Biff Brannon [proprietor of the New York Café] came to the mute's room one night. But as he could never stay away from the restaurant for long, he left in a half-hour.

Singer was always the same to everyone. He sat in a straight chair by the window with his hands stuffed tight into his pockets, and nodded or smiled to show his guests that he understood.

If he did not have a visitor in the evening, Singer went to a late movie. He liked to sit back and watch the actors talking and walking about on the screen. He never looked at the title of a picture before going into a movie, and no matter what was showing he watched each scene with equal interest.

Then, one day in July, Singer suddenly went away without warning. He left the door of his room open, and on the table in an envelope addressed to Mrs. Kelly there were four dollars for the past week's rent. His few simple possessions were gone and the room was very clean and bare. When his visitors came and saw this empty room they went away with hurt surprise. No one could imagine why he had left like this.

Singer spent all of his summer vacation in the town where Antonapoulos was being kept in the asylum. For months he had planned this trip and imagined about each moment they would have together. Two weeks beforehand his hotel reservation had been made and for a long time he had carried his railroad ticket in an envelope in his pocket.

Antonapoulos was not changed at all. When Singer came into his room he ambled placidly to meet his friend. He was even fatter than before, but the dreamy smile on his face was just the same. Singer had some packages in his arms and the big Greek gave them his first attention. His presents were a scarlet dressing-gown, soft bedroom slippers, and two mono-grammed nightshirts. Antonapoulos looked beneath all the tissue papers in the boxes very carefully. When he saw that nothing good to eat had been concealed there, he dumped the gifts disdainfully on his bed and did not bother with them any more.

The room was large and sunny. Several beds were spaced in a row together. Three old men played a game of slapjack in a corner. They did not notice Singer or Antonapoulos, and the two friends sat alone on the other side of the room.

It seemed to Singer that years had passed since they had been together. There was so much to say that his hands could not shape the signs with speed enough. His green eyes burned and sweat glittered on his forehead. The old feeling of gaiety and bliss was so quick in him again that he could not control himself.

Antonapoulos kept his dark, oily eyes on his friend and did not move. His hands fumbled languidly with the crotch of his trousers. Singer told him, among other things, about the visitors who had been coming to see him. He told his friend that they helped take his mind away from his lonesomeness. He told Antonapoulos that they were strange people and always talking — but that he liked to have them come. He drew quick sketches of Jake Blount and Mick and Doctor Copeland. Then as soon as he saw that Antonapoulos was not interested Singer crumpled the sketches and forgot about them. When the attendant came in to say that their time was up, Singer had not finished half of the things he wanted to say. But he left the room very tired and happy.

The patients could receive their friends only on Thursday and Sunday. On the days when he could not be with Antonapoulos, Singer walked up and down in his room at the hotel.

His second visit to his friend was like the first, except that the old men in the room watched them listlessly and did not play slapjack.

After much trouble Singer obtained permission to take Antonapoulos out with him for a few hours. He planned each detail of the little excursion in advance. They drove out into the country in a taxi, and then at four-thirty they went to the dining-room at the hotel. Antonapoulos greatly enjoyed this extra meal. He ordered half the dishes on the menu and ate very greedily. But when he had finished he would not leave. He held to the table. Singer coaxed him and the cab driver wanted to use force. Antonapoulos sat stolidly and made obscene gestures when they came too close to him. At last Singer bought a bottle of whiskey from the hotel manager and lured him into the taxi again. When Singer threw the unopened bottle out of the window Antonapoulos wept with disappointment and offense. The end of their little excursion made Singer very sad.

His next visit was the last one, for his two weeks' vacation was almost over. Antonapoulos had forgotten what had happened before. They sat in their same corner of the room. The minutes slipped by quickly. Singer's hands talked desperately and his narrow face was very pale. At last it was time for him to go. He held his friend by the arm and looked into his face in the way that he used to do when they parted each day before work. Antonapoulos stared at him drowsily and did not move. Singer left the room with his hands stuffed hard into his pockets.

Soon after Singer returned to his room at the boardinghouse, Mick and Jake Blount and Doctor Copeland began to come again. Each one of them wanted to know where he had been and why he had not let them know about his plans. But Singer pretended that he did not understand their questions, and his smile was inscrutable.

One by one they would come to Singer's room to spend the evening with him. The mute was always thoughtful and composed. His many-tinted gentle eyes were grave as a sorcerer's.

Mick Kelly and Jake Blount and Doctor Copeland would come and talk in the silent room — for they felt that the mute would always understand whatever they wanted to say to him. And maybe even more than that.

* * *

The town had not known a winter as cold as this one for years. Frost formed on the windowpanes and whitened the roofs of houses. The winter afternoons glowed with a hazy lemon light and shadows were a delicate blue. A thin coat of ice crusted the puddles in the streets, and it was said on the day after Christmas that only ten miles to the north there was a light fall of snow.

A change came over Singer. Often he went out for the long walks that had occupied him during the months when Antonapoulos was first gone. These walks extended for miles in every direction and covered the whole of the town. He rambled through the dense neighborhoods along the river that were more squalid than ever since the mills had been slack this winter. In many eyes there was a look of somber loneliness. Now that people were forced to be idle, a certain restlessness could be felt. There was a fervid outbreak of new beliefs. A young man who had worked at the dye vats in a mill claimed suddenly that a great holy power had come in him. He said it was his duty to deliver a new set of commandments from the Lord. The young man set up a tabernacle and hundreds of people came each night to roll on the ground and shake each other, for they believed that they were in the presence of something more than human. There was murder, too. A woman who could not make enough to eat believed that a foreman had cheated on her work tokens and she stabbed him in the throat. A family of Negroes moved into the end house on one of the most dismal streets, and this caused so much indignation that the house was burned and the black man beaten by his neighbors. But these were incidents. Nothing had really changed. The strike that was talked about never came off because they could not get together. All was the same as before. Even on the coldest nights the Sunny Dixie Show was open. The people dreamed and fought and slept as much as ever. And by habit they shortened their thoughts so that they would not wander out into the darkness beyond tomorrow.

Singer walked through the scattered odorous parts of town where the Negroes crowded together. There was more gaiety and violence here. Often the fine, sharp smell of gin lingered in the alleys. Warm, sleepy firelight colored the windows. Meetings were held in the churches almost every night. Comfortable little houses set off in plots of brown grass — Singer walked in these parts also. Here the children were huskier and more friendly to strangers. He roamed through the neighborhoods of the rich. There were houses, very grand and old, with white columns and intricate fences of wrought iron. He walked past the big brick houses where automobiles honked in driveways and where the plumes of smoke rolled lavishly from chimneys. And out to the very edges of the roads that led from the town to general stores where farmers came on Saturday nights and sat around the stove. He wandered often about the four main business blocks that were brightly lighted and then through the black, deserted alleys behind. There was no part of the town that Singer did not know. He watched the yellow squares of light reflect from a thousand windows. The winter nights were beautiful. The sky was a cold azure and the stars were very bright.

Often it happened now that he would be spoken to and stopped during these walks. All kinds of people became acquainted with him. If the person who spoke to him was a stranger, Singer presented his card so that his silence would be understood. He came to be known through all the town. He walked with his shoulders very straight and kept his hands always stuffed down into his pockets. His gray eyes seemed to take in everything around him, and in his face there was still the look of peace that is seen most often in those who are very wise or very sorrowful. He was always glad to stop with anyone who wished his company. For after all he was only walking and going nowhere.

Now it came about that various rumors started in the town concerning the mute. In the years before with Antonapoulos they had walked back and forth to work, but except for this they were always alone together in their rooms. No one had bothered about them then — and if they were observed it was the big Greek on whom attention was focused. The Singer of those years was forgotten.

So the rumors about the mute were rich and varied. The

Jews said that he was a Jew. The merchants along the main street claimed he had received a large legacy and was a very rich man. It was whispered in one browbeaten textile union that the mute was an organizer for the C.I.O. A lone Turk who had roamed into the town years ago and who languished with his family behind the little store where they sold linens claimed passionately to his wife that the mute was Turkish. He said that when he spoke his language the mute understood. And as he claimed this his voice grew warm and he forgot to squabble with his children and he was full of plans and activity. One old man from the country said that the mute had come from somewhere near his home and that the mute's father had the finest tobacco crop in all the county. All these things were said about him.

Antonapoulos! Within Singer there was always the memory of his friend. At night when he closed his eyes the Greek's face was there in the darkness — round and oily, with a wise and gentle smile. In his dreams they were always together.

It was more than a year now since his friend had gone away. This year seemed neither long nor short. Rather it was removed from the ordinary sense of time — as when one is drunk or half-asleep. Behind each hour there was always his friend. And this buried life with Antonapoulos changed and developed as did the happenings around him. During the first few months he had thought most of the terrible weeks before Antonapoulos was taken away — of the trouble that followed his illness, of the summons for arrest, and the misery in trying to control the whims of his friend. He thought of times in the past when he and Antonapoulos had been unhappy. There was one recollection, far in the past, that came back to him several times.

They had no friends. Sometimes they would meet other mutes — there were three of them with whom they became acquainted during the ten years. But something always happened. One moved to another state the week after they met him. Another was married and had six children and did not talk with his hands. But it was their relation with the third of these acquaintances that Singer remembered when his friend was gone.

The mute's name was Carl. He was a sallow young man who worked in one of the mills. His eyes were pale yellow and his teeth so brittle and transparent that they seemed pale yellow also. In his blue overalls that hung limp over his skinny little body he was like a blue-and-yellow rag doll.

They invited him to dinner and arranged to meet him beforehand at the store where Antonapoulos worked. The Greek was still busy when they arrived. He was finishing a batch of caramel fudge in the cooking room at the back of the store. The fudge lay golden and glossy over the long marble-topped table. The air was warm and rich with sweet smells. Antonapoulos seemed pleased to have Carl watch him as he glided the knife down the warm candy and cut it into squares. He offered their new friend a corner of the fudge on the edge of his greased knife, and showed him the trick that he always performed for anyone when he wished to be liked. He pointed to a vat of syrup boiling on the stove and fanned his face and squinted his eyes to show how hot it was. Then he wet his hand in a pot of cold water, plunged it into the boiling syrup, and swiftly put it back into the water again. His eyes bulged and he rolled out his tongue as though he were in great agony. He even wrung his hand and hopped on one foot so that the building shook. Then he smiled suddenly and held out his hand to show that it was a joke and hit Carl on the shoulder.

It was a pale winter evening, and their breath clouded in the cold air as they walked with their arms interlocked down the street. Singer was in the middle and he left them on the sidewalk twice while he went into stores to shop. Carl and Antonapoulos carried the sacks of groceries, and Singer held to their arms tightly and smiled all the way home. Their rooms were cozy and he moved happily about, making conversation with Carl. After the meal the two of them talked while Antonapoulos watched with a slow smile. Often the big Greek would lumber to the closet and pour out drinks of gin. Carl sat by the window, only drinking when Antonapoulos pushed the glass into his face, and then taking solemn little sips. Singer could not ever remember his friend so cordial to a stranger before, and he thought ahead with pleasure to the time when Carl would visit them often.

Midnight had passed when the thing happened that ruined the festive party. Antonapoulos returned from one of his trips to the closet and his face had a glowering look. He sat on his bed and began to stare repeatedly at their new friend with expressions of offense and great disgust. Singer tried to make eager conversation to hide this strange behavior, but the Greek was persistent. Carl huddled in a chair, nursing his bony knees, fascinated and bewildered by the grimaces of the big Greek. His face was flushed and he swallowed timidly. Singer could ignore the situation no longer, so at last he asked Antonapoulos if his stomach pained him or if he perhaps felt bad and wished to go to sleep. Antonapoulos shook his head. He pointed to Carl and began to make all the gestures of obscenity which he knew. The disgust on his face was terrible to see. Carl was small with fear. At last the big Greek ground his teeth and rose from his chair. Hurriedly Carl picked up his cap and left the room. Singer followed him down the stairs. He did not know how to explain his friend to this stranger. Carl stood hunched in the doorway downstairs, limp, with his peaked cap pulled down over his face. At last they shook hands and Carl went away.

Antonapoulos let him know that while they were not noticing, their guest had gone into the closet and drunk up all the gin. No amount of persuasion could convince Antonapoulos that it was he himself who had finished the bottle. The big Greek sat up in bed and his round face was dismal and reproachful. Large tears trickled slowly down to the neck of his undershirt and he could not be comforted. At last he went to sleep, but Singer was awake in the dark a long time. They never saw Carl again.

Then years later there was the time Antonapoulos took the rent money from the vase on the mantelpiece and spent it all on the slot machines. And the summer afternoon Antonapoulos went downstairs naked to get the paper. He suffered so from the summer heat. They bought an electric refrigerator on the installment plan, and Antonapoulos would suck the cubes of ice constantly and even let a few of them melt in the bed with him as he slept. And the time Antonapoulos got drunk and threw a bowl of macaroni in his face.

Those ugly memories wove through his thoughts during the first months like bad threads through a carpet. And then they were gone. All the times that they had been unhappy were forgotten. For as the year went on his thoughts of his friend spiraled deeper until he dwelt only with the Antonapoulos whom he alone could know.

115

This was the friend to whom he told all that was in his heart. This was the Antonapoulos who no one knew was wise but him. As the year passed his friend seemed to grow larger in his mind, and his face looked out in a very grave and subtle way from the darkness at night. The memories of his friend changed in his mind so that he remembered nothing that was wrong or foolish — only the wise and good.

He saw Antonapoulos sitting in a large chair before him. He sat tranquil and unmoving. His round face was inscrutable. His mouth was wise and smiling. And his eyes were profound. He watched the things that were said to him. And in his wisdom he understood.

This was the Antonapoulos who now was always in his thoughts. This was the friend to whom he wanted to tell things that had come about. For something had happened in this year. He had been left in an alien land. Alone. He had opened his eyes and around him there was much he could not understand. He was bewildered.

He watched the words shape on their lips.

We Negroes want a chance to be free at last. And freedom is only the right to contribute. We want to serve and to share, to labor and in turn consume that which is due to us. But you are the only white man I have ever encountered who realizes this terrible need of my people.

You see, Mister Singer? I got this music in me all the time. I got to be a real musician. Maybe I don't know anything now, but I will when I'm twenty. See, Mister Singer? And then I mean to travel in a foreign country where there's snow.

Let's finish up the bottle. I want a small one. For we were thinking of freedom. That's the word like a worm in my brain. Yes? No? How much? How little? The word is a signal for piracy and theft and cunning. We'll be free and the smartest will then be able to enslave the others. But! But there is another meaning to the word. Of all words this one is the most dangerous. We who know must be wary. The word makes us feel good — in fact the word is a great ideal. But it's with this ideal that the spiders spin their ugliest webs for us.

The last one rubbed his nose. He did not come often and he did not say much. He asked questions.

The four people had been coming to his rooms now for more than seven months. They never came together — always alone. And invariably he met them at the door with a cordial smile. The want for Antonapoulos was always with him — just as it had been the first months after his friend had gone — and it was better to be with any person than to be too long alone. It was like the time years ago when he had made a pledge to Antonapoulos (and even written it on a paper and tacked it on the wall above his bed) — a pledge that he would give up cigarettes, beer, and meat for one month. The first days had been very bad. He could not rest or be still. He visited Antonapoulos so much at the fruit store that Charles Parker was unpleasant to him. When he had finished all the engraving on hand he would dawdle around the front of the store with the watchmaker and the salesgirl or wander out to some soda fountain to drink a Coca-Cola. In those days being near any stranger was better than thinking alone about the cigarettes and beer and meat that he wanted.

At first he had not understood the four people at all. They talked and they talked — and as the months went on they talked more and more. He became so used to their lips that he understood each word they said. And then after a while he knew what each one of them would say before he began, because the meaning was always the same.

His hands were a torment to him. They would not rest. They twitched in his sleep, and sometimes he awoke to find them shaping the words in his dreams before his face. He did not like to look at his hands or to think about them. They were slender and brown and very strong. In the years before he had always tended them with care. In the winter he used oil to prevent chapping, and he kept the cuticles pushed down and his nails always filed to the shape of his finger-tips. He had loved to wash and tend his hands. But now he only scrubbed them roughly with a brush two times a day and stuffed them back into his pockets.

When he walked up and down the floor of his room he would crack the joints of his fingers and jerk at them until they ached. Or he would strike the palm of one hand with the fist of the other. And then sometimes when he was alone and his thoughts were with his friend his hands would begin to shape the words before he knew about it. Then when he realized, he was like a man caught talking aloud to himself. It was almost as though he had done some moral wrong. The shame and the sorrow mixed together and he doubled his hands and put them behind him. But they would not let him rest.

Singer stood in the street before the house where he and Antonapoulos had lived. The late afternoon was smoky and gray. In the west there were streaks of cold yellow and rose. A ragged winter sparrow flew in patterns against the smoky sky and at last came to light on a gable of the house. The street was deserted.

His eyes were fixed on a window on the right side of the second story. This was their front room, and behind was the big kitchen where Antonapoulos had cooked all of their meals. Through the lighted window he watched a woman move back and forth across the room. She was large and vague against the light and she wore an apron. A man sat with the evening newspaper in his hand. A child with a slice of bread came to the window and pressed his nose against the pane. Singer saw the room just as he had left it — with the large bed for Antonapoulos and the iron cot for himself, the big overstuffed sofa and the camp chair. The broken sugar bowl used for an ash tray, the damp spot on the ceiling where the roof leaked, the laundry box in the corner. On late afternoons like this there would be no light in the kitchen except the glow from the oil-burners of the big stove. Antonapoulos always turned the wicks so that only a ragged fringe of gold and blue could be seen inside each burner. The room was warm and full of the good smells from the supper. Antonapoulos tasted the dishes with his wooden spoon and they drank glasses of red wine. On the linoleum rug before the stove the flames from the burners made luminous reflections — five little golden lanterns. As the milky twilight grew darker these little lanterns were more intense, so that when at last the night had come they burned with vivid purity. Supper was always ready by that time and they would turn on the light and draw their chairs to the table.

Singer looked down at the dark front door. He thought of them going out together in the morning and coming home at

night. There was the broken place in the pavement where Antonapoulos had stumbled once and hurt his elbow. There was the
mailbox where their bill from the light company came each
month. He could feel the warm touch of his friend's arm against
his fingers.

The street was dark now. He looked up at the window
once more and he saw the strange woman and the man and the
child in a group together. The emptiness spread in him. All was
gone. Antonapoulos was away; he was not here to remember.
The thoughts of his friend were somewhere else. Singer shut
his eyes and tried to think of the asylum and the room that
Antonapoulos was in tonight. He remembered the narrow white
beds and the old men playing slapjack in the corner. He held
his eyes shut tight, but that room would not become clear in
his mind. The emptiness was very deep inside him, and after a
while he glanced up at the window once more and started down
the dark sidewalk where they had walked together so many times.

It was Saturday night. The main street was thick with people.
Shivering Negroes in overalls loitered before the windows of
the ten-cent store. Families stood in line before the ticket box
of the movie and young boys and girls stared at the posters
on display outside. The traffic from the automobiles was so
dangerous that he had to wait a long time before crossing the
street.

He passed the fruit store. The fruits were beautiful inside the
windows — bananas, oranges, alligator pears, bright little kum-
quats, and even a few pineapples. But Charles Parker waited
on a customer inside. The face of Charles Parker was very ugly
to him. Several times when Charles Parker was away he had
entered the store and stood around a long while. He had even
gone to the kitchen in the back where Antonapoulos made the
candies. But he never went into the store while Charles Parker
was inside. They had both taken care to avoid each other since
that day when Antonapoulos left on the bus. When they met in
the street they always turned away without nodding. Once when
he had wanted to send his friend a jar of his favorite tupelo
honey he had ordered it from Charles Parker by mail so as
not to be obliged to meet him.

Singer stood before the window and watched the cousin
of his friend wait on a group of customers. Business was always

119

good on Saturday night. Antonapoulos sometimes had to work as late as ten o'clock. The big automatic popcorn popper was near the door. A clerk shoved in a measure of kernels and the corn whirled inside the case like giant flakes of snow. The smell from the store was warm and familiar. Peanut hulls were trampled on the floor.

Singer passed on down the street. He had to weave his way carefully in the crowds to keep from being jostled. The streets were strung with red and green electric lights because of the holidays. People stood in laughing groups with their arms about each other. Young fathers nursed cold and crying babies on their shoulders. A Salvation Army girl in her red-and-blue bonnet tinkled a bell on the corner, and when she looked at Singer he felt obliged to drop a coin into the pot beside her. There were beggars, both Negro and white, who held out caps or crusty hands. The neon advertisements cast an orange glow on the faces of the crowd.

He reached the corner where he and Antonapoulos had once seen a mad dog on an August afternoon. Then he passed the room above the Army and Navy Store where Antonapoulos had had his picture taken every pay-day. He carried many of the photographs in his pocket now. He turned west toward the river. Once they had taken a picnic lunch and crossed the bridge and eaten in a field on the other side.

Singer walked along the main street for about an hour. In all the crowd he seemed the only one alone. At last he took out his watch and turned toward the house where he lived. Perhaps one of the people would come this evening to his room. He hoped so.

He mailed Antonapoulos a large box of presents for Christmas. Also he presented gifts to each of the four people and to Mrs. Kelly. For all of them together he had bought a radio and put it on the table by the window. Doctor Copeland did not notice the radio. Biff Brannon noticed it immediately and raised his eyebrows. Jake Blount kept it turned on all the time he was there, at the same station, and as he talked he seemed to be shouting above the music, for the veins stood out on his forehead. Mick Kelly did not understand when she saw the radio. Her face was very red and she asked him over and over if it was really his and whether she could listen. She worked with a dial for several minutes before she got it to the place that suited her. She sat leaning forward in her chair with her hands on her knees, her mouth open and a pulse beating very fast in her temple. She seemed to listen all over to whatever it was she heard. She sat there the whole afternoon, and when she grinned at him once her eyes were wet and she rubbed them with her fists. She asked him if she could come in and listen sometimes when he was at work and he nodded yes. So for the next few days whenever he opened the door he found her by the radio. Her hand raked through her short rumpled hair and there was a look in her face he had never seen before.

One night soon after Christmas all four of the people chanced to visit him at the same time. This had never happened before. Singer moved about the room with smiles and refreshments and did his best in the way of politeness to make his guests comfortable. But something was wrong.

Doctor Copeland would not sit down. He stood in the doorway, hat in hand, and only bowed coldly to the others. They looked at him as though they wondered why he was there. Jake Blount opened the beers he had brought with him and the foam spilled down on his shirtfront. Mick Kelly listened to the music from the radio. Biff Brannon sat on the bed, his knees crossed, his eyes scanning the group before him and then becoming narrow and fixed.

Singer was bewildered. Always each of them had so much to say. Yet now that they were together they were silent. When they came in he had expected an outburst of some kind. In a vague way he had expected this to be the end of something. But in the room there was only a feeling of strain. His hands worked nervously as though they were pulling things unseen from the air and binding them together.

Jake Blount stood beside Doctor Copeland. "I know your face. We run into each other once before — on the steps outside."

Doctor Copeland moved his tongue precisely as though he clipped out his words with scissors. "I was not aware that we were acquainted," he said. Then his stiff body seemed to shrink. He stepped back until he was just outside the threshold of the room.

Biff Brannon smoked his cigarette composedly. The smoke lay in thin blue layers across the room. He turned to Mick and when he looked at her a blush reddened his face. He half-closed his eyes and in a moment his face was bloodless once more. "And how are you getting on with your business now?"

"What business?" Mick asked suspiciously.

"Just the business of living," he said. "School — and so forth."

"O.K., I reckon," she said.

Each one of them looked at Singer as though in expectation. He was puzzled. He offered refreshments and smiled.

Jake rubbed his lips with the palm of his hand. He left off trying to make conversation with Doctor Copeland and sat down on the bed beside Biff. "You know who it is that used to write those bloody warnings in red chalk on the fences and walls around the mills?"

"No," Biff said. "What bloody warnings?"

"Mostly from the Old Testament. I been wondering about that for a long time."

Each person addressed his words mainly to the mute. Their thoughts seemed to converge in him as the spokes of a wheel lead to the center hub.

"The cold has been very unusual," Biff said finally. "The other day I was looking through some old records and I found that in the year 1919 the thermometer got down to ten degrees Fahrenheit. It was only sixteen degrees this morning, and that's the coldest since the big freeze that year."

"There were icicles hanging off the roof of the coal house this morning," Mick said.

"We didn't take in enough money last week to meet the payroll," Jake said.

They discussed the weather some more. Each one seemed to be waiting for the others to go. Then on an impulse they all rose to leave at the same time. Doctor Copeland went first and the others followed him immediately. When they were gone Singer stood alone in the room, and as he did not understand the situation he wanted to forget it. He decided to write to Antona-poulos that night.

The fact that Antonapoulos could not read did not prevent Singer from writing to him. He had always known that his friend was unable to make out the meaning of words on paper, but as the months went by he began to imagine that perhaps he had been mistaken, that perhaps Antonapoulos only kept his knowledge of letters a secret from everyone. Also, it was possible there might be a deaf-mute at the asylum who could read his letters and then explain them to his friend. He thought of several justifications for his letters, for he always felt a great need to write to his friend when he was bewildered or sad. Once written, however, these letters were never mailed. He cut out the comic strips from the morning and evening papers and sent them to his friend each Sunday. And every month he mailed a postal money order. But the long letters he wrote to Antonapoulos accumulated in his pockets until he would destroy them.

When the four people had gone, Singer slipped on his warm gray overcoat and his gray felt hat and left his room. He always wrote his letters at the store. Also, he had promised to deliver a certain piece of work the next morning, and he wanted to finish it now so that there would be no question of delay. The night was sharp and frosty. The moon was full and rimmed with a golden light. The rooftops were black against the starlit sky. As he walked he thought of ways to begin his letter, but he had already reached the store before the first sentence was clear in his mind. He let himself into the dark store with his key and switched on the front lights.

He worked at the very end of the store. A cloth curtain separated his place from the rest of the shop so that it was like a small private room. Besides his workbench and chair there was a heavy safe in the corner, a lavatory with a greenish mirror, and shelves full of boxes and worn-out clocks. Singer rolled up the top of his bench and removed from its felt case the silver platter he had promised to have ready. Although the store was cold he took off his coat and turned up the blue-striped cuffs of his shirt so that they would not get in his way.

For a long time he worked at the monogram in the center of the platter. With delicate, concentrated strokes he guided the scriver on the silver. As he worked his eyes had a curiously penetrating look of hunger. He was thinking of his letter to his friend Antonapoulos. Midnight had passed before the work was finished. When he put the platter away his forehead was damp with excitement. He cleared his bench and began to write. He loved to shape words with a pen on paper and he formed the letters with as much care as if the paper had been a plate of silver.

My Only Friend:

I see from our magazine that the Society meets this year at a convention in Macon. They will have speakers and a four-course banquet. I imagine it. Remember we always planned to attend one of the conventions but we never did. I wish now that we had. I wish we were going to this one and I have imagined how it would be. But of course I could never go without you. They will come from many states and they will all be full of words and long dreams from the heart. There is also to be a special service at one of the churches and some kind of a contest with a gold medal for the prize. I write that I imagine all of this. I both do and do not. My hands have been still so long that it is difficult to remember how it is. And when I imagine the convention I think of all the guests being like you, my Friend.

I stood before our home the other day. Other people live in it now. Do you remember the big oak tree in front? The branches were cut back so as not to interfere with the telephone wires and the tree died. The limbs are rotten and there is a hollow place in the trunk. Also, the cat here at the store (the one you used to stroke and fondle) ate something poisonous and died. It was very sad.

Singer held the pen poised above the paper. He sat for a long while, erect and tense, without continuing the letter. Then he stood up and lighted himself a cigarette. The room was cold and the air had a sour stale odor — the mixed smells of kerosene and silver polish and tobacco. He put on his overcoat and muffler and began writing again with slow determination.

You remember the four people I told you about when I was there. I drew their pictures for you, the black man, the young girl, the one with the mustache, and the man who owns the New York Café. There are some things I should like to tell you about them but how to put them in words I am not sure.

They are all very busy people. In fact they are so busy that it will be hard for you to picture them. I do not mean that they work at their jobs all day and night but that they have much business in their minds always that does not let them rest. They come up to my room and talk to me until I do not understand how a person can open and shut his or her mouth so much without being weary. (However, the New York Café owner is different — he is not just like the others. He has a very black beard so that he has to shave twice daily, and he owns one of these electric razors. He watches. The others all have something they hate. And they all have something they love more than eating or sleeping or wine or friendly company. That is why they are always so busy.)

The one with the mustache I think is crazy. Sometimes he speaks his words very clear like my teacher long ago at the school. Other times he speaks such a language that I cannot follow. Sometimes he is dressed in a plain suit, and the next time he will be black with dirt and smelling bad and in the overalls he wears to work. He will shake his fist and say ugly drunken words that I would not wish you to know about. He thinks he and I have a secret together but I do not know what it is. And let me write you something hard to believe. He can drink three pints of Happy Days whiskey and still talk and walk on his feet and not wish for the bed. You will not believe this but it is true.

I rent my room from the girl's mother for $16 per month. The girl used to dress in short trousers like a boy but now she wears a blue skirt and a blouse. She is not yet a young lady. I like her to come and see me. She comes all the time now that I have a radio for them. She likes music. I wish I knew what it is she hears. She knows I am deaf but she thinks I know about music.

The black man is sick with consumption but there is not a good hospital for him to go to here because he is black. He is a doctor and he works more than anyone I have ever seen. He does not talk like a black man at all. Other Negroes I find it hard to understand because their tongues do not move enough for the words. This black man frightens me sometimes. His eyes are hot and bright. He asked me to a party and I went. He has many books. However, he does not own any mystery books. He does not drink or eat meat or attend the movies.

Yah Freedom and pirates. Yah Capital and Democrats, says the ugly one with the mustache. Then he contradicts himself and says, Freedom is the greatest of all ideals. I just got to get a chance to write this music in me and be a musician. I got to have a chance, says the girl. We are not allowed to serve, says the black Doctor. That is the Godlike need of my people. Aha, says the owner of the New York Café. He is a thoughtful one.

That is the way they talk when they come to my room. Those words in their heart do not let them rest, so they are always very busy. Then you would think when they are together they would be like those of the Society who meet at the convention in Macon this week. But that is not so. They all came to my room at the same time today. They sat like they were from different cities. They were even rude, and you know how I have always said that to be rude and not attend to the feelings of others is wrong. So it was like that. I do not understand, so I write it to you because I think you will understand. I have queer feelings. But I have written of this matter enough and I know you are weary of it. I am also.

It has been five months and twenty-one days now. All of that time I have been alone without you. The only thing I can imagine is when I will be with you again. If I cannot come to you soon I do not know what.

Singer put his head down on the bench and rested. The smell and the feel of the slick wood against his cheek reminded him of his schooldays. His eyes closed and he felt sick. There was only the face of Antonapoulos in his mind, and his longing for his friend was so sharp that he held his breath. After some time Singer sat up and reached for his pen.

The gift I ordered for you did not come in time for the Christmas box. I expect it shortly. I believe you will like it and be amused. I think of us always and remember everything. I long for the food you used to make. At the New York Café it is much worse than it used to be. I found a cooked fly in my soup not long ago. It was mixed with the vegetables and the noodles like letters. But that is nothing. The way I need you is a loneliness I cannot bear. Soon I will come again. My vacation is not due for six months more but I think I can arrange it before then. I think I will have to. I am not meant to be alone and without you who understand.

Always,

JOHN SINGER

It was two o'clock in the morning before he was home again. The big, crowded house was in darkness, but he felt his way carefully up three flights of stairs and did not stumble. He took from his pockets the cards he carried about with him, his watch, and his fountain pen. Then he folded his clothes neatly over the back of his chair. His gray-flannel pajamas were warm and soft. Almost as soon as he pulled the blankets to his chin he was asleep.

Out of the blackness of sleep a dream formed. There were dull yellow lanterns lighting up a dark flight of stone steps. Antonapoulos kneeled at the top of these steps. He was naked and he fumbled with something that he held above his head and gazed at it as though in prayer. He himself knelt halfway down the steps. He was naked and cold and he could not take his eyes from Antonapoulos and the thing he held above him. Behind him on the ground he felt the one with the mustache and the girl and the black man and the last one. The knelt naked and he felt their eyes on him. And behind them there were uncounted crowds of kneeling people in the darkness. His own hands were huge windmills and he stared fascinated at the unknown thing that Antonapoulos held. The yellow lanterns swayed to and fro in the darkness and all else was motionless. Then suddenly there was a ferment. In the upheaval the steps collapsed and he felt himself falling downward. He awoke with a jerk. The early light whitened the window. He felt afraid.

Such a long time had passed that something might have happened to his friend. Because Antonapoulos did not write to him he would not know. Perhaps his friend had fallen and hurt himself. He felt such an urge to be with him once more that he would arrange it at any cost — and immediately.

In the post-office that morning he found a notice in his box that a package had come for him. It was the gift he had ordered for Christmas that did not arrive in time. The gift was a very fine one. He had bought it on the installment plan to be paid for over a period of two years. The gift was a moving-picture machine for private use, with a half-dozen of the Mickey Mouse and Popeye comedies that Antonapoulos enjoyed.

Singer was the last to reach the store that morning. He handed the jeweler for whom he worked a formal written request for leave on Friday and Saturday. And although there were four weddings on hand that week, the jeweler nodded that he could go.

He did not let anyone know of the trip beforehand, but on leaving he tacked a note to his door saying that he would be absent for several days because of business. He traveled at night, and the train reached the place of his destination just as the red winter dawn was breaking.

In the afternoon, a little before time for the visiting hour, he went out to the asylum. His arms were loaded with the parts of the moving-picture machine and the basket of fruit he carried his friend. He went immediately to the ward where he had visited Antonapoulos before.

The corridor, the door, the rows of beds were just as he remembered them. He stood at the threshold and looked eagerly for his friend. But he saw at once that though all the chairs were occupied, Antonapoulos was not there.

Singer put down his packages and wrote at the bottom of one of his cards, "Where is Spiros Antonapoulos?" A nurse came into the room and he handed her the card. She did not understand. She shook her head and raised her shoulders. He went out into the corridor and handed the card to everyone he met. Nobody knew. There was such a panic in him that he began motioning with his hands. At last he met an interne in a white coat. He plucked at the interne's elbow and gave him the card. The interne read it carefully and then guided him through several halls. They came to a small room where a young woman sat at a desk before some papers. She read the card and then looked through some files in a drawer.

Tears of nervousness and fear swam in Singer's eyes. The young woman began deliberately to write on a pad of paper, and he could not restrain himself from twisting around to see immediately what was being written about his friend.

Mr. Antonapoulos has been transferred to the infirmary. He is ill with nephritis. I will have someone show you the way.

On the way through the corridors he stopped to pick up the packages he had left at the door of the ward. The basket of fruit had been stolen, but the other boxes were intact. He followed the interne out of the building and across a plot of grass to the infirmary.

Antonapoulos! When they reached the proper ward he saw him at the first glance. His bed was placed in the middle of the room and he was sitting propped with pillows. He wore a scarlet dressing-gown and green silk pajamas and a turquoise ring. His skin was a pale yellow color, his eyes very dreamy and dark. His black hair was touched at the temples with silver. He was knitting. His fat fingers worked with the long ivory needles very slowly. At first he did not see his friend. Then when Singer stood before him he smiled serenely, without surprise, and held out his jeweled hand..

A feeling of shyness and restraint such as he had never known before came over Singer. He sat down by the bed and folded his hands on the edge of the counterpane. His eyes did not leave the face of his friend and he was deathly pale. The splendor of his friend's raiment startled him. On various occasions he had sent him each article of the outfit, but he had not imagined how they would look when all combined. Antonapoulos was more enormous than he had remembered. The great pulpy folds of his abdomen showed beneath his silk pajamas. His head was immense against the white pillow. The placid composure of his face was so profound that he seemed hardly to be aware that Singer was with him.

Singer raised his hands timidly and began to speak. His strong, skilled fingers shaped the signs with loving precision. He spoke of the cold and of the long months alone. He mentioned old memories, the cat that had died, the store, the place where he lived. At each pause Antonapoulos nodded graciously. He spoke of the four people and the long visits to his room. The eyes of his friend were moist and dark, and in them he saw the little rectangled pictures of himself that he had watched a thousand times. The warm blood flowed back to his face and his hands quickened. He spoke at length of the black man and the one with the jerking mustache and the girl. The designs of his hands shaped faster and faster. Antonapoulos nodded with slow gravity. Eagerly Singer leaned closer and he breathed with long, deep breaths and in his eyes there were bright tears.

Then suddenly Antonapoulos made a slow circle in the air with his plump forefinger. His finger circled toward Singer and at last he poked his friend in the stomach. The big Greek's smile grew very broad and he stuck out his fat, pink tongue. Singer laughed and his hands shaped the words with wild speed. His shoulders shook with laughter and his head hung backward. Why he laughed he did not know. Antonapoulos rolled his eyes. Singer continued to laugh riotously until his breath was gone and his fingers trembled. He grasped the arm of his friend and tried to steady himself. His laughs came low and painfully like hiccoughs.

Antonapoulos was the first to compose himself. His fat little feet had untucked the cover at the bottom of the bed. His smile faded and he kicked contemptuously at the blanket. Singer hastened to put things right, but Antonapoulos frowned and held up his finger regally to a nurse who was passing through the ward. When she had straightened the bed to his liking the big Greek inclined his head so deliberately that the gesture seemed one of benediction rather than a simple nod of thanks. Then he turned gravely to his friend again.

As Singer talked he did not realize how the time had passed. Only when a nurse brought Antonapoulos his supper on a tray did he realize that it was late. The lights in the ward were turned on and outside the windows it was almost dark. The other patients had trays of supper before them also. They had put down their work (some of them wove baskets, others did leatherwork or knitted) and they were eating listlessly. Beside Antonapoulos they all seemed very sick and colorless. Most of them needed a haircut and they wore seedy gray nightshirts slit down the back. They stared at the two mutes with wonder.

Antonapoulos lifted the cover from his dish and inspected the food carefully. There was fish and some vegetables. He picked up the fish and held it to the light in the palm of his hand for a thorough examination. Then he ate with relish. During supper he began to point out the various people in the room. He pointed to one man in the corner and made faces of disgust. The man snarled at him. He pointed to a young boy and smiled and nodded and waved his plump hand. Singer was too happy to feel embarrassment. He picked up the packages from the floor and laid them on the bed to distract his friend. Antonapoulos took off the wrappings, but the machine did not interest him at all. He turned back to his supper.

Singer handed the nurse a note explaining about the movie. She called an interne and then they brought in a doctor. As the three of them consulted they looked curiously at Singer. The news reached the patients and they propped up on their elbows excitedly. Only Antonapoulos was not disturbed.

Singer had practiced with the movie beforehand. He set up the screen so that it could be watched by all the patients. Then he worked with the projector and the film. The nurse took out the supper trays and the lights in the ward were turned off. A Mickey Mouse comedy flashed on the screen.

Singer watched his friend. At first Antonapoulos was startled. He heaved himself up for a better view and would have risen from the bed if the nurse had not restrained him. Then he watched with a beaming smile. Singer could see the other patients calling out to each other and laughing. Nurses and orderlies came in from the hall and the whole ward was in commotion. When the Mickey Mouse was finished Singer put on a Popeye film. Then at the conclusion of this film he felt that the entertainment had lasted long enough for the first time. He switched on the light and the ward settled down again. As the interne put the machine under his friend's bed he saw Antonapoulos slyly cut his eyes across the ward to be certain that each person realized that the machine was his.

Singer began to talk with his hands again. He knew that he would soon be asked to leave, but the thoughts he had stored in his mind were too big to be said in a short time. He talked with frantic haste. In the ward there was an old man whose head shook with palsy and who picked feebly at his eyebrows. He envied the old man because he lived with Antona-poulos day after day. Singer would have exchanged places with him joyfully.

His friend fumbled for something in his bosom. It was the little brass cross that he had always worn. The dirty string had been replaced by a red ribbon. Singer thought of the dream and he told that, also, to his friend. In his haste the signs sometimes became blurred and he had to shake his hands and begin all over. Antonapoulos watched him with his dark, drowsy eyes. Sitting motionless in his bright, rich garments he seemed like some wise king from a legend.

The interne in charge of the ward allowed Singer to stay for an hour past the visiting time. Then at last he held out his thin, hairy wrist and showed him his watch. The patients were settled for sleep. Singer's hand faltered. He grasped his friend by the arm and looked intently into his eyes as he used to do each morning when they parted for work. Finally Singer backed himself out of the room. At the doorway his hands signed a broken farewell and then clenched into fists.

During the moonlit January nights Singer continued to walk about the streets of the town each evening when he was not engaged. The rumors about him grew bolder. An old Negro woman told hundreds of people that he knew the ways of spirits come back from the dead. A certain pieceworker claimed that he had worked with the mute at another mill somewhere else in the state — and the tales he told were unique. The rich thought that he was rich and the poor considered him a poor man like themselves. And as there was no way to disprove these rumors they grew marvelous and very real. Each man described the mute as he wished him to be.

* * *

The time had come for Singer to go to Antonapoulos again. The journey was a long one. For, although the distance between them was something less than two hundred miles, the train meandered to points far out of the way and stopped for long hours at certain stations during the night. Singer would leave the town in the afternoon and travel all through the night and until the early morning of the next day. As usual, he was ready far in advance. He planned to have a full week with his friend this visit. His clothes had been sent to the cleaner's, his hat blocked, and his bags were in readiness. The gifts he would carry were wrapped in colored tissue paper — and in addition there was a de luxe basket of fruits done up in cellophane and a crate of late shipped strawberries. On the morning before his departure Singer cleaned his room. In his ice box he found a bit of left-over goose liver and took it out to the alley for the neighborhood cat. On his door he tacked the same sign he had posted there before, stating that he would be absent for several days on business. During all these preparations he moved about leisurely with two vivid spots of color on his cheekbones. His face was very solemn.

Then at last the hour for departure was at hand. He stood on the platform, burdened with his suitcases and gifts, and watched the train roll in on the station tracks. He found himself a seat in the day coach and hoisted his luggage on the rack above his head. The car was crowded, for the most part with mothers and children. The green plush seats had a grimy smell. The windows of the car were dirty and rice thrown at some recent bridal pair lay scattered on the floor. Singer smiled cordially to his fellow-travelers and leaned back in his seat. He closed his eyes. The lashes made a dark, curved fringe above the hollows of his cheeks. His right hand moved nervously inside his pocket.

For a while his thoughts lingered in the town he was leaving behind him. He saw Mick and Doctor Copeland and Jake Blount and Biff Brannon. The faces crowded in on him out of the darkness so that he felt smothered. He thought of the quarrel between Blount and the Negro. The nature of this quarrel was hopelessly confused in his mind — but each of them had on several occasions broken out into a bitter tirade against the other, the absent one. He had agreed with each of them in turn, though what it was they wanted him to sanction he did not know. And Mick — her face was urgent and she said a good deal that he did not understand in the least. And then Biff Brannon at the New York Café. Brannon with his dark, iron-like jaw and his watchful eyes. And strangers who followed him about the streets and buttonholed him for unexplainable reasons. The Turk at the linen shop who flung his hands up in his face and babbled with his tongue to make words the shape of which Singer had

133

never imagined before. A certain mill foreman and an old black woman. A businessman on the main street and an urchin who solicited soldiers for a whorehouse near the river. Singer wriggled his shoulders uneasily. The train rocked with a smooth, easy motion. His head nodded to rest on his shoulder and for a short while he slept.

When he opened his eyes again the town was far behind him. The town was forgotten. Outside the dirty window there was the brilliant midsummer countryside. The sun slanted in strong, bronze-colored rays over the green fields of the new cotton. There were acres of tobacco, the plants heavy and green like some monstrous jungle weed. The orchards of peaches with the lush fruit weighting down the dwarfed trees. There were miles of pastures and tens of miles of wasted, washed-out land abandoned to the hardier weeds. The train cut through deep green pine forests where the ground was covered with the slick brown needles and the tops of the trees stretched up virgin and tall into the sky. And farther, a long way south of the town, the cypress swamps — with the gnarled roots of the trees writhing down into the brackish waters, where the gray, tattered moss trailed from the branches, where tropical water flowers blossomed in dankness and gloom. Then out again into the open beneath the sun and the indigo-blue sky.

Singer sat solemn and timid, his face turned fully toward the window. The great sweeps of space and the hard, elemental coloring almost blinded him. This kaleidoscopic variety of scene, this abundance of growth and color, seemed somehow connected with his friend. His thoughts were with Antonapoulos. The bliss of their reunion almost stifled him. His nose was pinched and he breathed with quick, short breaths through his slightly open mouth.

Antonapoulos would be glad to see him. He would enjoy the fresh fruits and the presents. By now he would be out of the sick ward and able to go on an excursion to the movies, and afterward to the hotel where they had eaten dinner on the first visit. Singer had written many letters to Antonapoulos, but he had not posted them. He surrendered himself wholly to thoughts of his friend.

The half-year since he had last been with him seemed neither a long nor a short span of time. Behind each waking moment there had always been his friend. And this submerged communion with Antonapoulos had grown and changed as though they were together in the flesh. Sometimes he thought of Antonapoulos with awe and self-abasement, sometimes with pride — always with love unchecked by criticism, freed of will. When he dreamed at night the face of his friend was always before him, massive and wise and gentle. And in his waking thoughts they were eternally united.

The summer evening came slowly. The sun sank down behind a ragged line of trees in the distance and the sky paled. The twilight was languid and soft. There was a white full moon, and low purple clouds lay over the horizon. The earth, the trees, the unpainted rural dwellings darkened slowly. At intervals mild summer lightning quivered in the air. Singer watched all of this intently until at last the night had come, and his own face was reflected in the glass before him.

Children staggered up and down the aisle of the car with dripping paper cups of water. An old man in overalls who had the seat before Singer drank whiskey from time to time from a Coca-Cola bottle. Between swallows he plugged the bottle carefully with a wad of paper. A little girl on the right combed her hair with a sticky red lollipop. Shoeboxes were opened and trays of supper were brought in from the dining-car. Singer did not eat. He leaned back in his seat and kept desultory account of all that went on around him. At last the car settled down. Children lay on the broad plush seats and slept, while men and women doubled up with their pillows and rested as best they could.

Singer did not sleep. He pressed his face close against the glass and strained to see into the night. The darkness was heavy and velvety. Sometimes there was a patch of moonlight or the flicker of a lantern from the window of some house along the way. From the moon he saw that the train had turned from its southward course and was headed toward the east. The eagerness he felt was so keen that his nose was too pinched to breathe through and his cheeks were scarlet. He sat there, his face pressed close against the cold, sooty glass of the window, through most of the long night journey.

The train was more than an hour late, and the fresh, bright summer morning was well under way when they arrived. Singer went immediately to the hotel, a very good hotel where he had made reservations in advance. He unpacked his bags and arranged the presents he would take Antonapoulos on the bed. From the menu the bellboy brought him he selected a luxurious breakfast — broiled bluefish, hominy, French toast, and hot black coffee. After breakfast he rested before the electric fan in his underwear. At noon he began to dress. He bathed and shaved and laid out fresh linen and his best seersucker suit. At three o'clock the hospital was open for visiting hours. It was Tuesday and the eighteenth of July.

At the asylum he sought Antonapoulos first in the sick ward where he had been confined before. But at the doorway of the room he saw immediately that his friend was not there. Next he found his way through the corridors to the office where he had been taken the time before. He had his question already written on one of the cards he carried about with him. The person behind the desk was not the same as the one who had been there before. He was a young man, almost a boy, with a half-formed, immature face and a lank mop of hair. Singer handed him the card and stood quietly, his arms heaped with packages, his weight resting on his heels.

The young man shook his head. He leaned over the desk and scribbled loosely on a pad of paper. Singer read what he had written and the spots of color drained from his cheekbones instantly. He looked at the note a long time, his eyes cut sideways and his head bowed. For it was written there that Antonapoulos was dead.

On the way back to the hotel he was careful not to crush the fruit he had brought with him. He took the packages up to his room and then wandered down to the lobby. Behind a potted palm tree there was a slot machine. He inserted a nickel but when he tried to pull the lever he found that the machine was jammed. Over this incident he made a great to-do. He cornered the clerk and furiously demonstrated what had happened. His face was deathly pale and he was so beside himself that tears rolled down the ridges of his nose. He flailed his hands and even stamped once with his long, narrow, elegantly shoed foot on the plush carpet. Nor was he satisfied when his coin was refunded, but insisted on checking out immediately. He packed his bag and was obliged to work energetically to make it close again. For in addition to the articles he had brought with him he carried away three towels, two cakes of soap, a pen and a bottle of ink, a roll of toilet paper, and a Holy Bible. He paid his bill and walked to the railway station to put his belongings in custody. The train did not leave until nine in the evening and he had the empty afternoon before him.

This town was smaller than the one in which he lived. The business streets intersected to form the shape of a cross. The stores had a countrified look; there were harnesses and sacks of feed in half of the display windows. Singer walked listlessly along the sidewalks. His throat felt swollen and he wanted to swallow but was unable to do so. To relieve this strangled feeling he bought a drink in one of the drugstores. He idled in the barber shop and purchased a few trifles at the ten-cent store. He looked no one full in the face and his head drooped down to one side like a sick animal's.

The afternoon was almost ended when a strange thing happened to Singer. He had been walking slowly and irregularly along the curb of the street. The sky was overcast and the air humid. Singer did not raise his head, but as he passed the town pool room he caught a sidewise glance of something that disturbed him. He passed the pool room and then stopped in the middle of the street. Listlessly he retraced his steps and stood before the open door of the place. There were three mutes inside and they were talking with their hands together. All three of them were coatless. They wore bowler hats and bright ties. Each of them held a glass of beer in his left hand. There was a certain brotherly resemblance between them.

Singer went inside. For a moment he had trouble taking his hand from his pocket. Then clumsily he formed a word of greeting. He was clapped on the shoulder. A cold drink was ordered. They surrounded him and the fingers of their hands shot out like pistons as they questioned him.

He told his own name and the name of the town where he lived. After that he could think of nothing else to tell about himself. He asked if they knew Spiros Antonapoulos. They did not know him. Singer stood with his hands dangling loose. His head was still inclined to one side and his glance was oblique. He was so listless and cold that the three mutes in the bowler hats looked at him queerly. After a while they left him out of their conversation. And when they had paid for the rounds of

137

beers and were ready to depart they did not suggest that he join them.

Although Singer had been adrift on the streets for half a day he almost missed his train. It was not clear to him how this happened or how he had spent the hours before. He reached the station two minutes before the train pulled out, and barely had time to drag his luggage aboard and find a seat. The car he chose was almost empty. When he was settled he opened the crate of strawberries and picked them over with finicky care. The berries were of a giant size, large as walnuts and in full-blown ripeness. The green leaves at the top of the rich-colored fruit were like tiny bouquets. Singer put a berry in his mouth and though the juice had a lush, wild sweetness there was already a subtle flavor of decay. He ate until his palate was dulled by the taste and then rewrapped the crate and placed it on the rack above him. At midnight he drew the window-shade and lay down on the seat. He was curled in a ball, his coat pulled over his face and head. In this position he lay in a stupor of half-sleep for about twelve hours. The conductor had to shake him when they arrived.

Singer left his luggage in the middle of the station floor. Then he walked to the shop. He greeted the jeweler for whom he worked with a listless turn of his hand. When he went out again there was something heavy in his pocket. For a while he rambled with bent head along the streets. But the unrefracted brilliance of the sun, the humid heat, oppressed him. He returned to his room with swollen eyes and an aching head. After resting he drank a glass of iced coffee and smoked a cigarette. Then when he had washed the ash tray and the glass he brought out a pistol from his pocket and put a bullet in his chest.

Singer's suicide is not the end of the story, as it rarely is — especially for the living. For the living there is the period of guilt, of wondering, of rethinking possibilities and relationships. Singer's associates (who are not well met in these excerpts) had come to his room to talk and be listened to by the deaf man. They all look down at his grave and weep. Mick, the young friend who came to listen to the radio, cries so hard that she almost chokes.

Could not Singer have replaced Antonapoulos with other friends? Recall how different the two deaf men were: one a slow, lumbering, poorly educated, uncommunicative, childlike hulk of a man, and the other a bright, sensitive, literate Jewish intellectual. Together, they made an odd couple. They were in some ways like all deaf people and in some ways like none.

Note the early description of the two as they walk arm in arm down the street to work — the names, the manner of dress, the physiques, the expressions, and the attitudes. Despite the differences in background and interests, though, they do share and relate. Then one begins to see the increasing emotional disintegration of Antonapoulos and Singer's despair in helping his friend. When Antonapoulos is finally hospitalized, Singer in his loneliness recalls his early life as an orphan in an institution for the deaf and how he had learned to read, to sign, to follow the movement of people's lips, to understand spoken language. He had learned to speak but felt uncomfortable doing so. McCullers describes it well: "It was not natural to him and his tongue felt like a whale in his mouth."

Is it ironic for Singer, a deaf man, to be perceived as a good listener by his hearing and speaking friends? Biff, owner of the New York Cafe, wonders whether Singer really understands what is said, but he continues to come. Biff concludes that Singer does understand but is a little slow since he smiles appropriately but always several seconds after a funny remark. Singer listens to all of them — Blount, the fighting and often bloodied revolutionary; Mick, the bubbling adolescent; Dr. Copeland, the black physician, and Portia, his daughter; and others. Of his four talkative acquaintances, Singer comments: "The words in their hearts do not let them rest."

Is Singer's final action understandable or preventable? Suicide is no more common among the deaf than the hearing. For some persons it may be the only means of victory over loneliness. Singer undoubtedly could "listen," but it did not appease the loss of his deaf friend. Perhaps things would have been different had there been another deaf person who needed

139

companionship and to whom Singer could relate and love as he did Antonapoulos.

The heart is indeed a lonely hunter — and love an elusive target. The sheer terror of loneliness, of being without another caring person, is the ego's greatest challenge. "Little do men perceive what solitude is," wrote Francis Bacon, "and how far it extendeth. For a crowd is not company; and faces are but a gallery of pictures; and talk but a tinkling cymbal where there is no love."[3]

---

[3] Francis Bacon, "Essays," XXVII 1625, in *A New Dictionary of Quotations*, ed. H. L. Mencken (New York: Knopf, 1962), p. 1126.

QUESTIONS FOR DISCUSSION

1. In what ways do Singer and Antonapoulos act like deaf men and in what ways do they not? On what evidence do you support your answers?

2. Suppose Singer and Antonapoulos had both been blind instead of deaf. What might have been the consequences of Antonapoulos' hospitalization on Singer?

3. To what extent are the events besetting Singer, Antonapoulos, and the others a product of the setting (the South of the 1930's)? If the same events had occurred in a large Northern, Midwestern, or Western city in the 1960s or 1970s, what differences in outcomes might be expected?

4. No social, welfare, private, or public agencies are mentioned as possible aids to Antonapoulos or Singer. Assuming that they had been available, what do you think might have happened?

5. With reference to Question 4, if Singer and Antonapoulos had been blind instead of deaf, more private and public agencies would be available to assist these gentlemen. Why? If Singer had been retarded how would that have changed the situation?

6. What makes Singer a good listener despite his inability to hear? Think of someone you know who listens well. What differentiates him or her from others?

7. The fact that Antonapoulos could not read did not discourage Singer from writing to him. Singer knew this but continued to write. Why?

8. Using Singer and Antonapoulos as protagonists and the others as presented, outline a story titled *"The Heart is a Happy Hunter."*

ADDITIONAL READINGS

- Carr, Virginia S. *The Lonely Hunter. A Biography of Carson McCullers.* New York: Doubleday, 1976.
- Field, Rachel. *And Now Tomorrow.* New York: Macmillan, 1942.
- Furth, Hans G. *Deafness and Learning: A Psychosocial Approach.* Belmont, CA: Wadsworth, 1973.
- Greenberg, Joanne. *In This Sign.* New York: Holt, Rinehart and Winston, 1970.
- Rainer, John; Altshuler, Kenneth; Kallman, Franz; and Deming, W. Edwards, eds. *Family and Mental Health Problems in a Deaf Population.* 3d ed. Springfield, IL: Charles C Thomas, 1969.
- Schlesinger, Hilde S., and Meadow, Kay P. *Sound and Sign: Childhood Deafness and Mental Health.* Berkeley: University of California Press, 1972.
- Yates, Elizabeth. *Hue and Cry.* New York: Coward-McCann, 1953.
- Zuckerkandl, Victor. *Sound and Symbol.* Princeton: Princeton University Press, 1954.

"Obviously it may be good for one not to know too much"

4

The Secret Agent

Joseph Conrad

4

Conrad's story is "a simple tale" (as subtitled) of a simple boy surrounded and overwhelmed by political, social, and personal passions. The book was originally published in 1907, when it would be fair to say that mental retardation was not exactly an open and discussable topic. Apparently its publication set off vibrations akin to a giant piece of chalk squeaking across a Victorian chalkboard. When it was republished in 1921, Conrad saw fit to write an introduction to justify what critics had called the "sordid nature and moral squalor" of the story. He made clear in the introduction that he was not defending himself against such criticisms but simply taking the opportunity to explain that "there was no perverse intention, no secret scorn for the natural sensibilities of mankind at the bottom of my impulses."

And what was so sordid as to upset readers? *Secret Agent,* despite its title, is the story of a retarded boy, Stevie, and his family, primarily his sister Winnie, whose life is devoted to caring for and sheltering her brother. Stevie is certainly not a severely retarded youngster since he had learned to read and write under what Conrad characterizes as the British "excellent system of compulsory education." But Stevie is slow, cannot remember, is easily diverted and often lost in the streets of London. He is readily upset, often to the point of stuttering and squinting. Conrad notes that Stevie never has had any fits, so we may assume that he is, in our professional jargon, a familial, somewhat slow child with mild to moderate learning difficulties.

If the descriptive terms and labels used in the field of learning handicaps appear to be fuzzy and ultraconditional, those in the field of mental retardation seem clean, concise, and consensual. This is because of the aura of trust and confidence in dimensions of human behavior that can be designated by numerals. In the old days these designations led to such classifi-

145

cations as *idiot, imbecile,* and *moron.* These labels were followed by more descriptive terms like *severely, moderately,* and *mildly retarded,* and/or *trainable* and *educable retarded.* In tracing the history of mental retardation, one also encounters *feebleminded, simpleton, fool, ament, mentally deficient, mental subnormality,* and a host of other terms rarely used today.

It is worthy of note that the so-called "IQ scale," devised by the two French psychologists Binet and Simon at the beginning of the twentieth century, was constructed to help identify and place retarded children into more suitable educational environments. Such scales as later revised and interpreted became measures of innate intellectual capacity and provided a basis for other mystical notions.

Reliable measures of anything can take on a halo of truth and accuracy despite the fact that one may not be entirely clear about the phenomenon one is measuring. A thermometer may be fairly accurate in assessing body temperature, but it can offer only occasional clues as to what may be wrong when a reading is above or below the norm.

We certainly don't know enough about Stevie to be sure of the etiology of his limited and confused functioning. But, after all, Conrad was not concerned with Stevie's IQ score or specific diagnosis. As an observer and interpreter of the human condition, that author needed Stevie as the prime mover in the interplay of his mother, his sister, Mr. Verloc, and aspects of English society in the early twentieth century. A typical child would not have sufficed for Conrad's story. Nor would the counterpoint of interpersonal relations have been played out in shocking denoument if, for example, the child had been blind or deaf or orthopedically handicapped.

Stevie's mother wants the child to be accepted as a son in the Verloc's home, so she moves out. Winnie wants her husband to grow fond of the boy, to praise his usefulness and dependability. Mr. Verloc responds to his wife's wishes in friendly and cooperative attempts to "father" his wife's brother. Stevie, always wishing to please, stumbles into the explosive tragedy.

Intellectual or cognitive lacks are perceived and treated by cultures and societies past and present in vastly different ways. In some developing countries with large, unified families, retarded members have found acceptable roles and responsibilities without much ado or strain. In one country of my observation, an entire family, including a retarded youngster, worked on building a house. The boy was assigned tasks well within his physical and intellectual abilities. In such cultures "retardation" is not perceived or reacted to as in more industrialized societies.

In a sense, the more industrialized and individualistically oriented a society is, the more retarded a retarded child becomes. A technological, highly competitive society speeds up and increases the complexity of its symbol systems, communication processes, and human interactions. Jobs and opportunities for the under-educated are reduced by "smarter" machines. Test scores, grades, units, and similar quantifiable variables loom as virtually impossible barriers for the slow and retarded. Intellectual achievement in individualistic oriented societies is so valued that failure to so achieve is often tantamount to total failure.

More subtly, a society like ours — and to some extent all Western cultures — places great emphasis on individual responsibility for success in life, and at the same time strives to ensure equality of opportunity. Although this ideal is far from real, we tend to respond to children as if success is a product of their diligence, hard work, and ambition. We tend to equate virtue with winning and evil with losing. Success in school and in learning cognitive skills becomes a key arena for such self and social evaluations. Perhaps the impact of retardation on children has been successfully reduced in some families, neighborhoods, and schools but, generally, despite all one may do, retarded children rarely can emerge from a sustained school environment feeling competent in their limited abilities and good about self.

This prevailing atmosphere was evident in the English culture of the early twentieth century, as it is today. Victorian England wanted to know why an author of Conrad's reputation could place an innocent retarded boy into such an ugly plot. Conrad described how the story came to him and how Stevie's handicap became the necessary bridge between Winnie's passion and that of the anarchists. In whatever manner Conrad conceived and created Stevie, his characterization throughout is insightful, knowledgeable, and intuitively correct.

The excerpts concentrate on Stevie and Stevie's relationships. Stevie lives in a home with Mr. Verloc, who is married to Winnie, Stevie's older sister. In her choice of spouse, Winnie had taken great pains to ensure a home for Stevie as well as one for her mother. Mr. Verloc owns a small book and stationery store which serves as a front for meetings of socialists and anarchists.

Conrad first presents the major players and the theme. Mr. Verloc leaves his shop in charge of his brother-in-law, who we later discover to be a retarded, highly sensitive lad of fifteen. Obviously, Mr. Verloc has other fish to fry than what he is selling (empty boxes, ink, rubber stamps, revolutionary books, obscure newspapers, etc.) in his shop. Mr. Verloc's friends (as you will discover) are anarchists and revolutionaries for whom dynamite outrages are a form of protest. Mr. Verloc is also a secret agent serving the interests of a foreign government. He can leave his brother-in-law, Stevie, in charge of the shop because his wife, Winnie, is a dutiful and conscientious supervisor of the boy.

We also meet Mrs. Verloc's mother. Winnie's mother had wishes that her daughter would have children of her own but in her heart is not entirely displeased that Winnie does not. If she had no children of her own, perhaps Stevie would have a better chance of being accepted as a "child" in the family. Winnie is fond of Stevie. Indeed, it is suggested that she married Mr. Verloc, in part, to provide a home for the boy.

Stevie has learned to read and write in school, and probably with a little help from Winnie. But the boy is forgetful, easily diverted from tasks, often lost in the streets, and led astray by other boys.

THE SECRET AGENT

Joseph Conrad

Mr. Verloc, going out in the morning, left his shop nominally in charge of his brother-in-law. It could be done, because there was very little business at any time, and practically none at all before the evening. Mr. Verloc cared but little about his ostensible business. And, moreover, his wife was in charge of his brother-in-law.

The shop was small, and so was the house. It was one of those grimy brick houses which existed in large quantities before the era of reconstruction dawned upon London. The shop was a square box of a place, with the front glazed in small panes. In the daytime the door remained closed; in the evening it stood discreetly but suspiciously ajar.

The window contained photographs of more or less undressed dancing girls; nondescript packages in wrappers like patent medicines; closed yellow paper envelopes, very flimsy, and marked two-and-six in heavy black figures; a few numbers of ancient French comic publications hung across a string as if to dry; a dingy blue china bowl, a casket of black wood, bottles of marking ink, and rubber stamps; a few books, with titles hinting at impropriety; a few apparently old copies of obscure newspapers, badly printed, with titles like *The Torch, The Gong* — rousing titles. And the two gas-jets inside the panes were always turned low, either for economy's sake or for the sake of the customers.

These customers were either very young men, who hung about the window for a time before slipping in suddenly; or men of a more mature age, but looking generally as if they were

Excerpts from *The Secret Agent*, by Joseph Conrad. Copyright © 1907 by Doubleday & Co., Inc. Used by permission of Doubleday.

not in funds. Some of that last kind had the collars of their overcoats turned right up to their moustaches, and traces of mud on the bottom of their nether garments, which had the appearance of being much worn and not very valuable. And the legs inside them did not, as a general rule, seem of much account either. With their hands plunged deep in the side pockets of their coats, they dodged in sideways, one shoulder first, as if afraid to start the bell going.

The bell, hung on the door by means of a curved ribbon of steel, was difficult to circumvent. It was hopelessly cracked; but of an evening, at the slightest provocation, it clattered behind the customer with impudent virulence.

It clattered; and at that signal, through the dusty glass door behind the painted deal counter, Mr. Verloc would issue hastily from the parlour at the back. His eyes were naturally heavy; he had an air of having wallowed, fully dressed, all day on an unmade bed. Another man would have felt such an appearance a distinct disadvantage. In a commercial transaction of the retail order much depends on the seller's engaging and amiable aspect. But Mr. Verloc knew his business, and remained undisturbed by any sort of aesthetic doubt about his appearance. With a firm, steady-eyed impudence, which seemed to hold back the threat of some abominable menace, he would proceed to sell over the counter some object looking obviously and scandalously not worth the money which passed in the transaction: a small cardboard box with apparently nothing inside, for instance, or one of those carefully closed yellow flimsy envelopes, or a soiled volume in paper covers with a promising title. Now and then it happened that one of the faded, yellow dancing girls would get sold to an amateur, as though she had been alive and young.

Sometimes it was Mrs. Verloc who would appear at the call of the cracked bell. Winnie Verloc was a young woman with a full bust, in a tight bodice, and with broad hips. Her hair was very tidy. Steady-eyed like her husband, she preserved an air of unfathomable indifference behind the rampart of the counter. Then the customer of comparatively tender years would get suddenly disconcerted at having to deal with a woman, and with rage in his heart would proffer a request for a bottle of marking ink, retail value sixpence (price in Verloc's shop one-and-sixpence), which, once outside, he would drop stealthily into the gutter.

The evening visitors — the men with collars turned up and soft hats rammed down — nodded familiarly to Mrs. Verloc, and with a muttered greeting, lifted up the flap at the end of the counter in order to pass into the back parlour, which gave access to a passage and to a steep flight of stairs. The door of the shop was the only means of entrance to the house in which Mr. Verloc carried on his business of a seller of shady wares, exercised his vocation of a protector of society, and cultivated his domestic virtues. These last were pronounced. He was thoroughly domesticated. Neither his spiritual, nor his mental, nor his physical needs were of the kind to take him much abroad. He found at home the ease of his body and the peace of his conscience, together with Mrs. Verloc's wifely attentions and Mrs. Verloc's mother's deferential regard.

Winnie's mother was a stout, wheezy woman, with a large brown face. She wore a black wig under a white cap. Her swollen legs rendered her inactive. She considered herself to be of French descent, which might have been true; and after a good many years of married life with a licenced victualler of the more common sort, she provided for the years of widowhood by letting furnished apartments for gentlemen near Vauxhall Bridge Road in a square once of some splendour and still included in the district of Belgravia. This topographical fact was of some advantage in advertising her rooms; but the patrons of the worthy widow were not exactly of the fashionable kind. Such as they were, her daughter Winnie helped to look after them. Traces of the French descent which the widow boasted of were apparent in Winnie, too. They were apparent in the extremely neat and artistic arrangement of her glossy dark hair. Winnie had also other charms: her youth; her full, rounded form; her clear complexion; the provocation of her unfathomable reserve, which never went so far as to prevent conversation, carried on on the lodger's part with animation, and on hers with an equable amiability.

It must be that Mr. Verloc was susceptible to these fascinations. Mr. Verloc was an intermittent patron. He came and went without any very apparent reason. He generally arrived in London (like the influenza) from the Continent, only he arrived unheralded by the Press; and his visitations set in with great severity. He breakfasted in bed, and remained wallowing there with an air of quiet enjoyment till noon every day — and sometimes even to a later hour. But when he went out he seemed to experience a great difficulty in finding his way back to his temporary home in the Belgravian square. He left it late, and returned to it early — as early as three or four in the morning; and on waking up at ten addressed Winnie, bringing in the breakfast tray, with jocular, exhausted civility, in the hoarse, failing tones of a man who had been talking vehemently for many hours together. His prominent, heavy-lidded eyes rolled sideways amorously and languidly, the bedclothes were pulled up to his chin, and his dark smooth moustache covered his thick lips capable of much honeyed banter.

In Winnie's mother's opinion Mr. Verloc was a very nice gentleman. From her life's experience gathered in various "business houses" the good woman had taken into her retirement an ideal of gentlemanliness as exhibited by the patrons of private-saloon bars. Mr. Verloc approached that ideal; he attained it, in fact.

"Of course, we'll take over your furniture, mother," Winnie had remarked.

The lodging-house was to be given up. It seems it would not answer to carry it on. It would have been too much trouble for Mr. Verloc. It would not have been convenient for his other business. What his business was he did not say; but after his engagement to Winnie he took the trouble to get up before noon, and descending the basement stairs, make himself pleasant to Winnie's mother in the breakfast-room downstairs where she had her motionless being. He stroked the cat, poked the fire, had his lunch served to him there. He left its slightly stuffy cosiness with evident reluctance, but, all the same, remained out till the night was far advanced. He never offered to take Winnie to theatres, as such a nice gentleman ought to have done. His evenings were occupied. His work was in a way political, he told Winnie once. She would have, he warned her, to be very nice to his political friends. And with her straight, unfathomable glance she answered that she would be so, of course.

How much more he told her as to his occupation it was impossible for Winnie's mother to discover. The married couple took her over with the furniture. The mean aspect of the shop surprised her. The change from the Belgravian square to the narrow street in Soho affected her legs adversely. They became of an enormous size. On the other hand, she experienced a complete relief from material cares. Her son-in-law's heavy good nature inspired her with a sense of absolute safety. Her daughter's future was obviously assured, and even as to her son Stevie she need have no anxiety. She had not been able to conceal from herself that he was a terrible encumbrance, that poor Stevie. But in view of Winnie's fondness for her delicate brother, and of Mr. Verloc's kind and generous disposition, she felt that the poor boy was pretty safe in this rough world. And in her heart of hearts she was not perhaps displeased that the Verlocs had no children. As that circumstance seemed perfectly indifferent to Mr. Verloc, and as Winnie found an object of quasi-maternal affection in her brother, perhaps this was just as well for poor Stevie.

For he was difficult to dispose of, that boy. He was delicate and, in a frail way, good-looking, too, except for the vacant droop of his lower lip. Under our excellent system of compulsory education he had learned to read and write, notwithstanding the unfavourable aspect of the lower lip. But as errand-boy he did not turn out a great success. He forgot his messages; he was easily diverted from the straight path of duty by the attractions of stray cats and dogs, which he followed down narrow alleys into unsavoury courts; by the comedies of the streets, which he contemplated open-mouthed, to the detriment of his employer's interests; or by the dramas of fallen horses, whose pathos and violence induced him sometimes to shriek piercingly in a crowd, which disliked to be disturbed by sounds of distress in its quiet enjoyment of the national spectacle. When led away by a grave and protecting policeman, it would often become apparent that poor Stevie had forgotten his address — at least for a time. A brusque question caused him to stutter to the point of suffocation. When startled by anything perplexing he used to squint horribly. However, he never had any fits (which was encouraging); and before the natural outbursts of impatience on the part of his father he could always, in his childhood's days, run for protection behind the short skirts of his sister Winnie. On the other hand, he might have been suspected of hiding a fund of reckless naughtiness. When he had reached the age of fourteen a friend of his late father, an agent for a foreign preserved milk firm, having given him an opening as office-boy, discovered him one foggy afternoon, in the chief's absence, busy letting off fireworks on the staircase. He touched off in quick succession a set of fierce rockets, angry catherine wheels, loudly exploding squibs — and the matter might have turned out very serious. An awful panic spread through the whole building. Wild-eyed, choking clerks stampeded through the passages full of smoke, silk hats and elderly business men could be seen rolling independently down the stairs. Stevie did not seem to derive any personal gratification from what he had done. His motives for this stroke of originality were difficult to discover. It was only later on that Winnie obtained from him a misty and confused confession. It seems that two other office-boys in the building had worked upon his feelings by tales of injustice and oppression till they had wrought his compassion to the pitch of that frenzy. But his father's friend, of course, dismissed him summarily as likely to ruin his business. After that altruistic exploit Stevie was put to help wash the dishes in the basement kitchen, and to black the boots of the gentlemen patronizing the Belgravian mansion. There was obviously no future in such work. The gentlemen tipped him a shilling now and then. Mr. Verloc showed himself the most generous of lodgers. But altogether all that did not amount to much either in the way of gain or prospects; so that when Winnie announced her engagement to Mr. Verloc her mother could not help wondering, with a sigh and a glance towards the scullery, what would become of poor Stephen now.

It appeared that Mr. Verloc was ready to take him over together with his wife's mother and with the furniture, which was the whole visible fortune of the family. Mr. Verloc gathered everything as it came to his broad, good-natured breast. The furniture was disposed to the best advantage all over the house, but Mrs. Verloc's mother was confined to two back rooms on the first floor. The luckless Stevie slept in one of them. By this time a growth of thin fluffy hair had come to blur, like golden mist, the sharp line of his small lower jaw. He helped his sister with blind love and docility in her household duties. Mr. Verloc thought that some occupation would be good for him. His spare time he occupied by drawing circles with compass and pencil on a piece of paper. He applied himself to that pastime with great industry, with his elbows spread out and bowed low over the kitchen table. Through the open door of the parlour at the back of the shop Winnie, his sister, glanced at him from time to time with maternal vigilance.

* * *

Such was the house, the household, and the business Mr. Verloc left behind him on his way westward at the hour of half-past ten in the morning. It was unusually early for him; his whole person exhaled the charm of almost dewy freshness; he wore his blue cloth overcoat unbuttoned; his boots were shiny; his cheeks, freshly shaven, had a sort of gloss; and even his heavy-lidded eyes, refreshed by a night of peaceful slumber, sent out glances of comparative alertness. Through the park railings these glances beheld men and women riding in the Row, couples cantering past harmoniously, others advancing sedately at a walk, loitering groups of three or four, solitary horsemen looking unsociable, and solitary women followed at a long distance by a groom with a cockade to his hat and a leather belt over his tight-fitting coat. Carriages went bowling by, mostly two-horse broughams, with here and there a victoria with the skin of some wild beast inside and a woman's face and hat emerging above the folded hood. And a peculiarly London sun — against which nothing could be said except that it looked blood-shot — glorified all this by its stare. It hung at a moderate eleva-tion above Hyde Park Corner with an air of punctual and benign vigilance. The very pavement under Mr. Verloc's feet had an old-gold tinge in that diffused light, in which neither wall, nor tree, nor beast, nor man cast a shadow. Mr. Verloc was going westward through a town without shadows in an atmosphere of powdered old gold. There were red, coppery gleams on the roofs of houses, on the corners of walls, on the panels of carriages, on the very coats of the horses, and on the broad back of Mr. Verloc's overcoat, where they produced a dull effect of rustiness. But Mr. Verloc was not in the least conscious of having got rusty. He surveyed through the park railings the evidence of the town's opulence and luxury with an approving eye. All these people had to be protected. Protection is the first necessity of opulence and luxury. They had to be protected; and their horses, carriages, houses, servants had to be protected; and the source of their wealth had to be protected in the heart of the city and the heart of the country; the whole social order favourable to their hygienic idleness had to be protected against the shallow enviousness of unhygienic labour. It had to — and Mr. Verloc would have rubbed his hands with satisfaction had he not been constitutionally averse from every superfluous exertion. His idleness was not hygienic, but it suited him very well. He was in a manner devoted to it with a sort of inert fanaticism, or perhaps rather with a fanatical inertness. Born of industrious parents for a life of toil, he had embraced indolence from an impulse as profound, as inexplicable, and as imperious as the impulse which directs a man's preference for one particular woman in a given thousand. He was too lazy even for a mere demagogue, for a workman orator, for a leader of labour. It was too much trouble. He required a more perfect form of ease; or it might have been that he was the victim of a philosophical unbelief in the effectiveness of every human effort. Such a form of indolence requires, implies, a certain amount of intelligence. Mr. Verloc was not devoid of intelligence — and at the notion of a menaced social order he would perhaps have winked to himself if there had not been an effort to make in that sign of scepticism. His big, prominent eyes were not well adapted to winking. They were rather of the sort that closes solemnly in slumber with majestic effect.

Undemonstrative and burly in a fat-pig style, Mr. Verloc, without either rubbing his hands with satisfaction or winking sceptically at his thoughts, proceeded on his way. He trod the pavement heavily with his shiny boots, and his general get-up was that of a well-to-do mechanic in business for himself. He might have been anything from a picture-frame maker to a locksmith; an employer of labour in a small way. But there was also about him an indescribable air which no mechanic could have acquired in the practice of his handicraft however dishonestly exercised: the air common to men who live on the vices, the follies, or the baser fears of mankind; the air of moral nihilism common to keepers of gambling halls and disorderly houses; to private detectives and inquiry agents; to drink sellers and, I should say, to the sellers of invigorating electric belts and to the inventors of patent medicines. But of that last I am not sure, not having carried my investigations so far into the depths. For all I know, the expression of these last may be perfectly diabolic. I shouldn't be surprised. What I want to affirm is that Mr. Verloc's expression was by no means diabolic.

* * *

A bright band of light fell through the parlour door into the part of the shop behind the counter. It enabled Mr. Verloc to ascertain at a glance the number of silver coins in the till. These were but few; and for the first time since he opened his shop he took a commercial survey of its value. This survey was unfavourable. He had gone into trade for no commercial reasons. He had been guided in the selection of this peculiar line of business by an instinctive leaning towards shady transactions, where money is picked up easily. Moreover, it did not take him out of his own sphere — the sphere which is watched by the police. On the contrary, it gave him a publicly confessed standing in that sphere, and as Mr. Verloc had unconfessed relations which made him familiar with yet careless of the police, there was a distinct advantage in such a situation. But as a means of livelihood it was by itself insufficient.

He took the cash-box out of the drawer, and turning to leave the shop, became aware that Stevie was still downstairs.

What on earth is he doing there? Mr. Verloc asked himself. What's the meaning of these antics? He looked dubiously at his brother-in-law, but he did not ask him for information. Mr. Verloc's intercourse with Stevie was limited to the casual mutter of a morning, after breakfast, "My boots," and even that was more a communication at large of a need than a direct order or request. Mr. Verloc perceived with some surprise that he did not know really what to say to Stevie. He stood still in the middle of the parlour, and looked into the kitchen in silence. Nor yet did he know what would happen if he did say anything. And this appeared very queer to Mr. Verloc in view of the fact, borne upon him suddenly, that he had to provide for this fellow, too. He had never given a moment's thought till then to that aspect of Stevie's existence.

Positively he did not know how to speak to the lad. He watched him gesticulating and murmuring in the kitchen. Stevie prowled round the table like an excited animal in a cage. A tentative "Hadn't you better go to bed now?" produced no effect whatever; and Mr. Verloc, abandoning the stony contemplation of his brother-in-law's behaviour, crossed the parlour wearily, cash-box in hand. The cause of the general lassitude he felt while climbing the stairs being purely mental, he became alarmed by its inexplicable character. He hoped he was not sickening for anything. He stopped on the dark landing to examine his sensations. But a slight and continuous sound of snoring pervading the obscurity interfered with their clearness. The sound came from his mother-in-law's room. Another one to provide for, he thought — and on this thought walked into the bedroom.

Mrs. Verloc had fallen asleep with the lamp (no gas was laid upstairs) turned up full on the table by the side of the bed. The light thrown down by the shade fell dazzlingly on the white pillow sunk by the weight of her head reposing with closed eyes and dark hair done up in several plaits for the night. She woke up with the sound of her name in her ears, and saw her husband standing over her.

"Winnie! Winnie!"

At first, she did not stir, lying very quiet and looking at the cash-box in Mr. Verloc's hand. But when she understood that her brother was "capering all over the place downstairs" she swung out in one sudden movement on to the edge of the bed. Her bare feet, as if poked through the bottom of an un-adorned, sleeved calico sack buttoned tightly at neck and wrists, felt over the rug for the slippers while she looked upward into her husband's face.

"I don't know how to manage him," Mr. Verloc explained, peevishly. "Won't do to leave him downstairs alone with the lights."

She said nothing, glided across the room swiftly, and the door closed upon her white form.

Mr. Verloc deposited the cash-box on the night table, and began the operation of undressing by flinging his overcoat on to a distant chair. His coat and waistcoat followed. He walked about the room in his stockinged feet, and his burly figure, with the hands worrying nervously at his throat, passed and repassed across the long strip of looking-glass in the door of his wife's wardrobe. Then after slipping his braces off his shoulders he pulled up violently the venetian blind, and leaned his forehead against the cold window-pane — a fragile film of glass stretched between him and the enormity of cold, black, wet, muddy, inhospitable accumulation of bricks, slates, and stones, things in themselves unlovely and unfriendly to man.

Mr. Verloc felt the latent unfriendliness of all out of doors with a force approaching to positive bodily anguish. There is no occupation that fails a man more completely than that of a secret agent of police. It's like your horse suddenly falling dead under you in the midst of an uninhabited and thirsty plain. The comparison occurred to Mr. Verloc because he had sat astride various army horses in his time, and had now the sensation of an incipient fall. The prospect was as black as the window-pane against which he was leaning his forehead. And suddenly the face of Mr. Vladimir, clean-shaved and witty, appeared enhaloed in the glow of its rosy complexion like a sort of pink seal impressed on the fatal darkness.

This luminous and mutilated vision was so ghastly physically that Mr. Verloc started away from the window, letting down the venetian blind with a great rattle. Discomposed and speechless with the apprehension of more such visions, he beheld his wife re-enter the room and get into bed in a calm, businesslike manner which made him feel hopelessly lonely in the world. Mrs. Verloc expressed her surprise at seeing him up yet.

"I don't feel very well," he muttered, passing his hands over his moist brow.

"Giddiness?"

"Yes. Not at all well."

Mrs. Verloc, with all the placidity of an experienced wife, expressed a confident opinion as to the cause, and suggested the usual remedies; but her husband, rooted in the middle of the room, shook his lowered head sadly.

"You'll catch cold standing there," she observed.

Mr. Verloc made an effort, finished undressing, and got into bed. Down below in the quiet, narrow street measured footsteps approached the house, then died away, unhurried and firm, as if the passer-by had started to pace out all eternity, from gas-lamp to gas-lamp in a night without end; and the drowsy ticking of the old clock on the landing became distinctly audible in the bedroom.

Mrs. Verloc, on her back, and staring at the ceiling, made a remark.

"Takings very small to-day."

Mr. Verloc, in the same position, cleared his throat as if for an important statement, but merely inquired:

"Did you turn off the gas downstairs?"

"Yes; I did," answered Mrs. Verloc, conscientiously. "That poor boy is in a very excited state to-night," she murmured, after a pause which lasted for three ticks of the clock.

Mr. Verloc cared nothing for Stevie's excitement, but he felt horribly wakeful, and dreaded facing the darkness and silence that would follow the extinguishing of the lamp. This dread lead him to make the remark that Stevie had disregarded his suggestion to go to bed. Mrs. Verloc, falling into the trap, started to demonstrate at length to her husband that this was not "impudence" of any sort, but simply "excitement." There was no young man of his age in London more willing and docile than Stephen, she affirmed; none more affectionate and ready to please, and even useful, as long as people did not upset his poor head. Mrs. Verloc, turning towards her recumbent husband, raised herself on her elbow, and hung over him in her anxiety that he should believe Stevie to be a useful member of the family. That ardour of protecting compassion exalted morbidly in her childhood by the misery of another child tinged her sallow cheeks with a faint dusky blush, made her big eyes gleam under the dark lids. Mrs. Verloc then looked younger; she looked as young as Winnie used to look, and much more animated than the Winnie of the Belgravian mansion days had ever allowed herself to appear to gentlemen lodgers. Mr. Verloc's anxieties had prevented him attaching any sense to what his wife was saying. It was as if her voice was talking on the other side of a very thick wall. It was her aspect that recalled him to himself.

He appreciated this woman, and the sentiment of this appreciation, stirred by a display of something resembling emotion, only added another pang to his mental anguish. When her voice ceased he moved uneasily, and said:

"I haven't been feeling well for the last few days."

He might have meant this as an opening to a complete confidence; but Mrs. Verloc laid her head on the pillow again, and staring upward, went on:

"That boy hears too much of what is talked about here. If I had known they were coming to-night I would have seen to it that he went to bed at the same time I did. He was out of his mind with something he overheard about eating people's flesh and drinking blood. What's the good of talking like that?"

There was a note of indignant scorn in her voice. Mr. Verloc was fully responsive now.

"Ask Karl Yundt," he growled, savagely.

Mrs. Verloc, with great decision, pronounced Karl Yundt "a disgusting old man." She declared openly her affection for Michaelis. Of the robust Ossipon, in whose presence she always felt uneasy behind an attitude of stony reserve, she said nothing whatever. And continuing to talk of that brother, who had been for so many years an object of care and fears:

"He isn't fit to hear what's said here. He believes it's all true. He knows no better. He gets into his passions over it."

Mr. Verloc made no comment.

"He glared at me, as if he didn't know who I was, when I went downstairs. His heart was going like a hammer. He can't help being excitable. I woke mother up, and asked her to sit with him till he went to sleep. It isn't his fault. He's no trouble when he's left alone."

Mr. Verloc made no comment.

"I wish he had never been to school," Mrs. Verloc began again, brusquely. "He's always taking away those newspapers from the window to read. He gets a red face poring over them. We don't get rid of a dozen numbers in a month. They only take up room in the front window. And Mr. Ossipon brings every week a pile of these F. P. tracts to sell at a halfpenny each. I wouldn't give a halfpenny for the whole lot. It's silly reading — that's what it is. There's no sale for it. The other day Stevie got hold of one, and there was a story in it of a German soldier officer tearing half-off the ear of a recruit, and nothing was done to him for it. The brute! I couldn't do anything with Stevie that afternoon. The story was enough, too, to make one's blood boil. But what's the use of printing things like that? We aren't German slaves here, thank God. It's not our business — is it?"

Mr. Verloc made no reply.

"I had to take the carving knife from the boy," Mrs. Verloc continued, a little sleepily now. "He was shouting and stamping

161

and sobbing. He can't stand the notion of any cruelty. He would have struck that officer like a pig if he had seen him then. It's true, too! Some people don't deserve much mercy." Mrs. Verloc's voice ceased, and the expression of her motionless eyes became more and more contemplative and veiled during the long pause. "Comfortable, dear?" she asked in a faint, far-away voice. "Shall I put out the light now?"

The dreary conviction that there was no sleep for him held Mr. Verloc mute and hopelessly inert in his fear of darkness. He made a great effort.

"Yes. Put it out," he said at last in a hollow tone.

[Both Winnie and her mother have been working on ways to get Mr. Verloc to be more of a father to Stevie. Winnie's mother has decided that if she were no longer in the house, Stevie would in fact be the Verloc child. She, in secret, seeks and gains admission to an almshouse as a widow.]

Having infused by persistent importunities some sort of heat into the chilly interest of several licenced victuallers (the acquaintances once upon a time of her late unlucky husband), Mrs. Verloc's mother had at last secured her admission to certain almshouses founded by a wealthy innkeeper for the destitute widows of the trade.

This end, conceived in the astuteness of her uneasy heart, the old woman had pursued with secrecy and determination. That was the time when her daughter Winnie could not help passing a remark to Mr. Verloc that "mother has been spending half-crowns and five shillings almost every day this last week in cab fares." But the remark was not made grudgingly. Winnie respected her mother's infirmities. She was only a little surprised at this sudden mania for locomotion. Mr. Verloc, who was sufficiently magnificent in his way, had grunted the remark impatiently aside as interfering with his meditations. These were frequent, deep, and prolonged; they bore upon a matter more important than five shillings. Distinctly more important, and beyond all comparison more difficult to consider in all its aspects with philosophical serenity.

Her object attained in astute secrecy, the heroic old woman had made a clean breast of it to Mrs. Verloc. Her soul was triumphant and her heart tremulous. Inwardly she quaked, because she dreaded and admired the calm, self-contained character of her daughter Winnie, whose displeasure was made redoubtable by a diversity of dreadful silences. But she did not allow her inward apprehensions to rob her of the advantage of venerable placidity conferred upon her outward person by her triple chin, the floating ampleness of her ancient form, and the impotent condition of her legs.

The shock of the information was so unexpected that Mrs. Verloc, against her usual practice when addressed, interrupted the domestic occupation she was engaged upon. It was the dusting of the furniture in the parlour behind the shop. She turned her head towards her mother.

"Whatever did you want to do that for?" she exclaimed, in scandalized astonishment.

The shock must have been severe to make her depart from that distant and uninquiring acceptance of facts which was her force and her safeguard in life.

"Weren't you made comfortable enough here?"

She had lapsed into these inquiries, but next moment she saved the consistency of her conduct by resuming her dusting, while the old woman sat scared and dumb under her dingy white cap and lustreless dark wig.

Winnie finished the chair, and ran the duster along the mahogany at the back of the horsehair sofa on which Mr. Verloc loved to take his ease in hat and overcoat. She was intent on her work, but presently she permitted herself another question.

"How in the world did you manage it, mother?"

As not affecting the inwardness of things, which it was Mrs. Verloc's principle to ignore, this curiosity was excusable. It bore merely on the methods. The old woman welcomed it eagerly as bringing forward something that could be talked about with much sincerity.

She favoured her daughter by an exhaustive answer full of names and enriched by side comments upon the ravages of time as observed in the alteration of human countenances. The names were principally the names of licenced victuallers — "poor daddy's friends, my dear." She enlarged with special appreciation on the kindness and condescension of a large brewer, a Baronet and an M.P., the Chairman of the Governors of the Charity. She expressed herself thus warmly because she had been allowed to interview by appointment his Private Secretary — "a very polite gentleman, all in black, with a gentle, sad voice, but so very, very thin and quiet. He was like a shadow, my dear."

Winnie, prolonging her dusting operations till the tale was told to the end, walked out of the parlour into the kitchen (down two steps) in her usual manner, without the slightest comment.

Shedding a few tears in sign of rejoicing at her daughter's mansuetude in this terrible affair, Mrs. Verloc's mother gave play to her astuteness in the direction of her furniture, because it was her own; and sometimes she wished it hadn't been. Heroism is all very well, but there are circumstances when the disposal of a few tables and chairs, brass bedsteads, and so on, may be big with remote and disastrous consequences. She required a few pieces herself, the Foundation which, after many importunities, had gathered her to its charitable breast, giving nothing but bare planks and cheaply papered bricks to the objects of its solicitude. The delicacy guiding her choice to the least valuable and most dilapidated articles passed unacknowledged, because Winnie's philosophy consisted in not taking notice of the inside facts; she assumed that mother took what suited her best. As to Mr. Verloc, his intense meditation, like a sort of Chinese wall, isolated him completely from the phenomena of this world of vain effort and illusory appearances.

Her selection made, the disposal of the rest became a perplexing question in a particular way. She was leaving it in Brett Street, of course. But she had two children. Winnie was provided for by her sensible union with that excellent husband, Mr. Verloc. Stevie was destitute — and a little peculiar. His position had to be considered before the claims of legal justice and even the promptings of partiality. The possession of the furniture would not be in any sense a provision. He ought to have it — the poor boy. But to give it to him would be like tampering with his position of complete dependence. It was a sort of claim which she feared to weaken. Moreover, the susceptibilities of Mr. Verloc would perhaps not brook being beholden to his brother-in-law for the chairs he sat on. In a long experience of gentlemen lodgers, Mrs. Verloc's mother had acquired a dismal but resigned notion of the fantastic side of human nature. What if Mr. Verloc suddenly took it into his head to tell Stevie to take his blessed sticks somewhere out of that? A division, on the other hand, however carefully made, might give some cause of offence to Winnie. No. Stevie must remain destitute and dependent. And at the moment of leaving Brett Street she had said to her daughter: "No use waiting till I am dead, is there? Everything I leave here is altogether your own now, my dear."

Winnie, with her hat on, silent behind her mother's back, went on arranging the collar of the old woman's cloak. She got her handbag, an umbrella, with an impassive face. The time had come for the expenditure of the sum of three-and-sixpence on what might well be supposed the last cab drive of Mrs. Verloc's mother's life. They went out at the shop door.

The conveyance awaiting them would have illustrated the proverb that "truth can be more cruel than caricature," if such a proverb existed. Crawling behind an infirm horse, a metropolitan hackney carriage drew up on wobbly wheels and with a maimed driver on the box. This last peculiarity caused some embarrassment. Catching sight of a hooked iron contrivance protruding from the left sleeve of the man's coat, Mrs. Verloc's mother lost suddenly the heroic courage of these days. She really couldn't trust herself. "What do you think, Winnie?" She hung back. The passionate expostulations of the big-faced cabman seemed to be squeezed out of a blocked throat. Leaning over from his box, he whispered with mysterious indignation. What was the matter now? Was it possible to treat a man so? His enormous and unwashed countenance flamed red in the muddy stretch of the street. Was it likely they would have given him a licence, he inquired desperately, if —

The police constable of the locality quieted him by a friendly glance; then addressing himself to the two women without marked consideration, said:

"He's been driving a cab for twenty years. I never knew him to have an accident."

"Accident!" shouted the driver in a scornful whisper.

The policeman's testimony settled it. The modest assemblage of seven people, mostly under age, dispersed. Winnie followed her mother into the cab. Stevie climbed on the box. His vacant mouth and distressed eyes depicted the state of his mind in regard to the transactions which were taking place. In the narrow streets the progress of the journey was made sensible to those within by the near fronts of the houses gliding past slowly and shakily, with a great rattle and jingling of glass, as if about to collapse behind the cab; and the infirm horse, with the harness hung over his sharp backbone flapping very loose about his thighs, appeared to be dancing mincingly on his toes with infinite patience. Later on, in the wider space of Whitehall, all visual evidences of motion became imperceptible. The rattle and jingle of glass went on indefinitely in front of the long Treasury building — and time itself seemed to stand still.

At last Winnie observed: "This isn't a very good horse."

Her eyes gleamed in the shadow of the cab straight ahead, immovable. On the box, Stevie shut his vacant mouth first, in order to ejaculate earnestly: "Don't."

The driver, holding high the reins twisted around the hook, took no notice. Perhaps he had not heard. Stevie's breast heaved.

"Don't whip."

The man turned slowly his bloated and sodden face of many colours bristling with white hairs. His little red eyes glistened with moisture. His big lips had a violet tint. They remained closed. With the dirty back of his whip-hand he rubbed the stubble sprouting on his enormous chin.

"You mustn't," stammered out Stevie, violently, "it hurts."

"Mustn't whip?" queried the other in a thoughtful whisper, and immediately whipped. He did this, not because his soul was cruel and his heart evil, but because he had to earn his fare. And for a time the walls of St. Stephen's, with its towers and pinnacles, contemplated in immobility and silence a cab that jingled. It rolled, too, however. But on the bridge there was a commotion. Stevie suddenly proceeded to get down from the box. There were shouts on the pavement, people ran forward, the driver pulled up, whispering curses of indignation and astonishment. Winnie lowered the window, and put her head out, white as a ghost. In the depths of the cab, her mother was exclaiming, in tones of anguish: "Is that boy hurt? Is that boy hurt?"

Stevie was not hurt, he had not even fallen, but excitement as usual had robbed him of the power of connected speech. He could do no more than stammer at the window: "Too heavy. Too heavy." Winnie put out her hand on to his shoulder.

"Stevie! Get up on the box directly, and don't try to get down again."

"No. No. Walk. Must walk."

In trying to state the nature of that necessity he stammered himself into utter incoherence. No physical impossibility stood in the way of his whim. Stevie could have managed easily to keep pace with the infirm, dancing horse without getting out of breath. But his sister withheld her consent decisively. "The idea! Who ever heard of such a thing! Run after a cab!" Her mother, frightened and helpless in the depths of the conveyance, entreated:

"Oh, don't let him, Winnie. He'll get lost. Don't let him."

"Certainly not. What next! Mr. Verloc will be sorry to hear of this nonsense, Stevie — I can tell you. He won't be happy at all."

The idea of Mr. Verloc's grief and unhappiness acting as usual powerfully upon Stevie's fundamentally docile disposition, he abandoned all resistance, and climbed up again on the box, with a face of despair.

The cabby turned at him his enormous and inflamed countenance truculently. "Don't you go for trying this silly game again, young fellow."

After delivering himself thus in a stern whisper, strained almost to extinction, he drove on, ruminating solemnly. To his mind the incident remained somewhat obscure. But his intellect, though it had lost its pristine vivacity in the benumbing years of sedentary exposure to the weather, lacked not independence or sanity. Gravely he dismissed the hypothesis of Stevie being a drunken young nipper.

Inside the cab the spell of silence, in which the two women had endured shoulder to shoulder the jolting, rattling, and jingling of the journey, had been broken by Stevie's outbreak. Winnie raised her voice.

"You've done what you wanted, mother. You'll have only yourself to thank for it if you aren't happy afterwards. And I don't think you'll be. That I don't. Weren't you comfortable enough in the house? Whatever people'll think of us — you throwing yourself like this on a Charity?"

"My dear," screamed the old woman earnestly above the noise, "you've been the best of daughters to me. As to Mr. Verloc — there —"

Words failing her on the subject of Mr. Verloc's excellence, she turned her old tearful eyes to the roof of the cab. Then she averted her head on the pretence of looking out of the window, as if to judge of their progress. It was insignificant, and went on close to the curbstone. Night, the early dirty night, the sinister, noisy, hopeless, and rowdy night of South London, had overtaken her on her last cab drive. In the gaslight of the low-fronted shops her big cheeks glowed with an orange hue under a black and mauve bonnet.

Mrs. Verloc's mother's complexion had become yellow by the effect of age and from a natural predisposition to biliousness, favoured by the trials of a difficult and worried existence, first as wife, then as widow. It was a complexion that under the influence of a blush would take on an orange tint. And this woman, modest indeed but hardened in the fires of adversity, of an age, moreover, when blushes are not expected, had positively blushed before her daughter. In the privacy of a four-wheeler, on her way to a charity cottage (one of a row) which by the exiguity of its dimensions and the simplicity of its accommodation, might well have been devised in kindness as a place of training for the still more straitened circumstances of the grave, she was forced to hide from her own child a blush of remorse and shame.

Whatever will people think? She knew very well what they did think, the people Winnie had in her mind — the old friends of her husband, and others too, whose interest she had solicited with such flattering success. She had not known before what a good beggar she could be. But she guessed very well what inference was drawn from her application. On account of that shrinking delicacy, which exists side by side with aggressive brutality in masculine nature, the inquiries into her circumstances had not been pushed very far. She had checked them by a visible compression of the lips and some display of an emotion determined to be eloquently silent. And the men would become suddenly incurious, after the manner of their kind. She congratulated herself more than once on having nothing to do with women, who being naturally more callous and avid of details, would have been anxious to be exactly informed by what sort of unkind conduct her daughter and son-in-law had driven her to that sad extremity. It was only before the Secretary of the great brewer M. P. and Chairman of the Charity, who, acting for his principal, felt bound to be conscientiously inquisitive as to the real circumstances of the applicant, that she had burst into tears outright and aloud, as a cornered woman will weep. The thin and polite gentleman, after contemplating her with an air of being "struck all of a heap," abandoned his position under the cover of soothing remarks. She must not distress herself. The deed of the Charity did not absolutely specify "childless widows." In fact, it did not by any means disqualify her. But the discretion of the Committee must be an informed discretion. One could understand very well her unwillingness to be a burden, etc., etc. Thereupon, to his profound disappointment, Mrs. Verloc's mother wept some more with an augmented vehemence.

The tears of that large female in a dark, dusty wig, and ancient silk dress festooned with dingy white cotton lace, were the tears of genuine distress. She had wept because she was heroic and unscrupulous and full of love for both her children. Girls frequently get sacrificed to the welfare of the boys. In this case she was sacrificing Winnie. By the suppression of truth she was slandering her. Of course, Winnie was independent, and need not care for the opinion of people that she would never see and who would never see her; whereas poor Stevie had nothing in the world he could call his own except his mother's heroism and unscrupulousness.

The first sense of security following on Winnie's marriage wore off in time (for nothing lasts), and Mrs. Verloc's mother, in the seclusion of the back bedroom, had recalled the teaching of that experience which the world impresses upon a widowed woman. But she had recalled it without vain bitterness; her store of resignation amounted almost to dignity. She reflected stoically that everything decays, wears out, in this world; that the way of kindness should be made easy to the well disposed; that her daughter Winnie was a most devoted sister, and a very self-confident wife indeed. As regards Winnie's sisterly devotion, her stoicism flinched. She excepted that sentiment from the rule of decay affecting all things human and some things divine. She could not help it; not to do so would have frightened her too much. But in considering the conditions of her daughter's married state, she rejected firmly all flattering illusions. She took the cold and reasonable view that the less strain put on Mr. Verloc's kindness the longer its effects were likely to last. That excellent man loved his wife, of course, but he would, no doubt, prefer to keep as few of her relations as was consistent with the proper display of that sentiment. It would be better if its whole effect were concentrated on poor Stevie. And the heroic old woman resolved on going away from her children as an act of devotion and as a move of deep policy.

The "virtue" of this policy consisted in this (Mrs. Verloc's mother was subtle in her way), that Stevie's moral claim would be strengthened. The poor boy — a good, useful boy, if a little peculiar — had not a sufficient standing. He had been taken over with his mother, somewhat in the same way as the furniture of the Belgravian mansion had been taken over, as if on the ground of belonging to her exclusively. What will happen, she asked herself (for Mrs. Verloc's mother was in a measure imaginative), when I die? And when she asked herself that question it was with dread. It was also terrible to think that she would not then have the means of knowing what happened to the poor boy. But by making him over to his sister, by going thus away, she gave him the advantage of a directly dependent position. This was the more subtle sanction of Mrs. Verloc's mother's heroism and unscrupulousness. Her act of abandonment was really an arrangement for settling her son permanently in life. Other people made material sacrifices for such an object, she in that way. It was the only way. Moreover, she would be able to see how it worked. Ill or well she would avoid the horrible incertitude on her death-bed. But it was hard, hard, cruelly hard.

The cab rattled, jingled, jolted; in fact, the last was quite extraordinary. By its disproportionate violence and magnitude it obliterated every sensation of onward movement; and the effect was of being shaken in a stationary apparatus like a mediaeval device for the punishment of crime, or some very new-fangled invention for the cure of a sluggish liver. It was extremely distressing; and the raising of Mrs. Verloc's mother's voice sounded like a wail of pain.

"I know, my dear, you'll come to see me as often as you can spare the time. Won't you?"

"Of course," answered Winnie, shortly, staring straight before her.

And the cab jolted in front of a steamy, greasy shop in a blaze of gas and in the smell of fried fish.

The old woman raised a wail again.

"And, my dear, I must see that poor boy every Sunday. He won't mind spending the day with his old mother —"

Winnie screamed out stolidly:

"Mind! I should think not. That poor boy will miss you something cruel. I wish you had thought a little of that, mother."

Not think of it! The heroic woman swallowed a playful and inconvenient object like a billiard ball, which had tried to jump out of her throat. Winnie sat mute for a while, pouting at the front of the cab, then snapped out, which was an unusual tone with her.

"I expect I'll have a job with him at first, he'll be that restless —"

"Whatever you do, don't let him worry your husband, my dear."

Thus they discussed on familiar lines the bearings of a new situation. And the cab jolted. Mrs. Verloc's mother expressed some misgivings. Could Stevie be trusted to come all that way alone? Winnie maintained that he was much less "absent-minded" now. They agreed as to that. It could not be denied. Much less — hardly at all. They shouted at each other in the jingle with comparative cheerfulness. But suddenly the maternal anxiety broke out afresh. There were two omnibuses to take, and a short walk between. It was too difficult! The old woman gave way to grief and consternation.

Winnie stared forward.

"Don't you upset yourself like this, mother. You must see him, of course."

"No, my dear. I'll try not to."

She mopped her streaming eyes.

"But you can't spare the time to come with him, and if he should forget himself and lose his way and somebody spoke to him sharply, his name and address may slip his memory, and he'll remain lost for days and days —"

The vision of a workhouse infirmary for poor Stevie — if only during inquires — wrung her heart. For she was a proud woman. Winnie's stare had grown hard, intent, inventive.

"I can't bring him to you myself every week," she cried. "But don't you worry, mother. I'll see to it that he don't get lost for long."

They felt a peculiar bump; a vision of brick pillars lingered before the rattling windows of the cab; a sudden cessation of atrocious jolting and uproarious jingling dazed the two women. What had happened? They sat motionless and scared in the profound stillness, till the door came open, and a rough, strained whispering was heard:

" 'Ere you are!"

A range of gabled little houses, each with one dim yellow window, on the ground floor, surrounded the dark open space of a grass plot planted with shrubs and railed off from the patchwork of lights and shadows in the wide road, resounding with the dull rumble of traffic. Before the door of one of these tiny houses — one without a light in the little downstairs window — the cab had come to a standstill. Mrs. Verloc's mother got out first, backwards, with a key in her hand. Winnie lingered on the flagstone path to pay the cabman. Stevie, after helping to carry inside a lot of small parcels, came out and stood under the light of a gas-lamp belonging to the Charity. The cabman looked at the pieces of silver, which, appearing very minute in his big, grimy palm, symbolized the insignificant results which reward the ambitious courage and toil of a mankind whose day is short on this earth of evil.

He had been paid decently — four one-shilling pieces — and he contemplated them in perfect stillness, as if they had been the surprising terms of a melancholy problem. The slow transfer of that treasure to an inner pocket demanded much laborious groping in the depths of decayed clothing. His form was squat and without flexibility. Stevie, slender, his shoulders a little up, and his hands thrust deep in the side pockets of his warm over-coat, stood at the edge of the path, pouting.

The cabman, pausing in his deliberate movements, seemed struck by some misty recollection.

"Oh! 'Ere you are, young fellow," he whispered. "You'll know him again — won't you?"

Stevie was staring at the horse, whose hind quarters appeared unduly elevated by the effect of emaciation. The little stiff tail seemed to have been fitted in for a heartless joke; and at the other end the thin, flat neck, like a plank covered with old horse-hide, drooped to the ground under the weight of an enormous bony head. The ears hung at different angles, negligently; and the macabre figure of that mute dweller on the earth steamed straight up from ribs and backbone in the muggy stillness of the air.

The cabman struck lightly Stevie's breast with the iron hook protruding from a ragged, greasy sleeve.

"Look 'ere, young feller. 'Ow'd *you* like to sit behind this 'oss up to two o'clock in the morning p'raps?"

Stevie looked vacantly into the fierce little eyes with red-edged lids.

"He ain't lame," pursued the other, whispering with energy. "He ain't got no sore places on 'im. 'Ere he is. 'Ow would *you* like —"

His strained, extinct voice invested his utterance with a character of vehement secrecy. Stevie's vacant gaze was changing slowly into dread.

"You may well look! Till three and four o'clock in the morning. Cold and 'ungry. Looking for fares. Drunks."

His jovial purple cheeks bristled with white hairs; and like Virgil's Silenus, who, his face smeared with the juice of berries, discoursed of Olympian Gods to the innocent shepherds of Sicily, he talked to Stevie of domestic matters and the affairs of men whose sufferings are great and immortality by no means assured.

"I am a night cabby, I am," he whispered, with a sort of boastful exasperation. "I've got to take out what they will blooming well give me at the yard. I've got my missus and four kids at 'ome."

The monstrous nature of that declaration of paternity seemed to strike the world dumb. A silence reigned, during which the flanks of the old horse, the steed of apocalyptic misery, smoked upwards in the light of the charitable gas-lamp.

The cabman grunted, then added in his mysterious whisper:

"This ain't an easy world."

Stevie's face had been twitching for some time and at last his feelings burst out in their usual concise form.

"Bad! Bad!"

His gaze remained fixed on the ribs of the horse, self-conscious and sombre, as though he were afraid to look about him at the badness of the world. And his slenderness, his rosy lips and pale, clear complexion, gave him the aspect of a delicate boy, notwithstanding the fluffy growth of golden hair on his cheeks. He pouted in a scared way like a child. The cabman, short and broad, eyed him with his fierce little eyes that seemed to smart in a clear and corroding liquid.

"'Ard on 'osses, but dam' sight 'arder on poor chaps like me," he wheezed just audibly.

"Poor! Poor!" stammered out Stevie, pushing his hands deeper into his pockets with convulsive sympathy. He could say nothing; for the tenderness to all pain and all misery, the desire to make the horse happy and the cabman happy, had reached the point of a bizarre longing to take them to bed with him. And that, he knew, was impossible. For Stevie was not mad. It was, as it were, a symbolic longing; and at the same time it was very distinct, because springing from experience, the mother of wisdom. Thus when as a child he cowered in a dark corner scared, wretched, sore, and miserable with the black, black misery of the soul, his sister Winnie used to come along, and carry him off to bed with her, as into a heaven of consoling peace. Stevie, though apt to forget mere facts, such as his name and address for instance, had a faithful memory of sensations. To be taken into a bed of compassion was the supreme remedy, with the only one disadvantage of being difficult of application on a large scale. And looking at the cabman, Stevie perceived this clearly, because he was reasonable.

The cabman went on with his leisurely preparations as if Stevie had not existed. He made as if to hoist himself on the box, but at the last moment, from some obscure motive, perhaps merely from disgust with carriage exercise, desisted. He approached instead the motionless partner of his labours, and stooping to seize the bridle, lifted up the big, weary head to the height of his shoulder with one effort of his right arm, like a feat of strength.

"Come on," he whispered, secretly.

Limping, he led the cab away. There was an air of austerity in this departure, the scrunched gravel of the drive crying out under the slowly turning wheels, the horse's lean thighs moving with ascetic deliberation away from the light into the obscurity of the open space bordered dimly by the pointed roofs and the feebly shining windows of the little almshouses. The plaint of the gravel travelled slowly all round the drive. Between the lamps of the charitable gateway the slow cortège reappeared, lighted up for a moment, the short, thick man limping busily, with the horse's head held aloft in his fist, the lank animal walking in stiff and forlorn dignity, the dark, low box on wheels rolling behind comically with an air of waddling. They turned to the left. There was a pub down the street, within fifty yards of the gate.

Stevie left alone beside the private lamp-post of the Charity, his hands thrust deep into his pockets, glared with vacant sulkiness. At the bottom of his pockets his incapable, weak hands were clinched hard into a pair of angry fists. In the face of anything which affected directly or indirectly his morbid dread of pain, Stevie ended by turning vicious. A magnanimous indignation swelled his frail chest to bursting, and caused his candid eyes to squint. Supremely wise in knowing his own powerlessness, Stevie was not wise enough to restrain his passions. The tenderness of his universal charity had two phases as indissolubly joined and connected as the reverse and obverse sides of a medal. The anguish of immoderate compassion was succeeded by the pain of an innocent but pitiless rage. Those two states expressing themselves outwardly by the same signs of futile bodily agitation, his sister Winnie soothed his excitement without ever fathoming its two-fold character. Mrs. Verloc wasted no portion of this transient life in seeking for fundamental information. This is a sort of economy having all the appearances and some of the advantages of prudence. Obviously it may be good for one not to know too much. And such a view accords very well with constitutional indolence.

On that evening on which it may be said that Mrs. Verloc's mother having parted for good from her children had also departed this life, Winnie Verloc did not investigate her brother's psychology. The poor boy was excited, of course. After once more assuring the old woman on the threshold that she would know how to guard against the risk of Stevie losing himself for very long on his pilgrimages of filial piety, she took her brother's arm to walk away. Stevie did not even mutter to himself, but with the special sense of sisterly devotion developed in her earliest infancy, she felt that the boy was very much excited indeed. Holding tight to his arm, under the appearance of leaning on it, she thought of some words suitable to the occasion.

"Now, Stevie, you must look well after me at the crossings, and get first into the bus, like a good brother."

This appeal to manly protection was received by Stevie with his usual docility. It flattered him. He raised his head and threw out his chest.

"Don't be nervous, Winnie. Mustn't be nervous! 'Bus all right," he answered in a brusque, slurring stammer partaking of the timorousness of a child and the resolution of a man. He advanced fearlessly with the woman on his arm, but his lower lip dropped. Nevertheless, on the pavement of the squalid and wide thoroughfare, whose poverty in all the amenities of life stood foolishly exposed by a mad profusion of gas-lights, their resemblance to each other was so pronounced as to strike the casual passers-by.

Before the doors of the public-house at the corner, where the profusion of gas-light reached the height of positive wickedness, a four-wheeled cab standing by the curbstone, with no one on the box, seemed cast out into the gutter on account of irremediable decay. Mrs. Verloc recognized the conveyance. Its aspect was so profoundly lamentable, with such a perfection of grotesque misery and weirdness of macabre detail, as if it were the Cab of Death itself, that Mrs. Verloc, with that ready compassion of a woman for a horse (when she is not sitting behind him), exclaimed vaguely:

"Poor brute!"

Hanging back suddenly, Stevie inflicted an arresting jerk upon his sister.

"Poor! Poor!" he ejaculated, appreciatively. "Cabman poor, too. He told me himself."

The contemplation of the infirm and lonely steed overcame him. Jostled, but obstinate, he would remain there, trying to express the view newly opened to his sympathies of the human and equine misery in close association. But it was very difficult. "Poor brute, poor people!" was all he could repeat. It did not seem forcible enough, and he came to a stop with an angry splutter: "Shame!" Stevie was no master of phrases, and perhaps for that very reason his thoughts lacked clearness and precision. But he felt with greater completeness and some profundity. That

176

little word contained all his sense of indignation and horror at one sort of wretchedness having to feed upon the anguish of the other — at the poor cabman beating the poor horse in the name, as it were, of his poor kids at home. And Stevie knew what it was to be beaten. He knew it from experience. It was a bad world. Bad! Bad!

Mrs. Verloc, his only sister, guardian, and protector, could not pretend to such depths of insight. Moreover, she had not experienced the magic of the cabman's eloquence. She was in the dark as to the inwardness of the word "Shame." And she said placidly:

"Come along, Stevie. You can't help that."

The docile Stevie went along; but now he went along without pride, shamblingly, and muttering half words, and even words that would have been whole if they had not been made up of halves that did not belong to each other. It was as though he had been trying to fit all the words he could remember to his sentiments in order to get some sort of corresponding idea. And, as a matter of fact, he got it at last. He hung back to utter it at once.

"Bad world for poor people."

Directly he had expressed that thought he became aware that it was familiar to him already in all its consequences. This circumstance strengthened his conviction immensely, but also augmented his indignation. Somebody, he felt, ought to be punished for it — punished with great severity. Being no sceptic, but a moral creature, he was in a manner at the mercy of his righteous passions.

"Beastly!" he added, concisely.

It was clear to Mrs. Verloc that he was greatly excited.

"Nobody can help that," she said. "Do come along. Is that the way you're taking care of me?"

Stevie mended his pace obediently. He prided himself on being a good brother. His morality, which was very complete, demanded that from him. Yet he was pained at the information imparted by his sister Winnie — who was good. Nobody could help that! He came along gloomily, but presently he brightened up. Like the rest of mankind, perplexed by the mystery of the universe, he had his moments of consoling trust in the organized powers of the earth.

"Police," he suggested, confidently.

"The police aren't for that," observed Mrs. Verloc, cursorily, hurrying on her way.

Stevie's face lengthened considerably. He was thinking. The more intense his thinking, the slacker was the droop of his lower jaw. And it was with an aspect of hopeless vacancy that he gave up his intellectual enterprise.

"Not for that?" he mumbled, resigned but surprised. "Not for that?" He had formed for himself an ideal conception of the metropolitan police as a sort of benevolent institution for the suppression of evil. The notion of benevolence especially was very closely associated with his sense of the power of the men in blue. He had liked all police constables tenderly, with a guileless trustfulness. And he was pained. He was irritated, too, by a suspicion of duplicity in the members of the force. For Stevie was frank and as open as the day himself. What did they mean by pretending then? Unlike his sister, who put her trust in face values, he wished to go to the bottom of the matter. He carried on his inquiry by means of an angry challenge.

"What are they for then, Winn? What are they for? Tell me."

Winnie disliked controversy. But fearing most a fit of black depression consequent on Stevie missing his mother very much at first, she did not altogether decline the discussion. Guiltless of all irony, she answered yet in a form which was not perhaps unnatural in the wife of Mr. Verloc, Delegate of the Central Red Committee, personal friend of certain anarchists, and a votary of social revolution.

"Don't you know what the police are for, Stevie? They are there so that them as have nothing shouldn't take anything away from them who have."

She avoided using the verb "to steal," because it always made her brother uncomfortable. For Stevie was delicately honest. Certain simple principles had been instilled into him so anxiously (on account of his "queerness") that the mere names of certain transgressions filled him with horror. He had been always easily impressed by speeches. He was impressed and startled now, and his intelligence was very alert.

"What?" he asked at once, anxiously. "Not even if they were hungry? Mustn't they?"

The two had paused in their walk.

"Not if they were ever so," said Mrs. Verloc, with the equanimity of a person untroubled by the problem of the distribution of wealth, and exploring the perspective of the roadway for an omnibus of the right colour. "Certainly not. But what's the use of talking about all that? You aren't ever hungry."

She cast a swift glance at the boy, like a young man, by her side. She saw him amiable, attractive, affectionate, and only a little, a very little peculiar. And she could not see him otherwise, for he was connected with what there was of the salt of passion in her tasteless life — the passion of indignation, of courage, of pity, and even of self-sacrifice. She did not add: "And you aren't likely ever to be as long as I live." But she might very well have done so, since she had taken effectual steps to that end. Mr. Verloc was a very good husband. It was her honest impression that nobody could help liking the boy. She cried out suddenly:

"Quick, Stevie. Stop that green 'bus."

And Stevie, tremulous and important with his sister Winnie on his arm, flung up the other high above his head at the approaching 'bus, with complete success.

An hour afterwards Mr. Verloc raised his eyes from a newspaper he was reading, or at any rate looking at, behind the counter, and in the expiring clatter of the door-bell beheld Winnie, his wife, enter and cross the shop on her way upstairs, followed by Stevie, his brother-in-law. The sight of his wife was agreeable to Mr. Verloc. It was his idiosyncrasy. The figure of his brother-in-law remained imperceptible to him because of the morose thoughtfulness that lately had fallen like a veil between Mr. Verloc and the appearances of the world of senses. He looked after his wife fixedly, without a word, as though she had been a phantom. His voice for home use was husky and placid, but now it was heard not at all. It was not heard at supper, to which he was called by his wife in the usual brief manner: "Adolf." He sat down to consume it without conviction, wearing his hat pushed far back on his head. It was not devotion to an outdoor life, but the frequentation of foreign cafes which was responsible for that habit, investing with a character of unceremonious impermanency Mr. Verloc's steady fidelity to his own fireside. Twice at the clatter of the cracked bell he arose without a word, disappeared into the shop, and came back silently. During these absences Mrs. Verloc, becoming acutely aware of the vacant place at her right hand, missed her mother very much, and stared stonily; while Stevie, from the same reason, kept on shuffling his feet, as though the floor under the table were uncomfortably hot. When Mr. Verloc returned to sit in his place, like the very embodiment of silence, the character of Mrs. Verloc's stare underwent a subtle change, and Stevie ceased to fidget with his feet, because of his great and awed regard for his sister's husband. He directed at him glances of respectful compassion. Mr. Verloc was sorry. His sister Winnie had impressed upon him (in the omnibus) that Mr. Verloc would be found at home in a state of sorrow, and must not be worried. His father's anger, the irritability of gentlemen lodgers, and Mr. Verloc's predisposition to immoderate grief, had been the main sanctions of Stevie's self-restraint. Of these sentiments, all easily provoked, but not always easy to understand, the last had the greatest moral efficiency — because Mr. Verloc was *good*. His mother and his sister had established that ethical fact on an unshakable foundation. They had established, erected, consecrated it behind Mr. Verloc's back, for reasons that had nothing to do with abstract morality. And Mr. Verloc was not aware of it. It is but bare justice to him to say that he had no notion of appearing good to Stevie. Yet so it was. He was even the only man so qualified in Stevie's knowledge, because the gentlemen lodgers had been too transient and too remote to have anything very distinct about them but perhaps their boots; and as regards the disciplinary measures of his father, the desolation of his mother and sister shrank from setting up a theory of goodness before the victim. It would have been too cruel. And it was even possible that Stevie would not have believed them. As far as Mr. Verloc was concerned, nothing could stand in the way of Stevie's belief. Mr. Verloc was obviously yet mysteriously *good*. And the grief of a good man is august.

Stevie gave glances of reverential compassion to his brother-in-law. Mr. Verloc was sorry. The brother of Winnie had never before felt himself in such close communion with the mystery of that man's goodness. It was an understandable sorrow. And Stevie himself was sorry. He was very sorry. The same sort of sorrow. And his attention being drawn to this unpleasant state,

Stevie shuffled his feet. His feelings were habitually manifested by the agitation of his limbs.

"Keep your feet quiet, dear," said Mrs. Verloc, with authority and tenderness; then turning towards her husband in an indifferent voice, the masterly achievement of instinctive tact: "Are you going out tonight?" she asked.

The mere suggestion seemed repugnant to Mr. Verloc. He shook his head moodily, and then sat still with downcast eyes, looking at the piece of cheese on his plate for a whole minute. At the end of that time he got up, and went out — went right out in the clatter of shop-door bell. He acted thus inconsistently, not from any desire to make himself unpleasant, but because of an unconquerable restlessness. It was no earthly good going out. He could not find anywhere in London what he wanted. But he went out. He led a cortège of dismal thoughts along dark streets, through lighted streets, in and out of two flash bars, as if in a half-hearted attempt to make a night of it, and finally back again to his menaced home, where he sat down fatigued behind the counter, and they crowded urgently round him, like a pack of hungry black hounds. After locking up the house and putting out the gas he took them upstairs with him — a dreadful escort for a man going to bed. His wife had preceded him some time before, and with her ample form defined vaguely under the counterpane, her head on the pillow, and a hand under the cheek, offered to his distraction the view of early drowsiness arguing the possession of an equable soul. Her big eyes stared wide open, inert and dark against the snowy whiteness of the linen. She did not move.

She had an equable soul. She felt profoundly that things do not stand much looking into. She made her force and her wisdom of that instinct. But the taciturnity of Mr. Verloc had been lying heavily upon her for a good many days. It was, as a matter of fact, affecting her nerves. Recumbent and motionless, she said placidly:

"You'll catch cold walking about in your socks like this."

This speech, becoming the solicitude of the wife and the prudence of the woman, took Mr. Verloc unawares. He had left his boots downstairs, but he had forgotten to put on his slippers, and he had been turning about the bedroom on noiseless pads like a bear in a cage. At the sound of his wife's voice he stopped and stared at her with a somnambulistic, expressionless gaze so long that Mrs. Verloc moved her limbs slightly under the bed-clothes. But she did not move her black head sunk in the white pillow, one hand under her cheek and the big, dark, unwinking eyes.

Under her husband's expressionless stare, and remembering her mother's empty room across the landing, she felt an acute pang of loneliness. She had never been parted from her mother before. They had stood by each other. She felt that they had, and she said to herself that now mother was gone — gone for good. Mrs. Verloc had no illusions. Stevie remained, however. And she said:

"Mother's done what she wanted to do. There's no sense in it that I can see. I'm sure she couldn't have thought you had enough of her. It's perfectly wicked, leaving us like that."

Mr. Verloc was not a well-read person; his range of allusive phrases was limited, but there was a peculiar aptness in circumstances which made him think of rats leaving a doomed ship. He very nearly said so. He had grown suspicious and embittered. Could it be that the old woman had such an excellent nose? But the unreasonableness of such suspicion was patent, and Mr. Verloc held his tongue. Not altogether, however. He muttered, heavily:

"Perhaps it's just as well."

He began to undress. Mrs. Verloc kept very still, perfectly still, with her eyes fixed in a dreamy, quiet stare. And her heart for the fraction of a second seemed to stand still, too. That night she was "not quite herself," as the saying is, and it was borne upon her with some force that a simple sentence may hold several diverse meanings — mostly disagreeable. *How* was it just as well? And why? But she did not allow herself to fall into the idleness of barren speculation. She was rather confirmed in her belief that things did not stand being looked into. Practical and subtle in her way, she brought Stevie to the front without loss of time, because in her the singleness of purpose had the unerring nature and the force of an instinct.

"What I am going to do to cheer up that boy for the first few days I'm sure I don't know. He'll be worrying himself from morning till night before he gets used to mother being away. And he's such a good boy. I couldn't do without him."

Mr. Verloc went on divesting himself of his clothing with the unnoticing inward concentration of a man undressing in the solitude of a vast and hopeless desert. For thus inhospitably did this fair earth, our common inheritance, present itself to the mental vision of Mr. Verloc. All was so still without and within that the lonely ticking of the clock on the landing stole into the room as if for the sake of company.

Mr. Verloc, getting into bed on his own side, remained prone and mute behind Mrs. Verloc's back. His thick arms rested abandoned on the outside of the counterpane like dropped weapons, like discarded tools. At that moment he was within a hair's breadth of making a clean breast of it all to his wife. The moment seemed propitious. Looking out of the corners of his eyes, he saw her ample shoulders draped in white, the back of her head, with the hair done for the night in three plaits tied up with black tapes at the ends. And he forbore. Mr. Verloc loved his wife as a wife should be loved — that is, maritally, with the regard one has for one's chief possession. This head arranged for the night, those ample shoulders, had an aspect of familiar sacredness — the sacredness of domestic peace. She moved not, massive and shapeless like a recumbent statue in the rough; he remembered her wide-open eyes looking into the empty room. She was mysterious, with the mysteriousness of living beings. The far-famed secret agent $\triangle$ of the late Baron Stott-Wartenheim's alarmist despatches was not the man to break into such mysteries. He was easily intimidated. And he was also indolent, with the indolence which is so often the secret of good nature. He forbore touching that mystery out of love, timidity, and indolence. There would be always time enough. For several minutes he bore his sufferings silently in the drowsy silence of the room. And then he disturbed it by a resolute declaration.

"I am going on the Continent to-morrow."

His wife might have fallen asleep already. He could not tell. As a matter of fact, Mrs. Verloc had heard him. Her eyes remained very wide open, and she lay very still, confirmed in her instinctive conviction that things don't bear looking into very much. And yet it was nothing very unusual for Mr. Verloc to take such a trip. He renewed his stock from Paris and Brussels. Often he went over to make his purchases personally. A little select connection of amateurs was forming around the shop in

Brett Street, a secret connection eminently proper for any business undertaken by Mr. Verloc, who, by a mystic accord of temperament and necessity, had been set apart to be a secret agent all his life.

He waited for a while, then added: "I'll be away a week or perhaps a fortnight. Get Mrs. Neale to come for the day."

Mrs. Neale was the charwoman of Brett Street. Victim of her marriage with a debauched joiner, she was oppressed by the needs of many infant children. Red-armed, and aproned in coarse sacking up to the arm-pits, she exhaled the anguish of the poor in a breath of soap-suds and rum, in the uproar of scrubbing, in the clatter of tin pails.

Mrs. Verloc, full of deep purpose, spoke in the tone of the shallowest indifference.

"There is no need to have the woman here all day. I shall do very well with Stevie."

She let the lonely clock on the landing count off fifteen ticks into the abyss of eternity, and asked:

"Shall I put the light out?"

Mr. Verloc snapped at his wife huskily.

"Put it out."

* * *

Mr. Verloc, returning from the Continent at the end of ten days, brought back a mind evidently unrefreshed by the wonders of foreign travel and a countenance unlighted by the joys of home-coming. He entered in the clatter of the shop-bell with an air of sombre and vexed exhaustion. His bag in hand, his head lowered, he strode straight behind the counter, and let himself fall into the chair, as though he had tramped all the way from Dover. It was early morning. Stevie, dusting various objects displayed in the front windows, turned to gape at him with reverence and awe.

"Here!" said Mr. Verloc, giving a slight kick to the gladstone bag on the floor; and Stevie flung himself upon it, seized it, bore it off with triumphant devotion. He was so prompt that Mr. Verloc was distinctly surprised.

Already at the clatter of the shop-bell Mrs. Neale, blackleading the parlour grate, had looked through the door, and rising from her knees had gone, aproned, and grimy with everlasting

184

toil, to tell Mrs. Verloc in the kitchen that "there was the master come back."

Winnie came no farther than the inner shop door.

"You'll want some breakfast," she said from a distance.

Mr. Verloc moved his hands slightly, as if overcome by an impossible suggestion. But once enticed into the parlour he did not reject the food set before him. He ate as if in a public place, his hat pushed off his forehead, the skirts of his heavy overcoat hanging in a triangle on each side of the chair. And across the length of the table covered with brown oilcloth Winnie, his wife, talked evenly at him the wifely talk, as artfully adapted, no doubt, to the circumstances of this return as the talk of Penelope to the return of the wandering Odysseus. Mrs. Verloc, however, had done no weaving during her husband's absence. But she had had all the upstairs rooms cleaned thoroughly, had sold some wares, had seen Mr. Michaelis several times. He had told her the last time that he was going away to live in a cottage in the country, somewhere on the London, Chatham, and Dover line. Karl Yundt had come, too, once, led under the arm by that "wicked old housekeeper of his." He was "a disgusting old man." Of Comrade Ossipon, whom she had received curtly, entrenched behind the counter with a stony face and a faraway gaze, she said nothing, her mental reference to the robust anarchist being marked by a short pause, with the faintest possible blush. And bringing in her brother Stevie as soon as she could into the current of domestic events, she mentioned that the boy had moped a good deal.

"It's all along of mother leaving us like this."

Mr. Verloc neither said "Damn!" nor yet "Stevie be hanged!" And Mrs. Verloc, not let into the secret of his thoughts, failed to appreciate the generosity of this restraint.

"It isn't that he doesn't work as well as ever," she continued. "He's been making himself very useful. You'd think he couldn't do enough for us."

Mr. Verloc directed a casual and somnolent glance at Stevie, who sat on his right, delicate, pale-faced, his rosy mouth open vacantly. It was not a critical glance. It had no intention. And if Mr. Verloc thought for a moment that his wife's brother looked uncommonly useless, it was only a dull and fleeting thought, devoid of that force and durability which enables sometimes a thought to move the world. Leaning back, Mr. Verloc uncovered his head. Before his extended arm could put down the hat Stevie pounced upon it, and bore it off reverently into the kitchen. And again Mr. Verloc was surprised.

"You could do anything with that boy, Adolf," Mrs. Verloc said, with her best air of inflexible calmness. "He would go through fire for you. He —"

She paused attentive, her ear turned towards the door of the kitchen.

There Mrs. Neale was scrubbing the floor. At Stevie's appearance she groaned lamentably, having observed that he could be induced easily to bestow for the benefit of her infant children the shilling his sister Winnie presented him with from time to time. On all fours amongst the puddles, wet and begrimed, like a sort of amphibious and domestic animal living in ashbins and dirty water, she uttered the usual exordium: "It's all very well for you, kept doing nothing like a gentleman." And she followed it with the everlasting plaint of the poor, pathetically mendacious, miserably authenticated by the horrible breath of cheap rum and soapsuds. She scrubbed hard, snuffling all the time, and talking volubly. And she was sincere. And on each side of her thin red nose her bleared, misty eyes swam in tears, because she felt really the want of some sort of stimulant in the morning.

In the parlour Mrs. Verloc observed, with knowledge:

"There's Mrs. Neale at it again with her harrowing tales about her little children. They can't be all so little as she makes them out. Some of them must be big enough by now to try to do something for themselves. It only makes Stevie angry."

These words were confirmed by a thud as of a fist striking the kitchen table. In the normal evolution of his sympathy Stevie had become angry on discovering that he had no shilling in his pocket. In his inability to relieve at once Mrs. Neale's "little 'uns'" privations, he felt that somebody should be made to suffer for it. Mrs. Verloc rose, and went into the kitchen to "stop that nonsense." And she did it firmly but gently. She was well aware that directly Mrs. Neale received her money she went round the corner to drink ardent spirits in a mean and musty public-house — the unavoidable station on the *via dolorosa* of her life. Mrs. Verloc's comment upon this practice had an unexpected profundity, as coming from a person disinclined to look under the surface of things. "Of course, what is she to do to keep up? If I were like Mrs. Neale I expect I wouldn't act any different."

In the afternoon of the same day, as Mr. Verloc, coming with a start out of the last of a long series of dozes before the parlour fire, declared his intention of going out for a walk, Winnie said from the shop:

"I wish you would take that boy out with you, Adolf."

For the third time that day Mr. Verloc was surprised. He stared stupidly at his wife. She continued in her steady manner. The boy, whenever he was not doing anything, moped in the house. It made her uneasy; it made her nervous, she confessed. And that from the calm Winnie sounded like exaggeration. But, in truth, Stevie moped in the striking fashion of an unhappy domestic animal. He would go up on the dark landing, to sit on the floor at the foot of the tall clock, with his knees drawn up and his head in his hands. To come upon his pallid face, with its big eyes gleaming in the dusk, was discomposing; to think of him up there was uncomfortable.

Mr. Verloc got used to the startling novelty of the idea. He was fond of his wife as a man should be — that is, generously. But a weighty objection presented itself to his mind, and he formulated it.

"He'll lose sight of me perhaps, and get lost in the street," he said.

Mrs. Verloc shook her head competently.

"He won't. You don't know him. That boy just worships you. But if you should miss him —"

Mrs. Verloc paused for a moment, but only for a moment.

"You just go on, and have your walk out. Don't worry. He'll be all right. He's sure to turn up safe here before very long."

This optimism procured for Mr. Verloc his fourth surprise of the day.

"Is he?" he grunted, doubtfully. But perhaps his brother-in-law was not such an idiot as he looked. His wife would know best. He turned away his heavy eyes, saying huskily: "Well, let him come along, then," and relapsed into the clutches of black care, that perhaps prefers to sit behind a horseman, but knows also how to tread close on the heels of people not sufficiently well off to keep horses — like Mr. Verloc, for instance.

Winnie, at the shop door, did not see this fatal attendant upon Mr. Verloc's walks. She watched the two figures down the squalid street, one tall and burly, the other slight and short, with a thin neck, and the peaked shoulders raised slightly under the large semi-transparent ears. The material of their overcoats was the same, their hats were black and round in shape. Inspired by the similarity of wearing apparel, Mrs. Verloc gave rein to her fancy.

"Might be father and son," she said to herself. She thought also that Mr. Verloc was as much of a father as poor Stevie ever had in his life. She was aware also that it was her work. And with peaceful pride she congratulated herself on a certain resolution she had taken a few years before. It had cost her some effort, and even a few tears.

She congratulated herself still more on observing in the course of days that Mr. Verloc seemed to be taking kindly to Stevie's companionship. Now, when ready to go out for his walk, Mr. Verloc called aloud to the boy, in the spirit, no doubt, in which a man invites the attendance of the household dog, though, of course, in a different manner. In the house Mr. Verloc could be detected staring curiously at Stevie a good deal. His own demeanour had changed. Taciturn still, he was not so listless. Mrs. Verloc thought that he was rather jumpy at times. It might have been regarded as an improvement. As to Stevie, he moped no longer at the foot of the clock, but muttered to himself in corners instead in a threatening tone. When asked "What is it you're saying, Stevie?" he merely opened his mouth, and squinted at his sister. At odd times he clenched his fists without apparent cause, and when discovered in solitude would be scowling at the wall, with the sheet of paper and the pencil given him for drawing circles lying blank and idle on the kitchen table. This was a change, but it was no improvement. Mrs. Verloc, including all these vagaries under the general definition of excitement, began to fear that Stevie was hearing more than was good for him of her husband's conversations with his friends. During his "walks" Mr. Verloc, of course, met and conversed with various persons. It could hardly be otherwise. His walks were an integral part of his outdoor activities, which his wife had never looked deeply into. Mrs. Verloc felt that the position was delicate, but she faced it with the same impenetrable calmness which impressed and even astonished the customers of the shop and made the other visitors keep their distance a little wonderingly. No! She feared that there were things not good for Stevie to hear of, she told her husband. It only excited the poor boy, because he could not help them being so. Nobody could.

It was in the shop. Mr. Verloc made no comment. He made no retort, and yet the retort was obvious. But he refrained from pointing out to his wife that the idea of making Stevie the companion of his walks was her own, and nobody else's. At that moment, to an impartial observer, Mr. Verloc would have appeared more than human in his magnanimity. He took down a small cardboard box from a shelf, peeped in to see that the contents were all right, and put it down gently on the counter. Not till that was done did he break the silence, to the effect that most likely Stevie would profit greatly by being sent out of town for a while; only he supposed his wife could not get on without him.

"Could not get on without him!" repeated Mrs. Verloc, slowly. "I couldn't get on without him if it were for his good! The idea! Of course, I can get on without him. But there's nowhere for him to go."

Mr. Verloc got out some brown paper and a ball of string; and meanwhile he muttered that Michaelis was living in a little cottage in the country. Michaelis wouldn't mind giving Stevie a room to sleep in. There were no visitors and no talk there. Michaelis was writing a book.

Mrs. Verloc declared her affection for Michaelis: mentioned her abhorrence of Karl Yundt, "nasty old man"; and of Ossipon she said nothing. As to Stevie, he could be no other than very pleased. Mr. Michaelis was always so nice and kind to him. He seemed to like the boy. Well, the boy was a good boy.

"You, too, seem to have grown quite fond of him of late," she added, after a pause, with her inflexible assurance.

Mr. Verloc, tying up the cardboard box into a parcel for the post, broke the string by an injudicious jerk, and muttered several swear words confidentially to himself. Then raising his tone to the usual husky mutter, he announced his willingness to take Stevie into the country himself, and leave him all safe with Michaelis.

He carried out this scheme on the very next day. Stevie offered no objection. He seemed rather eager, in a bewildered sort of way. He turned his candid gaze inquisitively to Mr. Verloc's heavy countenance at frequent intervals, especially when his sister was not looking at him. His expression was proud, apprehensive, and concentrated, like that of a small child entrusted for the first time with a box of matches and the permission to strike a light. But Mrs. Verloc, gratified by her brother's docility, recommended him not to dirty his clothes unduly in the country. At this Stevie gave his sister, guardian, and protector a look, which for the first time in his life seemed to lack the quality of perfect childlike trustfulness. It was haughtily gloomy. Mrs. Verloc smiled.

"Goodness me! You needn't be offended. You know you do get yourself very untidy when you get a chance, Stevie."

Mr. Verloc was already gone some way down the street.

Thus in consequence of her mother's heroic proceedings, and of her brother's absence on this villeggiatura, Mrs. Verloc found herself oftener than usual all alone not only in the shop, but in the house. For Mr. Verloc had to take his walks. She was alone longer than usual on the day of the attempted bomb outrage in Greenwich Park, because Mr. Verloc went out very early that morning and did not come back till nearly dusk. She did not mind being alone. She had no desire to go out. The weather was too bad, and the shop was cosier than the streets. Sitting behind the counter with some sewing, she did not raise her eyes from her work when Mr. Verloc entered in the aggressive clatter of the bell. She had recognized his step on the pavement outside.

She did not raise her eyes, but as Mr. Verloc, silent, and with his hat rammed down upon his forehead, made straight for the parlour door, she said, serenely:

"What a wretched day. You've been perhaps to see Stevie?"

"No! I haven't," said Mr. Verloc, softly, and slammed the glazed parlour door behind him with unexpected energy.

For some time Mrs. Verloc remained quiescent, with her work dropped in her lap, before she put it away under the counter and got up to light the gas. This done, she went into the parlour on her way to the kitchen. Mr. Verloc would want his tea presently. Confident of the power of her charms, Winnie did not expect from her husband in the daily intercourse of their married life a ceremonious amenity of address and courtliness of manner;

vain and antiquated forms at best, probably never very exactly observed, discarded nowadays even in the highest spheres, and always foreign to the standards of her class. She did not look for courtesies from him. But he was a good husband, and she had a loyal respect for his rights.

Mrs. Verloc would have gone through the parlour and on to her domestic duties in the kitchen with the perfect serenity of a woman sure of the power of her charms. But a slight, very slight, and rapid rattling sound grew upon her hearing. Bizarre and incomprehensible, it arrested Mrs. Verloc's attention. Then as its character became plain to the ear she stopped short, amazed and concerned. Striking a match on the box she held in her hand, she turned on and lighted, above the parlour table, one of the two gas-burners, which, being defective, first whistled as if astonished, and then went on purring comfortably like a cat.

Mr. Verloc, against his usual practice, had thrown off his overcoat. It was lying on the sofa. His hat, which he must also have thrown off, rested overturned under the edge of the sofa. He had dragged a chair in front of the fireplace, and his feet planted inside the fender, his head held between his hands, he was hanging low over the glowing grate. His teeth rattled with an ungovernable violence, causing his whole enormous back to tremble at the same rate. Mrs. Verloc was startled.

* * *

"You here!" muttered Mr. Verloc, heavily. "Who are you after?"

"No one," said Chief Inspector Heat in a low tone. "Look here, I would like a word or two with you."

Mr. Verloc, still pale, had brought an air of resolution with him. Still he didn't look at his wife. He said:

"Come in here, then." And he led the way into the parlour.

The door was hardly shut when Mrs. Verloc, jumping up from the chair, ran to it as if to fling it open, but instead of doing so fell on her knees, with her ear to the keyhole. The two men must have stopped directly they were through, because she heard plainly the Chief Inspector's voice, though she could not see his finger pressed against her husband's breast emphatically.

"You are the other man, Verloc. Two men were seen entering the park."

And the voice of Mr. Verloc said:

"Well, take me now. What's to prevent you? You have the right."

"Oh, no! I know too well whom you have been giving yourself away to. He'll have to manage this little affair all by himself. But don't you make a mistake, it's I who found you out."

Then she heard only muttering. Inspector Heat must have been showing to Mr. Verloc the piece of Stevie's overcoat, because Stevie's sister, guardian, and protector heard her husband a little louder.

"I never noticed that she had hit upon that dodge."

Again for a time Mrs. Verloc heard nothing but murmurs, whose mysteriousness was less nightmarish to her brain than the horrible suggestions of shaped words. Then Chief Inspector Heat, on the other side of the door, raised his voice:

"You must have been mad."

And Mr. Verloc's voice answered, with a sort of gloomy fury:

"I have been mad for a month or more, but I am not mad now. It's all over. It shall all come out of my head, and hang the consequences."

There was a silence, and then Private Citizen Heat murmured:

"What's coming out?"

"Everything," exclaimed the voice of Mr. Verloc, and then sank very low.

After a while it rose again.

"You have known me for several years now, and you've found me useful, too. You know I was a straight man. Yes, straight."

This appeal to old acquaintance must have been extremely distasteful to the Chief Inspector.

His voice took on a warning note.

"Don't you trust so much to what you have been promised. If I were you I would clear out. I don't think we will run after you."

Mr. Verloc was heard to laugh a little.

"Oh, yes; you hope the others will get rid of me for you — don't you? No, no; you don't shake me off now. I have been a straight man to those people too long, and now everything must come out."

"Let it come out, then," the different voice of Chief Inspector Heat assented. "But tell me now how did you get away?"

"I was making for Chesterfield Walk," Mrs. Verloc heard her husband's voice, "when I heard the bang. I started running then. Fog. I saw no one till I was past the end of George Street. Don't think I met any one till then."

"So easy as that!" marvelled the voice of Chief Inspector Heat. "The bang startled you, eh?"

"Yes; it came too soon," confessed the gloomy, husky voice of Mr. Verloc.

Mrs. Verloc pressed her ear to the keyhole; her lips were blue, her hands cold as ice, and her pale face, in which the two eyes seemed like two black holes, felt to her as if it were enveloped in flames.

On the other side of the door the voices sank very low. She caught words now and then, sometimes in her husband's voice, sometimes in the smooth tones of the Chief Inspector. She heard this last say:

"We believe he stumbled against the root of a tree."

There was a husky, voluble murmur, which lasted for some time, and then the Chief Inspector, as if answering some inquiry, spoke emphatically:

"Of course. Blown to small bits: limbs, gravel, clothing, bones, splinters — all mixed up together. I tell you they had to fetch a shovel to gather him up with."

Mrs. Verloc sprang up suddenly from her crouching position, and stopping her ears, reeled to and fro between the counter and the shelves on the wall towards the chair. Her crazed eyes noted the sporting sheet left by the Chief Inspector, and as she knocked herself against the counter she snatched it up, fell into the chair, tore the optimistic, rosy sheet right across in trying to open it, then flung it on the floor. On the other side of the door, Chief Inspector Heat was saying to Mr. Verloc, the secret agent:

"So your defence will be practically a full confession?"

"It will. I am going to tell the whole story."

"You won't be believed as much as you fancy you will."

And the Chief Inspector remained thoughtful. The turn this affair was taking meant the disclosure of many things — the laying waste of fields of knowledge, which, cultivated by a capable man, had a distinct value for the individual and for the society. It was sorry, sorry meddling. It would leave Michaelis unscathed; it would drag to light the Professor's home industry; disorganize the whole system of supervision; make no end of a row in the papers, which, from that point of view, appeared to him by a sudden illumination as invariably written by fools for the reading of imbeciles. Mentally he agreed with the words Mr. Verloc let fall at last in answer to his last remark.

"Perhaps not. But it will upset many things. I have been a straight man, and I shall keep straight in this —"

"If they let you," said the Chief Inspector, cynically. "You will be preached to, no doubt, before they put you into the dock. And in the end you may yet get let in for a sentence that will surprise you. I wouldn't trust too much the gentleman who's been talking to you."

Mr. Verloc listened, frowning.

"My advice to you is to clear out while you may. I have no instructions. There are some of them," continued Chief Inspector Heat, laying a peculiar stress on the word "them," "who think you are already out of the world."

"Indeed!" Mr. Verloc was moved to say. Though since his return from Greenwich he had spent most of his time sitting in the tap-room of an obscure little public-house, he could hardly have hoped for such favourable news.

"That's the impression about you." The Chief Inspector nodded at him. "Vanish. Clear out."

"Where to?" snarled Mr. Verloc. He raised his head, and gazing at the closed door of the parlour, muttered feelingly: "I only wish you would take me away to-night. I would go quietly."

"I daresay," assented sardonically the Chief Inspector, following the direction of his glance.

The brow of Mr. Verloc broke into slight moisture. He lowered his husky voice confidentially before the unmoved Chief Inspector.

"The lad was half-witted, irresponsible. Any court would have seen that at once. Only fit for the asylum. And that was the worst that would've happened to him if —"

The Chief Inspector, his hand on the door handle, whispered into Mr. Verloc's face:

"He may've been half-witted, but you must have been crazy. What drove you off your head like this?"

Mr. Verloc, thinking of Mr. Vladimir, did not hesitate in the choice of words.

"A Hyperborean swine," he hissed, forcibly. "A what you might call a — a gentleman."

The Chief Inspector, steady-eyed, nodded briefly his comprehension, and opened the door. Mrs. Verloc, behind the counter, might have heard but did not see his departure, pursued by the aggressive clatter of the bell. She sat at her post of duty behind the counter. She sat rigidly erect in the chair with two dirty pink pieces of paper lying spread at her feet. The palms of her hands were pressed convulsively to her face, with the tips of the fingers contracted against the forehead, as though the skin had been a mask which she was ready to tear off violently. The perfect immobility of her pose expressed the agitation of rage and despair, all the potential violence of tragic passions, better than any shallow display of shrieks, with the beating of a distracted head against the walls, could have done. Chief Inspector Heat, crossing the shop at his busy, swinging pace, gave her only a cursory glance. And when the cracked bell ceased to tremble on its curved ribbon of steel nothing stirred near Mrs. Verloc, as if her attitude had the locking power of a spell. Even the butterfly-shaped gas flames posed on the ends of the suspended T-bracket burned without a quiver. In that shop of shady wares fitted with deal shelves painted a dull brown, which seemed to devour the sheen of the light, the gold circlet of the wedding ring on Mrs. Verloc's left hand glittered exceedingly with the untarnished glory of a piece from some splendid treasure of jewels, dropped in a dust-bin.

And so it ends like a Greek tragedy without chorus — all of Winnie's striving for good for Stevie, for acceptance and love, ending in shreds and pieces of an untimely bomb. Prophetically, her earlier statement to Mr. Verloc that "Stevie would go through fire for you" becomes all too true.

As Conrad spins this tale, it becomes clear that Stevie's role as a dependent, protected, trusting, and deeply feeling person is crucial to the interplay of plot and passion. This is not to say that children with retarded intellectual development are always compensated with great emotional sensitivity. Emotional sensitivity and empathy do not follow an IQ score. But many individuals like Stevie who feel alone and confused in a world not of their own making respond appropriately to the emotional retardation of their "normal" peers and adults.

Interestingly, H. G. Wells, who was a supporter and fan of Conrad's, felt that Conrad's works were too highly rated because Conrad perceived and wrote about people emotionally. "That gave him superiorities in many directions," wrote H. G., "but the very coldness and flatness of my perceptions gave me a readier apprehension of relationships, put me ahead of him in mathematics and drawing (which after all is a sort of abstraction of form) and made it easier for me later on to grasp general ideas in biology and physics."[1] Writers like Conrad are hard to educate, Wells goes on to say, because their abundant emotional impressions and expressions cannot be disciplined or subdued.

Consider the consequences if Wells had succeeded in "educating" Conrad. Compare, for example, the characterizations in "Country of the Blind" with Winnie, Stevie, and Adolf Verloc.

---

[1] H. G. Wells, *Experiment in Autobiography* (New York: AMS Press, 1934), p. 528.

QUESTIONS FOR DISCUSSION

1. What would you suggest as a better descriptive term than "mentally retarded" for someone like Stevie?

2. Rewrite a section of the story using the same major characters and the same plot but changing the year to 1980 and the locale to the largest city nearest you.

3. If you were to search the research literature and attempt to come up with a profile of a moderately retarded child like Stevie, what do you think you would find? How close

did Conrad come in 1907 to depicting a real Stevie?

4. Conrad strongly suggests (or does he?) that retarded individuals are more sensitive to the brutalities and injustices of humans to each other and to animals. To what extent is this supported or rejected by evidence?

5. Stevie's unfortunate fate is a byproduct of his handicap, but more a result of Winnie's desire for him to be accepted and loved by his surrogate father. Would the outcome have been different if Stevie had been a normal child? If yes, suggest how the events might have turned out differently if Stevie had not been retarded.

6. What was lacking in Stevie's life that might have reduced Winnie's protective relationship? Would things be different for Winnie and Stevie today? How?

7. Can you think of a plot like that of *The Secret Agent* in which Stevie would be blind instead of retarded? Try orthopedically handicapped, hard of hearing, or emotionally disturbed for Stevie, with Winnie and Mr. Verloc as is. Focus on the bombing incident.

ADDITIONAL READINGS

- Bettelheim, Bruno. *The Empty Fortress: Infantile Autism and the Birth of the Self.* New York: Free Press, 1967.
- Farber, B. *Mental Retardation: Its Social Context and Social Consequences.* Boston: Houghton Mifflin, 1968.
- Faulkner, William. *The Sound and the Fury.* New York: Random House, 1929.
- Haywood, H. D., ed. *Social-Cultural Aspects of Mental Retardation.* New York: Appleton-Century-Crofts, 1970.
- Hunt, Nigel. *The World of Nigel Hunt. The Diary of a Mongoloid.* New York: Garrett, 1967.
- Itard, Jean-Marc. *The Wild Boy of Aveyron.* New York: Appleton-Century-Crofts, 1932.
- Keyes, Daniel. *Flowers for Algernon.* New York: Harcourt, Brace & World, 1959. (also Bantam)
- Philips, Irving, ed. *Prevention and Treatment of Mental Retardation.* New York: Basic Books, 1966.
- Spencer, Elizabeth. *The Light in the Piazza.* New York: McGraw-Hill, 1960.
- Steinbeck, John. *Of Mice and Men.* New York: Viking Press, 1937.

Imperious voices from inner and outer reality . . .

5

The Secret Life of Algernon Pendleton

Russell H. Greenan

5

Of all the afflictions to which human beings are heir, none is more difficult to understand, conceptualize, or assess than that called "emotional." Emotional handicaps are possible in all persons including those with other sensory, motor, and intellectual handicaps. Also unlike most other human malfunctions, emotional handicaps may come and go. A person may suffer an emotional breakdown, recover, and never experience the disorder again. Further, measures of emotional stability or mental health can hardly be compared in conceptualization and reliability with achievement or aptitude measures. One can more easily conceptualize and identify the negative or handicapping aspects of emotional processes than the positive, enhancing ones.

What is an emotional handicap? First, one should not consider emotion as one does intellect. More intellect or intelligence is better under prevailing societal values than is less intellect. More emotion is not necessarily better than less nor is less better than more. In addition, emotional response has a qualitative nature and various responses may be considered appropriate and positive in one setting and inappropriate and negative in another. Emotion is energizing. It can be converted into aggression and hatred toward others, or aggression and hatred can be directed toward self. The same basic emotion can direct the behavior of the person who hurts others and the person who enters a psychological cocoon to escape from the hurt of others. Responses to emotional handicaps may lead a person on to personal and professional successes or to misery and failure. In the story by E. J. Kahn, Jr., "The Philologist," Dale Maple is highly successful as a student apparently because he finds little else in life emotionally rewarding. In other circumstances, emotional handicaps would most likely affect learning and behavior in more predictable ways.

It is normal to respond to the usual slings and arrows of life emotionally. We are happy with good fortune. We grieve when a loved one dies. We love, hate, become lonely, aggressive, and confused as befits the occasion. Emotions, however, become handicapping when responses are outside the range of normal appropriateness, intensity, and duration. When emotions act to prolong or freeze behavior beyond normal limits, the individual's behavior becomes restrictive and ritualistic and, in most cases, maladaptive. In one sense, the behavior of these individuals is frozen because in that state they lack freedom or some degree of freedom to respond to change.

One way to better understand such restriction of freedom is to understand the differences between emotional thinking and cognitive thinking. Consider that the human animal is a symbol user and processor par excellence. Humans are uniquely structured as biological organisms to create images, use a cognitive-affective system of communication called language, create and use a pure cognitive system of communication called mathematics, create and respond to a system of sounds called music, and with all of these, create creators and cosmologies. In both cognitive and emotional ways we "play" with these images, words, mathematical constructs, and tones. When our emotional ways of playing are shut down or cut off from our cognitive ways of thinking, though, our behavior becomes less flexible and adaptive. An effective cognitive and emotional relationship within a person enhances integrative and creative capacities; an ineffective relationship produces emotional handicap (i.e., reduction in behavioral flexibility).

The term *primary process* has been and is used to denote emotional/dream thinking. Such thinking is the more primitive, more powerful, more pervasive mode of symbolizing experiences. Most of life is enjoyed and suffered in this modality of thought. It gives rise to laughter, tears, anger, loneliness, life, and hope. Rational or secondary process thinking seems to be a late bloomer in the human evolutionary experience; indeed, some may argue that there is little evidence that such processes have yet bloomed. Secondary processes are geared to the physical world — the world of our five senses. Through language and mathematics, secondary processes help establish a rational, rule abiding way of life, including sciences, technologies, philosophies, and health.

Primary and secondary processes operate on different assumptions. The primary process can "talk" the secondary process into being logical for illogical reasons. Note, as you read the conversations between Eulalia and Algernon, how Eulalia, particularly, maneuvers the secondary process thinking of Algernon into specious, illogical behaviors. Primary process has greater executive impact on ego and greater influence on behavior, especially when it is poorly connected or cut off from secondary process. Whereas secondary process thinking is directed toward maintaining the organism in close and accurate touch with outer reality, primary process seems to focus on the principle of "I want what I want when I want it." Such thinking can move the human organism toward physical aggression, childish tantrums, seclusiveness, revenge, or apathy. In any event, when primary processes operate inadequately in conjunction with secondary processes, we speak of personality disorders, primary behavior disorders, or neuroses. When primary processes and secondary processes become disjointed or completely separated in their waking state functioning, we speak of borderline schizophrenia or psychosis.

Rarely are emotional handicaps considered to be unalterable or beyond help. Indeed, despite the difficulties in understanding and modifying its negative consequences, emotional difficulty is seen as something one can do something about. Nevertheless, its manifestations in children, especially school children, produce (1) an inability to learn despite normal intellectual, sensory, and health conditions; (2) an inability to develop and maintain satisfactory relationships with adults and peers; (3) inappropriate behavior or feelings; (4) a general mood of agitation, depression, or apathy; (5) a tendency toward illnesses, pains, and fears associated with stressful situations.[1] These factors may occur singly or in combinations, and they may vary in their intensity or extent from time to time. When they occur repeatedly over time and seemingly cannot be managed or reduced, children exhibiting those characteristics are emotionally handicapped to some degree.

Greenan, through Algernon Pendleton, is illustrating a serious emotional handicap (or is he?) in a way that makes some readers laugh and some angry. I have no idea how one would classify or diagnose Algernon. What's secret about Algernon's life is a vase named Eulalia with whom (which?) Algernon converses on highly significant matters.

Because the excerpts selected for reading omit some of the background material, a brief summary of the plot is:

Algernon, a 51-year-old bachelor, lives in an old, old family house in Brookline, Massachusetts. Algernon's great grandfather,

---

[1] These are discussed in greater detail in Eli M. Bower, *Early Identification of Emotionally Handicapped in School*, 2nd ed. (Springfield, IL: Charles C Thomas, 1969).

an eminent Egyptologist, had built the house and stocked it with a host of archeological ushabti and valuable artifacts. To keep himself and Eulalia from receivership, Algernon sells an occasional artifact to a Turkish art dealer, Mahir Suleyman. Algernon is visited by an old wartime buddy, Norbie Hess, who it turns out is attempting suicide by massive ingestions of food. The day before Norbie arrives, however, Algernon had destroyed a playful puppy that someone had left in his driveway because Eulalia — situated as she was on a rickety, occasional table — had feared for her porcelain life should the playful pup upset her. Convinced by Eulalia that killing the puppy was a rational, sane, and merciful thing to do, Algernon decided to do it, via a .45 automatic. His secondary process is helped by Eulalia to reason that: If I turn the pup loose, a car would certainly get it. if given to the S.P.C.A., it would be gassed. This way is swifter and surer.

Norbie is depressed and suicidal. It appears to Algernon that he can help his friend achieve his goal in a decisive, helpful manner. Eulalia convinces Algernon that he ought to be as much help to Norbie as he was to the puppy. Algernon does the "best" thing and dispatches Norbie.

Next on the scene is Madge Clerisy, an Associate Professor of Archeology who happens to find one of grandfather's ushabti in the shop of the Turkish merchant (who I might mention in passing has also been dispatched by Algernon). Madge, however, is more than a match for Algernon. She convinces and conjoles Algernon to let her do research on the treasures and mysteries left in the house by grandfather A. Edward Pendleton.

The excerpts included here give (1) an illustration of Algernon's relationship with Eulalia; (2) Madge's discovery of Algernon's relationship with Eulalia; (3) Madge's destruction of Eulalia; (4) Algernon's final dilemma: Which voices are real?

THE SECRET LIFE OF ALGERNON PENDLETON

Russell H. Greenan

CONVERSATION WITH MY FRIEND

Later I returned to the second floor and called on Eulalia in the library. She was standing as she usually did on a doily in the center of the rope-legged occasional table, and appeared to be in a good humor. I related the complete story of my visit to Mahir Suleyman.

"And did he pay as much money as the last time?" she asked.

"Yes, forty dollars," I said. "It's a fair price. He'll make a good profit, I'm sure, though not enough to take him back to his beloved Istanbul, poor chap."

I then told her of my daydream, of being well off again and presenting the Turk with a grand gift of twelve thousand dollars as a kind of gesture. "Think what a magnificent deed it would be! And when it came time for my metempsychosis, I'd be granted a splendid body in the next world. Wouldn't I, Eulalia — for such a fine disinterested action?"

"No doubt, but remember you haven't the money," she replied in her melodious voice. "Why worry about that fellow, anyhow? I'll bet he's rich as blazes, actually. You're the one who's poor, Al. What will you do when you've sold the last of Great-grampy's curios? What will you do then, Al?"

"Oh, my! I don't know. I haven't given it much thought. Start on the furniture, I guess."

Eulalia snickered. "You're impossible. No sense of money at all. One day you'll peddle me to Suleyman."

Excerpts from *The Secret Life of Algernon Pendleton,* by Russell Greenan. Copyright © 1949 by Alfred A. Knopf Inc. and Russell Greenan. Used by permission.

"Sell you? Never! That's an awful remark to make!" I exclaimed, shocked. "How can you suggest it even in fun? Why, I'd sooner sell my soul, Eulalia — really I would."

"Yes, so you say, but I'm not sure I believe you. There are times when I think you don't care for me as much as you pretend to."

"Oh, now!"

"I mean it! Yesterday you hardly spoke to me, Al, and on Monday you left the window open so wide that when it rained I was drenched. Had the wind been any stronger the curtains would have knocked me to the floor."

"I know, I know. I'm awfuly sorry, my dear. I saw it clouding up and I wanted to get back, but the bank was crowded and I had to wait to see Mr. Mayhew."

"If you had gone earlier, instead of fooling with that dog, you'd have had no trouble. Banks are always crowded at lunchtime," she said, while the sun, sifting through the leaves of the oak in the yard, danced upon her glittering fluted body. "Thank goodness you got rid of that mongrel! The way he bounded about, bumping into things."

"How did you know?" I asked.

"Know what?"

"That I got rid of him. I don't recall telling you. It was only last night that I did it, Eulalia."

"Yes, and you came here immediately afterward. Your memory is not what it was, Al," said she, though I needed no reminder of that debilitation. "But what about Mr. Mayhew? Was he friendly? Do you think he'll take the house?"

"Oh, no — I don't believe he'd do that. Not while I'm alive, he wouldn't. He was cordial enough. He simply said that he couldn't lend me any more money. Not a sou."

"And why should he? Why should Mr. Mayhew lend money on a property that for all intents and purposes he already owns? You're such a fool, Al! If you had managed the last mortgage money better, instead of squandering it on that Irish widow you picked up at Hall's Pond, you wouldn't be short now. You wouldn't listen to me, though."

As I did not want to start a spat by again attempting to explain that nothing had ever passed between Mrs. Clancy and myself — which, worse luck, was the absolute truth — I merely countered my friend's argument by itemizing the many debts I'd settled with those funds, and by pointing out that we were virtually free and clear for another six months.

"Perhaps by then," I continued cheerily, "Aunt Beaty down in Ellsworth might pass on, and leave me a few miles of that Maine shoreline she owns. What do you think?"

"I think you're a child," Eulalia said. Then she sighed once and added, "You really ought to go there and throttle her, you know."

"Throttle Aunt Beaty? What a thing to say!"

"Why not? The creature's eighty-nine years old. She'd be much better off. Expected inheritances are all well and good, but they can't compare with hard cash — and hard cash is what you require, Al. Mr. Mayhew, cordial or not, will foreclose if you don't make your payments."

That was a disturbing idea. Both of us fell silent. A fly came in the open window, inspected the room and departed. I must install that screen, I thought.

Meanwhile the sunbeams went on flecking and flashing across Eulalia's delicately curved spout, her graceful strap handle and her dainty bowl. How very lovely she was! Perfectly formed. Not a firing blemish of any sort. Nor was there a chip, a nick nor a single age crack on her pear-shaped body.

My father, who had bought her at Grosser's auction rooms in 1939 and who was a connoisseur of such things, unequivocally proclaimed her "the finest Worcester porcelain pitcher in the whole damn world." She was his favorite piece. Of course, not being attuned, he never heard her speak. Neither did I in those far-off days, for that matter. It was only after the war, by which time Dad had died of stroke, that my ears were finally able to distinguish the soft sound of Eulalia's lyric voice. When it happened I was quite taken aback, I need scarcely mention, but I did have sense enough to accept the phenomenon for what it was, and not pretend it was some baseless fantasy. After all, people of acute awareness are familiar with much stranger things than talking china jugs. The universe teems with marvels.

Even before I heard her, however, Eulalia's beauty attracted me. I could sit for hours gazing at her in deep fascination. Keats' *Ode on a Grecian Urn* expresses clearly the warm, euphoric sensations that filled me during these interludes. On one side of her bowl there is a scene in a cartouche which is an incomparably sweet and beguiling reverie — a kind of innocent dream of the type preadolescent children sometimes have. In a bucolic setting a rose-cheeked milkmaid lounges on a grassy knoll, one white arm supported by an overturned milk pail, while her lustrous blue eyes are raised in manifest adoration to a smiling shepherd boy who looms above her, his right leg crossed in front of his left and his languid weight sustained by a slender, knobby crook. Over their pretty heads a pair of stylized larks in a stylized tree sing them a silent madrigal. The middle-distance contains a few fat cows grazing peacefully in a meadow, and beyond that there is a tiny thatched cottage from whose chimney pearly smoke ascends to the lucid azure sky.

How enchanting it is! One longs to enter it, as Alice entered her looking-glass. The tableau is circled by pinkish-purple scrolls, and the rest of the smoothly glazed surface is abundantly adorned with sprigs of fruits and berries and sprays of leaves and flowers — the whole done in the mellowest greens, oranges, sienna browns, crimsons and buttercup yellows.

"What are you daydreaming about now?" she asked abruptly, dispelling my thoughts.

"Oh, nothing . . . nothing," I answered. "I was dwelling on Aunt Beatrice. You say the old doll is eighty-nine? Do you believe I might live so long, Eulalia?"

"Not without money, Al," she remarked dryly. "Not without money."

MORE THAN WHAT MEETS THE EAR

Though a habitual reader, I cannot lay claim to being a genuinely studious man. My knowledge is considerable, but too diverse to make me an authority in any field. I am not sufficiently disciplined for scholarly labors, and so read only those books that provide me with easy pleasure. For this reason I've never acquired a sound store of scientific erudition, which lack I keenly feel. Nevertheless, I'm sure I can explain satisfactorily to anyone with an open mind how it is that an English porcelain pitcher can speak.

Of the universe in which we live, we know comparatively little. It is an established fact, for instance, that there are colors we cannot see, like infrared and ultraviolet, whose wavelengths are outside the narrow range of radiation visible to our imperfect eye. There are also forms that are too large or too small for man's comprehension, substances too bland for his taste, pressures too light for him to feel, and odors too feeble to stimulate his organs of olfaction. The most famous of all these limitations, however, is that of sound. Who has not heard of (though not heard) those dog whistles whose pitch exceeds the adequacy of the human ear, while remaining fully audible to Fido or Rover? We are deaf to half the tones and tunes that charge the air around us. The wail of the wind, the songs of birds and insects, the crack of thunder and the roaring of the sea are all filtered and muffled before they register on our brains.

These are facts, as I have said, and quite beyond dispute. On the strength of them I submit that all the objects in creation have voices, but that we are unable to hear their speech because our ears were not designed for that sort of reception.

How, then, do I hear Eulalia — and occasionally other "in-animate" entities — if such is the case? I confess I do not know exactly. Once a medium told me that I was "clairaudient" — that the voices were really those of dead people — but I can't believe that; I can't believe it, I mean, in the sense that she intended. The voices belong to the objects as surely as my voice belongs to me. I've always been extraordinarily sensitive and perceptive. In my childhood I often saw and felt things that others missed completely. Then, during the war I suffered a brain concussion which I suspect altered and enlarged the wavelength range of my hearing. These two elements — my innate impressibility and the effects of cerebral shock — are in all likelihood responsible for my possession of this exceptional gift.

Perhaps the above explanation will seem like nonsense to some. I make no apology. The matter of vocal cords and all the other physiological accouterments of speech, the question of "inorganic" articles having brains and senses — these are mysteries I must leave for sages to solve.

Eddington, the illustrious astronomer and physicist, observes somewhere that any true law of nature is liable to seem irrational to rational man. Berkeley, Leibnitz, Descartes, Spinoza and all the other great minds of science unanimously recognized that our powers of observing and of knowing are inhibited by the deficiencies of our bodies. What is science, indeed, if not a determined effort to expand the bounds of human perception? The incomparably brilliant Albert Einstein, with whom I actually had several conversations when I was an undergraduate at Princeton, revealed with his theories of relativity and his wondrous concept of the four-dimensional space-time continuum, that the universe was a place far different from what we had previously imagined. Strange things occur out there.

And so, if one correlates the beliefs of the mathematicians and astrophysicists with those of the parapsychologists and metaphysical philosophers, it becomes impossible to deny the immortality of the soul and the ubiquity of life.

That I hear what I hear is beyond question. The voice of Eulalia is a reality. Why, then, should I pretend to myself that it doesn't exist, merely because those around me are unable to detect its mellifluous sound?

Yes, she speaks to me all right — and a very good thing, too! Before she did so, my life was a bit desolate, what with one problem and another. If it hadn't been for Eulalia I might well have slipped off the rails, somewhere along the way.

* * *

AT DINNER

Off we went to the Café Gubbio in the North End. A swart waiter with a cast in his eye ushered us to a trellised booth that was adorned with leafy vines, strings of garlic, bunches of grapes, clusters of variegated peppers, and garlands of flowers — all made of plastic. Reading from the Italian side of the menu and mutilating every word, Norbert Hess ordered for both of us.

The meal was colossal. It included a lavish fruit cup, an antipasto, a vellutina, ravioli, fish cooked in butter, and a grand casserole of capon, potatoes, onions and carrots. Halfway through my serving of chicken, I was forced to capitulate. I couldn't swallow another morsel. Across from me, however, my dinner partner continued to eat with undiminished enthusiasm. Mounds of gravy-soaked potatoes vanished into his busy mouth and speedily plunged down his throat; collops of capon quivered momentarily on his thin lips and then traveled the same road; rolls and butter, olives, stalks of celery, roasted green peppers and forkfuls of escarole joined in this relentless katabasis, aided in their passage by frequent glasses of a white wine called Lacrima d'Arno.

I was mesmerized by this awesome performance. He was like one of his own powerful pieces of construction machinery — something designed to scoop up debris or to fill excavations. Though around us people were laughing and talking, though Neapolitan ballads sung to the mellifluous strains of an accordion were drifting into our bower, Norbie was patently unaware of all but the food before him. Huge as the casserole was, it disappeared. Just in time, the strabismic waiter arrived bearing a platter of cold lamb and mint sauce.

"Another basket of garlic bread, signor!" my friend commanded, not skipping a beat in his gulping. "And don't forget that tufoli, will you? Bring a fresh jug of vino, too, and save yourself a trip."

Down went the lamb and in came the tufoli — an oversized macaroni like lengths of white garden hose, each tube crammed with meat. Norbie smothered it in Romano cheese and disposed of it with a flurry of elbow and jaw movements. Really, it was frightening. I remembered the man as a hearty eater, but what I was now witnessing seemed pathological. He ate in a frenzy like a long-starved timber wolf, barely pausing to sink his teeth in the food before swallowing it.

More dishes were brought to the table, graced the air for a brief while with their spicy redolence, and then departed into his inexorable maw. At last, after a flan the size of a brick and a double scoop of lemon sherbet, he burped a couple of times, plucked the napkin from his shirt front, and in a manner grotesquely genteel patted his wet mouth.

"That wasn't bad," he conceded, speaking to me for only the second time in almost an hour.

"Yes, delicious," I said, wondering how he could have possibly enjoyed it, bolting it the way he had.

With our coffee we had brandy and panetellas.

"Italians are great when it comes to chow," he remarked, stroking his distended stomach with a dimpled hand. "Rico Cremona — remember what a cook he was? He even made that New Zealand mutton taste good."

I left off wondering about Norbie's dining prowess and recalled Rico. He'd had a red face, a thin nose, a high-pitched voice, and a wife and two children. At Mare Island he'd listened to soap operas every afternoon like a man in a coma.

Contemplating the cigar smoke as it wound sinuously through the fake leaves on the trellis, I said, "After the war I visited Cremona."

Norbie gave me a sidelong glance. "How could you, Al? Cremona didn't make it. He went down with the ship."

"No, no, Norbie. Not Rico. I visited the city of Cremona in Italy. When I was in Milan I saw it on the map. It wasn't far, so I went. A lovely place, Cremona — famous for its violin makers."

We puffed in silence while the accordion played a saltarello.

At length I remarked, "Morison, the historian, considers the Battle of Savo Island to be the worst defeat the American Navy ever suffered."

"It figures," Norbie replied.

"Do you sometimes think about them?"

"Think about who, Al? All the guys, you mean?"

"Yes."

Norbie belched. "No, not any more," he said.

"I do. I have dreams, too. I see them floating in the green water — down the passageways, in the wardroom, in the engine room. They're like balloon figures — Larry, Artie Dolan, Richie Otis and the rest — swollen and white."

"Hey, come on! Don't get weird on me, buddy."

"Remember how hot it was, Norb? Everybody had a rash. When the flares exploded, where were you?"

"Aft. Natie Simons and me were standing under that hunk of canvas between the gun mounts, out of the rain."

As vivid as reality the scene came back to me. A silver curtain of rain, lightning blinking in the distance, and suddenly the star shells burst. A mistake, I thought. Grabbing a poncho to throw over my head, I ran out onto the port wing of the bridge. The fragrance of flowers filled my nostrils — hibiscus, or night-smelling orchids, or maybe frangipani — wafted from the island by the storm's wind. Like an aurora the flares danced in the sky. I could perceive two APD's anchored offshore, and then, without the least translation of time, I found myself in the sea gagging on salt water, and my brain a brazen chime clanging in the belfry of my skull.

"That fish was meant for the *Chicago*. We got in the way," Norbie said. "I went flying. By God, that ocean felt like concrete when I finally came down. Poor Natie! He wasn't one of the survivors, the poor bastard."

"I wouldn't have been one of the survivors, either, if it hadn't been for you," I pointed out quietly.

"That's a crock! I just gave you a little lift, is all. You'd have made it okay even if I hadn't."

"No, never. I was numb. I was helpless — frozen with fear. The reflection of the fire on the water made me think I was enveloped in flaming oil."

"Well, you weren't any more scared than I was. I kept thinking about the sharks we'd seen the day before. I was one happy guy when we got on that raft, let me tell you."

"Yes," I said, remembering how I'd sat weeping on the canvas bottom while Weaver beside me moaned and whimpered because his chest was caved in, and the *Davoran* — not a hundred yards away and still filled with people — capsized to starboard and slid into the sea in a mist of steam and smoke.

"What about another brandy, Al?"

"All right, Norbie."

He signaled the waiter.

"I still have that buzzing in my head," I declared.

"Honest to Pete? After all these years?" My friend looked surprised, and then just a trifle cautious. "But the voices — you don't hear them any more, do you?"

"Oh, no! The voices are gone," I answered quickly. As I did I crossed my fingers — the middle over the index — to counteract the lie. Though this was a childish habit, I knew, it was one I'd never been able to discard. As for the lie itself, I thought it best not to get into so complex a matter with someone as mundane as Norbie.

"That's good, buddy," he said, grinning broadly. "You were a wildman when I saw you that time in the sick bay on the *Josephson*. You told me you couldn't sleep because the pillows were yelling in your ears. You made the pharmacist's mates keep changing them. Bet you don't remember that."

He was wrong. I had no difficulty in remembering the ghastly, insinuating allegations of the pillows. However, I said nothing further.

When the bill came he insisted on paying for everything. We got a taxi on Salem Street. Since Norbie expressed a wish to view some historical sights, I instructed the driver to take us past Paul Revere's house, Faneuil Hall and King's Chapel. My companion gazed out the window at these old structures and for a while showed interest, but his attention soon flagged. He elicited the name of "a good place to get a drink" from the hackie and we sped off to the Hotel Sussex.

By this time I was weary. Still, under the circumstances, I could hardly raise an objection. I was therefore obliged to sit with him from ten in the evening till one in the morning, drinking Scotch and making dull and desultory conversation in a rather garish lounge-bar. Toward midnight a couple of bleached blondes entered the place, one of whom threw me a seductive glance. I was all for inviting them over to our table, but Norbie wouldn't hear of it.

"Hookers," he said, scowling. "I can spot them a mile off. Strictly hotel hookers, buddy. That one with the long hair looks as tough as a boiled owl."

Maybe he was right — I don't know. His attitude seemed strange to me, however. That was my last attempt to redeem the evening. With each drink — and he had four or five times as many as I did — Norbie's mood grew more somber. When at last we departed, he was almost morose.

Another cab returned us to the house. I saw Norbie to the guest room. He asked me if I would bring him a pitcher of ice water, which I did. Then I wished him a good night's sleep, and foggy-headed went to bed myself.

* * *

I PRESENT NORBIE

For lunch I prepared steaks, baked potatoes, canned string beans and a tossed salad. Norbie gobbled up everything and then ate a loaf of bread. To him it was a snack, I suspect — a mere refection. Afterward he went out on the porch, lay down on the iron-framed couch and was soon snoring clamorously. I washed the dishes, then went up to speak with Eulalia.

She knew of my visitor, of course, and since our lives — Eulalia's and mine — are not rich in incident, she was in a state of some excitement. Earlier in the day I had described our night on the town. Now I was asked for additional details and an account of all that had happened that morning. When I told of how I'd seen him weeping in his room, her interest was further quickened.

"Is he mad, do you suppose?" she asked. "Why haven't you brought him here so that I can see him?"

"I will. I will," I said.

"He sounds very peculiar, Al. You'd better watch yourself. He could be a raving maniac. When will you bring him?"

"Oh, five-thirty . . . or six. When he comes up to dress for dinner, my dear."

"If you forget, Al, I'll be furious."

I vowed not to. We gabbed for nearly an hour. I polished her with the chamois and moved the rope-legged table a little closer to the window so that she could see the field of daisies in the back of the garage. At three I left her.

On the porch Norbie still slept soundly, his batrachian visage like a Mardi Gras mask. I went to the supermarket. Returning a while later, I found that he had at last awakened and was watching a baseball game on television in the parlor, a glass of whiskey in his hand. I put the groceries away and joined him. It proved to be a suspenseful game, not being decided until the ninth inning when a Red Sox player scored on a long fly ball. Norbie enjoyed it thoroughly. After draining his glass, he struggled out of the chair, said he was going to take a shower and then lumbered up the stairs. I followed, and on the pretext of showing him the books that my great-grandfather had written, steered him into the library.

"Gracious me, he's gigantic!" exclaimed Eulalia as we entered. "He's a whale! A hippopotamus! An absolute monster!"

Though Norbie couldn't hear these crude remarks, they made me uncomfortable nonetheless. My little pitcher — because of loneliness, I suppose — often behaves in a somewhat hostile manner toward strangers. It's a paradox, like so many things on this planet. And, of course, in the presence of strangers I can't openly rebuke her for her rudeness without appearing peculiar. At the time of my mother's death I did on one occasion forget myself and chastised Eulalia in front of Reverend Wayne, our minister. Luckily, the good man attributed this queer conduct to my recent bereavement, but it was a bad gaffe just the same. I hesitate, therefore, to take people into the library.

Norbie, clearly indifferent, looked at the dusty volumes I showed him, and uttered a few polite comments.

Eulalia chattered on. "In those old photographs, dressed in his blue uniform, he was handsome," she said, "but now he's disgusting. Doesn't he have a face just like a frog's, Al? Do you think it's really him? Maybe he's an impostor. He's too ugly for words. And why has he come here to visit us?"

Behind my back I made frantic motions for her to be quiet — all in vain. She continued to bombard me with inquiries, knowing perfectly well that I couldn't answer them.

"How did he ever get so blubbery, Al? Why don't you ask him? He's a blimp! Have you noticed how he wobbles when he walks? His arms are so fat that they stick out from his sides like penguin's wings. Don't bring him near me, please! He's bound to jostle the table and knock me off."

I pretended deafness, though it wasn't easy. To talk with Norbie I was obliged to drown her out, which apart from being a trifle ungentlemanly was very confusing. She was still jabbering when we finally left the room.

* * *

THEY MAKE ME LOOK A FOOL

. . . I was very uneasy. All that morning I wandered restlessly around — to the Burying Ground, to Hall's Pond, to the supermarket, to the basement. I longed to talk again with Madge, but she didn't emerge from the library, even at lunchtime, and I dared not disturb her.

At two o'clock I went to see Eulalia in my mother's bedroom. Not having visited her for several days, I was given a poor reception. She refused to speak to me. From within her hollow bowl, only little sighs issued — sighs of the type that people make when they wish to express polite boredom. But I wouldn't go away.

Gently I polished her glittering surface with the chamois, and then I set her on top of the escritoire so that she might enjoy an unobstructed view of the park and get the full benefit of the sunshine. All the while I offered apologies for not having come to see her sooner.

Then I poured out the whole story. I told of how Madge had found Norbie, of our subsequent opening of Great-grampy's grave, of the tale of Ahmed Abderrasul, and finally, of Suleyman's appearance and his wild demands. As I spoke, Eulalia left off sighing. To anyone else, she might have seemed quite inanimate — an ordinary, though lovely piece of china — but to me it was obvious that she was listening intently to every word I said. I finished at last, sat on the side of my mother's bed and waited patiently.

A minute passed, and then another. She made a small snorting noise and said, "Why come to me? Take your troubles to the gypsy, Al. She's caused them. Let her cure them."

"Ah, well," I said. "It's true she never should have interfered, but the harm is done now, and that fool of a Turk will run to the police, Eulalia."

"Will he? And what about her? Do you think she can be trusted?"

"Madge? She doesn't want the police. She's only interested in finding her scraps of papyrus."

"Madge? So it's 'Madge,' is it? You've become great pals, haven't you? You're an idiot, Al. That cripple is playing a deep game. But why am I talking to you, anyway? You're as wicked as she is — a traitor, a false friend, a cheat, a ruffian."

"Now, now, don't carry on so, Eulalia," I said, trying to appease her. "The lady will be finished with her researches before too long, and then everything will go back to the way it was prior to her arrival."

"No, it'll never be the same again," she answered, and thereupon commenced to cry.

Until that moment I'd never heard Eulalia weep. It was a strange sound, rather like a shower of rain on tree leaves. In my nervous state it really vexed me.

"Oh, for God's sake!" I exclaimed. "Why are you bawling?" It's so silly. Stop it, please! Tears can't solve problems, my dear. I'm very surprised at your acting this way. You've always been such a steady, rational creature. You can't collapse now, Eulalia. Remember, it was you who first put the idea into my head — the idea to send poor Norbie on his way — so you have a share in this, too. Wailing like Niobe or Ariadne isn't going to help us out of our predicament."

Her crying, however, showed no signs of abatement. I shook my head angrily, and in the performance of this small action my eyes happened to traverse the bell-shaped mirror on my mother's chiffonier. In it, I espied Madge. She was watching me through the partially open door. I whirled around.

"To whom were you speaking?" she asked in her straight-forward manner, not at all abashed at having been caught eaves-dropping.

"Speaking?" I echoed feebly. "Why . . . why, no one. I was soliloquizing. It's a . . . a habit of mine."

"It was more than a soliloquy," she replied, her expression quizzical. "You were having a conversation — yes, a conversation with that pottery jug up there on the desk."

Treacherously misled by this statement, I made a rash assumption and blurted out, "Then you heard it speak, Madge?"

No sooner were the words out of my mouth than I realized I'd made an absolute ass of myself.

"Me? No," said she, smiling thinly. "I didn't hear it speak, Al, but it was very obvious that you did."

Only a Russian novelist — a Gogol or Dostoevsky — could have described my humiliation. How I longed to dash from the room! And while I stood there, hot with shame, Eulalia went on with her rain-shower weeping just as if nothing were happening.

The archaeologist came forward and murmured, "A talking Spode jug — intriguing. What opinions does it have?"

"Not Spode — Worcester," I mumbled. Then, getting up, I made a grave effort to gloss over the stupid remark I'd uttered earlier. "But the pitcher doesn't talk. What an idea!"

By this time Madge had reached the escritoire and was staring up at Eulalia, who now abruptly left off crying. Seeing the two of them together that way — face to face, as it were — only increased my discomfort.

"All right, Worcester then," the lady said. "Isn't it fancy, though? Much too baroque for my taste. I'm used to cruder, more primitive ware — and that usually in potsherds."

"It's silly to say that . . . that a pitcher can speak," I persisted. "It's absurd."

She glanced at me. "Is it? In that case, why have you crossed your fingers, Al? Is that a habit of yours, too? A little something you do automatically when you're telling lies?"

"Lying? I'm not! Why should I lie?" I asked, putting my hand in my pocket.

For a moment she regarded me in silence. Then she said, "We all have our idiosyncrasies, Al. No need to get upset. In any case, when you say the thing doesn't speak, you're telling the truth. It really doesn't. You only imagine that it does."

This line of reasoning — doubling back, as it did — compounded my confusion. "I don't imagine anything," I declared, sidling toward the door in hopes that she'd follow me out.

"You think the voice is real then?" said she, remaining where she was.

"Don't let her trick you, Al!" Eulalia suddenly chimed in.

"That's not what I meant," I said, halting.

"Yes, it is," Madge contradicted. "That's precisely what you meant."

The next thing I knew, she was questioning me so closely and relentlessly, and with such obvious pleasure, too, that I felt like a rat at the mercy of a terrier. At some time in her life she must have belonged to a debating society, for she could argue like a Jesuit. Her mind as incredibly nimble. All my replies were turned upside down, until I was no longer sure of what I was saying. It was harrowing. In the end she had me mouthing the most ridiculous contentions. Moreover, I twice referred to the pitcher as "she" and once even called it "Eulalia."

My position was impossible. I was driven into a corner and obliged to capitulate ignominiously. Feeling about the size of a gnat, I acknowledged that I had been talking to the piece of porcelain, that it was a living, feeling being, and that it was my good friend. I think it was the most difficult task I ever had to perform — making such an admission to a person like Madge Clerisy. But I had no choice, none at all.

"Eulalia — a pleasant-sounding name. It's sweet, romantic," she remarked, thoroughly amused by my confession. "Of course you know that she's no more than an auditory hallucination, Al — a kink in your mind."

"Oh, yes — I knew you'd think of it in those terms," I muttered, "but you couldn't be more mistaken. Really!"

Retrieving my composure after a few moments, I commenced an explanation of this admittedly rare phenomenon. I spoke of the limits placed on human senses, and of the vast unexplored areas beyond those limits; I dealt with cosmogony, cosmology, the space-time continuum, exobiology and many other related matters; I quoted Democritus, Albert Einstein, Bishop Berkeley, Lucretius and Sir James Jeans. Surprisingly, I was quite cogent, even eloquent. Nevertheless, though every word was irrefragably scientific, I accomplished nothing. On my listener's pretty face, disbelief was as evident as the time on the dial of a clock.

To make matters worse, at the end of my discourse Eulalia raised a fuss. "Stop gabbing like a simpleton," she said. "Get rid of this brazen gypsy. Give her a punch, Al. Kick her down the stairs right now. What are you waiting for?"

Madge shook her head. "Your arguments are rubbish, absolute nonsense," she declared contemptuously. "Where did you learn all that gobbledygook?" She then rested her stick against the desk, reached up and grasped the object of our discussion.

At once Eulalia squealed in alarm. "Don't let her touch me. Please! Make her put me down!" she wailed.

Frightened myself, I snatched the piece of porcelain from the woman's hands. My action startled her and she asked angrily, "Why did you do that? Did you think I might drop your precious Eulalia?"

"You might," I answered bluntly, transferring my old companion to the safety of the chiffonier.

"And would it matter if I did? You'd soon find something else to chat with, I'm sure," said Madge, laughing spitefully. "That's how it is with schizos. Instead of reading Einstein, Al, you should've looked into Freud. Your illness is one that he covers quite comprehensively. The china pitcher is only a prop — a kind of ventriloquist's dummy. It doesn't actually talk to you, but you talk to yourself through it. Do you understand?"

"Rubbish!" I said, paying her back in her own coin.

"It isn't."

"It is."

"Listen to me. You say the jug is alive — that it can think and feel, hear and speak. Can it see as well?"

"Yes, Eulalia can see — of course. The mechanics of the thing are a mystery to me, I admit, but —"

"How she does it doesn't matter. The point is, Al, that if she can see, I can prove I'm right and you're wrong," said Madge. "Here's what we'll do: you turn and face the door, and while you're looking away, I'll perform some simple action in full sight of the jug. Now, if Eulalia is a distinct being, you need only ask her what I've done and she can tell you. But if, as I claim, she's just an extension of yourself, she won't know any more about my action than you will."

"A splendid idea!" I exclaimed. "I agree completely. We'll settle the question at once and forever, my dear girl."

I whipped about smartly, then, and faced the doorway. A second later I heard a faint rustling, and a few seconds after that, my examiner said, "All right, Al, you may look now."

As I turned around again, I was unable to restrain a grin. "It's juvenile, this, but there are some who can learn only through concrete demonstrations," I crowed, delighted at having a chance to humble my tormentor. To my friend on the dresser, I said, "Very well, Eulalia — what was it she did?"

I waited, but Eulalia merely sighed.

"Well? Tell me what she did," I demanded.

"Who — your 'dear girl'?" Eulalia replied finally. "None of your business, Al, none of your business. If you wish to play games with your 'dear girl,' you must do so without my participation."

"Damn it!" I shouted. "What did she do?"

The jealous Eulalia would say nothing more, however. She sighed like a martyr and began to hum to herself.

Meanwhile, Madge Clerisy observed me with unconcealed glee — much as if I were a bear waltzing on his hind legs, or a sea lion balancing a ball on his nose. I was mortified, but beyond clenching my fists and stamping my foot on the floor, there wasn't a thing I could do. The pair of them had thwarted me completely.

So I swallowed my bile and growled, "Out of an imbecilic perversity, Eulalia refuses to be part of the charade."

The lady laughed gaily and picked up her Malacca stick.

"I don't care if you believe me or not," I told her. "You're the one, after all, who's deaf and blind."

Without a word she limped from the room. I heard her uneven tread go down the hall, and then the sound of the library door closing.

"Well, Eulalia, are you satisfied?" I asked bitterly.

"No," said she. "I'm not. And I won't be until you get rid of that detestable creature. Get rid of her, Al — do you hear me?"

I went down to the kitchen and made myself a cup of strong coffee.

* * *

THE CALAMITY

It was the sixteenth of July. Yes, the sixteenth — a Thursday. When I awoke that morning, I felt somewhat strange — unreal, otherworldly. I could almost imagine that I was ten years old again, that my mother and father and Great-grampy were downstairs having breakfast, and that Clarice was moving about in her room. I could hear the clatter of the dishes; I could even hear the *clop-clop* and creaking of a horse-and-wagon going along Beacon Street. This pleasant, dreamy condition lasted but a short time, however; it was hardly more than a spasm of sensation. Nevertheless, it relieved my mind of worry and put me in an excellent humor.

It was the sixteenth of July, I know, because I wrote the date down later. I washed, dressed, went to the kitchen and made myself four slices of French toast. I then came up to my mother's room to eat them. My early appearance caught Eulalia by surprise; she hadn't yet begun her day's brooding. Taking advantage of this, I remarked on how pretty she looked, followed with a few more innocent flatteries, told a little joke and swiftly guided her into a blithesome frame of mind. She was soon relating her own amusing stories. One of these was a description of Mrs. Binney's preslumber preparations — of how the old girl struggled out of her elaborate foundation garments, donned multiple nightgowns and a hairnet, applied numerous skin creams, searched under the bed and in the closet, and guzzled a glass of neat whiskey before finally climbing between the sheets. The poor thing had forgotten to lower her shade one night, and Eulalia had a ringside seat. It was very funny.

By the time I'd finished the toast and drunk the coffee, my friend was singing songs to me in her sweet voice. Her rendition of *Oh Dear, What Can the Matter Be? Johnny's Not Home from the Fair* was ineffably fine. Not to be outdone, I bellowed a few choruses of *Abdul Abulbul Ameer* — fairly ribald ones — which made Eulalia giddy with laughter. How animated she was! Her round, translucent cheeks glistened, while the lip of her spout appeared to curve in a broad, sensuous smile.

Barely had I finished my performance, however, than Madge Clerisy's irregular footsteps sounded on the staircase. She went past the door and into the library. At once, Eulalia lost her gaity. The old peevishness came back into her voice. She began to interrogate me. Why was the woman still in the house? What was she doing? Had the police come around yet, inquiring about the dead Turk? Why hadn't I taken her advice and told the whole story to the authorities.

My carefree mood evaporated, and my anxiety returned. As it happened, a young policeman had been to the door the preceding day, ostensibly checking the number of occupants in the building for the town directory. Though his sudden appearance had upset me a bit, there was nothing bogus about his manner, so I'd dismissed him from my thoughts. Now, because of Eulalia's remarks, the visit assumed sinister aspects. I told her about it.

"Ah! You see?" said she, seizing on it immediately. "They're after you, Al. The town directory! What an obvious lie! As if anyone would take a census in the middle of summer, with everybody away on vacation. Give yourself up, Al, while there's time. Since it was an accident, you have nothing to fear. And it's a way of making amends for the wrong you did to Mahir. Think of your next reincarnation, Al."

On and on she went, until my head was swimming. I did argue with her, but not too forcefully, as I suspected she was right. Because I was getting old, she pointed out, what happened to me in this life was much less important than what was in store for me in the life to come. There was no denying that, was there? One must look to the future.

So engrossed were we that we did not hear Madge approach the room. Suddenly the door was flung open, and there she stood. She glanced at me, then at Eulalia, then at me again. A scowl came to her lips.

"Have you seen my bag?" she inquired curtly.

"What? Your bag?" I asked, uncomprehending.

"Yes, yes — my handbag. I've lost it somewhere."

"Oh. No, I haven't. When did you see it last?"

"Yesterday afternoon. I may have left it on the streetcar. Damn! There wasn't much money in it, but there were papers — and a half-completed letter to a friend of mine." She regarded me closely with those piercing amber eyes of hers. "Are you quite certain you haven't seen it, Al?"

"Absolutely," I replied a trifle frostily, since the question struck me as accusatory. "Why should I say it if it weren't true?"

"Well, I've been all over the library, without turning it up," she answered. "I suppose I'll have to call the transit system people, hopeless though it will be."

During this exchange Eulalia had remained silent, but now she said to me, "Tell her that you're going to the police station, Al."

But I paid no attention to her. Madge was clearly in a bad mood; it was no time to broach such a subject, I felt. Miffed, Eulalia became more insistent. The archaeologist, meanwhile, was asking me for the full name of the trolley company, and where she could find the nearest telephone booth. With the two voices assaulting my ears, I became rattled. And so, without really intending to, I stated loudly, "Eulalia wants me to go to the authorities and tell them about Mahir Suleyman's death. She thinks it would be best."

The abruptness of this remark threw Madge off her stride. She looked at me blankly for a few seconds, then her fair features gradually reddened. Even before she opened her mouth, I knew she was infuriated. "Eulalia does, does she?" the woman sneered. "She wants you to confess — is that it, Al?"

I nodded, ill at ease.

"You'll do nothing of the sort — do you hear me?" she said. "You'll keep your big mouth shut."

"But why? If we explained all the circumstances, surely they'd be lenient," I mumbled.

Madge's reply took the form of invective. She called Eulalia an unflattering name, and me another — one I hadn't heard since I left the Navy. Not content with that, she delivered a tirade to us that was as profane as it was prolix.

"Defend yourself!" Eulalia shouted at me, contributing her share to the tumult. "Don't let that coarse creature — that gypsy — treat you like a weak-brained child. Be a man and stand up to her. Don't let her insult you that way, Al!"

Their voices mingled, sounding like one of those wild ultra-modern symphonies — a Charles Ives work, perhaps. Soon my thoughts were as confused and discordant as the noise of their scolding.

"Eulalia says that you should stop insulting me," I exclaimed above the pandemonium.

"Damn Eulalia!" said Madge brutally.

"Oh, what a common alley cat she is!" said Eulalia.

Determined not to be bullied, I boomed out, "Eulalia's right! She's right and you're wrong."

As Madge's face had been growing redder and redder, it was now the color of a glass of Beaujolais, and her eyes had narrowed to slits. "Eulalia? Eulalia?" she said in a tone that was all of a sudden deceptively soft. "I'll see to Eulalia!"

She rushed by me then, raised the walking stick as if it were a flail and brought it down upon my poor friend. So swiftly did she act that I had time to neither move nor cry out. Dumb, I watched the cane fly up, heard it whirr through the air, felt Eulalia's shriek of terror stab into my brain, heard the explosion — like the bursting of a grenade — as the iron ferrule made contact with the thin porcelain, listened to the anguished scream die in a gruesome crackling, and stared in frozen agony as my old companion's beautiful, fragile body came apart in a hundred ragged fragments which poured, in a sparkling cataract, down the bowed front of the mahogany secretary.

"Now what does she say?" Madge asked in a razor-edged voice.

"You killed her!" I gasped, stupefied by the immensity of the crime. Eulalia had disappeared. What had been Eulalia was now only a scattering of china chips on the floor.

"I've cured you of an hallucination," said Madge, with open satisfaction.

"But you killed Eulalia," I whispered huskily, still grappling with this incredible idea.

The woman made another remark, which I didn't understand, and started around me toward the door. I took hold of her then and threw her against the wall. Again she brought up the walking stick; before she could use it on me, however, I tore it from her grip and flung it away. My hands circled her slender neck. I could feel the cartilage of her throat under my thumbs as I began to strangle her.

At first her eyes continued insolent, but suddenly they gleamed with a lunatic fear. It was this hideous aspect of fright that saved her from death. Little by little, as I looked upon her contorted features, my mind cleared and my rage abated. When I released her she slumped to the floor and sprawled there, noisily sucking in air.

I staggered out, stumbled down the hall to my room, and weeping and groaning, fell across my bed. Never had I felt such pangs of sorrow.

* * *

DUMBFOUNDING DISCOVERY

Because the windows of the charnel house have no glass — only iron grilles — squirrels occasionally nest in the little building. As they clutter the place with dead leaves and other woodland debris, this can be a bother. What's more, when they spring up suddenly and dart past your nose toward the open door, they can give you a most unpleasant turn. That is exactly what happened to me about a week ago while I was rummaging for a hatchet. The animal's flight was so abrupt and my alarm so great that I staggered backward against the wheelbarrow, which tipped over onto the stone floor, producing an ear-piercing clang. As I was righting it, something called out to me. The sound was faint, but unmistakable.

"Al! Al!" is what I heard.

I glanced around. Since the voice had a hollow ring to it — a halloo-in-a-tunnel quality — I thought initially that it had come from an empty nail keg that stood atop some cordwood on my right. Staring at it, I waited.

"Is it you, Al?" came a second cry, no louder than the first and no less resonant.

However, it was obvious to me now that it wasn't emanating from the keg; it had come from a different direction.

"Yes, yes," I replied curtly, having small desire to engage in conversation with some silly rake or hoe. "What do you want? And who are you?"

"It's me, Al — Madge!" said the voice.

"Madge?" I asked, nearly upsetting the wheelbarrow a second time. "Madge?" Had I received a bolt of lightning in my ear, I could not have been more shocked. "Did you say . . . did you actually say 'Madge'?"

"Yes! Yes! Yes! I'm here — under the ground," the faint voice responded fervently. "Thank God! Thank God! I never thought it would happen. I never thought you'd find me — never! I was at the end of my tether, Al."

Well, incredible as it may appear, it really and truly was Madge Clerisy — I immediately recognized her voice — and she really and truly was beneath the earth. Naturally, I assumed at first that she had died somewhere and was now an astral communicant, but this was far from the case, as I shall explain.

Her cries came from the north side of the room, where the floor consisted of a single slab of granite, rectangular in shape and as large as the top of a kitchen table. I had noticed this mammoth slab for the first time on the day that I'd moved the old headstones from it — that distant day when Madge had insisted on reading all the epitaphs. It had impressed me with its bulk, since it was so much bigger than the other paving stones, but I'd given it no further thought. Now I regarded it with new eyes.

Dropping to my knees, I began brushing away with my hands the spider webs, leaves, chestnut husks and pine cones that littered its surface. In the hard soil, a few inches from one corner of the thing, I then discovered a small, almost circular hole. When Madge next spoke, it was from this hole — which was somewhat larger than a half dollar — that her voice issued. A funny little aperture it was, for it entered the ground at an angle. I guessed that it was the work of a mole or similar creature. Putting my eye to it, I saw a wan, fuzzy light, but that was all.

During the time that I made these investigations, the woman kept up a steady stream of talk. I couldn't apprehend her remarks, however. She babbled on about light and darkness, about silence, about the passage of the days, about solitude, about hope, and about a variety of other abstractions.

"Are you listening to me, Al?" she asked, at length.

"Yes," I said.

"Shout, Al — shout. It's far. It's quite a distance. Please shout. You can't know how wonderful it is for me to hear your voice."

"All right," I bellowed into the opening. "But tell me what has happened, and where you have got to."

She gave a giddy sort of laugh and said, "I've been here for more than a month. I'm not sure exactly how long. I tried to keep track of the days by the light in that hole, but I became muddled. It's been so terrible."

"More than a month?" I asked, mystified. "You've been buried more than a month, Madge? How is it possible?"

"Yes, yes. It was a trap, you see — a trap. Everything came down. What you will have to do is this, Al — hire a man with a crane, and have him lift that granite block. Do you understand?"

I shook my head — then, realizing she couldn't see the gesture, said, "No, not really."

"The walls muffle the sound," she said, thinking that her words hadn't reached me. "I'll speak louder, and you listen closely. Telephone a construction-equipment rental company — there'll be several in the Yellow Pages — and have them send a small power crane immediately. Tell them how urgent it is. Say that you need it to lift a heavy stone — that someone has fallen into a hole and that the stone is blocking the entrance. Once they've removed it, you can lower a knotted rope and I can climb the hell out of here."

"But how did you get into such a predicament in the first place, Madge? I can't make head or tail of what you're saying. What's down there — an abandoned well?"

Again she laughed, and again it sounded slightly delirious. "No, no, no, no! What's down here is A. Edward Pendleton's tomb! Yes, his tomb! I found it, Al. It's an underground apartment. There are four little rooms, and in one of them is his body, in a stone coffin. You'll hear all about it soon enough, though. Hurry now and make that call."

"Great-grampy's tomb? Welladay! Great-grampy's tomb? Really? Down there? Who would believe it!"

"You'll see it all shortly. Now get a move-on, Al."

My mind grappled with this amazing news. The old man's grave had been beneath the charnel house right along.

"Have you gone?" she called, rousing me from my contemplations.

"Oh, no. I've been thinking," I replied. "Wouldn't it be better to get the fire department? They have ladders . . ."

"Absolutely not! I don't want any damn officials in on this. They'll ask too many questions. Do you follow what I mean? This is my discovery, and I want it kept a strict secret for the time being. Stop making silly suggestions. Hurry off to the telephone. The crane operator need only know what I've instructed you to tell him."

She spoke with characteristic condescension, which irked me. "But why won't you tell me how it all happened, Madge?" I asked.

"Why? Why do you suppose? I want to get the hell out of this dungeon! I've been here an eternity — buried alive, you ninny! Can't you realize what it's been like?"

"No reason to be rude," I said, further offended. "I would think that since you've been there so long, another few minutes wouldn't matter too much."

I put my eye to the hole again, hoping I could catch a glimpse of her, but the wan glow was all that was visible. Accidentally my knee sent a pebble tumbling down the opening.

"Be careful, for God's sake!" she shouted instantly. "Don't try to move it by yourself. The whole thing might collapse. Get the machine! Get the crane!"

Sitting on my haunches, I considered the problem. How could I do what she asked? It was mad. The situation was fantastic — unreal.

"A crane would never fit through the lich gate," I said. "Besides, it would have to run over some of the graves to get here. And the police are sure to ask questions. I'll have to give them a reasonable explanation."

She yelled an oath up to me. The word she used was one that I'd always found abhorrent, even from the lips of men. "Stop chattering, and make the call," she said venomously. "If you have to knock the gate down, then knock it down — you damn boobie!"

I could feel my temper struggling to wrest control from my reason; I could feel my cheeks flush with warm blood; and I could hear the buzzing inside my head grow to a surf-like roar. Yet at all costs I was determined to maintain my self-possession.

"You haven't convinced me, Madge," I answered coldly. "I'm going back to the house and mull things over."

The briefest pause ensued, during which the lady archaeologist speedily reappraised our relative positions. "Don't go!" she exclaimed then in alarm. "Don't go, Al! I didn't mean what I said. I apologize. I never meant to insult you, Al — it's only that I'm overwrought, that I'm half out of my senses from all this being alone. I'm really very sorry that I spoke that way to you."

"That's all right," I said. "But tell me the story, won't you?"

"Very well. Very well, I will. And after I do, you'll make the telephone call. Okay, Al?"

"Yes."

"Do you promise?" she asked, attempting to sound playful, though the result was a bit grotesque.

"Yes," I repeated.

THE NETHER PLACE

For a moment she was silent. Outside in the Burying Ground, a cicada drummed vigorously. It's late in the season for a cicada, I thought.

"The day you drove off to Philadelphia, I happened to wander into the charnel house, and that huge granite slab caught my eye," she said, commencing her narrative. "It reminded me of granite blocks I'd seen in Egypt, at the Temple of Khafra. What struck me was that this one was not only larger than the other paving stones, it was far more precisely cut."

Inspecting the slab myself, I saw at once what she meant. The edges had been tailored with a fine accuracy.

She went on. "I started to poke around it with an old iron paling. It didn't take me long to discover that the stone was hinged on a thick steel rod, and that the ends of it were fixed in adjacent pieces of granite. When I jumped up and down on it, it wobbled slightly. I concluded from this that it was counterweighted. Using the paling, I tried to prize it open, and to my amazement found that the task was relatively easy. It came up inch by inch; as it did, I shoved logs into the gap to act as supports. Eventually the counterweight assumed most of the load, so that when I gave a good hard push, the enormous rock swung back as smoothly as an overhead garage door.

"I was excited, needless to say. Before me was a flight of nearly vertical stone steps leading into total darkness. I switched on my flashlight, and down I went. It was a long descent — I counted more than forty steps — but at last I reached the bottom. There I trod on yet another slab — one that was square, like a platform. As I did so, it lurched beneath my feet. I tried to keep my balance by leaning on my cane; the ferrule slipped on the hard surface, however, and I fell forward. I then heard an ominous, crackling noise, even as I was hurtling wildly through the air. Though I landed all in a heap, somehow the flashlight remained in my hand. Instinctively I directed its beam up the shaft and saw the huge granite door fall back into place, sealing the entrance. Simultaneously another heavy stone — the one that had served as the counterweight — broke loose and dropped on the topmost step of the long flight. The next thing I knew, the entire stairway came tumbling down like an avalanche.

"Do you see, Al? It was a trap. My weight on the platform had triggered the hellish thing. It was intended to crush intruders. Fortunately, however, my fall had pitched me a couple of yards to the side, and I had time to roll even farther away. But you can't imagine what it was like. It was worse than an earthquake. The noise was thunderous, and the dust blinding. Everything vibrated. Four or five of the massive steps — each one must weigh a hundred pounds — bounced in my direction. How they failed to land on me I'll never know! I was uninjured, but I was damn shaken up. It was a good while before I dared move from where I lay huddled."

Madge here left off speaking. I could hear her take a deep breath and release it in an exaggerated sigh.

"Absolutely fantastic!" I exclaimed into the aperture. "It's like one of those old tales about the pyramids. You know the kind — secret passages, deadfalls, and the Pharaoh's curse. But then what happened? What happened next, Madge?"

Coughing a couple of times, she complained about having to shout such a long story over so great a distance. Nevertheless, I was able to persuade her to continue.

"When the dust settled, I saw that I was in a cubicle. It was like an oubliette I'd seen once in an Italian castle. The only exit seemed to be the shaft, which was — in addition to being closed — far too steep to climb. I was unwilling to accept that this elaborate arrangement led only to a cul-de-sac, and I started to scrutinize the walls. After fifteen minutes or so, I came to the conclusion that they were as solid as the walls of the Grand Canyon.

"Panic suddenly took hold of me. I imagined that the air was bad, that I was already on the brink of asphyxiation. It wasn't true, of course, but I believed it. I stood there, panting and sweating, for I don't know how long. Then, as swiftly as the terror had come, so too did it leave me. My confidence and my reason returned. Calmly and methodically, I began an examination of the floor. Almost at once my probing fingers detected a crevice in the mortar, which I traced around a quadrangular stone. Though it was only half the size of the block above, I knew for certain that it was another door. When I located the hinge, I nearly danced for joy. Quickly I piled chunks of the broken staircase on the short end of the slab, until the weight was such that it swung open. The chunks of rock slid noisily into the space below.

"Shining the light in the hole I saw an iron ladder, and around it stacks and stacks of boxes. It was a second cubicle. Very warily I climbed down into it. The air was stale and dry. Through an alley between rows of cartons, I was able to make out a stone doorway, and I walked toward it cautiously. As I drew near, I was astonished to see a light switch fastened to the side of this arch. I glanced up and there in the low ceiling was a bulb and fixture. Standing well back and using the tip of my cane, I flicked the switch. The place was instantly filled with bright light.

"A most fantastic scene appeared before me. A short hall ran from the doorway to a third room. From this room, which was bigger than the others, a glistening basalt lion glared out at me with gold-and-turquoise eyes. At his side was an alabaster sphinx, fully three feet high and marvelously made. Beyond them, I saw a gilded couch, a beaten-gold screen, and a superb bronze statue of the jackal-headed god, Anubis.

"I rushed down the passage and found myself in the burial chamber of A. Edward Pendleton. Occupying the center of the floor was an Egyptian pink-granite sarcophagus — a Pharaoh's, though which Pharaoh's I haven't been able to figure out because the cartouche is not one I'm familiar with. Surrounding it were incredible things — a fabulous harp, a magnificent diorite falcon, a perfectly preserved sunboat, a sheath of gold-headed arrows. There were several ebony trays, beautifully set with nacre; there was a bronze woman, inlaid with silver, gold and gems. In one corner I discovered an ivory-and-cedarwood chest. In it were drinking cups of gold, gold rings and bracelets, gold pectorals, gold buckles, gold fibulae, and jewelry and beads of every description. In the opposite corner lay a dismantled chariot, all plated with hammered gold. But, Al, until you see these wonders yourself, you can't possibly appreciate how breath-taking, how absolutely astounding they really are."

Throughout Madge's recitation, I crouched motionless with my ear glued to the little hole in the hard earth, so utterly entranced was I. Yet I could scarcely believe what I heard.

"A Pharaoh's tomb!" I said now. "A Pharaoh's tomb, right here in the Burying Ground! Just imagine! Why, it's staggering! Still, it's exactly the sort of thing Great-grampy would do. Yes, exactly the sort of thing, Madge. And it explains the Italian stonecutters that Mr. Piero hired. I recall now a particular spring vacation from school. The yard was so cluttered with stones that it looked like a quarry, and my mother told me to keep out of the way and not go near the charnel house. But Great-grampy said he was making the place into a temple. Well, by God, I guess he was — in a sense."

"It's a pity you didn't mention that to me earlier," said the archaeologist a trifle caustically.

"Didn't I? Oh, I guess not. Think of all that gold, though. Poor, poor Mahir. He was right, wasn't he?" I said. "But what else is down there?"

"You'll see soon enough, Al. There's a fourth room — a chapel, and very tiny. It's crowded with figurines of Horus and Isis and the rest of the deities. According to my calculations, the apartment is almost fifty feet under the ground. It was quite a project, all right. You can't hear anything going on above. The only noise comes from the electric motor."

"Electric motor?"

"Yes. The light switch also turned on a blower. I didn't notice it at first, but afterward I felt the current and heard the hum. There's an open pipe in the garage up there that used to puzzle me. I believe now that the air is sucked in through that."

"Oh. But why would a dead man want fresh air?"

"You mean you don't understand it yet?" she asked, again sounding irritable. "Why did he want any of this stuff? He thought he was going to come back to life, that's why. Like a true Pharaoh, he provided himself with everything he'd need in this world or the next. A good thing, too, or I'd have died of suffocation the first day." She laughed shortly. "Well, I've told you the whole tale. Run now and make that telephone call."

My legs were awfully cramped from squatting all this time, but I'd been so intrigued that I hadn't dared stand up and stretch them for fear of missing something. I peeked into the hole once more. The disc of dim light was all that could be discerned. Something about the woman's story didn't jibe with reality, and my mind had been struggling with this inconsistency. Suddenly, I realized what it was.

"Madge," I called. "How could you have survived? It's almost six weeks since I went to Philadelphia — and you've had no nourishment!"

"Ah, but I've had plenty," she said, chuckling. "That room filled with cartons was the old bird's storeroom. Do you remember telling me that he liked buying food by the carton? That food is down here. Canned soup, canned vegetables, sardines, fruit salad, bully beef, baked beans, tuna fish — they've kept me alive. My one complaint is that he didn't think to put in a hot plate; I've had to eat everything cold."

"Amazing! And the food was good after all this time?"

"Except for some hash that tasted a little strange, and which I didn't use, yes. The old dungeon is remarkably dry. Yes, Al — your Great-grampy took good care of me. He provided linens, blankets, soap and towels, books to read (he liked Edgar Wallace, didn't he?), a wind-up phonograph and albums of opera records — even several cases of French wine. I didn't drink much of it, though. I stuck to water. There's a small sink here, with a single tap. It handled my thirst and my washing-up needs very nicely. By the way, haven't you heard me banging on the pipes? I'm sure they must connect with the house. I beat them until I thought they'd burst."

"Yes, yes — I did hear a lot of knocking," I admitted, "but I assumed it was only the usual racket that old plumbing often makes. Imagine, that was you signaling! My brain's in a whirl.

I really can't comprehend it all. The gold and the statues, for example — did he buy these things from that Ahmed fellow?"

"That's right. I found a couple of more notebooks in the burial chamber, and in them he tells the whole story. He got the lot for a trunkful of English sovereigns. Ahmed was foolish to sell so much for so little, but I guess he needed ready cash. I think, too, that A. Edward — who learned about the secret from a Luxor whore — threatened the Arab with exposure. When you consider that the prize item was a *rishi* coffin of Ramses the Second, it's clear that the price he paid was very low. The *rishi* coffin is the innermost one. Your great-grandfather is lying in it right now. We'll see it after we open the sarcophagus. It's a casket made of solid gold and encrusted with precious stones, and alone worth a fortune."

"A coffin of gold — just like Tutankhamen!"

"Probably a better one than that. Ramses the Second was a much more powerful king. That's the story, then. Now, Al, run out and phone. When the man comes, tell him to raise the front end of the slab until it pivots back on the hinge; after that, it can be tied in position with heavy ropes."

She stopped. I could almost hear her waiting for me to speak — and this was the moment I'd been unconsciously putting off. I stood and stretched my legs, licking my lips and wishing sincerely that life were not so complicated.

"Al?" she called.

I knelt again. "I think," I said into the opening, "that I'm going to have to leave you down there."

"What!" she cried. "You can't be serious!"

"I am, though. Yes, Madge, I am. I know it's awful, but I really think it's the right thing to do."

"Don't talk nonsense! How can it be the right thing to do? Are you mad?" she yelled up, her voice tremulous.

"No, it's . . . it's only that you've caused so much trouble," I said slowly, while trying to sort everything out in my head. "And if I set you free, you'll cause more. Take Great-grampy, for instance. What right have you to disturb him after all the effort he went to, to ensure his repose? Why should you violate his mausoleum? Why should he be dumped from his coffin, merely to satisfy the curiosity of scholars? That's certainly not right, Madge."

As far away as she was, the sound of her heavy breathing reached me through the narrow aperture. I listened to it for what seemed a long time.

"Very well, Al," she replied finally. "I'm certainly not prepared to remain entombed, just for an archaeological discovery. Life is more precious to me than even these chests of treasure . . . or academic acclaim. If my stay in this hole has taught me anything, it's been that. I give you my solemn word that I will never, as long as I live, reveal what I have found. I swear that I won't tell anyone. Get me out of here, Al, and I'll go away immediately. You'll never hear from me again."

"Of course," I said sadly.

Hesitantly she asked, "Of course you'll let me out?"

"No — oh, no. I meant, of course you would make promises like that — but once you were safe, you'd do just as you pleased. The difficulty is that you're much cleverer than I am. You'd have me jumping through hoops in no time, Madge. The trip to Philadelphia that I made is a case in point. Off I went, like Don Quixote. And why did you send me there? Because you knew, or had strong suspicions, that the tomb was under this slab, and you couldn't risk my interference. The day you went down those steps, you didn't just happen to have a flashlight — you were expecting to explore. Yes, and it was your intention to grab whatever you found and run off with it like a common thief. However, you underestimated Great-grampy, and he caught you."

"Al, Al! Don't talk this way," she said, striving to control her voice. "You can't mean what you're saying. You're playing one of your little jokes, aren't you? Don't, Al. It's too cruel."

"I'm not joking."

"But if you abandon me — that would be murder."

"Why? I'm not to blame for your predicament. You're where you are through your own folly. In any event, where does murder enter into it? You're far from being dead, and you've told me that you have everything down there that you could possibly need."

The nasty letter that I'd found in her handbag came to my thoughts, and I almost mentioned it. I didn't, though. It would have been brutal, too like taunting a vanquished foe. Instead I said, "I'm going back to the house."

236

"No — wait! Wait, Al! You've forgotten something, haven't you?" she called hastily. "Don't you remember making a promise to me a little while ago? You said that if I explained how I got down here, you'd telephone for the man with the crane." Her tone was a ghastly imitation of a mother humoring a recalcitrant child. "You remember that, Al, I'm sure you wouldn't ever go back on your word."

"When I made that promise, I had my fingers crossed," I replied. "You couldn't know it, of course, but nevertheless it means I'm not bound by what I said."

"Fingers crossed? Fingers crossed?" she screamed then.

"Don't go to pieces," I implored quickly, alarmed by her reaction. "Listen to me, Madge. It's a big decision for me to make, and though I believe I'm right in wanting to keep you there, I don't want to seem arbitrary. I'll get a second opinion on the matter, my dear."

I heard her suck in her breath. "Whose?" she asked hopefully.

"Eulalia's," said I. "Her advise is usually very sound."

"Eulalia. Eulalia is a china pitcher," Madge declared in a dead voice. "Eulalia. Eulalia isn't a person — she's a thing. Anyhow, I broke her to pieces, Al. Have you forgotten that?"

"No, I haven't. I glued her back together, though."

"I see. I see. And she's talking again?"

"Oh, yes. I know it's not easy to believe, but it's true. After all that, she's still alive. It's a miracle."

"A miracle? It isn't a miracle, Al — it's madness. She doesn't exist, your Eulalia. Her voice is inside your head. It's you talking to yourself — can't you realize that?"

"No, she exists all right," I answered, laughing. Then an interesting idea occurred to me. "Yes, Eulalia exists just as surely as you exist, Madge. Think about it. I can see Eulalia, but I can't see you. Here I am, kneeling on the ground and talking into a little hole. If what you say is so — if truth and reality consist only in what we can see and touch — then our conversation today must be adjudged no more than an illusionary dialogue, whipped up by my fancy. Do you understand? Who knows? You may be far away in Philadelphia (after all, that's surely a likelier possibility), but my imagination insists on pretending you've never left. I hear your voice rising from beneath the earth. What could be more bizarre than that? It must be that I am talking to myself, as you contend — that the sounds are all inside my skull."

"Have the stone lifted, then. Have it lifted, if you don't believe I'm here!"

"And appear a prize boobie when there's nothing underneath but moldly soil and centipedes? I think not. Now, Madge, I really have to go."

"Not yet, Al!"

"Yes — but I'll be back," I said soothingly. "And in the meantime I'll have a word with Eulalia and see what she recommends."

The woman began to shriek. The shrill cries sent chilling tremors down my spine. I got to my feet. Though she continued with her yelling, so little of the sound escaped from the tiny opening that it might have been mistaken for the faint squeaking of a mouse. When I reached the door of the charnel house, I no longer heard it at all. Only the drumming of the cicada was audible.

One of the characteristics of seriously disturbed persons is sometimes the hearing of voices that seem to originate within the person. People who have heard such voices report that one has no choice but to listen. The voices are imperious and compelling. If one were to be clinical about Algernon and Eulalia, one might agree with Madge, who regards Eulalia as no more than an auditory hallucination — a kink in Algernon's mind. Whether real or no, Eulalia acts like a bitchy, whining child. She wants Algernon to herself, goads him into multiple murders, guilt, and confession. In fact, Eulalia is shattered literally and figuratively by Madge after almost convincing Algernon to confess his murders to the police. "I've cured you of an hallucination," boasts Madge — and then is almost strangled by a distraught Algernon. But Eulalia is the winner after all. Restored with love and Elmer's Glue-all, she rises to the occasion in the final confrontation.

When Algernon returns from the wild goose chase to Philadelphia, he finds that Madge has gone. But has she? It appears that Madge got rid of Algernon to have time to search for and discover the underground tomb of Grand-pappy A. Edward Pendleton. Unfortunately, in her haste and clumsiness she had dislodged a heavy stone now blocking the entrance and exit. This underground tomb is well-ventilated, stocked with food, has adequate toilet and laundry facilities and books, including a splendid assortment of Edgar Wallace mysteries. Apparently, when Grand-pappy Pendleton died, he did not mean to stay dead for long.

Madge can now converse with Algernon only through a long tube. She is, of course, relieved to be alive but does not want to consider the tomb (alive or dead) as a permanent residence. Algernon promises to make a phone call for a man with a crane to lift the rock and release Madge. After thinking it over, however, he decides to do nothing. He acknowledges his promise to a now desperate Madge but quickly disposes of his pledge by indicating that he had his fingers crossed when he so promised. And as any child knows, a promise with fingers crossed doesn't amount to a hill of beans. Eulalia exists again, Algernon tells Madge, "just as surely as you exist . . . Think about it. I can see Eulalia, but I can't see you. Here I am, kneeling on the ground and talking into a little hole. If what you say is so — if truth and reality consist only in what we can see and touch — then our conversation today must be adjudged no more than an illusionary dialogue, whipped up by my fancy . . . Who knows? You may be far away in Philadelphia (after all, that's surely a likelier possibility), but my imagination insists on pretending you've never left. I hear your voice rising from beneath the earth. What could be more bizarre than that? It must be that I am talking to myself as you contend — that the sounds are all inside my skull."

Madge has only one last card to play — lift the stone and see if I'm really here, she pleads. But Algernon can't risk it and leaves to talk it over with Eulalia. He hears Madge's screams and shrill cries, which Algernon acknowledges could easily be mistaken for the faint squeaking of mice.

The story, especially the denouement, poses the classic confrontation between dream and reality, between inner and outer data, between neural and sensory stimuli, and between primary and secondary processes of thought.

Is Algernon "mentally ill?" Is he emotionally disturbed? Is he in need of psychotherapy? To what extent is he handicapped? Is he overly anxious? (Apparently, this occurs only when he is chided by Eulalia or unable to talk with Eulalia). Does Algernon function well? Does he make friends and influence people? One can conceive of Algernon and Eulalia living happily together ever after even with Madge (if she's really there) underfoot.

A major problem posed by someone like Algernon and others who converse with real and imagined Eulalias is to differentiate between "different" and "pathological," between dysfunctional and functional behavior. Almost all of us have had imaginary friends and may have spoken to objects here and there, including pictures, automobiles, letters, and mirrors. In fact, studies of creative and talented children have indicated that, overall, they tend to have more imaginary companions than the rest of humanity.

Listening to voices is another matter. All is well if one can listen to such voices with freedom to turn them off, to reject their demands, or to not listen. This is apparently not possible for seriously disturbed persons. Algernon *must* listen to Eulalia. He truly considers the import of her "reasoning," which technically results in murders, including those of the Turkish merchant and the real or imagined Madge. Yet, in Algernon's mind these acts were all done as altruistic and helpful gestures.

Probably, the wellspring of new ideas and creations is in primary processes. Whatever and however these "voices" communicate with us, once they begin to command us, we are in trouble. Undoubtedly, highly creative artists and renowned scientists have had active primary processes connected to well organized secondary processes. At times the connections may have been broken — as in Joan of Arc, Van Gogh, Frederick Nietzsche, Ernest Hemingway, Robert Schumann, and others. But many creative persons

240

have maintained good primary and secondary process connections throughout their lifetimes.

There is much we do not know about the Algernon Pendletons of this world. There is much we do not understand about our thinking processes and how they are related. Somewhere among the ushabti of our past, there ought to be a Eulalia that is less evasive.

QUESTIONS FOR DISCUSSION

1. What evidence would you present to convince a court that Algernon was not mentally competent? What evidence would you present to oppose this designation?

2. If you were a scenic designer and asked to stage the last scene with Madge in the tomb, Algernon at sea level, and Eulalia somewhere around, could you suggest some structural and dramatic ways of presenting the inner and outer world of Algernon?

3. Discuss your own emotional reactions to the mix of humor and the macabre in this selection.

4. Of all household objects with which one might wish to converse, a vase somehow seems particularly suitable. Do you agree? For what reasons? What other objects might offer companionship and conversation?

5. How would you characterize Eulalia's personality?

6. If Madge is really trapped in the tomb, how do you think Eulalia might convince Algernon to dig her up? Write a brief alternate ending to document this possibility.

7. If emotional disturbance reduces one's degrees of behavioral freedom, how is this concept illustrated in Algernon's behavior? in Eulalia's behavior? in their relationship?

ADDITIONAL READINGS

- Freud, Sigmund. "Formulations Regarding the Two Principles in Mental Functioning." In *Collected Papers,* vol. 4. New York: Basic Books, 1959.

- Hilgard, Ernest. "Impulsive Versus Realistic Thinking: An Examination of the Distinction Between Primary and Secondary Processes in Thought." *Psychological Bulletin* 59 (1962): 477-88.
- Vonnegut, Mark. *The Eden Express*. New York: Farrar, Straus, 1949.
- Jones, Richard M. *Fantasy and Feeling in Education*. New York: New York University Press, 1968.
- Long, Nicholas; Morse, William; and Newman, Ruth. *Conflict in the Classroom*. 2nd ed. Belmont, CA: Wadsworth, 1971.

"Good God, man, what would you be now
if you had been able to read"'

6

The Verger

W. Somerset Maugham

6

Reading seems to be one of those unique human aptitudes that, given half a biological and cultural chance, flourishes and prospers in most children. And in this world of cascading words, one can hardly contest its importance as a survival skill.

Without reading skills, a child's school life can only become more and more frustrating and hopeless. Unquestionably, reading disabilities in children cause parents to push panic buttons. Few persons — except perhaps a rare individual like Albert Edward Foreman, protagonist of "The Verger" — would argue the reality of such panic (and it *is* nice to have "The Verger" to remind us that all is not lost for all people with reading problems).

The research literature on reading disabilities is vast and complex, ranging as it does from specific medical, genetic, organic, emotional, motivational, and cultural deprivation as causes. To some extent reading problems are examined and described much like the proverbial elephant perceived by the cluster of blind men. Physicians and neurologists are particularly sensitive to organic and genetic causes and to specific etiologies called *dyslexias.* Psychologists and psychiatrists tend to focus on emotional and family related sources; ophthalmologists and opticians investigate the possibility of faulty eye movements associated with poor eye-hand and eye-motor coordination. Pediatricians look for indications of abnormal or slow maturation and other uneven growth factors. Sociologists and early childhood educators may suspect culturally related deprivations or inadequate language experiences. While these perceptual rigidities may be somewhat overdrawn, the tendency for reading disabilities to be fenced in by this or that profession is all too common.

Within our present boundaries of knowledge, reading disability can be compared to a high fever: The condition could have a number of causes, often interacting and overlapping. A child might

245

have a maturational lag, get pushed into reading, fail, become emotionally upset by his or her perceived stupidity, and strenuously avoid any further contact with the experience. Or early reading may be taught to children in so mundane and uninteresting a manner that a child's motivation to read is all but destroyed.

Reading is, after all, a sparking between a written squiggle and a mind. It's the sparking that connects the two — the electricity and excitement of imagination. It has always seemed to me that reading failure is in one sense a blunting of a child's imagination. And the relationship between juvenile delinquency and reading failure has been convincingly found to be positive, high, and reinforcing. In one study of reading disability among boys, adjudged delinquents had an incidence of eighty-three percent as compared to thirty-three percent in a normal population.[1]

Whenever excitement and adventure cannot be obtained through one's imagination and thoughts, one needs to seek it in the real world. In James T. Farrell's book *Studs Lonigan,* he reminisces about his childhood in South Chicago, recalls the usual street corner conversations among him and his friends in which a poverty of imagination and a lack of resources (What do you want to do? I don't know — what do you want to do? etc.) produced the crime-maker of childhood boredom.[2] Farrell recalls his leaving the group because of his interest in books and ideas, while his colleagues go off seeking excitement in the real world without success.

Claude Brown, author of *Manchild in the Promised Land,* recalls how this was with him.[3] By the time he was sixteen he had been in and out of several so-called correctional institutions. Despite his apparent ability, he had never learned to read until he was cajoled into it by the kindly wife of the superintendent of Warwick. The first book he read was the autobiography of some woman (as Brown puts it) named Mary McLeod Bethune. He gets interested and with the help of the superintendent's wife wades through specially written biographies of Jackie and Sugar Ray Robinson, Einstein, and Schweitzer. He was about sixteen at the time, but these stories really turned him on. "I kept reading and I kept enjoying it. I used to just sit around in the cottage reading.

---

[1] A. A. Fabian, "Reading Disability: An Index of Pathology," *American Journal of Orthopsychiatry* 35 (April 1955): 319-328.
[2] James T. Farrell, *Studs Lonigan* (New York: Avon, 1977).
[3] Claude Brown, *Manchild in the Promised Land* (New York: Macmillan, 1965).

I didn't bother with people and nobody bothered me. This was a way to be in Warwick and not to be there at the same time" (p. 151).

An old New England proverb strongly suggests that too much reading will rot the brain. Reading is not intended to replace living in the real world but to help make it more pleasant and enjoyable. Above all, it is the greatest invention for managing time, especially boredom. It is a magical resource unique to humans. How, then, did A. E. Foreman get along without it?

THE VERGER

W. Somerset Maugham

There had been a christening that afternoon at St. Peter's, Neville Square, and Albert Edward Foreman still wore his verger's gown. He kept his new one, its folds as full and stiff as though it were made not of alpaca but of perennial bronze, for funerals and weddings (St. Peter's, Neville Square, was a church much favoured by the fashionable for these ceremonies) and now he wore only his second-best. He wore it with complacence, for it was the dignified symbol of his office, and without it (when he took it off to go home) he had the disconcerting sensation of being somewhat insufficiently clad. He took pains with it; he pressed it and ironed it himself. During the sixteen years he had been verger of this church he had had a succession of such gowns, but he had never been able to throw them away when they were worn out and the complete series, neatly wrapped up in brown paper, lay in the bottom drawers of the wardrobe in his bedroom.

The verger busied himself quietly, replacing the painted wooden cover on the marble font, taking away a chair that had been brought for an infirm old lady, and waited for the vicar to have finished in the vestry so that he could tidy up in there and go home. Presently he saw him walk across the chancel, genuflect in front of the high altar and come down the aisle; but he still wore his cassock.

"What's he 'anging about for?" the verger said to himself. "Don't 'e know I want my tea?"

The vicar had been but recently appointed, a red-faced energetic man in the early forties, and Albert Edward still regretted

"The Verger," copyright © 1929, by W. Somerset Maugham, from *Cosmopolitans* in *The Complete Short Stories of W. Somerset Maugham*. Used by permission of Doubleday & Co.

his predecessor, a clergyman of the old school who preached leisurely sermons in a silvery voice and dined out a great deal with his more aristocratic parishioners. He liked things in church to be just so, but he never fussed; he was not like this new man who wanted to have his finger in every pie. But Albert Edward was tolerant. St. Peter's was in a very good neighbourhood and the parishioners were a very nice class of people. The new vicar had come from the East End and he couldn't be expected to fall in all at once with the discreet ways of his fashionable congregation.

"All this 'ustle," said Albert Edward. "But give 'im time, he'll learn."

When the vicar had walked down the aisle so far that he could address the verger without raising his voice more than was bcoming in a place of worship he stopped.

"Foreman, will you come into the vestry for a minute. I have something to say to you."

"Very good, sir."

The vicar waited for him to come up and they walked up the church together.

"A very nice christening, I thought, sir. Funny 'ow the baby stopped cryin' the moment you took him."

"I've noticed they very often do," said the vicar, with a little smile. "After all I've had a good deal of practice with them."

It was a source of subdued pride to him that he could nearly always quiet a whimpering infant by the manner in which he held it and he was not unconscious of the amused admiration with which mothers and nurses watched him settle the baby in the crook of his surpliced arm. The verger knew that it pleased him to be complimented on his talent.

The vicar preceded Albert Edward into the vestry. Albert Edward was a trifle surprised to find the two churchwardens there. He had not seen them come in. They gave him pleasant nods.

"Good-afternoon, my lord. Good-afternoon, sir," he said to one after the other.

They were elderly men, both of them, and they had been churchwardens almost as long as Albert Edward had been verger. They were sitting now at a handsome refectory table that the old vicar had brought many years before from Italy and the vicar sat down in the vacant chair between them. Albert Edward faced them, the table between him and them, and wondered with slight uneasiness what was the matter. He remembered still the occasion on which the organist had got into trouble and the bother they had all had to hush things up. In a church like St. Peter's, Neville Square, they couldn't afford a scandal. On the vicar's red face was a look of resolute benignity, but the others bore an expression that was slightly troubled.

"He's been naggin' them, he 'as," said the verger to himself. "He's jockeyed them into doin' something, but they don't 'alf like it. That's what it is, you mark my words."

But his thoughts did not appear on Albert Edward's clean-cut and distinguished features. He stood in a respectful but not obsequious attitude. He had been in service before he was appointed to his ecclesiastical office, but only in very good houses, and his deportment was irreproachable. Starting as a page-boy in the household of a merchant-prince, he had risen by due degrees from the position of fourth to first footman, for a year he had been single-handed butler to a widowed peeress and, till the vacancy occurred at St. Peter's, butler with two men under him in the house of a retired ambassador. He was tall, spare, grave and dignified. He looked, if not like a duke, at least like an actor of the old school who specialised in dukes' parts. He had tact, firmness and self-assurance. His character was unimpeachable.

The vicar began briskly.

"Foreman, we've got something rather unpleasant to say to you. You've been here a great many years and I think his lordship and the general agree with me that you've fulfilled the duties of your office to the satisfaction of everybody concerned."

The two churchwardens nodded.

"But a most extraordinary circumstance came to my knowledge the other day and I felt it my duty to impart it to the churchwardens. I discovered to my astonishment that you could neither read nor write."

The verger's face betrayed no sign of embarrassment.

"The last vicar knew that, sir," he replied. "He said it didn't make no difference. He always said there was a great deal too much education in the world for 'is taste."

"It's the most amazing thing I ever heard," cried the general. "Do you mean to say that you've been verger of this church for sixteen years and never learned to read or write?"

"I went into service when I was twelve, sir. The cook in the first place tried to teach me once, but I didn't seem to 'ave the knack for it, and then what with one thing and another I never seemed to 'ave the time. I've never really found the want of it. I think a lot of these young fellows waste a rare lot of time readin' when they might be doin' something useful."

"But don't you want to know the news?" said the other church-warden. "Don't you ever want to write a letter?"

"No, me lord, I seem to manage very well without. And of late years now they've all these pictures in the papers I get to know what's goin' on pretty well. Me wife's quite a scholar and if I want to write a letter she writes it for me. It's not as if I was a bettin' man."

The two churchwardens gave the vicar a troubled glance and then looked down at the table.

"Well, Foreman, I've talked the matter over with these gentlemen and they quite agree with me that the situation is impossible. At a church like St. Peter's, Neville Square, we cannot have a verger who can neither read nor write."

Albert Edward's thin, sallow face reddened and he moved uneasily on his feet, but he made no reply.

"Understand me, Foreman, I have no complaint to make against you. You do your work quite satisfactorily; I have the highest opinion both of your character and of your capacity; but we haven't the right to take the risk of some accident that might happen owing to your lamentable ignorance. It's a matter of prudence as well as of principle."

"But couldn't you learn, Foreman?" asked the general.

"No, sir, I'm afraid I couldn't, not now. You see, I'm not as young as I was and if I couldn't seem able to get the letters in me 'ead when I was a nipper I don't think there's much chance of it now."

"We don't want to be harsh with you, Foreman," said the vicar. "But the churchwardens and I have quite made up our minds. We'll give you three months and if at the end of that time you cannot read and write I'm afraid you'll have to go."

Albert Edward had never liked the new vicar. He'd said from the beginning that they'd made a mistake when they gave him St. Peter's. He wasn't the type of man they wanted with a classy congregation like that. And now he straightened himself a little.

He knew his value and he wasn't going to allow himself to be put upon.

"I'm very sorry, sir, I'm afraid it's no good. I'm too old a dog to learn new tricks. I've lived a good many years without knowin' 'ow to read and write, and without wishin' to praise myself, self-praise is no recommendation, I don't mind sayin' I've done my duty in that state of life in which it 'as pleased a merciful providence to place me, and if I *could* learn now I don't know as I'd want to."

"In that case, Foreman, I'm afraid you must go."

"Yes, sir, I quite understand. I shall be 'appy to 'and in my resignation as soon as you've found somebody to take my place."

But when Albert Edward with his usual politeness had closed the church door behind the vicar and the two churchwardens he could not sustain the air of unruffled dignity with which he had borne the blow inflicted upon him and his lips quivered. He walked slowly back to the vestry and hung up on its proper peg his verger's gown. He sighed as he thought of all the grand funerals and smart weddings it had seen. He tidied everything up, put on his coat, and hat in hand walked down the aisle. He locked the church door behind him. He strolled across the square, but deep in his sad thoughts he did not take the street that led him home, where a nice strong cup of tea awaited him; he took the wrong turning. He walked slowly along. His heart was heavy. He did not know what he should do with himself. He did not fancy the notion of going back to domestic service; after being his own master for so many years, for the vicar and churchwardens could say what they liked, it was he that had run St. Peter's, Neville Square, he could scarcely demean himself by accepting a situation. He had saved a tidy sum, but not enough to live on without doing something, and life seemed to cost more every year. He had never thought to be troubled with such questions. The vergers of St. Peter's, like the popes of Rome, were there for life. He had often thought of the pleasant reference the vicar would make in his sermon at evensong the first Sunday after his death to the long and faithful service, and the exemplary character of their late verger, Albert Edward Foreman. He sighed deeply. Albert Edward was a non-smoker and a total abstainer, but with a certain latitude; that is to say he liked a glass of beer with his dinner and when he was tired he enjoyed a cigarette. It occurred to him now that one would comfort him and since he did not carry them he looked about him for a shop where he could buy a packet of Gold Flakes. He did not at once see one and walked on a little. It was a long street, with all sorts of shops in it, but there was not a single one where you could buy cigarettes.

"That's strange," said Albert Edward.

To make sure he walked right up the street again. No, there was no doubt about it. He stopped and looked reflectively up and down.

"I can't be the only man as walks along this street and wants a fag," he said. "I shouldn't wonder but what a fellow might do very well with a little shop here. Tobacco and sweets, you know."

He gave a sudden start.

"That's an idea," he said. "Strange 'ow things come to you when you least expect it."

He turned, walked home, and had his tea.

"You're very silent this afternoon, Albert," his wife remarked.

"I'm thinkin'," he said.

He considered the matter from every point of view and next day he went along the street and by good luck found a little shop to let that looked as though it would exactly suit him. Twenty-four hours later he had taken it and when a month after that he left St. Peter's, Neville Square, for ever, Albert Edward Foreman set up in business as a tobacconist and newsagent. His wife said it was a dreadful come-down after being verger of St. Peter's, but he answered that you had to move with the times, the church wasn't what it was, and 'enceforward he was going to render unto Caesar what was Caesar's. Albert Edward did very well. He did so well that in a year or so it struck him that he might take a second shop and put a manager in. He looked for another long street that hadn't got a tobacconist in it and when he found it, and a shop to let, took it and stocked it. This was a success too. Then it occurred to him that if he could run two he could run half a dozen, so he began walking about London, and whenever he found a long street that had no tobacconist and a shop to let he took it. In the course of ten years he had acquired no less than ten shops and he was making money hand over fist. He went round to all of them himself every Monday, collected the week's takings and took them to the bank.

One morning when he was there paying in a bundle of notes and a heavy bag of silver the cashier told him that the manager would like to see him. He was shown into an office and the manager shook hands with him.

"Mr. Foreman, I wanted to have a talk to you about the money you've got on deposit with us. D'you know exactly how much it is?"

"Not within a pound or two, sir; but I've got a pretty rough idea."

"Apart from what you paid in this morning it's a little over thirty thousand pounds. That's a very large sum to have on deposit and I should have thought you'd do better to invest it."

"I wouldn't want to take no risk, sir. I know it's safe in the bank."

"You needn't have the least anxiety. We'll make you out a list of absolutely gilt-edged securities. They'll bring you in a better rate of interest than we can possibly afford to give you."

A troubled look settled on Mr. Foreman's distinguished face. "I've never 'ad anything to do with stocks and shares and I'd 'ave to leave it all in your 'ands," he said.

The manager smiled. "We'll do everything. All you'll have to do next time you come in is just to sign the transfers."

"I could do that all right," said Albert uncertainly. "But 'ow should I know what I was signin'?"

"I suppose you can read," said the manager a trifle sharply.

Mr. Foreman gave him a disarming smile.

"Well, sir, that's just it. I can't. I know it sounds funny-like, but there it is, I can't read or write, only me name, an' I only learnt to do that when I went into business."

The manager was so surprised that he jumped up from his chair.

"That's the most extraordinary thing I ever heard."

"You see, it's like this, sir, I never 'ad the opportunity until it was too late and then some'ow I wouldn't. I got obstinate-like."

The manager stared at him as though he were a prehistoric monster.

"And do you mean to say that you've built up this important business and amassed a fortune of thirty thousand pounds without being able to read or write? Good God, man, what would you be now if you had been able to?"

"I can tell you that, sir," said Mr. Foreman, a little smile on his still aristocratic features. "I'd be verger of St. Peter's, Neville Square."

During my search for literature for this volume, a colleague called to recommend this story. "I'll tell you frankly," he said, "I don't like Maugham, but this story really tickled me." As for me, I do like Maugham and have never really lost the excitement and suspense of the first reading of *Ashenden: Secret Agent,* whom I encountered as a youth.

Somerset Maugham started his career life as a physician specializing in obstetrics in nineteenth century England. Like Foreman, he gave up one career for another when, much to his surprise, some plays he had written were produced and praised. He then started to deliver more plays, short stories, and novels than babies, and dropped his initial career. His first major novel, *Of Human Bondage,* was about a physically handicapped medical student having a variety of what in today's parlance would be called "identity crises." Maugham himself, although delighting in conversation and chatter, was a heavy stutterer and highly sensitive to problems of the handicapped.

It is interesting that Maugham chose a verger to be his fortunate nonreader. Vergers are versatile workers in churches, serving as sacristans, ushers, caretakers, and handymen. St. Peter's, Neville Square, serves a well-heeled class of people in a good neighborhood. Can such an institution take the chance of having an illiterate person as a verger?

Despite all the data on reading disabilities, nothing in A. E. Foreman fits any of it. His lack of literacy bothers him not a whit. He admits without regret that he is "too old a dog to learn new tricks." Without wishing to praise himself, he has done well without this important skill. One recognizes immediately that Albert Edward is not your ordinary verger — with two recognizable first names of royalty and a fine surname, our protagonist is bound for better things!

In spite of his handicap, Albert Edward Foreman has learned a few things. He praises the vicar for doing well what the vicar himself was proud of doing well. Albert recalls that the last vicar wasn't bothered by illiteracy in a verger and added that there was "too much education in the world" anyway. Albert has gotten by all these years, so why change? ("If I couldn't seem able to get the letters in me 'ead when I was a nipper, I don't think there's much chance of it now.")

The tragedy of Albert Edward Foreman's "dyslexia" and illiteracy builds. His years of dutiful service in the church are over. Does he go out into the cruel world in search of a "fag" to smoke along the road to ruin? Not so. Like many of Maugham's creations, Albert thumbs his nose at convention, thinks his way to success, steps into his limousine, and rides off into the glorious sunset.

QUESTIONS FOR DISCUSSION

1. From all indications, what is your best guess on why A. E. Foreman never learned to read?

2. Why are reading disabilities fairly common in some countries like the United States and rather rare in other countries like Japan (for example)?

3. Would you agree or disagree with the churchwardens and the vicar in giving Foreman three months to learn to read and write or be fired? If you agree, also take Foreman's side and justify his action in objecting to this stipulation.

4. Why do you suppose Maugham selected the job of verger for Foreman? What other jobs might Foreman have had and survived?

5. Foreman seems not at all demeaned by or ashamed of his inability to read or write. Why do you think this is so?

6. How did you learn to read?

7. How would you differentiate reading a textbook from reading *Huckleberry Finn* or *The Hobbit*?

8. The vicar tells Foreman that he has no complaints about his work, his character, or his capacity, but he adds, "We haven't the right to take the risk of some accident that might happen owing to your lamentable ignorance." Can you think of any real or hypothetical accidents that the vicar might have had in mind? If not, what *did* he have in mind?

ADDITIONAL READINGS

- Bower, Eli M., ed. *Orthopsychiatry and Education.* Detroit: Wayne State University Press, 1971. (Section on reading as a significant skill including the rarity of reading disability in Japanese children, p. 181-255)
- Brown, Claude. *Manchild in the Promised Land.* New York: Macmillan, 1965.
- Coles, Gerald S. "The Learning-Disabilities Test Battery: Empirical and Social Issues." *Harvard Educational Review* 48 (Aug. 1978): 313-40.
- Fabian, A. A. "Reading Disability: An Index of Pathology." *American Journal of Orthopsychiatry* 35 (April 1955): 319-28.
- Miller, Alan D.; Margolin, Joseph B.; and Yolles, Stanley F. "Epidemiology of Reading Disabilities: Some Methodologic Considerations and Early Findings." *American Journal of Public Health* 47 (1957): 1250-56.
- White, Robert W. *Lives in Progress.* New York: Holt, Rinehart and Winston, 1952.
- Wright, Richard. *Black Boy.* New York: Signet Books, 1951.

"I'd repeat the alphabet slowly, 'A', and he'd say 'A' . . ."

7

Recovery with Aphasia

C. Scott Moss

7

"I'd repeat the alphabet slowly, 'A,' and he'd say 'A'; and I'd say 'B' and he'd say 'beh' and then I'd get on to 'D' and he'd say 'A' again." So it goes with Scott Moss being helped by his wife to recover from aphasia.

What is aphasia? Most definitions refer to impairment in the expression or reception of language as a result of some kind of brain injury. Because adults are rarely without language, some authorities differentiate between adult conditions, often called dysphasia, and aphasia in children. If language has not been acquired by a child, he or she may be said to have developmental or congenital aphasia. This is different from childhood aphasia, in which the impairment occurs after some language has been obtained.

Most investigators further differentiate aphasia into (a) expressive, (b) receptive, (c) mixed, (d) agrammatic, and (e) amnesic aphasias. Expressive aphasics cannot find words or expressions that fit their thoughts, or the words they come up with are off the mark. Receptive aphasics hear differently from what is said, or hear gibberish. Mixed aphasics have difficulty in both processes — as is often the case. Agrammatic aphasics have trouble with grammar, and amnesic aphasics with memory for objects and names. None of these classifications is exclusive, and neurologists or linguists do not universally agree upon any of the classifications. Some authorities question whether aphasia in the usual sense exists in childhood[1] or can be defined as above. Indeed, a conference of experts concluded that the problem of formulating a definition of aphasia was more than a trivial matter of rhetoric.[2]. To date, the debate and lack of consensus continue.

---

[1] Nancy Wood, *Language Disorders in Children* (Chicago: National Society for Cripped Children and Adults, 1959).

[2] Charles Osgood and Murray Miron, *Approaches to the Study of Aphasia* (Urbana: University of Illinois, 1963).

Of the selections in this volume, this is one of two nonfictional inclusions. My rationale for including it is that, notwithstanding its truth, it reads much like good fiction. In addition, I have discovered no other fiction or nonfiction that so well depicts the emotional and family interactive factors in speech and communicative disorders as does the Moss book. What is unique about this account of Scott Moss' stroke and subsequent recovery is his ability to recall, often in painstaking detail, how it all went, and to have his wife respond to and narrate the same events from her perspective. Scott Moss had been trained to be a keen observer of clinical and interpersonal detail. The reader finds that, despite the stroke, Moss does not lose his skill in observing the most difficult subject of all — self. Moss also exemplifies how unique are the mediations of handicaps and injuries. For Moss, aphasia was both a catastrophe and an opportunity.

The book from which this selection was extracted begins with the Moss family preparing to move from San Francisco (where Moss had been a psychologist in the regional office of the National Institute of Mental Health) to Champaign and the University of Illinois, where he had accepted a position in the Department of Psychology. After getting somewhat settled, Moss goes off to a symposium, attempts to get ready for his advising, and meets his colleagues and neighbors.

RECOVERY WITH APHASIA

C. Scott Moss

On Monday, October 30, I was working in my office at about four o'clock when a colleague of mine, Len Ullmann, came in. It was during this session that I experienced an abrupt coughing spell which I attributed to his cigarette smoke. I excused myself and went to the drinking fountain, and after a few minutes the coughing subsided. However, I noticed then that vision in my right eye had become askewed. Also, the thumb on my right hand had become numb. I attempted to continue working, but my vision prevented concentration on the written material. So at a few minutes before five I decided to go home. I commented to my wife on my peculiar symptoms, but actually regarded them as only minor, though troublesome, afflictions that I hoped would soon pass.

After dinner I again attempted to read the newspaper, but couldn't, and I began to experience a sharp pain that was at first in the back of my head and then moved to the left side of my temple. I have never been bothered by headaches and I suppose this should have alerted me that something was terribly amiss, but it didn't. My wife fixed a hot water bottle and I held it to the side of my head. By about ten o'clock the pain had somewhat subsided though my eyesight had not improved, and I settled down to try to watch a replay of a recent Green Bay-Bears game.

At about eleven o'clock I experienced another coughing spell, and this one would not stop. My wife became frightened and, wishing to believe that I was teasing her, turned off the TV. Despite my coughing I made a move toward the TV, only to find myself

Excerpts from *Recovery with Aphasia,* by C. Scott Moss. Copyright © 1972 by the University of Illinois Press. Used by permission of the author and the University of Illinois Press.

on the floor. Though I did not realize it at the time, the right side of my body had become paralyzed. Bette thought for a moment that I was malingering; however, as she explained to me much later, she knew something had happened when I tried to smile at her and only the left side of my face lit up. I heard her go to the phone and summon an ambulance. She then came back beside me and attempted to subdue my further efforts to rise.

I was conscious or at least semiconscious the whole time. I vaguely remember seeing the ambulance drivers coming in, being rolled onto a cot, feeling rain fall on my face, hearing the sound of the distant siren, and being taken to the emergency room at a local hospital. There was a nurse and also an attendant there who tried to speak with me. Things were hazy but I was in no pain, although I could not talk back to them. Eventually my wife arrived, having called the director of the clinical psychology division, Don Peterson, who came and stayed with the children while Bette came to the hospital. At about one o'clock the doctor in charge of the emergency calls arrived. I then did in retrospect an amazing thing: The paralysis had largely left me and I shifted over on my side and proceeded to engage in an appropriate conversation, experiencing only one or two blocks.

I was then wheeled upstairs to the pediatrics ward, since there were no beds on the adult wards. Bette stayed with me until almost three o'clock. For some reason I remember feeling very depressed. One could call it a premonition of things to come. Just that morning I had taken and passed my physical exam for incoming faculty members. Thinking about it months later, it became obvious to me that such examinations are limited in value in the absence of specific symptoms, since a few hours after the exam I was to suffer a debilitating stroke.

The next morning when I awoke, I was completely and totally aphasic. I was given a neurological examination, an EEG, and later a chest X-ray. As I learned later, the hospital simply lacked skilled clinicians to diagnose my case, though obviously I was a severely brain-damaged patient. On the fourth day, at the insistence of my wife, I was transferred by ambulance to Presbyterian-St. Luke's Hospital in Chicago. My wife and my mother accompanied me in the ambulance. For eight days the staff there pried and prodded me: a brain scan, spinal tap, skull films, and an angiogram were among the techniques utilized.

My life as a patient was uneventful. I was still in no pain. For the most part, I simply slept or dozed. I did comprehend somewhat vaguely what was said to me, but I could not answer except in gestures or by neologisms. I knew the language I used was not correct but I was quite unable to select the appropriate words. I recollect trying to read the headlines of the *Chicago Tribune* but they didn't make any sense to me at all. I didn't have any difficulty focusing; it was simply that the words, individually or in combination, didn't have any meaning, and even more amazing, I was only a trifle bothered by that fact.

My wife and my mother were with me and they helped comfort me, feeding me at mealtime and keeping me company. My appetite was largely delinquent, and in the next couple of weeks my weight fell twenty pounds. I did not have a bowel movement during the week I was hospitalized, and fortunately or otherwise, no one thought to check on it. I did feel critical (and still do) about the way I was handled by the two surgical residents assigned to my case. Quite unintentionally they imparted the feeling that they were only interested in my *neurological* impairment, and didn't respond to me as a whole human being, one filled with *psychological* reactions at having suffered a catastrophic accident. I attributed this initially to the fact that I couldn't communicate with them and therefore was not sensitive to their interactions with me. Now I realize that this was standard procedure for neurosurgeons, but I still think it is a shame not to treat the patient as a whole personality.

As I look back on it now, I had relatively little concern for the children, my wife, or the home — I was too far out of it to care. I had come so very close to death that I more or less welcomed it. It was indeed, as I experienced it, a very painless way to go. In fact, for a long time afterward I was confident that I was living on borrowed time, and I expected it to expire at any moment. It was as if the stroke had benumbed any emotional investment in the future and I simply shrugged at my perception of my imminent demise.

At the end of a full week, and again at the behest of my wife, I was discharged. A student and his wife drove our car to Chicago and I recall that I was slightly chagrined that I could not converse with them on the drive home. A colleague and his wife had stayed at the house with the children and apparently they all got along very well. It was nice to be in familiar surroundings again.

For a month I stayed in bed or lounged about the house in my bathrobe. A few words of halting, limited speech began to come back to me. Eventually it was time to go to the office again. My wife transported me to and from campus for the next three weeks. They were only token visits and I would stay for about half an hour. Later, when I began driving myself, it was at first strange. It was as if I were learning to coordinate the visual-motor function all over again. The members of the staff seemed glad to see me, and it was nice to be back again but the difference was simply enormous. I was unable to engage in even normal conversation, let alone deal with more elaborate conceptions. For instance, despite my best efforts I would block even on the most minimal words. Holding a minor conversation of even a few words would be quite taxing for me. I could never tell if what I had to say would come out right — even asking for a pencil from the secretary had to be elaborately planned and painfully carried out.

The second week I ran into a colleague who happened to mention that it must be very frustrating for me to be aphasic since prior to that I had been so verbally facile. I assured him that it was not upsetting and then later found myself wondering why it was not. I think part of the explanation was relatively simple. If I had lost the ability to converse with others, I had also lost the ability even to engage in self-talk. In other words, I did not have the ability to think about the future — to worry, to anticipate or perceive it — at least not with words. Thus, for the first five or six weeks after hospitalization I simply existed. So the fact that I could not use words even internally was, in fact, a safeguard. I imagine it was somewhat similar to undergoing a lobotomy or lobectomy in the dissociation from the future. It was as if without words I could not be concerned about tomorrow.

In the period of January 9 to January 23, I had two meetings in Chicago with Dr. Joseph Wepman, a psychological expert in aphasia. Bette accompanied me by train on the 125-mile trip. I was given a series of tests, and while my performance was of a high level compared to the average brain-damaged patient, nevertheless I was aware of some impairment on the items. I had extreme difficulty in following abstractions of a professional nature (I could follow the meaning of a single sentence but I had difficulty in comprehending the whole). Similarly, I had difficulty in following a digit span for more than five or six numbers (less backwards) and also in defining proverbs (I could still define them at an abstract level but now I had to work around to the answer rather than going directly to it as I had done before). I also had decided deficits in memory. Immediately upon my return from Presbyterian-St. Luke's, I sat down with my wife and tried to remember the names of people we had known in San Carlos; while I was able to picture them, I was completely unable to recall their names, even those of our two next-door neighbors.

It was with regard to a summary meeting with Dr. Wepman in about the middle of January that I found myself while in the bathtub actually beginning to anticipate the rudiments of a discussion that I would have with him.* Thus, for the first time I was aware that my inner speech was returning. It is difficult to explain what it was like to be entirely without internal verbalizations. I bathed, shaved, and selected my clothing with appropriateness, for instance, on the few occasions when I got dressed, but without words to express what I was doing, even to myself. It was as though I could perform the automatic habits that I had learned through a lifetime, but would be lost once the demands were made for increasing abstractness.

At this meeting on the 23rd, Dr. Wepman reported that I had improved greatly in the three-week interim, and that in several more months I should be largely restored. He did not have knowledge of what had actually happened to me, because he had not had access to the medical report. He assumed that fat had been given off from the heart, had blocked the carotid artery temporarily, and then had been dissolved. He stated that if the block had remained lodged for even four or five minutes, I would have become a "vegetable." He also said I would continue to manifest organic symptoms for the next several months, but he saw no reason to continue seeing me since I would readily improve. He would be happy to see me in the spring when I was recovered! He concluded that since I had absolutely no premorbid signs this was a "one-time" thing for me.

Finally, he stated that I would benefit little from seeing a speech therapist. From his point of view, time was the primary

*I used to love hot baths during this period. I liked to soak for 45 minutes to an hour, two or even three times a day. Lest the psychodynamically inclined be tempted to overinterpret, this was because the house we had rented turned out to be incompletely insulated.

factor in my recovery, and this was a physiological rather a psychological factor. It was in this conversation that he happened to remark that Dr. Erika Fromm (also at the University of Chicago) had worked for the past couple of years with hypnosis in simulating organic symptoms in normal subjects. I at once replied that I knew Erika and it would be interesting to provide her a brain-injured patient, myself, and see what she could do about restoring normality through hypnosis and age regression. Hypnosis and hypnotherapy had been an interest of mine throughout my professional career.

From that date until early in March I continued to improve. I could exchange pleasantries with a person as long as it was not expected that I would initiate topics or provide much information. I still was unable to handle the abstractions involved in clinical work. I could not read literature or really talk with my colleagues about professional issues. My wife and I nevertheless worked as hard as we were able to recapture my facility with professional jargon and to renew my acquaintance with abstract conceptions. Around the time that I began to visit my office again, we sat down to work on five papers which I had committed myself to complete. The first paper was a survey on the "Experimental Induction of Dreams." Fortunately, I had progressed considerably on the paper bfore my accident, but it still had to be finished, tidied up, and typed.

I cannot begin to describe how immensely difficult it was to read and summarize the various passages that still remained. It was an unholy, tortuous business. I attempted to dictate to Bette what I wanted to say, and not being able to do this, I reacted strongly at times, sometimes pounding my fists or simply repeating the same gibberish over and over. The normal anxiety over my immediate performance was obviously beginning to return. It seemed so much easier to have my wife read the passages and have me somehow, with her great assistance, manage to indicate what should be done with them. I would stumble about, trying somehow to voice the meaning, my wife would listen to me for some period of time, and then attempt to repeat the gist of what I had to say. Often we would go round and round on certain issues. The result was that the paper ended up half mine and half her own translation of what she thought I had meant to convey. The editors' acceptance of the paper a few weeks later greatly buoyed our spirits (Moss, 1968). Gradually, over some months, as I did a better job of dictating, these extremely difficult periods tended to subside, although I have always been critical about my performance without really being able to do much about it.

On February 1 I volunteered to take on a section of eight students, monitoring them in psychotherapy. Don Peterson was delighted, but I did this with considerable hesitance. It was again a matter of my walking a narrow line between what I was able to do and what I could not yet afford to do. I could not speak with the students at all in the way that I formerly had, being unable to discuss the therapy recordings in detail or their ramifications. Nevertheless, I could deal with questions in a sort of non-directive fashion, as long as too copious an answer wasn't demanded. I also listened to the student-client recordings between sessions and directed Bette to transcribe selected responses while trying not to rob the sessions of all their spontaneity in the process. I managed to complete the course in June, and the students were most generous in their ratings of my performance, though I felt much less than adequate.

It was of interest to me how in a day or even an hour I could feel relatively good and the next moment regress. This matter of recovery is an uncertain thing — it is an uphill struggle of a most uneven character. When I responded to external demands, I could marshal unusual effort for a limited time; for example, when talking on the telephone with the friends and acquaintances who called us I was probably at my optimum. It reminded me of having heard of stutterers who lose their speech defect on the phone. It may have had some relationship to the restricted number of stimuli which I was forced to cope with on the phone. But given time to sit around the house and dwell on my symptoms, or in any type of direct interpersonal relationship and every contact extended me, I was immediately reminded of my glaring deficiencies.

I also found that I was easily distracted; for example, I was not too restrained with the children. Before, I had been able to select what I wanted to watch on TV and noises had not bothered me. But now I found that any distraction was quite upsetting, and I reacted by removing the offender or turning up the volume on the TV until the noise became intolerable to others. On the other side, the TV was a great pacifier: I could vicariously enjoy the human interactions without being called upon to participate.

In February, 1968, I began therapy with the university speech department. I felt that there was virtue in giving my wife some respite from my many demands on her. I met twice a week with a young graduate trainee who was unstructured in her demands but who gave me her undivided attention for an hour each week. On February 27 I reported that for the first time since my accident I remembered a dream. It was of interest to me that for the four-month period I did not recall a single dream. This struck me as a curious state of affairs since for years I had been interested in the study and meaning of dreams; however, my stroke apparently impaired either the ability to have dreams or my capacity to remember them. I lay down each night for seven or eight hours of uninterrupted sleep. It was as if during the daytime I had no words to express what was happening and at night I had no dreams — it was a complete and total vacuum of self-speech for me.

Perhaps Greenberg and Dewan (1968) are correct in saying that in aphasia dreaming serves to integrate new information into existing past information stores. I tended to dream in pictures, of course, but without words the memory of these nocturnal images was lost. Since my big white boxer dog "dreams" every evening without words, for example, this leads to the speculation that perhaps I didn't dream during the recovery period from my accident. How else would one account for the fact that even today I hold many waking memories from my period of hospitalization and the first few months when I had no words to describe these events even to myself, but at the same time do not remember having dreamed at all during these four months. Further evidence is that as I recovered my internal verbalizations, the memory of noctural mentation began to recur.

When I entered into ordinary conversation after five or six months, I had progressed sufficiently to talk more or less normally until I came to a word on which I might block. Unlike former times at that juncture, *absolutely nothing* came to mind — it was an absolute zero — there were no alternatives from which to choose. I purchased a crossword puzzle book to give me facility in learning synonyms. The problem of dealing with abstractions also continued to plague me during this period. It took a great deal of effort for me to keep an abstraction in mind. For example, in talking with the speech therapist I would begin to give a definition of an abstract concern, but as I held it in mind it would sort of fade, and chances were that I'd end up giving a simplified version rather than one at the original level of conception. It was as though giving an abstraction required so much of my addled intelligence that halfway through the definition I would run out of the energy available to me and regress to a more concrete answer. Something like this happened again and again.

It was also fascinating to me how completely and totally fixed I was on the "here and now." Even former events just prior to my accident had faded. In regard to my professional work, I recognized the terms that were used, but in a sense they had receded into the distant past rather than being immediately in my awareness. And in the same vein, thought about the future was most difficult. So both the past and the future had faded for me, and I existed almost exclusively in the present. In working with my speech therapist, for instance, I had been attempting to explain the general conceptions of community health. As long as I stuck to the paper or an outline, I did relatively well. But without the outline I rapidly floundered, although I could answer specific questions that were asked. In essence, then, I was unable to keep in mind a verbal outline of what I had to say. This in broader perspective is what happened to me generally. I was unable to generate a gestalt of either my previous life or the future, and therefore life beyond the immediate situation was meaningless. This restriction held not only for my work but for all personal life as well. For example, five months after the accident I was able to recall occasionally the names of some people who were our San Carlos neighbors, but I could not embroider them with associations as I had formerly.

From March 14 through March 18 I was a patient at Michael Reese Hospital, where I had volunteered as an experimental subject for Dr. Doris Gruenewald, a colleague of Erika Fromm whom I had also met previously. I traveled to Chicago without my wife, which indicates that I was making some progress. It was Dr. Gruenewald's job, if possible, to induce me into hypnosis, cause me to regress beyond the time when I had suffered my stroke, and determine whether I had recovered, to any appreciable extent, my normal method of speaking and thinking. It was at best a far-out experimental effort which reflected my desperation that hypnotherapy might help.

271

I was admitted to a locked psychiatric ward in which most of the patients had partial "open-door privileges." It was a peculiar and unique personal experience for anyone, especially for a clinical psychologist who often had wondered what the experience would be like behind locked doors. I was treated exactly the same as all the other patients; for instance, the nurses immediately went through my suitcase and took my medicine and my razor. Prior to any attempts at hypnosis, I was given a complete physical and neurological examination. I passed the examination in excellent shape. I also had a prehypnotic EEG taken while I was in a drugged sleep. The reason for this phase of the study was a report by Kupper in 1945. Through hypnotic age-regression he had supposedly transported an epileptic patient back beyond the period of traumatic injury and what had previously been very morbid then turned into a normal-appearing electroencephalogram. I was extremely skeptical of this experiment; no one had replicated the study to my knowledge.

During the examination with Doris Gruenewald, it occurred to me to tell her of an experience which I had suffered twenty-two years before. I was stationed for the last year of military service in World War II with a B-29 group on Guam. When we were not busy with the planes, we used to play a great deal of bridge, often three to five hours a day. In the middle of February, 1946, I was transported back to the United States and in a couple of days was separated from service. Sometime that summer, a group of us were sitting around when I suggested that perhaps we could play bridge. None of the rest knew the game so I volunteered to teach them. I took a pack of cards, shuffled them, and then found I couldn't remember a thing about how to play bridge, that is, I couldn't remember how many cards were dealt, if you drew for some cards — in short, absolutely nothing. I had to buy a book to recapture how to play bridge. I attributed this experience to essentially two factors: (1) a complete change of setting so that past associations with bridge had been completely cut off, and (2) the repression with which I dealt with my combat experiences. During the period of military service, I had kept rather complete records of what I did. Later, in going through these diaries, I recalled the things that had happened to me, but in a very real sense I had intellectualized and isolated them from the associated affect. It was in a way as if I had never been in service at all. I

recalled this as a way of explaining my sense of distance from things both of a personal and professional nature prior to my accident.

Dr. Gruenewald, of course, suspected that perhaps I had an ulterior motive in telling her of this episode. It became increasingly clear to me as we talked that I had never really experienced any real affective discharge toward this stroke. For the first six or seven weeks I had experienced no emotion at all, then later, until now, I had experienced momentary frustrations toward internal or external obstacles, but again, no ventilation regarding my disability. I had in a sense treated my whole accident as if I were sort of an experimental subject, an "object" for investigation rather than a person who had experienced a terrible trauma. It was a defense consistent with my identity as a professional person interested in research. Each person adapts to his organicity with his in-built psychological mechanisms.

The first session brought home to me the degree to which I had suppressed the situation. I was not a good hypnotic subject, as I might have suspected from studies having to do with the susceptibility of other operators. Nevertheless, I listened to Doris' induction procedures on hypnosis and tried to follow them, although it was very difficult not to intellectualize the situation. I succeeded in going into a very modest trance or at least a hypnoidal state. During this initial session, Doris asked me to go back to San Carlos and, through a projective hypnotic technique, inquired what I was doing. I thought of the house and pictured Bette and me working outside, planting flowers. I was immediately caught up in what it had meant for Bette and the children to move to Illinois. It was quite a concession for her to have to cut herself off from her friends and her home there. Very soon the tears were flowing. Bette and the children had given up so much to come here, primarily for the furthering of my professional career, which had now been cut short.

In the second session, Doris relinquished her attempts at hypnosis and placed the responsibility directly on me. Again, I have the feeling that I was partially successful in inducing self-hypnosis, although we spoke mostly of my professional activities with NIMH. I recalled that the night before I had had what might be called a posthypnotic dream. I was back working for NIMH and was busy looking through a list of research-approved grants,

attempting to find out what happened to the grant of a colleague at the university. Then the scene was transformed and I was engaged in giving research consultation. I don't remember the details, but we were having an excellent time and I performed most adequately. This recalled in turn the first dream that I had had on February 27. In that dream I had accepted the fact that I was limited because of my stroke and had gone back to work at Fulton State Hospital (in Missouri). I was in charge of the psychology training program. Since I was unable to train people directly, because of my accident, I was looking through a file drawer of previous tapes that might be utilized for that purpose. We felt that the dream about NIMH was relatively positive in contrast to the earlier dream, which featured my acceptance of my disability.

Dr. Gruenewald had prepared a series of psychological tests based on my description of the areas in which I still suffered some deficit. On the day of my admission, I took a test battery in the waking condition and repeated it under hypnosis; but I do not think it was really successful. On Monday afternoon, prior to my departure from the hospital, I had a postexperimental battery. We tried hetero- and auto-hypnosis in relation to the test battery, but the effect, if any, soon wore off. In the EEG laboratory I attempted auto-hypnosis in lieu of drugs and surprisingly seemed to go to sleep without any medication. The lab technician at the time reported that I had been deeply asleep, but later in her written report of the examination stated that I was awake during the procedure, apparently because no medication was given to induce physiological sleep. The second EEG was essentially similar to the first. Six weeks later, a report from Doris on the psychological tests stated that there was no difference between the pre- and post-tests other than a slight positive finding on the post-test which could be attributable to a practice effect.

There is one other important event that bears mention in this brief period of hospitalization. I was interviewed by the ward psychiatrist, and in going over what had happened to me I recounted how the past and the future seemed to have lost all meaning for me. He dismissed this symptom as a variation of retrograde amnesia, although he admitted he had never heard a patient discuss the symptom quite as I had. In retrospect, I doubt very much that his conception could have been an explanation of what I had

experienced. As I understand it, the victim either organically blots out or represses the specific circumstances surrounding the time of his accident and the immediate events leading up to it. My problem was exactly the opposite: I remembered in great detail the situation leading up to my accident, and the trauma surrounding it. It was, in effect, an event that I remembered *too well* (even though I had no words to describe much of it at the time). The stroke acted as some sort of massive retroactive inhibition* which caused the gross dilution of all other experiences in my life.

Anyway, I came home from the hospital and for the next three weeks was deeply depressed. It was a most unusual depression for me since formerly I had tended to bounce back quickly from adversity. Bette was coming down with a cold and I did not tell her what had transpired except in very general terms. But when the depression lifted, the sense of distance from my past and future life was also gone. My life had become unified again! Somehow I connect my perception of the concept of *time* with this event. When I came to Illinois, I had an infinite amount of time to continue my professional career; after the accident, every minute was at a premium. It was as though in the instant of the accident I had been transformed from a very much alive, striving, professional person to a patient in a state of complete acceptance of death. Six months after the accident I still felt that if I could just interact in the next brief interpersonal exchange I would be thankful. I counted my objectives as measured by the hour, day, or, at most, a week.

BETTE'S PERCEPTION OF THE EVENTS

Upon my persistent urgings Bette finally sat down at the tape recorder in June of 1968 and dictated her memory of the accident

---

*This is a psychological-experimental term which in learning theory means the intervention of a strident stimulus that causes preceding learned stimuli to be forgotten or repressed. Much later, I ran across the term "cultural shock" which seemed to me to capture at least part of the original sharp constriction. Cultural shock refers to a world that one can no longer make sense of nor understand. It designates the massive psychic reaction which takes place within the individual plunged into a culture vastly different from his own. It seemed that this to me is what a brain-injured person also goes through in attempting to make sense of his former (now foreign) life.

seven months after it happened. I didn't listen to the tape for another six months, although I wouldn't maintain for a moment that these were independent observations. I think I sensed even then that my account of the initial stage of the accident was so clinical, detached and quite humorless — or at least it became manifest later on — that I wanted a much fuller account of the total impact of the stroke on my family. In a very real sense, my professionalism was against me in telling it in such a detached way — but this was my ultimate defense and quite obviously I could never have done it in any other way. Despite the effort to suppress it, the remembrances were still strong and frightening for my wife. This is her account of the episode and her very personal reactions to it. It coincides with my report but offers much more of the flavor of the effect of intense emotional upheaval upon the members of my family and what they were forced to go through.

BETTE: I often wonder if the move to Champaign had anything to do with the accident. I can remember our coming here in May [1967] and looking around at this flat farm land and saying, "Good heavens, we'd be out of our minds to leave California," even though we both had come from this area originally. And yet the opportunity to further Scott's career was just too good to pass up, plus the fact that his traveling was getting a bit tiresome, and we needed a daddy home more than he was. We got along all right and didn't complain, but it was a difficult type of life. I always felt sorry for women who ended up raising children by themselves and yet it almost bordered on this because on most weekdays the children and I were by ourselves much of the time. It did look like a chance to have a different style of life, snuggled into a little university town, and we didn't think we'd miss the big city that much. But I suppose it was the opportunity of the job itself which was most intriguing. There were compensations, we told ourselves, but I think we can say that we somewhat reluctantly agreed to leave the West Coast and come to Champaign.

There was the problem of selling the house [in San Carlos]. I worried a great deal about that and it didn't seem that that went smoothly at all. And then I suppose Scott's having to come on to Champaign without us concerned me because of Joel's accident in which he fell and broke his arm. The decision was made for us when the orthopedist said that Joel could not travel for a month. So the kids and I had to stay in San Carlos. We didn't get away until the third of October, when Scott arrived. In the meantime we had packed the house, our neighbors had packed the car, and the kids and I met Scott at the airport and proceeded east. It was kind of exciting to be on another new adventure. Joel was getting along O.K., and the little ones were excited about the move. Actually we had a pleasant trip east and everything went all right. We stopped in St. Louis for a couple of days to see my dad, and then on to Champaign.

Scott had rented a "metal monstrosity," but the house certainly looked like California and this helped us make the adjustment. So we settled in and I remember thinking that I was so glad that Scott liked to set up our various minor treasures which we had collected through the years. He really has a knack for arranging things, which I suppose is because of his art background. Anyway, I remember thinking that I was so glad that he had taken over those built-in shelves in our living room and put all those things on them because I'll bet I never would have got that done with all that happened. So Scott pitched right in and we managed to get the house livable.

We were there about a week when Scott had to go to Cincinnati for a meeting. I remember a couple of neighbors had asked us to come over for dessert, but he was gone and I didn't want to go without him. When Scott arrived in Cincinnati he called us, and just in that few short hours of the trip he had developed what seemed to be a terrific cold. He sounded very nasal, and his voice was quite husky the way it is when he gets a bad cold, but this seemed to come on quite suddenly. Anyway, Scott didn't feel well, which was quite obvious. When he returned, he had what appeared to be a bad cold, and the coughing irritated us the most. I remember thinking that he should go see somebody about that cough, but I knew full well he wouldn't, having learned from past experience that he didn't really trust or believe in doctors for minor afflictions. The cough was so severe — he was up two or three hours a night for a week — but we still thought it was linked with just the cold. The following weekend we went to a dinner at Lloyd Humphreys' [chairman of the psychology department] and he didn't feel good then, although I don't remember that the coughing was too bad.

277

On that fateful night, October 30, he came home from the office and told me about his vision, and he suggested that it was only in the right eye, and for whatever reason I asked if he was certain that it was only in the one eye, and then he discovered it was actually in both eyes [as it turned out, the vision in the top half of *both* eyes refused to coincide with that in the bottom]. But how do you ever know about every, illness that the human body is prone to develop unless you've experienced it or known someone who has? So there we were, ignorant of the whole thing. Even now, I don't know what we could have done, since finding out the inadequacies of the local physicians. I really think that in this instance ignorance was bliss. We might have suspected, as now I think we should have, that something was going wrong inside his brain. But if we had, who knows whom we would have got hold of, and anybody we might have called could have messed up the whole thing, so I guess to make me feel better I think it was well that we didn't suspect a stroke.

Anyway, Scott's headache that evening should have told us something, but we just didn't realize what in the world was going on. We think now that the cough had to do with the closing of the artery, but then we just didn't know, I suppose because Scott had always been so healthy, and outside of gaining weight in the winter which he lost in the summer he was in good physical health. When I think back on it, the one time that I did persuade Scott to go see "Uncle George" (we called him that because he had a long-sounding Greek name), he recommended that Scott go for further tests to the hospital. But Scott never did go because the trouble subsided and he was too busy traveling.

I don't like to have to go back and remember all this. People kept asking me, how did I know what to do? The answer was I didn't know what to do and I don't know that what I did was right. You don't stop and think at times like this. I saw him fall, and I still thought he was teasing because once in a while when we would kid each other Scott would stagger around. So I wanted to think that was what he was doing this time, but obviously he wasn't. He didn't stop coughing until he fell down, and then the coughing abruptly stopped. He was still reaching for that blamed TV just to watch the dumb Packers! He fell down on his knees and elbows, and I could see he was trying to get up and couldn't. He looked at me with a cockeyed smile where one side of his face didn't move; then of course I knew that something was terribly wrong. I was frightened and I was going to run to do something. I got the operator and asked her to send an ambulance. I didn't know what else to do, I didn't know any neighbors, and it was almost 11:30 at night. Scott was so hot, beads of perspiration stood out on his head. He kept trying to get up and kept looking at me, almost pleading with me to do something, but I didn't know what to do. He apparently could not talk. I simply tried to keep him quiet, which he was.

It wasn't long before the ambulance arrived. It was raining outside. It was a very nice man who came in and asked me where they should take him. I had no answer to this, but I remembered seeing a large medical center and that's where I thought we should go. The men were very, very nice, and asked if I wanted to go with them. I couldn't because our three children were asleep, but I promised to come over as soon as I could get someone to stay with the children. At this point I called Don Peterson. I told him something had happened to Scott, that I didn't know what, but that I'd had him taken to the hospital. I was in my pajamas at the time so I went in and got dressed and it didn't take Don fifteen minutes to get to the house. I don't remember what we said to each other; I was close to hysterics because I was so frightened and I didn't know what had happened, except I felt the world had suddenly caved in on us. First he said he would take me to the hospital, but I insisted I could drive myself, so he said he would stay with the children. The ambulance driver had called me in the meantime to say that they had my husband in the emergency room and did I know where it was. I said I would find it.

When I arrived, Scott was still in the emergency room. No one was in there with him, no doctor or anyone, he was simply lying on this cart. I don't know how long we waited but it was a heck of a long time for the doctor to arrive. It seems to me he didn't get there until about 1:30 a.m. He was an internist who happened to be on call. By this time the paralysis had left Scott's arm and leg. The doctor did the usual tapping and listening, and then he said, "Tell me what happened." I thought Scott couldn't talk, so I went through the account of what I thought had happened. And then he turned and said to Scott, "Now you tell me." And Scott spoke up and told him in effect what I had told him.

279

I remember being surprised that he could talk so fluently. Occasionally he'd block, but for the most part he gave the same accounting that I did. The doctor said that he didn't know what had happened, but he suggested that Scott stay the night and maybe they'd run a couple of tests on him the next day.

At that juncture Scott was wheeled up to pediatrics since they didn't have any other empty beds. They put him in a little room off in the corner and I stayed with him until about 3 a.m. The only thing I noticed while I was still there was that while Scott could talk to me, he was very cold, he had the chills, and I remember asking for blankets and heaping them on his bed. But he was still quite cold and I don't remember now how long that lasted. We agreed that possibly he should try to sleep and he actually dozed a little bit. I wasn't worried about his speech at all since we had engaged in considerable conversation. I then called Don at home and told him that I just about had him settled down, and I suppose I got back about 3:30 a.m. It's funny, too, I've often thought, that surely somewhere in the psychological studies one must have come across symptoms of a stroke, and yet trying to explain to Don how Scott appeared and what had happened, he didn't evidence any knowledge as to what had happened either.

In the morning, knowing they were going to run these tests, I called the hospital about 9 a.m. after sending the children off to school. I didn't tell Scott's mother he was in the hospital, since I didn't want to alarm her unnecessarily. The girl who answered the phone said that Dr. Moss was in having some tests run and she would have him call me when he came back. So I went on about what I was doing. I eventually called again and she said yes, he was in his room and she would put him on. She apparently gave Scott the phone and he uttered a sound but that's all that it was; I could not make head or tail of what he was trying to say to me. I remember feeling that I had just fallen down to China. My heart just dropped! And there he was just babbling something over the phone to me, but nothing that I could understand. At this juncture I knew that something was very wrong and I simply said to him, "Well, let's hang up the phone and I'll be there in a few minutes." I got over there as quickly as I could, and when I saw him he could say absolutely nothing to me. He just looked at me. Apparently he understood me but he couldn't say anything back. And as so often happens there were no doctors around to tell me anything. The nurses were in and out but I don't think they understood what was going on with Scott.

I remember sitting by his bed (by this time he had been moved into a double room), and I would talk to him and he'd just look at me. I'd try to get him to even answer questions where he could shake his head yes or no. He seemed to understand what I said. I guess I was simply not letting myself think that something was really that wrong with him. I just would not accept that. And so he and I played little games where I would try to get him to say different things. I'd repeat the alphabet, slowly, A — and he'd say "A"; and I'd say B — and he'd say "Beh"; and then I'd get on to D, and he'd say "A" again. That was all that I could get him to do, repeat A, B, C. He'd smile when he did this though, and whether he couldn't say the D or he simply didn't care — he was like a child who wanted to play games. So that's what we did while I was there with Scott — play games.

I remember mistakenly thinking, well, maybe he could write something to me. I'd say to him when I left, "Do you want me to bring you something? Can I bring you something to eat?" — because he wasn't eating anything. And he'd nod his head "yes." Then I'd say, "Well, what is it you want?" And then he'd babble something which I couldn't understand. And finally I decided that maybe Scott could write to me. So I gave him a pencil and a paper and asked him to write it down. I wish now that I had saved some of the things that he wrote to me, but I didn't have the foresight to save them. Of course what he wrote wasn't even letters, it was just little discrete markings. Eventually I began playing a game like Twenty Questions with him, in response to what he wanted. We always got around to a milkshake every time. So I'd stop downstairs on my way up and order a chocolate milkshake for him. He'd act as though he wanted it and maybe he'd take one or two swallows and then leave the rest.

I knew they had called in a neurologist but I never laid eyes on the man all the time Scott was in the hospital. The internist was rather vague, too. I knew they had run a series of tests on him, but after waiting until the second day I called the neurologist's office and received a runaround from the receptionist. I gave her half an hour and then called her back. I demanded to know what these tests were, that I was his wife and had a right to know what they'd found out. She replied that the neurologist had placed the results in a file and turned it over to the internist. At this point I called him and he wasn't there, so I left word for him to call me as soon as possible. At the end of that day, at 10 o'clock, he finally called and reported that they thought Scott had a primary brain tumor which meant it was operable or he had cancer that had begun in his lungs and had spread to his brain, and if this was so there was nothing they could do about it. They left me with those two choices for another day! It was unbearable; I almost went out of my mind — yet trying not to let Scott know that *I* knew there could be anything this wrong.

But Scott was in such a happy mood — he really didn't care one way or the other — he was in no pain. He dozed most of the time, or when I was there we'd play our little game or I'd talk to him and he'd listen and smile and act as though he understood. I'd say things like "Who am I? Do you know me?" And he'd nod his head "yes." And then I'd say, "Am I your sister?" No, I wasn't his sister. He acted as though he knew who I was. And then I'd say, "Do you have any children?" He'd indicate that he did. Then I'd say, "How many children do you have?" Sometimes he'd indicate four and sometimes five (we actually have three). And I never knew exactly but I still think that he didn't lose his sense of humor, because we've always played that way with each other. I think he was still displaying a sense of humor, which is just incredible. I knew perfectly well he really knew how many children he had — that he was simply playing with me.

Finally the internist called again on the third night and said there was no cancer of the lungs and they had decided that it was a primary brain tumor. His remark to me was that he would strongly suggest that I take him to Chicago because there was nobody here that he would let touch a member of his family. Well, that decided it for me — we would take him to Chicago. They subsequently made a referral to Presbyterian-St. Luke's and to Dr. Oldberg and his staff. We went two days later. I had the children to consider too, and Jean Peterson was marvelous; she did her best to find someone to come in and take care of them. I also had to tell the children about daddy and to try to explain to a five-, seven- and ten-year-old where we were going. When we came back from Chicago, I discovered how the older boy's school work had suffered. Joel is a quiet boy. He has feelings but they often aren't demonstrable, he hides them well, and really, in all the worry and concern about Scott, I thought the children were all right. As I found out later, his school work fell considerably. He was much more aware of the danger and the trouble we were in than I had realized.

The night that I found out what they thought at the hospital about a tumor was the first time I called my father in St. Louis and told him Scott was in the hospital. I didn't tell him too much about it except for the diagnosis and the fact that I was taking him to Chicago. He listened to me, of course, and asked what he could do. I said, "Nothing that I know of." He said not to worry about money because he would help out on that, and I knew he would if we needed it. But then the next morning he called back and of course he had had all evening to think about this, and he said he wanted to go to Chicago with me. "I can't bear to think of you going through this and being all alone." And when he said "all alone" my fears mounted and that was the beginning of the shaking up, because, going back a bit, of all the heartaches he has had in his life and some in mine — we had seen my little nephew operated on for what supposedly was a brain tumor, and as a result he was physically and intellectually maimed — so a brain operation was not exactly new to either of us and we knew what would lie ahead if the surgery was to take place. So Dad and I must have had this in the back of our minds. I remember crying very hard after I hung up the phone; he was feeling the same way I was — feeling for me.

I sat down with the children the night before we left and attempted to tell them that daddy was very ill, because at this point I thought he was going to have surgery. But this threatened my control — I didn't want to break down in front of the children. Up until now I had managed to hold myself together pretty well, probably because I still refused to believe that anything was going to happen to him. I saw him and I knew he was sick and that something was drastically wrong, but I would not accept the fact that he wouldn't be all right again. This is what held me together.

I also finally had to tell Scott's mother what was happening. I told her first that Scott had had this bad cough and I'd taken him to the hospital, still trying to spare her the hurt and the anxiety of knowing all this. When eventually I had to tell her, I hoped that she would stay with the children, but she said no, she wasn't up to staying with the children and she wanted to go to Chicago, too. So a young couple, he was an assistant professor here and they had no children, volunteered at the last minute to come in and live in the house, so that part of the problem was resolved. I called them every night after getting back from the hospital. Don Peterson made arrangements for us to stay at student housing in Chicago, and we took taxis back and forth.

The morning we left to go it was snowing. We had a very nice ambulance driver again and Scott's mother sat up in front with him while I sat in back by Scott. He was extremely quiet, of course, during the whole trip. I kept asking him if he was all right. He just sort of dozed — he didn't notice anything going on about him. We went right into Presbyterian-St. Luke's hospital and they got him settled in his room. Then the team came in, led by Dr. Matz, a resident neurosurgeon. I never did see Dr. Oldberg. Scott said later that he saw him once, when he was leading a group of interns; they looked him over for maybe five minutes. I remember when Matz came in to see him for the first time, I was sort of surprised that Scott mobilized himself to answer Matz's questions with "yes" and "no." At least he could understand him, but that was apparently the limit of his vocabulary at this time.

When we arrived at Presbyterian-St. Luke's it was on Friday, the beginning of the weekend. I knew they didn't run tests in hospitals on Saturday or Sunday, but I felt that time was of the essence. Dr. Matz did say that no one would be around on the weekend, and I asked if time didn't have something to do with Scott's condition, and why in the world would they let him lie there for two days before they did anything. So he said he would have some tests run Saturday. But I guess if I hadn't said anything, Scott would have just waited until Monday. The doctor did give him a preliminary examination, and there is the possibility he knew there was no urgency, but his thoughts weren't shared with me if such was the case.

They ran their own independent studies, which included an angiogram. They also called in a vascular team. At this point they discovered that the left artery was blocked and that surgery was not possible. They in effect could do nothing for him. They announced that time was the biggest element in his eventual recovery, whatever that might be. There was no medication given and they had no suggestions to make whatsoever. Of course Scott lost considerable weight. I also lost weight because of anxiety. Mother and I would go through the motions of trying to eat a meal or two but it didn't work very well.

As if we didn't have enough to think about, I also became ill with a hormone upset and had to seek out a gynecologist to get myself straightened out. It just added to the discomfort all the way around. Mostly our days were just spent going over to the hospital as soon as we were allowed in and sitting with him all day. I used to attempt to feed him when his lunch or dinner came but there wasn't much that he wanted to eat. I'd bring him a milkshake, and sometimes he'd drink a bit of that but not much. Drink was all that he did want, he wouldn't eat a meal at all. He was just content to lie in bed. We'd get the newspapers and I'd try to tell him what was going on. We also had a TV in the room and I turned on a football game or two; he looked at it some but I doubt that he was really interested.

I am reminded of something that happened in the hospital — he used to do things like this every now and then, even during the height of his illness. It is one of the things that really kept me going. In the hospital he wasn't saying anything but simply listening to me and watching me, and I got up from the chair by his bed to leave the room, and he patted me on the fanny. I turned around quickly and looked at him and there was that familiar twinkle in his eye, and I knew that I still had the same Scott I started with. I don't care what his outward appearance was, he was still basically the same person. This is another reason why I refused to believe that anything really, really could be wrong with him.

Our friends the Noltes dropped in from Decatur; we met them one night in the elevator when we were coming down to get something to eat. I was very glad to see them. Mary is a dear person; she had her nurse's uniform with her and was all set to stay and nurse Scott if we needed her. I'll never forget that Mary did this. When John and Mary came to the hospital, I sent them up to Scott's room, but I said that they shouldn't expect Scott to say anything although I was sure he would like to see them and would enjoy their talking to him. But after they did go on, I was quite nervous because I thought he wouldn't want me to have sent anyone up when he couldn't talk to them and I wasn't there. I felt a strong urge to run back to the room to protect him from being in that situation, feeling that he might be quite upset with me for having done this. But we went on and had a quick bite to eat anyway, and when we got back to the room he was just lying there smiling at them. They were sort of making small talk, and apparently it wasn't bothering him a bit to have them there. He didn't mind that he couldn't talk to them. I felt a great sense of relief.

There were many, many phone calls that came in on the phone by the bed. People called from all over to find out about him. The word had spread very quickly. I had called our friends the Scanderups in San Carlos to tell Dorothy and Dean about the accident and I asked them to call the Federal Building in San Francisco to inquire about whether Scott was still covered by federal group insurance. This immediately prompted a phone call from John Bell, the director of the mental health operation in the region, so the word got out, not only through neighbors in San Carlos but through NIMH in Washington. So calls were coming in constantly from people who knew Scott from all over. He had been doing so well in his field, and then to have this crashing blow — everybody felt for him and their concern was genuine; I really did appreciate it. When I would sit by his bed and repeat the name of the person, he would seem to know who it was and I would know he understood what I was saying to him.

They didn't tell me what was actually wrong with him until the evening before we went home. When they finally did tell me, they still said they were going to keep him a couple of days, and I said, "No, you're not! I want to get out of here in the morning, so sign us out; Scott is going to go home. If there is nothing you can do for him here, I can do a lot more at home. I can feed him and do exactly the same things and more than you're doing here." Dr. Matz was very nice and said he would try, and I said, "You do more than try, you get us out of here!" So he did. That evening I called Don Peterson and asked if he could get someone to drive our car up, because I didn't want to come back in the ambulance. Don did get a graduate student and his wife to drive up and get us. So we brought him home. The couple who had stayed with our children wouldn't take anything — she told me I would spoil everything they had done if I persisted in wanting to pay her. They had taken good care of the children and we were really most grateful for this.

We tried to reestablish some sort of a normal life — as normal as it could be. The children were glad to see daddy back, of course, and I remember all of them coming up and hugging him and trying to ask him things. Of course he didn't answer. I had to say to them that they should talk to daddy, and that though he might not want to talk, he would listen and understand what they were saying. I tried to tell them not to expect him to talk a lot to them, without trying to explain why he couldn't talk. They really accepted it very well, and they'd play little games with him, too. They were very good about it. As he got to where he could say a few words after some weeks, he would likely as not say things wrong, and they'd just laugh. We'd all laugh, including Scott. It wasn't anything that they minded at all — they just thought it was kind of funny and joked about it.

I tried to get some weight back on him — he was quite thin — and eventually he began to eat a little bit. He'd try to read the newspaper but he couldn't. I don't remember how long it was before he really talked much to me. I guess I became aware that he wasn't interested in anything. I ran the house and did all the things that had to be done, and he was like a star boarder. He ate and slept at our house but without much interaction. He was pleasant. Actually I thought, in the beginning, that he couldn't be taking this as well as he appeared to be. He understood what was wrong, and I would think, knowing him, that he should be very angry and upset over this turn of events, but he wasn't. He just accepted it and I suppose that this was all part of it. He really didn't care that much about anything. He didn't think about it, as I know now, so how could he be worried about it. In the beginning I thought he would be in a miserable mood all of the time and very irritated, but of course he wasn't. He was like a very pleasant guy who was just there. He'd eat as well as he could whatever I'd fix him and he'd sit and watch TV or just sit.

But it wasn't long before he decided that he was going to get busy. For example, he was going to try to read his professional journals, which was extremely difficult for him. He would pick up a journal and try to read something, but it didn't last long — he just couldn't keep the thoughts together. It seemed to go better if I would read to him. I spent all of my time with him, except getting meals, doing washing and ironing, and taking care of the children. But the rest of the time we spent together, talking, and trying to regain whatever we could that seemed to have been lost. He had no memory for past events. He knew vaguely that we had been in California, but he didn't remember people, even people that we really knew well. Perhaps he could picture them in his mind when I introduced the names, but he sure couldn't remember anybody's name, not a single person, even people that lived next door or people that he worked with. I would try to recall incidents that we had experienced or laughed about but he often didn't appear to recall them. His whole past seemed to have been wiped out. He was, in some ways, a cabbage, but not really.

I remember the first time that Lloyd Humphreys came over, someone whom he was very self-conscious about in his situation, which is one thing that I always felt was wrong in his attitude, and yet I couldn't expect him to act in any other way. He's always been a perfectionist so he was no different about this than anything else. He wasn't ashamed of what had happened but he seemed to feel that he had no right to act the way he was. He should try to act normally. I always felt that this was wrong. If you've had an accident it's not any fault of yours, and if you can't respond to something because of this, this is not any fault of yours. And why in the world did he have to put up some kind of a front and try to pretend that he was better than he was — but this is the difference in the way we look at things. If something like this had happened to me and my friends or associates came around, I could only act a certain way and I wouldn't try to act any differently. But he felt so bad for having had this happen to him — he just wouldn't accept the fact that something had happened in the brain that simply would not allow him to talk any better at the time.

But returning to Lloyd, I remember the three of us sat in the living room and we had a drink. Lloyd chatted away and Scott did his best to try to converse with him, but felt very ill at ease the whole time that Lloyd was there. I really didn't think that Lloyd expected him to do anything outstanding — after all, unless you've had it happen to you, you don't understand it (and we eventually found out Lloyd's mother had had a stroke and suffered from mild aphasia). No one expected Scott to do an outstanding job in anything but he seemed to feel that they expected him to. You can only do what you can and no one had any right to expect otherwise.

For the most part my feelings were, even at this time, that he would come out of this, that we'd work at it as we could, and actually at the beginning there was rapid improvement, and this brings us around to the positive side of perfectionism. I think if he had just sat and not tried to do anything his improvement would not have been as rapid — he pushed himself hard to do things. I think it is very good that he did it this way, that he wanted to do it this way. He was committed to writing a couple of articles and there was a deadline coming up on one of them. I felt that I had done a pretty good job of holding us together until this time and because he hadn't been angry about anything it had been rather pleasant, all things considered. But when we began to work on this article for the first time he became extremely angry with himself, and then began to shout at me. This is the first and possibly the only time when I felt sorry for myself. Having feelings of my own, I felt he didn't need to yell at me, but it only lasted a little while, and then I realized that it was a selfish thing for me to feel this way. After all, he couldn't help how he was acting under the pressure to begin speaking again. So I got over it quickly, and we went on working on the article. It was very difficult for me to try to understand what he was attempting to say to me. I guess I had read enough of what he had written and typed enough of his manuscripts so that I was a little familiar with his terminology. I could pick out what he would write in contrast to something written by another, that is, his style of writing, so I guess all of this helped me to try to put down what he was saying. But it was extremely difficult; as much as I wanted to help do it, it got to the point where I dreaded these sessions. It seemed to take so much out of him and it made me irritable too.

Even before the accident happened he would get angry at himself and would occasionally take it out on me, and this was always upsetting to me. I don't like to see people angry, I don't like to be around people who are angry, we don't like to be around couples who are constantly bickering. So when somebody gets angry at me it is very upsetting to me, although in this instance I should have realized why he was angry. He wasn't angry at me — he was angry at himself. Anyway, we stuck to the manuscript,

289

mailed it off, and they did accept the paper, which was just marvelous for us. From then on we began writing a little bit more. He worked on more and more, and I really think that being the type of person that he was, he was fortunate in this kind of an accident, because I don't know whether somebody else would have begun to work as soon as he did and would have kept at it as hard as he did. I feel that this was Scott doing this, not just a patient — it was his own personality that drove him so hard to get himself well. A lot of people would have given up or at the very least it would have taken them some time before they had the motivation to try to work and to force themselves to talk and read and understand.

Here is a note that Julie wrote about that time describing her recollection of the accident and the impression it had upon her:

My father had an accident not long ago and this is what I remember. It all happened at night when I was asleep so in the morning I went downstairs and Mom was crying. I asked her what was the matter? She said, "Daddy is sick and in the hospital." Well, I told her everything was going to be all right and said, "Please stop crying."

And then she went away to the hospital and the Clowers [Clores] stayed with us at our house. The next thing I remember is Mom came home with Dad. They came home and when Daddy stepped in the door he looked at us kids, he looked in sort of half surprise and half confused. Well, we hugged him and he said, "Hullow."

Now he stalls to think of words and his temper is much shorter. Sometimes he wants to call me and he says, "Kevin, ah Joel, ah Julie." But no matter how awkward he ever gets, we still love him just the same.

When Scott was here taking his graduate work, he happened to take a course under Joseph Wepman, who is one of the few experts in the country on aphasia. So he decided he wanted to go and talk to Joe. I set up an appointment with him. One cold morning Scott and I got on the train and had a nice trip into Chicago. It was enjoyable because we were hopeful that if anyone could help Scott it was Dr. Wepman. He could give Scott recommendations about what to do to improve. We had lunch first at the International House on the Chicago campus, where Scott lived during his internship. He showed me around a bit and we really had a nice time. Then we spent the afternoon with Dr. Wepman's assistants and they did some tests on him. I didn't talk to anybody then. We went home with the information that they would rerun the tests three weeks later. Anyway, Scott enjoyed seeing Joe and we both felt that maybe they would help him.

Then we went back again and at this point they talked with me, too. They retested Scott and in the three weeks' time they felt they saw a great deal of improvement, and this is the way we felt, too, because the improvement was very rapid at this time. But what it all boiled down to was Dr. Wepman telling him that there really wasn't anything that he could do to speed up the recovery, and that given a few more months or so he would probably be fully recovered and he would be very interested in seeing Scott at that time. So this buoyed our spirits considerably. I remember the train ride back on the Panama Limited and our sitting in the club car. We had a drink and then went back to the diner and had a nice dinner. We were just floating on clouds because we took to heart what Dr. Wepman had said to us and we really felt that in another couple of months Scott would be entirely recovered. Unfortunately, the prediction didn't turn out to be correct.

Scott continues to improve day by day but gradually the improvement has begun to slow down. It is no longer quite so spectacular, although I still see improvement in the various areas. For instance, at first he couldn't type at all, but he has stuck to it and little by little he types a little faster, with plenty of errors, but he remembers where to put his fingers. Probably the thing that has stayed the worst has been his handwriting, but before the accident his handwriting wasn't anything to brag about. I think that even that has improved a bit. He still finds that when he talks to people he cannot follow long, involved conversations. For his part, Scott can talk for a few minutes and everything's fine, but he simply needs time to put his words in order. If it gets to be an extended conversation, he is likely to lose the area of thought. And he can't take notes because he can't write that well.

No one had advised Scott to take any speech therapy; in fact, Dr. Wepman was against it, but Scott has gone to the speech department. It certainly can't hurt him any and it gives him a chance to talk to people other than me, because he is extremely self-conscious about talking to anyone else. He feels that he might make a mistake and then he'd block, and he doesn't want to do this. He just can't stand the fact that he doesn't talk exactly the way he used to. I'm constantly saying, "But people don't expect you to talk like you used to," and he'll end up getting angry with me. The point is that he wants to talk the way he remembers and he isn't going to have it any other way. If he can't talk that way, then he isn't going to talk! So there!

REFERENCES

Greenberg, R., and Dewan, E. "Aphasia and Dreaming: A Test of the Hypothesis." *Psychophysiology* (1968) 5:203-204.
Moss, Scott. "Experimental Manipulation of Dreams." In *Progress in Clinical Psychology,* edited by L. E. Abt and B. T. Perss. New York: Grune and Stratton, 1968, pp. 114-135.

Let me call your attention to some of the significant items in the initial response by Scott and Bette to Scott's stroke and aphasia. He tries to read the headlines of the paper but they make no sense to him. More significant in all this is his awareness that not only can he not read anymore but he is relatively unmoved emotionally by this realization.

Scott notes that at the time he had little concern over his family, his imagined imminent death, and his inability to converse with anyone. Later, when a colleague suggests that the aphasia must have been particularly frustrating to one so verbal, Scott assures him that it was not. Then he does what good clinicians often do — he responds to his own response with raised eyebrows and self inquiry: "Why indeed is my loss of this significant skill treated so lightly?" Having lost language, Scott is unable to converse with himself. He cannot conceptualize time, emotions, and his own reality. Without words, he is practically without self and the bindings of past experience. The only area in which he seems to have been somewhat emotionally sensitive is his treatment by the surgical residents, who he feels attend to him as if he is a battered brain rather than as a person who has suffered a catastrophic accident, a *whole* person. But he attributes this to his own lack of ability to communicate and accepts such treatment as standard for neurological patients.

Later he experiences "unholy, tortuous" attempts to recover language and speech, and directs his anger and rage at himself when all that comes out is gibberish. And, being interested in dreams, he recalls that from October 30, 1967, to February, 1968, he has no memory of dreaming at all. Thus, he has no words to express what is happening in his waking state and no dreams to express his sleeping state. For most of us, dreams are manifested as images that are programmed by primary or emotionally organized processes. But, as Scott hypothesizes, the dream cannot be integrated into the waking reality when no words surround it. Scott notes that his white boxer dog dreams often and well without words; of course, white boxer dogs have no spoken language to begin with. Did Scott really dream without being able to recall it in a waking state because of his wordlessness, or did he simply not dream at all?

He notes his difficulties with synonyms and abstractions and how difficult it is for him to move out conceptually and temporally from the "here and now." The past is dim, the future meaningless. Moreover, he becomes increasingly aware of his flattened affect and emotional nonchalance. He is treating all this as if Scott Moss[2] were outside Scott Moss, watching a "natural" psychological experiment. As he recovers and begins to unite the two Scott Mosses, he suggests that strokes can induce a massive retroactive inhibition of all experiences except those leading up to the stroke and the events surrounding it. He compares the state he has been in with a kind of "cultural shock" — the emotional reaction one sometimes has after moving from a familiar, known environment to a strange, new, unexperienced one.

In the second part, wife Bette recounts the events surrounding Scott's stroke as she experienced them. After the emergency, you see Bette rethinking what she did, what she perhaps might have done, getting the ambulance and someone to sit with the kids; and seeing her husband bedded down in the pediatrics ward because no empty beds were available elsewhere. She recalls her first reactions the next morning to his speechlessness. The absence of anyone to guide her wild thoughts and her attempts to help Scott are documented. She asks to know what's wrong with Scott, and the response presents two possibilities — primary brain tumor or cancer that had spread from the lungs. Then there is her day-to-day game playing with a husband who seems to feel no pain or anxiety and keeps his sense of humor throughout while she "administers" his treatment and attends to children, parents, friends, and household.

Scott finally is back home and on the long road to rehabilitation. As Scott has noted earlier about himself, his reaction to his stroke has deprived him of the wherewithal to be upset about it. Not so Bette. This is a most trying and challenging time for her.

What about Scott a year later? In the book's concluding statements, not excerpted here, he says he is sufficiently pleased about his recovery, and certainly we would not have had this book if he had not "recovered." He says that treatment for his brand of aphasia is still a mystery, and he has residual disabilities including an inability to recall significant and special words, to use precise and targeted speech. He recounts a story told by Harry Harlow about the porpoise (which Harlow contended God had created in a fit of malicious wrath). Scott writes, "Harlow maintained that he could think of nothing more damaging to the ego than to have an intelligent brain but no equipment for expressing it. Nor can I."[3]

---

[3] C. Scott Moss, *Recovery With Aphasia* (Urbana: University of Illinois Press, 1972), pp. 43-44.

QUESTIONS FOR DISCUSSION

1. Moss responds to his early hospitalization with the feeling that hospital personnel were concerned about his neurological impairment but unconcerned about him as a person. Would you want to change this and, if so, how?
2. What do you suppose are some factors that make research on aphasia more complex and difficult than research investigating other neurological impairments?
3. In what way was Moss' early emotional reaction similar to Johnny Bonham's in *Johnny Got His Gun?*
4. What does Moss conclude about having no dreams for several months? Do you agree? What are some alternative possibilities?
5. Moss suggests that his stroke acted as some sort of massive retroactive inhibition or cultural shock that diluted all other experiences in his life. What does he mean by this?
6. What are the essential differences between Scott's and Bette's perceptions of Scott's aphasia?
7. If you were to work with adult aphasics in a hospital or clinic, what insights do you gain from this husband/wife tale that might be helpful?

ADDITIONAL READINGS

- Farb, Peter. *Word Play.* New York: Bantam, 1975.
- Farrell, B. *Pat and Roald.* New York: Random House, 1969.
- Huizinga, Johan. *Homo Ludens.* Boston: Beacon Press, 1955.
- Langer, Susanne. *Philosophy in a New Key.* New York: Mentor, 1948.
- Osgood, Charles, and Miron, Murray, eds. *Approaches to the Study of Aphasia.* Urbana: University of Illinois Press, 1970.
- Ritchie, D. *Stroke: A Diary of Recovery.* London: Faber and Faber, 1966.

Excuse me for not rising . . .

8

People Will Always Be Kind

Wilfred Sheed

8

Much about Brian Casey, the protagonist of Sheed's novel, reminds one of Shakespeare's Richard Ⅲ. Both are crippled, misshapen — the one from birth, the other by disease. Both learn to use their physical deformities to control and obtain power over others. As Richard says:

> But I, that am not shaped for sportive tricks
> Nor made to court an amorous looking glass
> I, that am rudely stamp'd and want loves majesty
> To strut before a wanton ambling nymph;
> I, that am curtail'd of this fair proportion,
> Cheated of feature by dissembling nature,
> Deformed, unfinished, sent before my time
> Into this breathing world, scarce half made up
> . . .
> And therefore since I cannot prove a lover
> To entertain these fair well spoken days
> I am determined to prove a villain
> And hate the idle pleasures of these days.

Early in the story Brian is "rudely stamped" by one of the last recorded cases of poliomyelitis before the Salk and Sabin vaccines became available. Although it is hardly fair to compare the villainies of King Richard with those of Brian Casey, the relationships of orthopedic handicaps and personality traits are visible in both men. I quickly emphasize, however, that neither Richard nor Brian represents any particular syndrome or logical outcome of physical disability.

---

[1] As in William Shakespeare, "Richard Ⅲ," *Shakespeare's Complete Works*, Student's Cambridge Edition, ed. William Allan Neilson (Boston: Houghton Mifflin. Cambridge: Riverside Press, 1920), p. 731.

In any case, handicaps that are physically deforming can cause high stress levels, particularly concerning self image. One finds it difficult "to court an amorous looking glass." As Myerson[2] generalizes:

(1) Physique is a social stimulus.
(2) It arouses expectations for behavior.
(3) It is one of the criteria for assigning a person to a social role.
(4) The person perceives himself by comparison to others.
(5) Variation in physique in and of itself does not produce psychological maladjustment.
(6) Where physical disabilities produce emotional handicaps, such handicaps are produced by social variables.
(7) The critical variables are cultural and individual personality characteristics such as competitiveness, self acceptance, cognitive capacity and style and emotional maturity.

In today's society orthopedically handicapped persons like Brian or Richard can be considered normal for educational purposes. Both are bright. Both would be able to get into and out of the places in which formal learning is housed (e.g., lecture halls, libraries, laboratories). They are in no way handicapped in conceptualizing or receiving information via the printed page or through verbal intercourse. Former handicapping conditions have been reduced by city planners, building codes, legislation, and modern technological aids including individually tailored wheelchairs, electronic recording and writing devices, usable ramps sidewalks, and specially equipped bathrooms.

Even with functional access to transportation, buildings, self help, and other equalizing resources, though, orthopedically handicapped persons need other kinds of support. Many require daily physical therapy including speech therapy. Others require medical monitoring of specific health problems. Children with cerebral palsy or other nervous system difficulties, for example, may be subject to seizures, requiring properly prescribed and monitored medication. Children having juvenile diabetes must be watched for reactions to too much or too little insulin. Programs for children having cardiac conditions, sickle cell anemia, hemophilia, and other health problems must be geared to the personal medical needs of the child. An Individualized Education Program is required by Public Law 94-142 for students determined to have special needs.

---

[2] Lee Myerson, "Somatapsychology of Physical Disability," in *Psychology of Exceptional Children and Youth,* ed. W. M. Cruickshank (Englewood Cliffs, NJ: Prentice-Hall, 1971), pp. 1-60.

Often, these forms of support don't require any fancy or marked change in educational programs. Most of these children can learn and proceed in a manner comparable to any child. Some teachers may not like the idea of including in their classroom a drooling, cerebral palsied child or a child having occasional mild seizures, but if these children can learn and function with the others and pose no major problem to themselves or other students, they belong with their peers. Given the teachers' and schools' acceptance of such variance, along with positive peer reaction, other students' perceptions and outlooks can be broadened and enhanced by this opportunity to extend their concept of normality.

John Singer (see Chapter 3) is not a typical deaf person, nor is Algernon Pendleton (Chapter 5) a typical emotionally disturbed person. Brian Casey neither represents nor can be considered a typical post-polio person.

The reader will become quickly aware of the various interpersonal ploys that Brian uses to deal with his feelings of being cheated by "dissembling nature." The excerpts concentrate on Brian's development after his polio — as an adolescent, son, friend, student, and self-proclaimed cripple. In the second section of the book, the narration of Brian's story is by Sam Perkins, a reporter hired by then Senator Casey to assist him in his political campaign.

PEOPLE WILL ALWAYS BE KIND

Wilfred Sheed

The wall is straight at that point, although later he would always think of it as curved. He sat on it for some three hours, embarrassed to tears. The clock on Riverside Church kept him abreast of the hours, halves, quarters, who could tell? Night couples wandered past, glowing fiercely. A professor and his dog, nobody he knew. Fifty yards behind him cars hummed sweetly along the river edge, smiling to themselves. Their lights were blinding and the buildings in front of him blazed like an iron foundry. A sudden late-summer carnival was in the works. The professor's straw hat gleamed and his dog shot a golden arc under the street lamp. The number 5 bus rocked past like a holiday camper.

Brian didn't want to approach the blazing building just yet, the fiery elevator; his mother's face would be blackened with heat. It was cooler out here on the wall. Still, he couldn't stay all night. He lowered his feet to the sidewalk, and immediately his knees buckled. He was barely able to clamber back without being caught. In his bones he'd felt it coming. Two stumbles yesterday, followed by little reassuring gusts of strength. This evening the same, throwing some sweet forward passes, delicate as a jeweler, and sitting down with his back bursting and his throat too sore to speak. He'd felt lousy for three days and nights, and Dr. Devlin had said flu, as usual, but he'd told his mother he felt O.K. and had gone out and played football like a maniac. He knew all right.

A thin ribbon of thought slanted across his mind: he could make it from the tree to the railing, from the railing to the parked cars — but then what? How to cross the street? He would simply have to get down on his knees and paddle. In a few minutes, when the professor was out of sight, he might give it a shot.

Excerpts from *People Will Always Be Kind*. Copyright © 1973 by Wilfred Sheed. Reprinted with the permission of Farrar, Straus and Giroux, Inc.

The professor left, at last, a happy man on two good legs; but as Brian was about to make his move, a couple came and sat on a nearby bench and began laboriously to neck. The girl's dress was a sizzling white, the man's sailor suit, white white white. That particular year, people used to neck for distance. Even if they weren't going overseas the next day. It gave Brian a bitter taste tonight. He ached from his throat to his feet, and the wall was a gravelly slab gnawing at his rump. He couldn't wait for them to finish.

"Mister," he said to the man. Much too softly. "Mister" louder, and then no doubt some kind of scream. Brian had never asked for help in his life, and he made a hysterical mess of it. They carried him across the street, big firm hands in his armpits, all his problems solved. The apartment was cool as crystal. He was put to bed, and the fever had a chance to settle, and the next day he was off to the hospital, the twenty-third recorded polio case that August.

It was difficult to be solemn about a wise guy like Brian. "He was a great guy," Hennessy said. "He was neat," said Bernie Levine. Hennessy had heard somewhere that only the best physical specimens got it. "That lets you out," said Phil Marconi, who was usually best ignored. Levine suddenly remembered an act of kindness and Fatstuff came up with another. ("He wasn't that good," said Phil. "I mean he was just a guy." They stared at him in frozen horror.)

"I guess he was my best friend," said Fatstuff Hennessy.

"Mine too." "Definitely."

"He could understand what you were thinking before you thought it."

"How'd he do that?" said Marconi.

"Ah, shut up," said Fatstuff. "How would you like to get it, Marconi?"

Marconi was too tough to hit, so the thing to do was sort of whine at him.

"Hey listen — is that why you're being so nice about Casey?" said Phil. "Because you think you might get it yourself? It won't help, baby, believe me."

"Go fuck yourself," said Levine. "If you get it, I'm going to celebrate for three whole days."

"Sure, why not?" said skeptic Marconi. "Crying wouldn't help me."

The feeling was that arguing with Phil cheapened you. Phil was the kind of fellow who said that Germans were better soldiers than Americans. The Italian campaign in Africa and the jokes that ensued had made him bitter about things.

"I really got to know him in the last year," said Sam Hertz doggedly.

"Yeah, we all did," said Phil. "Never knew a guy with so many dear, dear friends."

"I'm really sorry for you, you know that, Marconi?" said Hennessy. "You're really twisted."

"Everyone crowd round Casey for luck, now. Touch the hunchback," said Marconi. "Anybody want to play some football? While we still got a leg to stand on?" Philadelphia matrons could not have looked more shocked. "Suit yourselves, sickies," said Marconi and wandered out, with his football under his arm.

There was fear in the air now. "Jesus," said somebody. "Football!"

"That guy ought to grow up."

"He makes me puke."

It was steaming forenoon in the Casey apartment, a fan carried soggy air around on its wings. The boys had come over to get the poop on Brian and give awkward comfort to his parents. But there was no one there except a slow-motion cleaning lady.

"It was funny that night," said Levine, trying to recapture the mood after Marconi's ravages, "how he wouldn't stop playing. You remember how it got dark, and we wanted to go to Loew's, and he'd say, 'Hey catch, Fatman,' or, 'Big Bernie, let's see the ball.'"

Hennessy could feel his own legs drain of strength as he listened. He moved them slightly to make sure. So did Hertz. Marconi would have pissed himself from laughing. So would Brian.

"How'd he get home finally?"

"I don't know," said Hennessy. "I couldn't see the ball no more. So he waved me to go on home. He was just standing there the last time I looked back." Brian's thin, mocking, Irish face looked in retrospect saintly: Christ in his garden. Hennessy had hung around simply because Brian had asked him to — which now made him the closest thing to a good disciple. The others had trickled off to Loew's long since. "Hey Fatstuff, don't jump through too many

305

flaming hoops now" was Marconi's parting word that night. But Hennessy's subservience now seemed prophetic insight.

Kevin Casey, Brian's father, came home from the hospital, looking grave. In sorrow, his thin, black-Irish face seemed younger than usual. The boys sat crushed and small as Mr. Casey talked. Brian's legs were their legs now. No man is an island, when there's an epidemic around. "It's too soon to tell," said Mr. Casey. "He's still delirious. We'll know the extent of the damage in a few days."

Hennessy stuttered. "Does he, *you* know, know?"

"I honestly can't say," said Mr. Casey.

Delirium was a golden garden where Brian wandered, with his football under his arm, while the dice were rolled for a piece of left leg, possibly a hand. Lungs? We'll see. That's a tough point to make. Mr. Casey explained what he had just learned himself, about how polio worked. Think of a switchboard in the spine, he said, think of nerves blowing out like fuses. This was certainly something new to worry about. Hennessy's chronic appendicitis moved around to the back. The virus was still mincing through town, swishing her purse. Maybe *you*, Hennessy. No, I won't go. Take Marconi. He deserves it, not me.

"When can we see him, Mr. Casey?"

"I can't say. I'll let you know."

The gang went off, sorrowing. Phil Marconi was still lounging on the stoop. "You're all scared shitless," he said "That's why you're so worried about Brian." He had stayed around just to say that. He spat it out hard, no joking this time. They heaved off in their different directions, not answering, not wanting to hear another blasphemous word.

Beatrice Casey had stayed longer at the hospital, straining her eyes in the bad light of her son's room. When she closed them, she could see nothing but running. Hadn't Brian ever walked anywhere? She couldn't remember it. Not in all his years. Legs of all ages pounding solemnly. Now his legs were swathed to the hip in hot soggy flannel. The room smelled like a laundry, it was hard to believe that anything healthy could come out of such a place.

She had been too foggy to notice much the night they brought their son here. She remembered entering the emergency hospital through a dim liver-tinted foyer. Why had he lied about his flu? Why had she believed him? And would it have helped to know sooner? She wanted to discuss all this with someone.

Brian was taken upstairs for processing. They were told to wait down here, and were swiftly forgotten about. They mingled with some old people who had been sitting here forever, as if waiting for Immigration to decide their cases. Bare pipes lined the off-yellow walls. "This is the kind of place Dickens got the English to abolish," said Kevin.

A pretty place might have been worse, was all she thought. A polite receptionist, a bowl of flowers would have made her cry. An old man with a bright black mustache daubed at her feet with a mop made of seaweed. Kevin had to walk over to the desk every few minutes and ask if it was time to go up yet. Otherwise, they would be squatting there yet, like the old people.

"Downtown Moscow," muttered Kevin. Why was he going on about the hospital? What difference did it make? As an architect he had a right to his interests, but there was a time for everything. She herself wanted a place that reminded her that life was short and foul.

Now, two days later, she saw Kevin's point. Brian needed sunlight at least, he would never get well in the dark. Think of the plants in city apartments. The fever was almost played out, and he looked as if nothing too serious had happened. She smiled at him with all the tenderness she could muster, and he smiled back politely. He obviously didn't know what a fix he was in yet.

The tenderness dried in her throat and stuck like paint. She could not for the moment look at her son naturally. It would take time and practice. She studied the nurse, for composure. Miss Withers moved in a brisk monotone, pumping up the bed, putting a napkin over the urine bottle as if it were vintage champagne — regulating the room's mood at a steady 70. No laughter please in the hospital zone, laughter is paid for later at night and you know who has to clean up. Tears? Just don't get them on the patient. As soon as Beatrice looked at her son again, tenderness came back like a blush. She got up to go. "Will he be all right?" she asked Nurse Withers. "I think he'll live," said the nurse, winking grotesquely. "Won't you, sonny?"

Living would hardly be enough, for a perpetual-motion machine like Brian. She could see him now, the size of her thumbnail, playing ball down in Riverside Park, making the trained-monkey moves of baseball: holding glove to mouth to jabber something, swinging three bats, and crouching down with the handles in his lap — none of it made any sense to her, so she watched with special attention, between swipes of the duster. Bend and straighten and jiggle and spit. Strange things to be doing, but he seemed to enjoy them.

She cried automatically when she got home. As soon as she saw the living-room furniture. (Yesterday, the hall closet brought it on.) And Kevin calmed her, an old practice of theirs, but not as satisfactory as usual. "Don't *you* ever cry?" she said.

"I just express myself differently," he said. Kevin was the worst man in the world to criticize. He took an awkward lurch on the arm of her chair. "I wouldn't think I'd have to prove how much I feel."

"I'm sorry," she said quickly, "I didn't mean anything like that." God's truth. It was just a point of manners. She had hoped vaguely that his response to grief would be perfect.

Kevin put his arm around her. They probably should love each other a little more consciously than they were accustomed to. Which meant that an agreed-upon dullness of bodies must be waived, and the hedgehog defenses of the spirit. He thought that perhaps lovemaking would help. She thought not. Not after just seeing Brian. Their cross-purposes made for an awkward seating arrangement. Kevin stood up and went looking for a cigarette or anything else he could find.

"There's a good sunset," he said. She could tell from the violet in the room that this must be so. A rich flush suffused the sofa cushions, the color of Christmas.

"Do you suppose he knows yet?" Kevin asked casually.

"Knows what? That he's got polio? I guess so. He must, don't you think?"

"I don't know. It's hard to think straight when you're in fever. Do you think he knows much *about* polio?"

"Oh, he must. All those pictures of little boys in leg irons." My God, was he one of *those* now? A March of Dimes poster? "You can't miss those pictures." Don't think. Just keep talking.

"I guess not. And our gallant President." He rocked with his hands in his pockets, and the sky flared in front of him. His shoulders looked skinny with the waistcoat hunched up on them. Beatrice thought, What is he doing, talking about sunsets and gallant Presidents? Has he no feelings? And thought, I must not get hysterical. Kevin was a dry, cheery man and you couldn't ask him to drop everything overnight. His style of mourning would be different from hers, equally acceptable in its own way. It seemed, in fact, to consist of an endless keeping up of morale, like the British in 1940 — even when you wanted morale to sag a little. It didn't mean he didn't feel things, though.

Father O'Monahan, expert in grief, turned up that afternoon. She was pleased: he might lay down some guidelines, about sunsets and jokes and things. She walked him along the corridor and into the living room. Kevin didn't fancy O'Monahan in a general way, but surely they would both be above personalities today. Kevin managed a greeting of sorts and winced over the priest's soft handshake, in a way that might have passed for sorrow, she hoped.

"This is a sad thing," said O'Monahan, sinking down in his favorite sofa . . .

"We think so," said Kevin, starting in on him right away.

"You'll need a lot of faith. And hope, too. They tell me cures are being found every day."

"Not for polio. You must be thinking of something else," said Kevin. "Will you be having a drink, Father?" Oh dear, an Irish accent.

"Er, the usual. A little Scotch and soda."

Kevin went out to the kitchen, wooden-faced and prickly. Beatrice was appalled. His sarcasm was usually as light as pastry . . . in fact, he used to be quite funny about O'Monahan, claiming that he couldn't believe in spiritual leaders over 250 pounds. But today he seemed vicious, as if O'Monahan were to blame for the whole thing; or as if, anyway, *some*one should be punished for it. She hoped he stayed in the kitchen until he came to his senses.

O'Monahan seemed ill at ease, for all his experience. She felt like telling him not to worry.

"How is the boy?"

"He's much better. He — smiled at me today." A flash flood of grief. Freeze it at once. Practice not crying every day, until your tears harden like cement. Women with strong faces. Beauty hint.

"That's wonderful. He'll be his old self in no time."

"Not quite," said Kevin, back at the door already. "He'll be missing a thing or two."

"But his wonderful spirit will still be there."

Kevin's face was ugly with mischief. The charm turned into poison.

"How do you know his spirit is wonderful?" said Kevin. "That's what we're about to find out, isn't it, Father?" He handed over the drink with elaborate disdain, which O'Monahan strove to ignore. Kevin was a *funny* man. Was this what happened to funny men under pressure?

"Give us your advice, Father," she said. "What should we tell Brian about his condition?"

"Yes, Father," said Kevin, "tell us about that."

O'Monahan writhed a fat man's writhe, and the sunset flashed across his chest. "Am I the only one that's drinking?" he asked.

"That's right," said Kevin.

"I don't care for one right now," Beatrice added more politely.

"Well, then," said the priest, looking at his glass wildly, as if wondering whom he could plant it on.

"Oh, go ahead and drink it," said Kevin.

O'Monahan took a temporizing sip and said, "I don't set up as an expert, Kevin." Then what the hell are we paying your salary for? said Kevin's face. "I've never had a son of my own, it goes without saying." All right then, don't say it, said the face. You've probably never even been sick, have you? Ah, but you read about it once, in the seminary, in Latin.

"But I think I would emphasize the miracles of modern science, the marvels that take place hourly in our labs." So that's it. Bow your knee to the man in the white coat, ye sinners. "And don't forget the power of prayer. It can move mountains, you know." Oh yes? Name one.

Beatrice's head was splitting. She had heard Kevin giving the works to Monsignor Sheen on the radio, settling scores with some old nun who had once slapped his face for talking back. She bet he was doing it now. She guessed she had hoped that the warm heart inside every comedian would be coaxed to Kevin's surface by tragedy; but perhaps it was cold hearts comedians had. Anyway, she hated to see O'Monahan all guileless, feeding her husband straight lines.

"Thank you, Father," said Kevin stiffly. "I'm sure that's very helpful."

O'Monahan got up. He knew the score, knew that he couldn't win. His cloth stood on end in the presence of an Irish anticleric. Kevin was usually politer than this, but the hatred was always there, for the connoisseur. Kevin was a good enough Catholic, outside of that. His confessions were dry and scrupulously correct. It didn't seem to mean any more to him than brushing his teeth, and O'Monahan sometimes thought he would be a mellower man if he just gave it up altogether: not that mellowness counts for much in the courts of the Lord.

Beatrice saw the priest out. "Kevin is upset today. I'm sorry if he was sharp with you."

"That's all right," he whispered back. "It may be one way I can help."

She stalled by the door. She would not go back in a temper. A fight would be just awful. "Who the hell is he to be giving us advice? This is a real problem, not one of those spiritual ones." Kevin purple and shaking with clown's rage. She went straight to her bedroom. Brian would sense it if they had been fighting. She credited her son now with supernatural powers. She tried briefly to feel sorry for Kevin and his ancient wounds, but she just couldn't. She felt quite isolated. A sarcastic man was no company at a time like this.

Later in the evening, Kevin told her that he hadn't meant to be critical of O'Monahan at all. Maybe a little tasteless joke at first, but what the hell, they were old friends. He was really most anxious to hear what O'Monahan had to say. And she really hoped that this was the truth.

* * *

"Good night, kid," said Nurse Withers. She seemed to be all right. He listened with half an ear while she told him about some fellow she was dating. He sounded like a real creep, but maybe it was the way she told it.

He would miss the opening of school, which was no great loss. It would probably take several months to fix this thing up. The doctor was vaguely optimistic about it. His mother's sad smile had puzzled him. He didn't know of anything that called for that. He lay in the dark now, feeling the wet ooze around his legs. The fact that the legs couldn't move was neither here nor there. He was used to it already. They would move again in their good time. But the hot packs were a nuisance. He felt as if he'd been out in the rain all day and was now drying out in front of a stove. But as soon as he got anywhere, the night nurse would dip some more flannel, and he would be back to go.

"Too bad you don't talk," he said to the nurse, a placid Russian lady.

"I talk a little," she said, nudging the pack under his knee.

"This priest, Father O'Monahan, one of God's holy fools, Dad calls him, he was in today, and he said, 'My son, you're being very plucky about this, hmmm, hmmm.' So I said, 'What's with pluck, Father? Lying in bed and being looked after by beautiful nurses is plucky?' And he shook his head, and told me I had a grand spirit. I don't know what gets into these people."

Night nurses should be able to talk. He felt lonely with nothing but his wet flannel. There was this to be said for the nurses, though; they didn't take it all so darn seriously. Madame Kutchakokov here could have been moving furniture, for all the concern she showed.

He shut his eyes and imagined the scene as he sauntered into a touch-football game on the block. "Hey, it's Casey." "Yeah, it's Casey. Fellas, it's Casey. You got out of the hospital, I see," etc. He hoped they would think of something more interesting to say when the time came, but right now, it was the best he could do for them. Admiring glances, soundless pats on the butt. Casey is back, "Shut up and just gimme the ball, will you?" Fatso came running and handed him the ball like a chalice. Marconi threw him a grudging smile. Not bad, not bad at all . . . Cut it out now, Casey. Nobody thinks you're that hot. But it was a pretty vision to sleep on.

The next few days were busy as a diplomat's. Visitors were whisked in and out, bearing flowers, magazines, and from his old man, detective stories. He began to distinguish between the "very plucky's" and the "how's the boy's," the tender smilers and the hearty laughers. It was quite a game adjusting to all of them. Even his friends, Bernie Levine and Fatstuff, had to be reconsidered.

They started out very solemn, dressed up as if for a job interview, and wound up chasing each other around the bed and knocking over his water jug. Fatstuff asked if Brian could feel anything in his legs, and he said, Go ahead and touch. I can see you're dying to. And Fatstuff touched, as if expecting the mummy's curse to strike him.

Bernie said, "How're the nurses? Are they any good?"

"Not bad, not bad." He had been too weak to think about it in that sense. "They're probably kind of cold, though."

Bernie giggled. "Do they, you know, wash you?"

"Oh for godsake," said Brian. "Yeah, sure, they wash you until you can't stand it." Fatstuff was looking at him as tenderly as a woman. Good grief, he thinks my balls have got it. "Of course, the nurses are frightened at first by my amazing proportions," he said, smothering his own panic. He really didn't know. The area was numb for the moment with the packs jammed against it.

"What happens when you have to take a crap?" asked Bernie, from his list of topical questions.

"They got pots and pans for that. You lose the taste for it after a while." Fact. He was brimming with constipation. But did they really want to hear about that? He sensed it was up to him to keep the conversation going. Stranded between jollity and reverence, his friends hardly knew where to turn.

"How's Phil?" he asked.

They glanced at each other. "Don't mention that guy," said Bernie. "Please."

"What's the matter? Burning candles to Mussolini again?"

"Nothing. He's just a rat, that's all."

"Go on, he must have done *something*."

"Well." They hesitated again.

"Come on fellas, you don't have to look at each other every time you talk. What'd the wop do?"

"Well," said Bernie, "we were talking about, you know, you, and what a lousy break you got, and he was kidding around, and he wouldn't take it seriously."

"Is that so?" How dare he not take it seriously? It was strange, being talked about at all. Brian didn't realize he was an issue. "It was nice of you guys to stick up for me. You *did* stick up for me, didn't you?"

"Definitely."

"What'd you say about me?"

"Well, you know, that you were a good guy and all. That you had a lot of guts." They obviously resented being made to say it, and would think twice about sticking up for him next time. Saints don't reach for compliments. He had certainly botched that one.

"Yeah sure, I'm a prince. What I really want to know is, what did Macaroni say that was so terrible?"

"He said that, *you* know, you were just a guy."

"Why, that's a *terrible* thing to say."

"Well, it was the way he said it, right Bernie? All sneery and *blech*."

"And he said we were just being nice to you because we were afraid of catching it ourselves."

Brian smiled. "That's interesting. Is there any truth in it?"

The silence was horrible. They had come to worship at the shrine, and the old saint had pointed a bony finger at them and told them they stank on ice. No more pilgrimages for them, boy. He would have to look for new clients, new friends; but right now he didn't care.

After that, things degenerated, and out of sheer social inadequacy, Bernie landed a punch on Fatstuff's biceps and the chase was on. Brian lay there, aware of his dead legs, thinking, Those guys are afraid of this, and I've already been there. A grotesque sense of power creamed through his veins, right down to his toes. Yes, his crotch was alive all right. He saw their horseplay as fear and weakness, the high thin farting of virgins, to use Marconi's favorite expression. They didn't know the secret of his power — that polio wasn't really that bad.

Nurse Withers threw them out, and they said a worried but fervent goodbye. The young diplomat figured it this way. They were on record as thinking he was a great guy, magically improved by polio; and they would stand on the record and try to forget what had happened in here today.

The next encounter was a surprise. Phil Marconi himself; a triumph. "What are you doing in here without a present, Phil? Don't you know that everyone brings me presents?"

"Yeah, I figured that. So I thought you wouldn't miss the one I didn't bring."

"You don't understand, you fascist pig. It isn't the present, it's the respect it shows."

You couldn't accuse Phil of sneering, because his lips were shaped that way and he didn't have to move them. "How come all the presents go to you, anyway? You sick or something? I think you should give some presents to your friends, to keep things even."

"You came here just to tell me that?"

"Yeah, I thought this place might be ruining your character. Which was shaky to begin with."

Phil would be a great guy if he could ever stop saying the same one thing, over and over. Fifty-seven variations of "you're not so hot."

"I hear you upset my friends, Phil. You told them I was just a guy."

"Nicest thing I ever said about you. Those little shits were sucking up to you for luck. Getting polio doesn't change anything in my books."

Yeah, maybe not. Phil was so desperate to get everything straight, after the wartime propaganda, he never knew when to stop. Brian was getting sick of the subject of polio, however cunningly served up.

"Have I missed any triumphs of the Italian forces?" he said.

"Boy, you guys are boring. If the enemy fights good, you call him a fanatical killer. If he fights bad, you call him a clown. Italians don't want this war and you should be grateful."

"Is it true they fought a draw with a flock of sheep?"

"You make me sick, Casey. When did you last hear from the Irish Army? Fifteen-oh-two, in the Battle of the Bog, was it? Unfortunately, the limeys routed them utterly."

It was good to shoot the crap like this. Marconi's Irish accent had to be heard.

"Den dere was de Battle of McGonnigle's britches in 1603, where alas de Irish was forced to flee, but [switch to solemn Edward R. Murrow voice] they got a great song out of it, which is still heard wherever free men gather." Marconi laughed rackingly at his own invention. "Yessir, the strains of 'McGonnigle's Britches' were heard above the battle at O'Donegal's Downfall and again the following year at O'Donovan's Disaster."

"You're full of shit," said Brian. His stomach felt drastically weak and any more laughter would blow it apart. Miss Withers came in to check on the racket. Marconi's laugh was a wheezing bark that could alarm anyone. He might be trying to kill someone in there.

"See you, Brian," he said abruptly and left, stumbling past Miss Withers.

Marconi was defiantly clumsy. He was the kind of guy who sneered at baseball and hit the ball a mile with a grudging, what's-it-to-you swing. In the movies he and Brian lived at, he would be the hero's best friend, the one who chewed him out about his values the night of the championship. It was no accident — they studied those parts closely. Brian saw himself as a natural John Garfield.

They rested him and fattened him up for the next round of visitors — his aunts, Brigid and Portia. There was no escape around here, except to get so sick *nobody* could see you. He felt more than ever like a mummy in a glass case, as the aunts looked him over. Brigid looked at his legs as if she expected them to tell her something. Portia stared above his head as if nothing had happened. People were really a scream, in this situation.

Aunt Portia had a leather shopping bag, Aunt Brigid's was made of wool. Brigid hauled out a missal stuffed with holy cards. "This one is St. Jude, patron of lost causes — not that your cause is lost, by any means. And here is St. Dismas, the good thief. He's always handy. I'd like you to keep these, Brian. They've done wonders in their time."

"And if you should want something a little more substantial, I've brought you some medical magazines." Aunt Portia sprayed her selection over Brian's knees. They looked like the kind of two-bit sun-and-health nudist magazines that Brian and his friends occasionally browsed for cheesecake.

"Do they say anything about polio?" he asked.

"Well, there's one about a Dr. Steinmetz who does nerve grafts. Here he is." She flipped to a marked page. There was a fuzzy picture of a small man in a two-piece bathing suit, standing next to a smiling brunette, twice his size. He had a chin beard, which looked hastily glued, and rimless glasses. The caption said the doctor was honeymooning in Atlantic City with his third wife, a former patient. Miss Olivia Schenk, if anyone wanted to know.

"Dr. Steinmetz has had a terribly hard time from the medical world," said Portia. "They hate new ideas, you know."

"Nerve grafts? What's that got to do with polio?"

Portia didn't blink. "I'm not sure. The article is mostly about amputations, I believe. But don't you think the same principles might apply?"

Maybe, maybe. His options were many at this point.

Brigid surged back into the picture. "The nuns at St. Cecilia's are praying their hearts out for you, Brian. And Father McShea mentions you in all his masses." He imagined a votive light burning through the night in a dark chapel. Just for him. Hot spit.

"You won't be needing medical help in that case," said Aunt Portia, who was something of a needler.

Brigid laughed. She was a big woman, not easily rattled. She had fifteen or twenty children. Brian couldn't remember which. Altar boys with sniffles, flower girls: you only saw them in church. "God prefers to work in natural ways if he can," she said. On another day, Portia would have given battle. "It's the only way he ever works, have you noticed?" Leaving the Church had been a convulsion for her, her moment of highest intensity, and she never missed a chance to rekindle it.

"There's no conflict between religion and science," said Brigid, and Portia gave a hopeless snort. "We'll both be working for Brian in our own ways," said Brigid.

Religion and science made sleepy, after-lunch peace in Brian's mind. They were both just ways of getting cured. He pictured nuns praying in shifts around the clock, scorching their wimples, trying to shake a miracle loose; while at the same time brilliant scientists worked feverishly in mile-long labs, holding test tubes to the light and squinting. "Come here a minute, Watson. I think I'm on to something." Also quacks in bathing suits, mad enough to try anything, grafting the legs of a goat, the heart of a chicken. Something had to come of it all.

Meanwhile Brigid and Portia fought with their eyes. Don't destroy the boy's faith. Well, don't you fill him with superstition then. Or rather, "My life good, your life bad." Brian had heard them at it, at family get-togethers, and didn't care. They were both right. Brigid had special powers. She breathed in time with the tides and had a baby every spring. She knew something. But Portia, his father's older sister, was pretty smart in her own way.

They left in uneasy truce, and Miss Withers scooped up their cards and magazines and stuffed them in his bedside drawer. "Open the cage and let my crazy relatives out," said Brian. "I've seen worse," said Miss Withers.

She seemed annoyed at having to fix his flowers and tidy his presents. He could understand that. Her petulance was comradely, us against them. "Those magazines are putting my aunt through college," he said. Miss Withers held up his urine bottle and he nodded — a sordid exchange in most instances, but Miss Withers made a fine thing of it. "How'd you make out last night?" he asked her.

"I don't know. They're all after the same thing, aren't they?" She said it provocatively, a little gift for Brian. He thought about that thing they were after for a moment, golden and glowing. Then felt tired and dizzy. The packs sagged cold on his legs and Miss Withers began to cook up a new batch. Dr. Samson looked in on him at that point, peeped under the packs, and nodded. What did he see? He asked Brian to flex his right knee. Brian couldn't, but the doctor nodded again anyway.

"How does it look, Doc?" he asked.

"Very good. No sign of atrophy," said Dr. Samson.

"Yeah, but is there any sign of life?"

The doctor smiled. "Don't be in such a hurry. These things take time."

You see, you see? He said I'm going to get better. Brian wasn't sure whether to press the inquiry and shoot for more specific assurance. O.K. — shoot. "What would you say the chances are, Doc?"

Samson looked at Nurse Withers, as if this were a routine they'd done together before. "These kids," he said. "Always trying to pin you down." Mis Withers looked back without expression, bless her. The doc straightened up and swung into a man-to-man match-up.

"Brian, I can't give you odds. People are working night and day on this thing. And your own spirit could make a big difference."

Ten years in medical school to learn that? Brian expected a better brand of cheese from this man.

"What about Nurse Kenny?" he said.

"Yes, well, she's done some very useful work. Mostly in cutting down atrophy. That's about all she's proved so far."

"What about Dr. Steinmetz then?"

"Dr. Who?"

Brian was embarrassed already. "Dr. Steinmetz. He does nerve grafts."

"*Nerve* grafts? For polio?"

It did sound pretty silly. His aunt had led him into this. Samson didn't laugh, because he didn't have to. "I'd rely on real scientists if I were you, Brian."

"I heard the medical profession was down on him."

"Is that so? Well, I'm not surprised. He probably should have his license revoked." Samson was an official in the American Medical Association, and he couldn't let it pass. "Men like that fatten on silly old ladies and make it that much harder for the rest of us. Don't you think that if he had a cure for polio, we'd know about it by now? Don't you think we'd *welcome* it?" The thought of Portia as a silly old lady was crushing. His own family didn't belong in those categories. Silly spinster, fat fool.

Samson's anger was so darn *distinguished.* "I'm sorry, Brian, but those people give me a swift pain. Nurse Kenny, too, if it comes to that. Just another exhibitionist, raising false hopes in sick people. Put your faith in real doctors, Brian. And in your own fighting spirit."

The doctor left, still smoothly raging. His neck was too thick for a doctor's. Brian's fighting spirit felt as hollow as Nurse Kenny. In defense of his stupid profession, Dr. Samson had just about admitted that there was no hope. Fighting spirit, indeed. If they were relying on that, the game was up.

He gathered from Miss Withers's expression that he must be showing some distress. "Don't worry about him, he's an old fud," she said. But the rows of scientists were waxworks figures now, and the nuns at prayer were just silly old ladies, baying at the moon. "What about Dr. Steinmetz?" he said ironically.

319

She frowned and said, "Well, maybe he's on to something. Dr. Samson would be the last to know."

Brian shut his eyes, too tired to feel seriously scared. There were some good things among Samson's ravings, weren't there? That you never could tell. That scientists were working. That these things take time. When he woke, he found he had regrouped and added Samson to the good tidings.

* * *

"I say we tell him."

"Tell him what, dear?"

"The score," said Kevin. "About his chances. You can't feed a boy of sixteen fairy tales. It's bad for him in the long run."

"Oh dear, not that again. We're *not* telling him fairy tales," said Beatrice. "There *are* such things as miracles. You believe that, don't you?"

They were in front of the window again. The back rooms were all as dark as underwater dungeons. So the Caseys met at the front window every evening. The trees in Riverside Park were beginning to shed, and the coming of winter had to be borne in mind.

"Yes, I guess so. Occasionally. Not too many miracles in New York, though," he muttered.

"There's not too much faith in New York, either. Do you suppose that might account for it?"

They looked at each other fearfully, as if they had both felt the first drop of the monsoon. "Look, let's not fight about it," said Kevin. "It's just one small point."

"I'm not fighting and personally I don't care *what* you think about miracles," said Beatrice, "though it seems a pity to have that emptiness in your life."

Kevin mumbled, more to himself than her, "I didn't say that they couldn't happen. Just that they don't."

"But I'm afraid you'll say something to Brian when he gets home," continued Beatrice.

He turned his head. Sick of memorizing the Jersey shore. Palisades Park was shut for the winter. The Crisco sign was out like a light. Everything dead or dying over there. Each time you have the same discussion, it gets a little bit worse. "I won't say anything at all to him until we've talked it over together. Meanwhile, I plan to do everything I know to make him happy.

O.K.?" Kevin always liked to cut domestic quarrels short, before
they got sloppy. But it was sometimes hard to do that and still
make his point. Brian was due home tomorrow and would spend
his days in the bright living room. From now on, they would
have to do their arguing in whispers, and in the bedroom. So,
if they wanted a last noisy one, this was the time for it.

"I'm sorry," said Beatrice. "I know you want what's best
for him."

"I do," said Kevin, reaching an arm for her shoulder. They
stood for a moment side by side, as if there were an altar in
front of them and a beaming priest. They had weathered some
standard-issue storms in eighteen years: miscarriages, hyster-
ectomy, no more children. Nothing terrible recently. Not much
more money of course, ambition flogged slowly to death like
most people's. They could surely survive this one.

"Look, I just want to ask this one thing," he said. "We agree
that Brian has got a fine spirit, right? So — why don't you think
he can face the facts?"

"Oh, can't you leave it alone? Why is it so important to
you?" She disengaged herself, and he began to prowl, to the
sofa, back, anywhere.

"I don't know." There was some other quarrel between them,
but they couldn't find it and had to keep settling for this one.
"I don't want my son living in an unreal world, that's all."

"You don't mean the Catholic Church, do you?"

"No, of course I don't. The Catholic Church is realistic."
Kevin groped. The Church taught a little of everything, didn't
they? What was the teaching for this? "They teach you to accept
suffering, not to run away from it, and they teach, I think they
teach, that it's presumptuous to expect miracles. But besides all
that — Don't you see that accepting the facts could make a
real man of him? If we lie to him, if we offer him a Hollywood
cure, we leave him a kid forever, like everyone else in this
damned country."

"It just so happens his own faith is a very important factor."

There was a sense of scandal and shock between them. They
had never really argued religion before. Kevin's anti-clericalism
was just a mannerism. They agreed about the essentials, because
the essentials never came up. And Kevin's good humor always
suggested that he would be right about them if they did.

"You and Father O'Monahan seem to think a healthy body is everything," he said. "Damnit, if the spirit is so important, why don't you concentrate on that for a while?"

"I don't understand you, Kevin. Don't you want your boy to be well?" Oh God, the power of a non sequitur. "Of course I do. But what if he isn't?"

"He will be. I know he will be." What monster of cold rationality could doubt it? "If it's God's will that he isn't, there'll be time enough to face it then. But how can you give up on him so soon?"

Lack of faith was a terrible accusation. It was better to be wrong than to be a doubter, a life-denier. He tried to rephrase it. "All right. I believe it. I believe that he very probably will get well. I don't see what we've ever done to rate a miracle, but maybe we'll land one anyway. More likely it will be science that does it."

"That's perfectly fine with me."

"But, anyway, *I* don't know —" silk cords of custom kept them from fighting properly and ending it. He wasn't allowed to say, You can't face it yourself, can you? You're more Hollywood than you thought, aren't you? And she wasn't allowed to say back, what she must be thinking, You're being very brave on your son's behalf, I must say. Could you have taken a blow like that yourself? Could you take it now? It was as if the sick boy were in the next room already and they must talk in flurried whispers.

At their last anniversary, Kevin had toasted the happiest couple he knew and the man who made it possible. Now, one badly phrased word could release old poisons they hadn't known about. They groped for that word and pulled away from it. To stall, Kevin gave her a good-old-boy squeeze and she responded slightly like a faithful chum.

The next day, Kevin Casey dropped by the hospital to assist at Brian's removal. It was a cold, raw day, a cold-blooded killer to all that grew, but Brian thought the fresh air was simply great as they slammed open the iron door and hoisted him down the ramp and into the ambulance. "I don't know when I've felt so great," he said. "Just feel that air, will you." Kevin's bones had long since turned to stone, but he did as he was told. And for a moment he shared his son's elation.

What could he do for this wonderful boy? Brian was talking thirteen to the dozen in the ambulance. His face must be the only one in town to have escaped the first frost. Outside people with grey faces peered in whenever the driver stopped for a red light (the ambulance was in no hurry) and it seemed as if their skin would fall off with the next wind and have to be raked away. Or line the gutters like rind. Legs or no legs, his son was at least alive.

Brian talked of the wonders of home, what he would do first, second, who he would like to see (not see), and the Grade A spookiness of hospital life. Miss Withers, he said, had broken with her creep and taken up with another equally creepy. She was plagued by sex fiends. The night nurse was hoping to get back to Russia and rejoin her "people" as soon as the war ended, and had actually managed to convey it in English. Brian had been patient with her, and she could now say words like "drop dead" and "so's your old man," with that sad, faraway smile of hers.

"It sounds as if you had a pretty good time after all," said Kevin.

"Yeah, except for things like the early-morning washing. I told you about that, didn't I? The night nurse likes to give you a last lick before she checks out. And then the morning nurse wakes you again for a quick scrub — mind you, you're still wet from the night nurse." He was more talkative than he used to be, almost like an actor. "And then there's temperature-taking practice. You know, after the first week, you don't really have a temperature to take any more, but boy, try telling that to the nurses. The trainees come sneaking in with their thermometers and whammo, in the mouth, under the arm, anyplace they feel like. Wow."

Any change was worrying. This was definitely a new boy. There was a smoothness about him, and the rattling charm of a salesman. Had he been listening to too many daytime radio shows? Or was this the tinny echo of somebody's bedside manner? Kevin hated blather; Brian sensed this, and slowed down a little. "It's funny about the temperature part," he said. "You know, polio only lasts about a week. What you have after that is the *remains* of polio."

Perhaps it was possible to become both glibber and more thoughtful. Anyway, the synthetic thing, the prattle, would become worse if the boy was lied to about his condition. (Why is this such a mania of yours, Kevin? Because I cannot bear to deceive him. Because he'll find out and say "You deceived me." Because I cannot bear it that *I* know and he not. Because. A good confession is never done.)

That morning, before picking Brian up, Kevin had talked with Dr. Samson, to make absolutely sure. Samson had been his usual evasive self, squirting smoke screens of "wait and see's" and "early to tell's," but when he saw that Kevin would settle only for the worst, he said, "Unless science comes up with something, I guess his chances are only fair."

God, he hated people like Samson. There was a sense of no Irish need apply about him. And of "Fordham? (pause) I see." "Less than fifty-fifty?" Kevin badgered. "*Much* less than fifty-fifty?" Let's have a little mental discipline, Yale.

The doctor nodded. "There should be *some* sign of life by now, Mr. Casey. The arms seem to be all right, especially the right one. He nearly broke my hand testing his grip. The neck and stomach are weak but hopeful." And then he launched into a stream of Latin names, *glibius flatulus, ponderus maximus,* not Latin a Catholic would use, indicating that Brian's legs were a wasteland where no life would stir again.

Was that what he wanted to hear? Pain was ambiguous, some people laughed from it. Kevin was delirious, flayed alive, laughing to death, but glad to *know.* Nothing could now get worse, that was the important thing. Jerk the adhesive off smartly. Brian could still live a wonderful life, but they must get started on it right away. No more prayers to St. Philomena.

"I wouldn't tell your wife about this," said Dr. Samson.

"What about my son?"

"Why tell him? He'll get used to his condition in a year or two, and he won't mind knowing then."

If Samson had his way, no one would ever be told anything. Everyone would pass through life knowing nothing at all, caressed by lies. His only medicine was anesthesia.

"You don't trust my son, is that it?" Kevin said as pleasantly as possible. "You don't think he's strong enough for the truth?"

"Few people are. Remember, Brian is only a boy of what? Sixteen? Precocious in some ways. But don't be misled by that. It will take all the courage he has, to face it when he has to."

Please, Doctor, spare us your wisdom, O.K.? You have utterly failed to help us professionally. In fact, you have done nothing at all, so far as I can see. So do not lecture us on how to live . . . Kevin felt for a mad moment that the doctor was to blame for the whole thing: his sly evasions, his passivity had held Brian in check for precious weeks.

Samson looked as if he was used to this. He came around the desk and stood by Kevin, ready to shake hands or whatever Kevin preferred. "I'm sorry, Mr. Casey. It's hard for you too, *I* realize that. It's your decision, of course. But I think Brian will figure it out at his own speed. The facts are there." Translated: everybody really knows that polio is incurable, don't they? I, Dr. Samson, have not deceived the public.

A weaselly compromise. Dr. Samson was paid by the minute, and his handshake was metered. Kevin was uncomfortable with professional men. Of course he was one himself, but he didn't feel like one. He left the doctor's office and had a couple of drinks for lunch to steady himself. It was indeed his decision to make. The truth hurt like hell, he could hardly bear to keep his own eye on it for more than a second. But two years of ghastly charade and dwindling hope were unthinkable. You wouldn't string out, say, an amputee for two years, would you? All right then. Whether Beatrice liked it or not, he would share the truth with his son and join him in battle. The truth could make Brian a hero: how many people ever get close to the truth? With only one son, you wanted to go all the way. It wasn't enough just to make him happy.

Kevin still had blood in his eye, with a little Scotch, as he joggled in the ambulance. But now Brian had lengthened his view from the first days at home and was burbling about the months ahead.

"Basketball, yah, who cares about basketball? I'm not tall enough anyway. The doctor says I'll never make seven feet. I expect to be out and around by then, of course, but it'll take awhile to get my legs back in shape. You can definitely put me down for the opening of the baseball season."

My God, he was talking like a child. The baseball season! Kevin jerked his head, but there was no place else to look in the narrow ambulance. Brian must have thought his old man was nuts, like all the others: trying to hide his fixed grin and his streaming eyes.

* * *

So Kevin gave up, for now, the idea of telling Brian his chances. He still thought he should, but he hadn't the heart to. As the only one in the neighborhood to face it, Kevin began to feel that he carried an unfair burden. He watched with heavy eyes the pantomime of cheerfulness and unreality forming around Brian: the holy-card vendors setting up their stands, Portia and her crazy magazines, the quacks with their optimism, ten dollars an ounce. He ached to scourge them away, and have everything very pure and simple, but he couldn't bring himself to do it. And every day he felt weaker and more out of it.

Brian didn't spot much of this. His father seemed his old brisk self — altogether too brisk in some ways. For instance, he brought up the question of schoolwork on Brian's second day home. "Can't that wait a little?" said Beatrice. Exactly Brian's feeling about it. "It's possible to get lazy in bed," said Kevin. No, no. Polio victims are a compendium of all the virtues. Brian knew his old man had a point, but felt nettled with him for bringing it up at this particular time.

It would be unspeakably dreary to have this thing and to have to study as well. What Brian wanted now was magazine subscriptions. He proposed to his mother that they put out for *Look, Collier's, Time,* and *The Sporting News,* a nicely balanced lineup. Kevin said, "You won't have time for anything else." "Nobody in the world has more time that I have," said Brian. They compromised on *Time* and *Look.*

The days were pleasant enough, except for the grunt and groan with the physiotherapist. Mrs. Schmidt demanded an hour's work and a pound of flesh, and a ten o'clock scholar. "You're not pushing," she'd say. "How can you tell? I don't have any strength there yet." "I can tell." She pumped his legs, as if she were training him for the Rockettes. When he didn't push, she noticed it, and when he did push, she accused him of doing it with his hip, a low form of cheating. There was no easy winning with Mrs. Schmidt.

"When am I going to get better?" he asked from time to time.

"Never, if you don't push."

"Yeah, but if I push?"

"Just keep pushing."

That was all the sense he could get out of her. But she was a good kid. She lit on a flickering muscle as if it were a gold strike. "Do that again." He usually couldn't. "I thought I saw something. All right, let's get back to work." She would never give up on any leg that came her way. But after a month or so, she began to allow herself a five-minute cigarette break. And it turned out she was quite different at rest. Her face smoothed out and she looked beautiful, for forty-two. She talked about music a lot, although Brian told her he had a tin ear. Never mind, he should hear about music anyway. It was part of being a civilized man. Did he speak German, no? 'Fraid not. He spoke French then, yes? Sorry, *Ach,* you Americans. One thing she wouldn't talk about under any circumstances was the war. It seemed she was some kind of refugee with a husband still over there. But whether this husband was in a concentration camp or the German High Command, there was no way of telling. Brian couldn't tell a Jew from anyone else, even though he'd lived in New York all his life. He didn't think he'd met any, although Levine might be one.

They had him in a cranked-up bed, and he sat by the window watching the grim last of the touch-football games and the appearance of mittens and sleds. There was no place for real sleighing down there, but they paddled along hopefully until they came to a rise. They were smaller than they used to be.

Enthroned in clean pajamas in the middle of the living room, he came in for a good deal of random attention. All the Caseys' visitors paid their frantic respects, the "how is everything" brigade, and the "you're looking wonderful" division. After which, they would forget him and talk business and politics, so that he went from being petted to being bored. The way it goes. He read a lot, mostly junk, but some good stuff. Damon Runyon, Chesterton, Plato's *Republic.* Decided Socratic questions were a crock: "Oh yes, Socrates, truly, Socrates; how do you want your ass kissed today, Socrates?" Still, he liked the book. Father O'Monahan came around and gave him the sacraments at Christmas. Very embarrassing to confess masturbation to a man who could actually see you, but there was no way round it. O'Monahan took it like a sport. A man came over to cut his hair, and a fine mess that was, trying to tilt his head around on the pillow. His neck was still weak as water and they talked about putting it in a brace — scare talk that came to nothing.

It was like living in a luxury hotel, where everything was brought to you on trays. Even the men's room was brought to you. He was embarrassed the first time his father took out the steaming bedpan. It was things like that which made him ache to get back on his feet. Otherwise, it was a pretty good life, at least in the daytime. People seemed to think he was going through something, and if he said he wasn't, their eyes glowed double with admiration.

The nights were kind of crumby. He prayed a lot (1) to get better and (2) to avoid the roaring temptations of the flesh. He didn't sleep well, for want of exercise, and he usually succumbed to number 2 around three in the morning, in agonies of remorse. Please don't hold this against me, Lord. I still want to get cured and will make this up to you eventually. No one in good health should ever have occasion to masturbate. Linking the problems like that gave him an exhilarating sense of purpose, and he slept serenely in his wet pajamas.

In February a little man came around with a roll of brown paper and began tracing his legs. It hadn't been explained to Brian, or he hadn't been listening, that he was about to be measured for leg braces. A disgusting idea. "What do I want those things for?" he bellowed at Mrs. Schmidt. "I'm going to walk on my own legs."

"*Ja,* but in the meantime . . . You don't want to spend all your life in this room, do you?"

It felt like a betrayal. His muscles would never come back in those iron grilles. He had seen people heaving along Broadway, dragging them like chains. In fact he even remembered throwing a pitying smile to one such — old fellow with a beard and a shiny black suit. God, what a horrible thing to do.

"You didn't even ask if I wanted them," he raged. "How can you make decisions like that for people?"

"I'm sorry, Brian. It's routine."

"Do my parents know about this? Get my mother."

Mrs. Schmidt was not someone you ordered about, but this time she went meekly enough and came back with Beatrice.

"What is it, Brian?"

He wanted his anger to hit her, level and hard. "Did you know about this, Mother? Did you know that Mrs. Schmidt was planning to put me in braces?" The little man shoved a second piece of paper under Brian's other leg and began sketching. He either was deaf or had heard it all before. "My God, not my right leg too. Mrs. *Schmidt!* You said my right leg was improving. Mother, *did* you know about this?"

Brian had not yelled at his mother since he was five, and he half-expected her to slap him sober, especially for saying "my God." But to his surprise, he got away with it. She bowed her head and said, "I'm sorry, Brian, Mrs. Schmidt said it was a normal part of your treatment."

"Oh, she did, eh? You thought that putting my legs in iron braces was going to bring them back to life, is that what you thought?" His mother was crying, and he felt a queasy mixture of contempt and confusion. "My God, Mother, why didn't you *tell* me about it? That's all I ask. I don't want things *done* to me . . ."

"I'm sorry," said Beatrice. She shook her head and then half-ran from the room. Did I do that? thought Brian. The cause and effect were of different sizes. It was weird the way the cheerfulness around him would spring these sudden cracks: his mother crying, his father making faces in the ambulance.

"This has nothing to do with whether you get cured or not," said Mrs. Schmidt coolly. "Your physiotherapy will continue as before. It is a healthy sign of progress that we've brought you this far."

When Mrs. Schmidt bursts into tears, *that* will be the day. The little man rolled up his papers and left. Brian tried to stay angry over the deception. He still thought he was going to get it in the neck from *some*one for shouting at his mother, and he wanted to maintain some righteous indignation for his defense. But when he next saw his mother, she was still very gentle and repentant. And when his father got home, Brian heard them murmuring in the hall, and then his father was very gentle, too.

The braces arrived, gaunt steel scaffoldings smothered in straps, and he was jimmied into them and strapped tight and hoisted aloft, like a knight helpless in his armor. It was a giddy feeling, lurching about at this altitude, with his feet trailing off in the distance. He jerked a leg in a memory of walking, and only Mrs. Schmidt, a former circus strong man, it turned out, kept him from crashing to the floor. His knees hurled themselves against the leather caps, they would certainly flop out in a moment. He was scared spitless that he would just fall apart if he tried to move again. Straw would fly out of his chest. But Mrs. Schmidt was everywhere, under his armpits, around his chest, doing it all.

She urged him forward in a stately waddle in strides of no more than six inches, all the way to the window. He felt giddy with achievement. It was a clear, sharp day, you would know it was New York blindfold. But looking at it *standing up* — now there was something. He rested his head lightly against the glass, savoring his sheer tallness. He had no idea how high five foot ten was. If somebody comes in now and talks about my gallant struggle, I can at least grab him and fall on top of him. Bite his leg, if necessary. Oh boy. He felt drunk up here and half-mad with power.

"Are you ready to walk back now?" asked Mrs. Schmidt. "Try not to do it all with the hip. And not so much drag, please. Keep the toes pointed." She was at it already, before he had even had his measure of gloating. What difference did it make which way his toes pointed? He'd be out of these things in a twinkling. However, something warned him not to raise the question right now. She would only say, "You'll never get better if you don't point the toes."

As she commenced her endless unstrapping, he thought, She's right, this isn't much of a triumph. He thought again of the old men heaving along Broadway, some of them not really old at all but solemn little boys in glasses: they had probably had their moments of glory like this, the first day up. It was no time to get complacent. The braces looked malignant when they were off: like something in an Amsterdam Avenue store window, between the pink trusses and the corrective corset. Dwarfs humping in to be measured for dwarf equipment. He didn't belong to that world, and never would.

"I hope you didn't pay too much for them," he told his parents over supper. "Because I don't intend to stick around in them for long."

He knew that this proclamation came under the heading of gallant struggle and fighting spirit, but for once it couldn't be helped. He had to put his intentions on the record. His mother said, "Of course you won't." And his father said, rather blankly, "We didn't pay too much." And then recovered himself to say, "Not that that makes any difference."

* * *

[The following sections were written by Sam Perkins, a writer working with Brian Casey.]

We were looking desperately for a candidate that year as usual. It was my first crack at the vote, and I didn't realize that one was always looking desperately for a candidate. This was the first election ever held as far as we were concerned, and if we didn't find our man, probably the last one. Grim.

Solemnly my friends and I stalked the state capitols, interviewing any charlatan or windbag willing to give time to a bunch of politically illiterate undergraduates. I formed a loathing then and there for minor politicians, who seemed as superficial as actors and nowhere near as entertaining, and who were at their absolute worst with children. No black man ever saw more condescension on the hoof than we did that winter. Nor do I ever wish to hear again a sermon on patience and how there are no easy solutions.

At the same time, I formed a grudging admiration for the stars, the ones who could charm the socks off you in the length of time it takes to shake out of the next urinal. These may turn up on any side of any issue, and in my slightly older opinion are a bloody menace and should be banned from public life.

Washington was a bit better. I'll take senators over governors any day — wider interests, I guess, and less encrusted in grey-faced hangers-on. At first, we were certain we would find our man here. The four most promising of them were thrillingly blunt with us, firing off opinions that would surely have shocked their constituents out of their tennis shoes. Washington was so unreal, and they were so buffered with immunity, they could say anything they liked.

Until that is, we got to the Issue. That was something on which even a minor senator might be quoted on the front page. A look of calculated vagueness came over our boys, then the patience sermon and allusions to top-level briefings. If we knew what they knew. This took out two of them, two of the best.

Since they had a real shot at the Presidency, they wouldn't take the one chance that would make it possible. At this writing, they're both still waiting, a little farther back in the pack than before.

This left us with Senators Jenkins and Casey. Jenkins had manifest dentures and no power base. He alone could speak out on the Issue and be guaranteed no hearing at all. A soft-on-Communism charge hung limply on him, and nobody could be bothered to remove it. Needless to say, he seemed ready to run at a moment's notice.

Casey had the opposite trouble. He was, at first glance, too slick, too good to be true. He had New York-power base to burn. He'd made some money of his own somewhere. And he'd come out on the Issue at just the right time — not too early with the cranks, or too late with the schemers. He was a star all right, young, presumably dynamic (who ever heard of a young listless politician?), handsome, with a look of stoic endurance that he'd obviously earned — notice the slight way he shuffles his legs, must be very painful for him. In researching Casey's past, I talked to a couple of old polio hands, and they said that that was one thing they couldn't stand about Casey: the way he reminded you. It was a violation of the code and made him a bad man. But then they didn't know politics. Also, they were terrific polio snobs. Nobody knew but them.

"Excuse me for not rising," said the senator.

"Hm, all right, of course." We grunted with alarm.

He asked what he could do for us, and we said, Run for President on the Issue. We were down to our last senator, and our finesse was shot to hell. The bastards had worn us out.

"Well, I'd need a little louder demand than that, wouldn't you say?" ·

"Sure, sure. But would you be interested?"

We named our groups, and they sounded pretty silly in a senator's office, but he nodded and said, "It's a start. I think student politics is going to have a good year. Anyone like a cigarette?" He flashed a silver case. "Only tobacco, I'm afraid. Amherst, Harvard, Radcliffe, and Tufts, eh? That's a pretty good concentration. Could you deliver New England for me?"

I guess we tittered. We had learned our political manners and recognized that heavy joshing style, the language of the heart for politicians. Casey almost made it attractive, though not quite. He had the voice — a touch of the New York streets, mixed with your favorite professor's intonations: impossible by now to tell which was laid on which. And of course, he was more intelligent than the others.

"It's a tempting suggestion. But you people would have to promise you wouldn't just play at it. You'd have to go out and find yourself a coalition and bring it back in here, kicking and screaming in a sack. And I never met a coalition that wasn't revolting. Union jackals and black con men and students — wait till you see the students you'd get. Not little ladies and gentlemen like yourselves."

"Yeah, well."

"And fund-raising — Christ, I wouldn't ask any decently raised child to plug into *that* sewer."

"Aren't you busy?" I asked. "I mean, I hate to take up your time."

"No, that's all right. I like to talk." He smiled at me. Down boy! "Leave when you get tired. There aren't many people here in Hellfire Swamp who really like politics. Gossip, now that's something else."

We were charmed, flattered, sold for life. He canceled two appointments, and made funny cracks about the dignitaries involved. Then a not-so-funny one. "Senator Smithers keeps a camera in his asshole to catch the perverts." Wrong joke for this group. Sold, unsold. As if he wanted to sell us all over again. You liked me as a nice guy, now try me as a rat. Let's get down to essences here. Trying to keep cool as the hot charm poured over my head. Something disturbing about his lunging playfulness, the big-dog virility some politicians have.

* * *

"If you ever got to like me," Casey said, almost to himself, "you wouldn't be so useful to me." This was just a warm-up toss. I was to find that something about car and plane travel brought on a rush of suspect illuminations. He always seemed playful in the back of a car. Also in a swimming pool, or any place where nobody else had legs either. Christ, he was hysterical in swimming pools.

"You'll be relieved to know I do not demand loyalty," he said. "Peerless efficiency will do."

We were driving back to Washington to clean up his desk, and were mauling around a fund-raising speech for the evening, breaking our toil with Casey's own special word game, which he called Sophistry. My reading of the above fortune cookie was (1) I enjoy playing Machiavelli. (2) I can make friends any time I want to. If you don't like me, it's because I choose it so. (3) and (4) and (5). I was working on these when the bell rang and he gave me another. "Friendship is a basically unfair relationship," he said. "Now where was I?"

I wanted to talk politics, not this stuff, and I hoped it would blow over soon. "What do you mean, about friendship?" I said, yawning mentally.

"Epigrams shouldn't have to be explained, just topped. Ten points off your score and back to undersecretary. All right, just this once, since you're new here. To put it Thomistically, friendship disturbs the balance of nature. In practice, it always means, 'I'll take something from him and give it to you, so you'll be my friend,' and at its worst, which is most of the time, it means, '*You'll* take something from him, won't you, honey, and give it to me, because I'm *your* friend.' It's an offense against *justitia* and *ipsud quod rem.*"

Was he serious? St. Thomas, *justitia,* a world without friends? "How does it feel to be trapped in a speeding car with a medieval fanatic?" he said.

Casey's idea of fund-raising was quite a ways from mine. In fact, I didn't see how he could worm a penny from anyone his way. It threatened to be one of the dullest speeches ever delivered. No jokes, no fervor. "It's all right. I'll read it with a throb in my voice and a twinkle in my eye," he said. "Just make sure the figures on steel are right. I may be using last year's."

"You mean you did them from memory?"

"That's right." Son of a bitch. This owl is God.

"One thing to remember, Sam. These are very important people. Jews on the way up, Wasps holding, Clyde Jasper, the dignified Negro. I wouldn't insult them with a lively speech." He smiled, wallowing in his plush throne. "They just want to know if they can trust this man with their children's teeth."

Out of the car, he was like a fish beached. For public appearances, he used a dignified wheelchair, but on private missions he heaved along on two canes, dragging his hips behind him. He seemed annoyed when I accidentally walked on ahead of him, but when I dropped back, he said, "Go on, go on." I never did work out how fast he wanted, or whether I was making up the whole problem myself— the kind of goofy impasse that has to be kept in mind throughout this account.

Now that was certainly the end of the day, right? I had learned enough *Realpolitik,* or fakepolitik, to last a year. Time now to go to bed and digest it all. But the phone was ringing even before I got in the room.

"Where the hell is Spritzer?" Casey's voice sounded German war movie.

"How the hell do I know where the hell is Spritzer? He lives his own life, thank God."

"Goddamnit, I've got to have Spritzer." Then, in a note of wheedle, "He's not in his room. Are you sure you haven't seen him?"

"That's right." Nobody could want Spritzer that much.

"Well — in that case, would you mind coming up yourself? Right away." He paused. "And bring some money." What money? I didn't have any money unless he needed thirty-two cents in a hurry. But he'd already rung off.

You go too far, Senator Bighead. I almost rang back to make a noise into the phone. But his voice had sounded peculiar, as if he was forcing the arrogance. I decided to take a look at him.

"Come in," he shouted, before I'd finished knocking. But I didn't have a key and he couldn't get to the door. "Come in, come in." He began to shout as if his bed were on fire. Then, in a lower voice, "Let him in, or I'll crawl over and do it myself."

Silence, My God, he'll do it. I don't want to see it — I could just picture Casey looking up at me from the doorknob. What the hell scene was I in for now? Had Fielding come to kill him or what? I found myself banging on the door like an idiot, there in the middle of the night in the middle of the Hilton.

The door opened slowly. I flinched, but it wasn't Casey. It was a blonde with her blouse ripped, paperback style. The odd thing was, she was holding one of Casey's braces in her hand.

335

She obviously didn't want to let me in, but she didn't know what else to do with me. She was a victim of one of Casey's situations. He was sitting up in bed to the left of our picture, with his legs folded under him and his face going three ways at once.

"Fielding must have sent her," he said quickly. "It's a frame. I let her in, I thought she was room service. And she began tearing off her clothes."

"How come your braces were off?" I don't know why I asked. It was as if we were checking his story for weaknesses.

"I wheeled over," he said carefully. "Then I got back into bed. That was a mistake, I admit."

"Crap," said the girl. "I don't know any Fielding. I just want my money."

"We'll have to pay her something," said Casey. "We can't afford a scandal at this stage of the campaign. Have you got a fifty, Sam?"

"For what you wanted, it's a hundred. If I did that stuff."

"So, you didn't do it. Give her fifty, Sam. And, baby, tell your friend Fielding that he'd better think of a better trick for next time. Nobody's going to believe I raped a big healthy girl like you. Not in my condition."

She didn't say anything. If he wanted his frame-up story, he was welcome to it, as a professional courtesy. It was just another john's fantasy to her. Son of a bitch thinks he's running for President. She held out her hand to me, still gripping the brace as a hostage.

That would have been that — except that I didn't have the fifty. "Couldn't you write a check?" I croaked.

"Not in my own name. Can't you see, that's just what Fielding wants? In Spritzer's name maybe, or yours."

"I don't take checks," said the blonde, her usual helpful self.

So there we were, me with my door handle and the blonde with her brace, and Casey fighting for control. Rosie or whatever her name was could not break the tie. Her mind had frozen. Did she take American Express? I wondered. Casey was trying to regain his TV form, and I was confident he would any moment. He stared at her imperiously, trying to break her proud stupidity; but she was strong. Meanwhile, I was working out ridiculous little deals that were too silly even to mention.

Don't ask me how long, an hour, thirty seconds, something like that: Casey's glare suddenly broke against her face, and astonishingly, his own face seemed to crumple completely. In a voice I'd never imagined, creamy with self-pity, he said. "Can't you see I'm helpless? I'm tired. We'll get you the money in the morning. I swear to God." He was close to crying.

The kindhearted prostitute stared back with utter contempt. She might be in a cheap line of work, but she'd never crawl like that to anyone. "Here —" she threw the brace at him and it clunked on the floor. "Keep your fucking money." She pushed my hand off the door handle and went out, without leaving a name or address.

Casey sat for a long time, in a species of trance. He didn't ask me to leave, and I didn't want to. I know it sounds crazy, but I honestly thought he might try to kill himself. I've never seen a face readier for it. "It weakens you in some ways," he said to himself. A regular hour must have gone by this time, and I saw light under the window blind. Maybe he was safe now.

I began to open the door, and he said, "You didn't believe a fucking word, did you? About Fielding and the frame-up?"

"It doesn't matter."

"You can quit when you like. Jack'll give you your money."

"I didn't say I wanted to quit."

"I didn't ask you." He wouldn't look at me even now. "I can't have someone working for me who's sorry for me."

I remember after that walking down the corridor, staring at the carpet with sanded eyes; and rocking gently in front of the elevator; and thinking, as *he* might have been thinking, Maybe he shouldn't be President after all.

* * *

Just to remind you of who we're talking about and to clear your mind of Mrs. Casey, let me give you a last blast of the authentic Casey sound: "A bastard who knows he's a bastard is the worst bastard of all. Still, he has some kind of inner life, and that's supposed to be pretty good, isn't it? Ah, what do *you* know, you little dash dash dash? . . . Black rage, eh? Tell me frankly, sir — would you rather be black or have polio? and who am I supposed to rage at? Don't tell me about your suffering, sir. I detest monopolies. Ah, forget it, Sam. They may have suffered, I sure as hell haven't . . . try it like this. So much injustice in past cannot hope cure now stop Suggest hands full cleaning up block stop. Okay, festoon it with gut rhetoric, and we got ourselves a broad base . . . The Jews? The national I.Q. would sink to 63 if they went away. However, they must expect to suffer for being so smart. Nobody likes people to be that smart. Meanwhile, Israel should have a phantom jet in every garage . . . You know something [yawn] Sam? The Master only calls lepers to the head table, so just admit you are one, and get up there boy. Fake the sores if you have to, no one's counting. Just *wanting* to have them is a sign of [yawn] I forget. Theology is very complicated. Anyway, Sam, just remember — a Casey can always beat a Perkins at that game. You'd make a lousy leper. Nothing personal, O.K.? Who wants to eat with a bunch of sick people anyway? I often wonder what the Master sees in them . . . Sinking fast. Take a letter here in vital heartland of New Jersey wheat capital of little man not one scintilla of one iota in allegations of my opponent who has unfortunately taken low road . . . you know something, Sam? God has been very good to me. Yes, he has, the old bastard [snore]."

They say it's going to be different next year. More kids and women and blacks than ever are going to take part in the electoral process, i.e., vote, partly inspired by Casey's run for the roses last time. I sincerely hope they will have the maturity to reject this man, who despises kids, exploits women, and — well, I don't know how he is with blacks because I never saw him with one (I guess he admires their gall, though, and he says they make great audiences). But I'm afraid he's just their cup of tea. Every one of those groups is masochistic in its own way, or so it seems to your little-league philosopher. Look at what I took from him — and didn't he know I would? So Casey will wheel his throne among them — seeing healthy people on their knees is all he asks of life, the rest is spinach — and they'll sing Hosanna and "Hail to the Chief" and other Christian hymns. A crippled king for a crippled world, they crucified him once but here he comes again. A nice act, but I have a hunch that Casey's father ain't in heaven.

At this late date in the manuscript, I thought I'd check some of my theories with an old political crony of Casey's. I knew he'd sneer at the politics, out of very pride. But I thought he'd at least be dazzled by the psychological insights. No dice. "He never talked like that to me or any of the guys," he said. "That religious stuff."

"Yeah, but he said those things."

"Well, he was just being literary." He withered me, the way they all did. Literary was make-believe, a case of milady's vapors. "Yeah, but he said them," I insisted.

He looked at me a moment with those boiled-potato eyes they issue to inner-city pols and said, "You know the one mistake I thought Casey was making was hiring young jerks like you. But I was wrong, and he was right, as usual. He's got every kid in the country on his side this time — and you know how he got them? From practicing on *you* every day." He laughed. "Jesus Christ, supergimp. That's a good one."

I couldn't believe it.

"Where did a clown like you get a smart idea like that?" I snarled.

"He *told* me. You were sitting in the front seat of the car one day and I said, 'That's some staff you got,' and he said, 'That's not a staff, that's my violin.' Christ what a politician. He could make DiMaggio think he was really a ballplayer at heart."

Big fat victim — it was you he was practicing on, not me. I got it right the first time. Literary is real, not that crap you deal in. Yeah, he saw you standing on a railroad platform years ago, on his way to Salt Rock, getting smaller and smaller and going nowhere. And he saw you next to his bed, rubbing your fat hands and telling him God was on his side, and picking him out of the snow and saying, Take it easy, son. And he said, Someday I'm going to get that mother. I know because he told me. I wrote the book, you see. He's my character.

The fat pol just laughed and laughed. Casey would probably have laughed too. Because I was on that railroad platform myself, dwindling to nothing, as Casey shot off into the night looking, once and for all and to hell with all of you, for that miracle cure they'd promised him. Not a cure for polio or anything trivial like that, just a cure for not being God.

The author has two advantages in constructing Brian Casey and the political milieu in which he later functions. Sheed went through the trauma of managing his own polio episode as an adolescent in England; and later, when he moved to the United States, he went along with Eugene McCarthy as a speech maker and writer when McCarthy ran for president.

In Phil Marconi we meet one of the bitter alter egos of Brian. While Brian's friends are being kind and sympathetic, Phil is digging, unmasking, fomenting. "Hey listen," he says, "is that why you're being so nice about Casey? Because you think you might get it yourself?" Later he suggests that they all crowd around Brian and touch the "hunchback" for luck: "Anyone want to play some football? While we still got a leg to stand on?"

Sheed presents us a clear and compelling picture of an adolescent using his disability to control and abuse his family, friends, nurses, physical therapists, and physicians. He becomes a master at increasing guilt in those close to him to serve any purpose he wishes. In portions of the book not excerpted here, he reads about an attractive rehabilitation center far from home and suggests to his father that he be sent there. And when his parents engage in some realistic grumbling about costs, Brian stabs back with, "I'm sorry I'm a burden on you."

Beatrice Wright's book on the psychology of physical disability[3] — although published 20 years ago — is still probably the best single source of research knowledge and clinical illustrations on the subject. In it, Harold Russell, who lost both hands in World War II and had them replaced by mechanical hooks, is cited extensively as an example of a person who had to work his way out of the image of "freak" to that of "normal fellow." Eventually, he was able to accept and act on the insight that "self respect and real pride are better fed by achievement than by concealment." In Brian Casey's case, his concealment was not so much his paralyzed legs but how he was using them to control and destroy others.

Again, as in *Recovery With Aphasia,* we have a family attempting to deal with its own ecological relationships. In *People Will Always Be Kind* Brian is using his handicap to push his parents to the brink. He searches for magic cures and miracles while eating up the meager resources of the Casey family.

---

[3] Beatrice Wright, *Physical Disability — A Psychological Approach* (New York: Harper and Brothers, 1960).

In the second part, the reader sees Brian through the eyes of Sam Perkins, a writer hired by then Senator Casey to help him get elected to the Presidency. Apparently, Brian't earlier reluctance to run things, as he voiced in Part 1, has disappeared. We see Perkins becoming more and more uncomfortable as Brian's house prig. Yet, Perkins justifies himself as a highminded, puritanical idealist in need of a vehicle through whom to shout. In time the house prig turns into house conscience as he and Brian confront each other.

One wonders what Brian's physical handicap has to do with all this and at times almost forgets this fact about Brian, except when Brian throws it into the arena. Is Brian attempting to stand tall because God or dissembling nature knocked him down, or is Brian going to show Him up by becoming His image? Certainly, the seeking of power and control by going into politics is not necessarily born of physical or other handicaps. Ego needs and processes are no different, no better or worse, in the halt and the lame than in the healthy. Perhaps Senator Casey would have been what he turns out to be without the impetus of crippling polio. Sam Perkins finally decides that Brian's redeeming quality is that he is a bastard who knows he is a bastard. Curiously, one can't help applauding and admiring the bastard. At least I did.

QUESTIONS FOR DISCUSSION

1. After Brian gets polio, cynical Phil suggests to Bernie and Fatstuff that they are being especially nice to Brian because "you think you might get polio." What do you think of Phil's suggestion?

2. There are several indications of the stress effect of Brian's illness on his family. Can you describe some of the specific ways in which Beatrice and Kevin Casey show this?

3. When Brian's father, Kevin, is visited by Father O'Monahan, an expert in grief, Kevin becomes angry and hostile. Suppose you had been Father O'Monahan — how might you have handled it? (This might be explored in a role-played simulation.)

4. What do you think of the advice Dr. Samson gives Kevin about telling Brian the true nature of his illness?

5. "If you ever got to like me you wouldn't be useful to me," says Casey, the Presidential hopeful, to Perkins, his staff aide. What does he mean by this?

6. In the aftermath of the encounter of Casey, Perkins, and the prostitute, Casey asks Perkins to quit working with him. "I can't have someone working for me who's sorry for me," Casey says. What does he mean?

7. What are some occupations other than politics that would have suited Brian's handicap and related needs?

ADDITIONAL READINGS

- Asch, Sholem. *East River.* New York: Putnam, 1946.
- Garrett, J. F., and Levine, E. S. *Psychological Practices With the Physically Disabled.* New York: Columbia University Press, 1962.
- Goffman, Erving. *Stigma: Notes on the Management of Spoiled Identity.* Englewood Cliffs, NJ: Prentice-Hall, 1963.
- Graham, Winston. *The Walking Stick.* New York: Doubleday, 1967.
- Hesse, Herman. *Gertrude.* Boston: G. K. Hall, 1974.
- Heyward, DuBose. *Porgy.* Dunwoody, GA: Berg, 1967.
- Lowery, Bruce. *Scarred.* New York: Vanguard Press, 1961.
- Maugham, W. Somerset. *Of Human Bondage.* New York: Random House, 1956.
- Melville, Herman. *Moby Dick.* New York: Modern Library, 1934.
- O'Connor, Flannery. "Good Country People." *Incomplete Stories.* New York: Farrar, Straus and Giroux, 1972.
- Shakespeare, William. "Richard Ⅲ." *Shakespeare's Complete Works.* Student's Cambridge Edition, edited by William Allan Neilson. Boston: Houghton Mifflin, 1920. (London: Isaac Iaggard and Ed. Blount, 1623).
- Shontz, F. C. *Perceptual and Cognitive Aspects of Body Experience.* New York: Academic Press, 1969.
- Zweig, Stefan. *Beware of Pity.* New York: Viking Press, 1939.

"He wants feeling . . ."

9

The Philologist

E. J. Kahn, Jr.

9

The gifted and talented are rarely considered handicapped although some of them have physical, sensory, and specific learning problems. People with a high degree of intellectual ability often receive high marks for additional abilities like good judgment, compassion, and human relationships — yet, highly gifted and creative individuals sometimes wander off on their own, using their intellect, judgment, and talent in highly restricted, asocial, or anti-social ways.

Humans think with the head and with the heart. We are indeed emotional as well as intellectual beings. In the waking state we process data in cognitive-affective chunks. If, for example, we learn to read in an atmosphere of boredom, ritual, or threat, our cognitive competence in this skill may be shaped and controlled by the emotional setting of the learning.

John Dewey and Sigmund Freud — one as educator-philosopher, the other as psychotherapist — made significant explorations into cognitive-affective relationships in thinking. While Freud was attempting to find ways of healing persons whose emotional thinking processes had been cut off from their reason, Dewey was trying to promote educational processes that would help children to experience concepts and data — i.e., to successfully integrate emotional and cognitive processes. In essence, Dewey sought a fully functioning intellect as Freud sought a fully functioning ego. Both read and admired each other's works and probably never met. Yet, as Levitt keenly observed, they both arrived at the central problem of human functioning — the relationship of intellect and emotion in development, creativity, and behavior. Freud was an ardent admirer of Dewey. Max Eastman reported that Freud once told him that John Dewey was one of the few men in the world for whom he had high regard.[1]

---

[1] M. Levitt, *Freud and Dewey on the Nature of Man* (New York: Philosophical Library, 1960).

Dale Maple, protagonist of the upcoming tale, could be considered a living legend of cognitive-affective splitting. Dale is not schizophrenic (a term meaning split personality in a pathological sense) but he would certainly win few awards as "mentally healthy citizen of the year." In tracing Dale's history, one is reminded of Hamlet's remarks to Horatio on this matter: "By their o'ergrowth of some complexion, oft breaking down the pales and forts of reason . . . shall in the general censure take corruption from that particular fault" (Act I, Scene IV). Later, Hamlet adds: "Thus conscience does make cowards of us all. And thus the native hue of resolution is sicklied o'er with the pale cast of thought" (Act III, Scene I).[2]

Apparently, Dale Maple, our philologist, has had sufficient emotional causes to break down the pales and forts of reason. Ironically, the forts of reason in Dale are well manned and well defended within certain borders. The need for heart/head relationships is nowhere more strongly evident than in such persons. Should we be surprised that gifted, creative persons like Dale can be somewhat slow-thinking and dull in some significant matters?

Dale Maple is not a typical example of a gifted or creative person. And his high IQ or any special gift is not requisite to trigger the events of this story. In any event, some bright, creative persons have a tendency to move within their own circles and thoughts and to be no better or worse than their normal peers in integrating their emotional and cognitive thinking processes.

Dewey cautioned that learning should be thought of as an active, integrative process and that students should learn and grow as persons through experiences combining cognitive and emotional processes. In the case of Dale Maple and other such children with or without high intellectual abilities, we are still searching for ways to enhance heart and head development.

---

[2] As in William Shakespeare, "Hamlet," *Shakespeare's Complete Works,* Student's Cambridge Edition, ed. William Allan Neilson (Boston: Houghton Mifflin; Cambridge: Riverside Press, 1920), pp. 901; 911.

THE PHILOLOGIST

E. J. Kahn, Jr.

A TRIP TO OLD PALOMAS

On the afternoon of February 18, 1944, a Mexican customs inspector named Medardo Martinez, whose seat of operations was the town of Las Palomas, just across the international border from Columbus, New Mexico, and sixty miles west of El Paso, was riding in a horse-drawn wagon, accompanied by a friend, on the outskirts of Old Palomas, a tiny village three miles south of Las Palomas. At four-thirty, they noticed three men, all carrying knapsacks, who were walking south through the desert, a hundred yards or so off the road. Two of the men were wearing blue denim shirts and trousers; one of this pair was hatless, and the other had on a black fedora. The third man was wearing a khaki shirt and blue denim trousers, a rumpled American Army field jacket, and a gray felt hat, its brim turned down all around. On being confronted with something out of the ordinary, Martinez reacted with the inquisitiveness characteristic of his calling. He stopped his wagon and hailed the three men. They walked over, and it was quickly evident that none of them could — or, at any rate, would — speak Spanish. Martinez had been in the customs service for fifteen years, but the dirt road through Las Palomas wasn't used heavily by American tourists and he had never learned English. His friend, however, could speak it a little, and so, it seemed, could one of the trio, the fellow with the gray hat. He was a clean-cut-looking young chap nearly six feet tall and weighing maybe a hundred and sixty-five, with straight brown hair, hazel eyes, even white teeth, and a full lower lip, the kind that requires only a slight adjustment to produce a pout. Except for a

Excerpted from an article in *The New Yorker*. Reprinted by permission; copyright © 1950, 1978, The New Yorker Magazine, Inc.

few days' stubble, he was handsome. Martinez, through his interpreter, asked the men where they were bound. The man with the gray hat said, haltingly and in a soft, low voice, that they were looking for work in Mexico. Martinez asked to see their passports or other identification papers. They didn't produce any, so he invited them to board his wagon, ride back to Las Palomas, and have an interview with the immigration people there. The three men didn't argue, possibly because they had noticed that, like most Mexican border officials, he was armed.

José Magnana, the chief immigration inspector in Las Palomas, couldn't speak English, either, and also had to talk with the strangers through an interpreter. The young man with the gray hat identified himself as Eduard Müller and his companions as Erhard Schwichtenberg and Heinrich Kikillus. This time he said that they were trying to work their way to Tuxtla, a seaport twelve hundred miles distant on the Gulf of Mexico, and thence to Germany. Magnana felt sure that they were German soldiers who had headed for Mexico after escaping from one of the prisoner-of-war camps in the Southwestern United States, as had happened before during the war, and he decided to turn them over to the United States, without going to the bother of holding formal deportation hearings. He telephoned his opposite number, William F. Bates, an inspector of the United States Immigration and Naturalization Service, at Columbus, a town of a couple of hundred, and asked him to step over into his country for a minute. Bates came to the Mexican customs point, a hundred yards across the border, and questioned the men. The man who called himself Müller said, in labored English with a thick German accent, that he and his friends were Jewish refugees from Europe, and Schwichtenberg and Kikillus tried, with more animation than logic, to add authority to this story by displaying some little German and Italian flags they had on them. Bates was not impressed. He knew that four German prisoners had fled not long before from a camp near Amarillo, Texas, and he thought it likely that he had three of them on his hands. He took the men to Columbus and telephoned the F.B.I. office in El Paso.

At two o'clock the following morning, four F.B.I. agents reached Columbus. They questioned the three men but didn't get anything particularly enlightening out of them. The agents then drove them ninety miles to Las Cruces, New Mexico, and deposited them in the Doña Ana County jail. The three men were stripped there and thoroughly searched. On them were found, among other things, several boxes of candy bars, a couple of pocketknives, a canteen apiece, and a compass. In Schwichtenberg's wallet was a letter, in German, that one would hardly have expected to find on the person of a Jewish refugee in the winter of 1944. "Believe me, when the hour comes, I shall without doubt gladly give my life for Germany," one passage read. "I don't want to live without Germany — but Germany alone must live, must be free and powerful, so that someday our people will live and act in freedom in a larger, more powerful, and united Reich. Every sacrifice is worthy of that time." The F.B.I. men, when they inspected the trio's knapsacks, must have been amused to note that all Müller's contained was a change of underwear, an electric razor, and a whole cured ham.

Shortly after noon, the F.B.I. force was augmented by the arrival of D. A. Bryce, the head of the El Paso office. His colleagues hadn't made any headway with Müller; in fact, they had been advised by him, helpfully, not to believe everything he said. They had, however, become convinced that the two other men actually were named Heinrich Kikillus and Erhard Schwichtenberg; that they had been, respectively, a *Stabswachtmeister* (master sergeant) and an *Unteroffizier* (corporal) in the Afrika Korps; and that they were fugitives from a prisoner-of-war camp — not the one at Amarillo but one at Camp Hale, Colorado, six hundred and fifty miles from Old Palomas. Mr. Bryce concentrated on the remaining man, who, in substantiation of his statement that he was named Eduard Müller, called attention to an official document in German that he had on him. It was an extract from the military pay record of *Unteroffizier* Eduard Müller, prisoner of war, twenty-four years old; born in Schwarzenholz, Saar; holder of the German-Italian Memorial Medal; captured at Casablanca; special identification marks, none. The man who called himself Müller amplified this terse biography by telling Bryce a good deal about the family he said he had in Germany and about the wartime experiences he said he had had in the Afrika Korps, and by adding that as a boy he had gone to school in England but that, as Bryce must have realized, his English had regrettably rusty become. Bryce interrogated him for three-quarters of an hour, at the end of which period the suspect confessed, in tears and in perfect English, without a trace of accent, that his real name was Dale Maple, that he was a private first class in the Army of the United States, and that his trip to Mexico had not been authorized by any military superior. Bryce abruptly stopped questioning him and made a couple of phone calls to nearby outposts of the Department of Justice. At five o'clock that afternoon, Dale Maple was arraigned before the Commissioner for the Federal District Court, at Las Cruces, on the charge of treason.

Maple's bail was set at a hundred thousand dollars, and since, understandably, he could not produce such an amount, he was taken to Albuquerque, New Mexico, and lodged in the Bernalillo County jail. There he was asked a great many questions and gave a great many answers. He told Bryce, who interviewed him on and off for most of a week, that he, too, had been stationed at Camp Hale, that he had left it shortly after noon on February 15th, with the two Germans in tow, and that they had hoped to go on from Mexico to Argentina, thence by ship to Spain, and from Spain, finally, to Germany — the place on earth where Kikillus, Schwichtenberg, and he wished most to be. He said that he was one of a group of around a hundred American soldiers sympathetic to Germany who had banded together to stop the war by such methods as sabotaging transportation and communication facilities in the United States. He also said that in July, 1941, before he had become a soldier, he had tried to go to Germany, under a false name and with a phony passport, to attend a school in Hamburg where he would have received instruction in the art of sabotage that he could put to pro-Nazi use back in the United States. He said that after Pearl Harbor he had again tried to get to Germany, this time to join its Army. When that didn't work out, he had enlisted in the American Army. He said that he had been treated very badly in the American Army, and that his fellow-conspirators had been, too. He described them as "men who were as enthusiastic in their love of Germany as I . . . men who were also as determined Nazis as I was." He said that they were interested "not in the military defeat of the United States but rather in the termination of what we considered to be an unjustified and undesirable war, and in the preservation of Germany." He added, "I had no intention of remaining in the United States after such a cessation of hostilities, but only of going to Germany as rapidly as possible."

Bryce must have been amazed when he began learning about Maple's background. The F.B.I. had, of course, had dealings before with Americans in cahoots with the enemy. For instance, there had been Max Stephan, a Detroit tavernkeeper and a naturalized citizen, who had been convicted of treason for briefly succoring and harboring a German prisoner of war who had escaped from an internment camp in Canada and was trying to make his way to Central America. But Stephan had been born in Germany, had belonged to the German-American Bund, and was on the whole a pretty miserable character; at the very moment of snarling "I am not a traitor and I am not afraid," he had become so weak in the knees that he had to sit down. Maple was something else. He hadn't a drop of German blood, had been born in the United States, had never been abroad, and had never strutted around with the Fritz Kuhn crowd. Aside from his momentary breakdown as he disclosed his identity, he was a calm and collected customer. He was a man, moreover, of considerable intellectual gifts and of many cultural accomplishments. A native of San Diego, he had been the top student of his high-school class there. He was a much better than average pianist, with many recitals to his credit. He had earned a Bachelor of Arts degree, *magna cum laude,* at Harvard in 1941. He was a member of Phi Beta Kappa. He had planned to make a career of teaching comparative philology, the science of linguistics. He had specialized in it at college, delving into Old Danish and Assyrian and poring over Babylonian cuneiform tablets. He was the first Harvard student ever to undertake the study of Maltese, a blend of Italian and Arabic. He had done half a year's graduate work in Russian, Polish, and Hungarian. Not only did he speak fluent German (with or without an American accent, depending on his mood) but there was scarcely any other European language, ancient or modern, with which he was not familiar. His literary tastes were broad; his library contained a Hungarian translation of the New Testament, "The Psychobiology of Language," "Modern Harmony," "A Complete Hebrew and Chaldee Lexicon," "Gulliver's Travels," "Das Lied von Bernadette," "Colloquial Japanese," "Das Nibelungenlied," and "Fifteen Selected Stories of O. O. McIntyre." Mr. Bryce was

351

rather impressed by him. "I have often made the statement since interviewing Mr. Maple," the F.B.I. man later declared, "that he was one of the most intelligent men I have ever had an opportunity to interview."

After the three men were caught, Kikillus and Schwichtenberg were not punished, for, of course, they had a right to escape. They were taken to a prisoner-of-war camp at Worland, Wyoming, perhaps on the theory that being interned at that northerly spot would discourage them from heading toward Latin America again. Kikillus stayed put, but Schwichtenberg, agreeable as ever, consented to join two other Germans in an escape. At ten o'clock one night in June, 1945, they cut the barbed-wire fencing of their stockade and set forth. Schwichtenberg didn't do nearly so well this time. He was captured after two and a half hours of freedom.

As for Maple, the Army couldn't try him for treason, because that crime is a civil one; it is nowhere mentioned by name in the Articles of War, the military code. The Army could, and did, try him for desertion and for two violations of the 81st Article, which has to do with relieving, corresponding with, or aiding the enemy, and is the military statute that most nearly approximates the civil treason law. A general court-martial appointed by the Seventh Service Command to hear Maple's case convened at Fort Leavenworth, Kansas, on April 17, 1944, and adjourned on May 8th. It listened to a good deal of testimony — including a remarkable statement of seven thousand words, some of them in Latin, composed and read by the accused — and then decided that Maple was guilty on all counts and should hang by the neck until dead.

The court had been instructed not to announce its verdict, and it didn't. Maple and his counsel were nevertheless fairly sure that he had been found guilty. He didn't learn his sentence for another seven months, which he spent, as he had spent the weeks of his trial and those immediately preceding it, in the United States Disciplinary Barracks at Fort Leavenworth. In December, the War Department, without going into detail, announced that Maple had been given a death sentence and that President Roosevelt had commuted it to life imprisonment at hard labor, dishonorable discharge, and forfeiture of all pay and allowances. The President's clement action was in keeping with an American tradition; no citizen of this country has ever been executed by the federal government for treason against it. Maple was then transferred to the United States Penitentiary at Leavenworth, a federal institution six miles from Fort Leavenworth. In April, 1946, the Army, in keeping with a tradition of its own, which calls for sweeping reductions in peacetime of punishments imposed by courts-martial during wartime, cut his sentence to ten years. If Maple gets the customary time off for good behavior, he will be released not later than February 21, 1951, and since he will then be only thirty, he will, in all actuarial probability, have many years of leisure ahead in which to reflect, if he cares to, on the fact that he holds the distinction of being the first American soldier ever to have been convicted of a crime that, but for the wording of the Articles of War, would be the crime of treason.

DISSONANCE IN THE TOWER

On October 9, 1940, in the tower of Lowell House, at Harvard University, the members of the Verein Turmwächter got together, as they did every second Wednesday, for an evening of carefree *Gemütlichkeit*. The Verein Turmwächter — literally, "Club of Tower Watchers" — was the university's German Club and, like its companion societies, the Cercle Français, the Circolo Italiano, the Slavic Circle, and the Spanish Club, existed to give students a chance to converse informally in their favorite foreign tongue with other young men and, now and then, young ladies from Radcliffe. At meetings of the Verein, the use of any language but German was, naturally, *verboten*. The club's sixty members were governed by very few other rules. They spent nearly all their time talking about German art, music, and literature, drinking beer, eating pretzels, and singing old German drinking songs — "Bier Her!," "Wenn die Vielchen Blühen," and "Die Lorelei" — and "Gaudeamus Igitur," an old Latin old German drinking song. The members' interests were catholic and their discussions covered all aspects of German culture, but they were careful to steer clear of contemporary German politics, lest the erroneous impression be circulated that they fancied the

cultural theories emanating from the tower of Dr. Joseph Goeb-
bels. So eager was the club to avoid suspicion that its faculty
adviser, an instructor in German, went to some pains to buy
songbooks untainted by the inclusion of certain numbers then
especially esteemed in Germany by young men's drinking-and-
singing societies — for instance, the Horst Wessel Song.

That October evening, a couple of dozen students turned
up at the Lowell House tower, among them the Verein's treasurer,
a twenty-year-old senior named Dale Maple. His knowledge of
German was excellent (he had even taught himself to write
German script), he liked to sing (he was a member of the
Harvard Glee Club, too), he liked to talk about German literature and music (he was an accomplished pianist), and he was so
enthusiastic in his admiration for all things German that he had
a plaster-of-Paris head of Adolf Hitler in his room in Dunster
House. Maple appeared for the meeting in an American Army
uniform. It included cavalry boots, since the Harvard unit of the
Reserve Officers' Training Corps, in which he was a cadet first
lieutenant, was a horse-artillery outfit. The costume was an odd
one for the occasion, not only because it gave an uncomfortably
Storm Trooperish air to the proceedings but because R.O.T.C.
students at Harvard usually wore their uniforms only when they
were attending sessions of the course, in the afternoon. Maple's
acquaintances felt, however, that he took the R.O.T.C. much
more to heart than the majority of the men in it. Some of them
were, like him, genuinely interested in soldiering; others, though,
considered it an easy way of earning credit toward graduation,
and still others took it because it provided an opportunity to
go horseback riding at the government's expense. (The Professor
of Military Science and Tactics was also coach of the polo
team.) It was thought that Maple was interested in the course,
and the Reserve commission that followed its successful completion, because there were special circumstances in his background. He had never talked much about his family, but he had
talked about it enough to give several acquaintances the impression that his father was a career officer — a colonel or general
in the Regular Army or a captain in the Regular Navy. So certain
was one of Maple's classmates that Dale's father was an eminent
naval officer that when the classmate went into the Navy in the
spring of 1941, he looked in the Navy Officers' Register for the

senior Maple. He was surprised to find nobody by that name listed. He would have been even more surprised if he had known that Dale's father (through no fault of his own but because he had foot trouble) had never served a day in the armed forces.

The meeting of the Verein proceeded without incident until it was just about to break up. Then Maple and a couple of undergraduates who had presumably agreed to follow his lead suddenly began singing "Die Wacht am Rhein." It was a number that had theretofore been tactfully avoided by the Verein. The faculty adviser, distressed by this ideologically embarrassing performance, asked the singers to stop. They did. Then, while the other members of the Verein were still off balance, Maple threw a good, hard punch. He began a rendition of the Horst Wessel Song. What with his being in uniform, the effect was astonishing. As soon as the faculty adviser recovered, he ordered Maple to leave the room, and on that strange and sour note the meeting was adjourned.

To the relief of the other members of the club, Maple submitted his resignation a day or so afterward, complaining that the Verein's attitude toward German culture was narrow-minded. The incident might have ended there, but Maple seemed anxious not to let it end. He prepared a statement about his resignation for the *Crimson,* the campus daily, and that paper ran a story about him, giving him approximately the same amount of space it had once devoted to some undergraduates who had momentarily diverted their fellow-students by swallowing live goldfish. The *Crimson* said:

Because his intense belief in Adolf Hitler and his methods of government by dictatorship clashes irreconcilably with the tenets of the Verein Turmwächter, Harvard's German Club, Dale Maple '41 formally resigned from the Club last week.

Making no secret of his unlimited support of the Third Reich, Maple stated his belief yesterday that the best of all possible methods of government is totalitarian. "Even a bad dictatorship is better than a good democracy," he claimed.

His support of the Nazi regime is nothing new, according to the testimony of friends and members of the Club. Maple even carries his support so far as to justify the worst of Hitler's atrocities under the pretext of "necessity" . . . and he openly voices his conviction that he and any other person could quite happy living under a totalitarian regime.

> Maple's resignation . . . brought to a climax a situation in which the Nazi sympathizer claimed that the Club could not concern itself with German culture while isolating the problem of the government of the country.
>
> "The present government of Germany is as much a part of German culture as the works of Beethoven, Wagner, Dürer, or Kant," Maple claimed in a statement yesterday. "A culture is an integrated whole, and any attempt to ignore a part of that whole necessarily ignores an essential part of that culture. . . ."

The Boston newspapers, always alert to make capital out of Harvard students, would probably have played up the story, but the *Crimson* published it on the day a local politician was demanding an investigation of the suspicious activities of Dr. Herbert Scholz, the German Consul General in Boston and, it was later established, the chief Gestapo agent in the United States, a post he had been accorded by virtue of a long and intimate friendship with Heinrich Himmler. All the Boston papers carried on at some length about Dr. Scholz, and only two bothered with Maple. Both described him, on an inside page, as "the university's most ardent Hitler sympathizer." A couple of weeks later, *Time* devoted a column of its "Education" department to him, presenting, under the heading "Making of a Nazi," what it called "the brief case history of a native U.S. Nazi." The *Time* article was reprinted in the *Free American and Deutscher Weekruf und Beobachter,* a Nazi weekly in Yorkville, which ran it on page 1, under the sulky headline:

HE ADMIRED HITLER
IT WOULD HAVE BEEN ALL RIGHT IF HE HAD ADMIRED
STALIN, CHIANG KAI-SHEK OR TROTSKY.

Maple attained this celebrity in the Yorkville paper on November 14, 1940, and on the same day, up in Cambridge, the *Crimson* dealt with him again. It reported that he had been "summarily dismissed" from the R.O.T.C. by the Professor of Military Science and Tactics, who had investigated him and had decided, evidently on the basis of his opinions of dictatorship and democracy, that he was "not fit material for an officer." Once again, the Boston papers paid little heed, this time because of their excitement over an announcement from Washington that the Dies Committee was about to investigate not only Dr. Scholz but all German and Italian consuls in the United States.

Many of Maple's classmates, scattered around the world in the armed forces, probably didn't read about him again until the spring of 1947, when they received the *Sexennial Report* of their class. It was a volume devoted largely to the war experiences of the men of '41, and it was dedicated to the thirty-eight members who had lost their lives in service. Nearly all the survivors contributed capsule autobiographies, but there was none following Maple's name — merely the words "Maple did not return a questionnaire." If he had, his entry could have gone something like this:

In December, 1941, while doing graduate work at Harvard, tried to go to Germany and join German Army. Didn't work out. Joined American Army. Eventually assigned to unit composed mainly of men suspected of being disloyal to United States. In February, 1944, while stationed at Camp Hale, Colorado, deserted. Was picked up in Mexico three days later. Had two German soldiers with me, whom I had helped escape from a prisoner-of-war camp. Was arraigned in civil court on charge of treason. Army claimed jurisdiction over me, tried me before blue-ribbon court-martial, sentenced me to hang. Sentence commuted to life imprisonment, afterward to ten years. Present address: General Prisoner 61364-L, United States Penitentiary, Leavenworth, Kansas. Probably get out of here, with time off for good behavior, early in 1951, in time for tenth reunion.

Maple was not tried for treason only because the Army does not list that crime as such in its Articles of War. He was the first American soldier ever to be found guilty of the military equivalent of treason. Few Americans have ever been tried for treason, and none have been executed for it by the federal government, although death is the customary punishment in other countries. Up to the Second World War, a mere handful of Americans had been convicted of treason, and nearly all these had ultimately been pardoned. Since the last war, nine Americans have been convicted of treason, principally people who made propaganda broadcasts for the enemy. One of the group is Martin James Monti, who got twenty-five years and a ten-thousand-dollar fine for stealing an American Army airplane and delivering it to a German airfield in Italy, along with himself, and then broadcasting for the Nazis. Monti was, like Maple, in the armed forces when he committed his traitorous act, but he was out of the Army before he was called to account. Monti, now also a prisoner at Leavenworth, was twenty-three at the time of his crime, was of high intelligence, came from a respectable, God-fearing, unimpugnably American family, had been a staunch isolationist before the war, and was a devout Catholic. He was sane, but psychiatrists who examined him said that he had "psychopathic and paranoid traits marked by oversensitivity and ego-eccentricity." Maple, for whatever significance the analogy may have, was also twenty-three, was of high intelligence, came from a respectable, God-fearing, unimpugnably American family, was a prewar isolationist and a devout Catholic, and, though sane, was oversensitive, egotistic, and eccentric, and, according to one psychiatrist, had psychopathic and paranoid traits. In the background of these two exceptional young men there is, however, one notable difference. Monti had two sisters and four brothers, all four of whom served honorably in the armed forces. Maple was an only, and lonely, child.

Maple was born in San Diego on September 10, 1920. His father was of English stock and a native of Illinois. His mother, of English and Irish origin, was born in Kentucky, where her father, a nomadic merchant, settled down for a while. They were married in 1915, at Colton, California. The elder Maple, nineteen, was an apprentice in the Atchison, Topeka & Santa Fe's San Bernardino repair shop. His wife, seventeen, was training to be a nurse. Both were Baptists, and when their son was born, he was baptized in that church. By that time, his father was working for the Standard Iron Works in San Diego. Soon he switched to the National Iron Works, and he has been there ever since. He is now in charge of its sheet-metal foundry. When Dale was a boy, the family, which lived in a five-room bungalow, never had much money, but they got along in reasonable comfort. From the time Dale was around eight, relations between his parents were exceedingly strained, and their incompatibility gave the household an atmosphere of profound uneasiness. Dale had been a shy, frail, nervous, and awkward boy all along; the difficulties his parents were having, plus the fact that he had no brothers or sisters, made him even more maladjusted. The only thing he seemed to care about was music.

When Dale was five, his parents bought him a second-hand piano and arranged for him to take lessons. He soon became so accomplished a performer, if not precisely in the child-prodigy class, that they got him a Steinway grand, although it was vastly out of line with their scale of living. Dale enjoyed playing the piano and listening to music; sometimes a passage would so move him that he would burst into tears. At the age of eight, he was appearing in recitals with other piano students. When he was thirteen, he gave a solo concert, at a San Diego hotel, that included Bach, Beethoven, Chopin, Schubert, Grieg, Schumann, Tchaikovsky, Bartók, Debussy, and Rachmaninoff. "The ambitious program material bespoke a commendable desire on the part of the young student to reach for the best in piano literature," said the critic of a San Diego newspaper. "Memorizing of the long and difficult program was no small achievement in itself." Friends and admirers pressed gifts upon the young artist — two bouquets of flowers, three one-pound boxes of candy, a music dictionary, a leather portfolio, and a dollar bill. Dale subsequently played at Townsend Club and Pythian Sisters meetings, aboard ships at the San Diego Naval Base, and in churches. In the fall of 1935, when he was fifteen, he was invited to perform at San Diego's California Pacific International Exposition, and was the youngest native son of his city to receive such an invitation. This time a critic said he had "genuine promise" and added that "he displays maturity in interpretation to a remarkable degree . . . and gives great promise of taking his place as a concert artist as he gains in further study and experience."

By then, Dale had decided to make a career out of concert work, an ambition that was frustrated. If he had kept to that resolve, he would probably not have had an easy time of it. For one thing, he had a slight case of syndactylism, or webbed fingers. It would have been hard for him to play with the speed and accuracy required of a virtuoso unless he had had an operation, and few pianists have ever gone to such trouble. Franz Liszt was one, but he had normal hands and merely wished to increase his span. For another thing, Maple was no Liszt; he played the piano very well, but he was not quite topnotch. "Dale enjoyed music, and had talent," one of his teachers has said, "but I was never sure that what he did accomplish wasn't more the result of intense application than of native musical ability. His chief characteristic always was that when he made up his mind to do something, he would stick to it with all the power of his being until it was done." His parents raised chows for a while, and

Dale, who sometimes handled the dogs in shows, applied himself to the task as determinedly as if the perpetuation of the breed rested wholly on his shoulders. He was never satisfied with the pedigrees of the dogs his family acquired, he went to libraries and spent hours doing further research on their genealogies. On occasion, Dale managed to get extraordinary results without application. When he was fourteen, a family friend urged the Maples to enter in a municipal flower show some sweet peas growing on the fence outside their house. Dale, who had had no experience in such matters, gathered an armful of flowers and vases, took them to the show, arranged them in a few minutes, and won three major awards in the sweet-pea competition: best vase, pink and white shades; best vase, lavender and blue shades; and best vase, purple and maroon shades.

Dale liked demonstrating his talents, for he craved attention and approbation, and was willing to go to extremes to get them. At the San Diego High School, from which he graduated in June, 1937, he got a good deal of attention but little approbation. It was a public school, with an enrollment of more than three thousand students. Dale easily established himself as the brightest boy in his class (aside from a B one semester in R.O.T.C., he never got a mark lower than A) and, like scholarly youngsters everywhere, one of the least popular. He had a prodigious imagination, and he gave it free rein. It was hard to know when he was telling the truth, but he was so plausible that he convinced a number of people in the school, including several members of its faculty, that he had travelled extensively, particularly in Germany — a country that even then figured importantly in his daydreams, undoubtedly because its music gave him pleasure. Popularity in school is often related to athletic accomplishment; Dale shied away from the ordinary sports and went in for bridge and chess. He had few close friends, and took to cultivating far-off pen pals, among them a girl in Germany with whom he corresponded about the music and literature of her country. His school friends were mostly in the R.O.T.C., an organization that, in the pacifistic early thirties, was considered by many young men to be attractive only to misfits incapable of developing timelier interests. Dale also tried out for the school orchestra. He found that several other boys could play the piano, though not so well as he, but that there was no bass fiddler. He offered to fill the vacancy, which he did satisfactorily after only a few swipes at the unfamiliar instrument.

Dale graduated first in a class of five hundred and eighty-five, and was awarded, among many other academic honors, the Wayne Gridley Simmons Scholarship Prize for "the highest average standing in all subjects throughout the entire high-school course." (Never a man to leave well enough alone, Maple testified at his court-martial, seven years afterward, that he had been first in a class of fifteen hundred, a statistic that was passed on without question, when his case was reviewed, in a letter Secretary of War Stimson wrote to President Roosevelt. Maple would doubtless have been pleased if he had known that his swollen view of his own singularity had been included in official correspondence on such a high level.) The normal studies were a cinch for him, and, to keep himself from going intellectually stale, he ventured into extracurricular fields. He decided to write a thesis on the trajectory of rifle bullets, and, to do it competently, first acquainted himself with differential calculus. "There's nothing to it," he said afterward. He was often bored with the topics assigned him for themes and substituted others more to his liking. Some of the faculty didn't mind this, on the theory that such outstanding gifts as his had to be handled with forbearance, but others were less tolerant. A teacher who was invited by a colleague to read some of Maple's youthful prose compositions told a friend, "I found his writing undistinguished and said so. He refused to write on the assigned topics and insisted on writing about a trip to Europe with his mother. After several such papers, I indicated my opinion that the American Express travel advertisements were better and that I disapproved of excessive adolescent snobbishness." Some of the faculty, however, held Dale up to their students as an example of virtue and industry worthy of imitation but probably inimitable. This didn't go over too well with the other students, and they showed their resentment in the kind of spontaneous demonstration of cruelty that comes so easily to the young. The occasion was a school concert. "Dale," a classmate recalls, "was to appear in one of those hodgepodge assemblies in which the harassed faculty member in charge tries to please both faculty and students by mixing classical acts, like Maple's, with popular, like the inevitable tap or soft-shoe dance to 'Cocktails for Two.' Dale came on after a particularly engaging and extremely popular girl dancer, who had brought down the house. When he walked out onto the stage — and it was a long walk from the wings to the big concert grand in the center — the audience broke into one loud, derogatory guffaw, because Dale didn't walk like the average high-school kid. He seemed to be curved backward in the middle, like a skinny half-moon. He had a horrible slouch, even for a high-schooler, and he had one of those mincing, self-conscious strides that are taken to mean that the guy isn't one of the gang. He looked exactly as the student body wanted a studious, brilliant grind to look — a queer, pale ugly duckling, a sissy. I am not certain, but I think the audience threw pennies at him, too."

On his high-school record, Maple won a scholarship to Harvard in 1937. His parents couldn't otherwise have afforded to send him to college. Characteristically, on learning that most Harvard courses involve a great deal of note-taking, he taught himself shorthand and after six weeks' study was able to beat a couple of professional stenographers with whom he had an informal competition. That fall, he went to Cambridge, by bus. His parents were divorced soon after. His father remarried. His mother, to whom Dale had always been closer, moved East to be near him and, having relatives in Newport, Rhode Island, settled there. From then on, Dale considered Newport his home town. His mother, too, got married, after a while. Her new husband was the proprietor of a small electrical-appliance store there — an earnest man, active in the local Kiwanis Club and the Chamber of Commerce, who shut up shop during the war to become a sheet-metal worker in the local Naval Torpedo Station but is now back in the business, assisted by his wife. During Dale's Harvard years, he spent his vacations with his mother and stepfather, and he often travelled from Cambridge to Newport, some seventy miles distant, for weekends; when he couldn't get down there, his mother generally went up to Harvard. Dale liked Newport, admired its fine big houses and their elegant occupants, and kept posted on the parties they gave. But, despite the fact that he was to be the only graduate of the Harvard College class of '41 to list Rhode Island as his home — a distinction a Newport paper mentioned with mixed pride and embarrassment when he was arraigned for treason — he didn't move in the social set and never was invited to any of the parties.

Dale breezed through his courses. He originally planned to concentrate throughout his four undergraduate years on history, largely to please his mother, who, once it seemed likely that he would not go into concert work, wanted him to have a diplomatic career. (He had predicted, shortly before leaving San Diego, that he was destined to become Ambassador to the Court of St. James.) At Harvard, though, he exhibited no more of the diplomatic knack of making friends than he had in high school. Just seventeen, retiring, unworldly, and vain, he didn't fit comfortably into any campus group. "You met him and kind of liked him at first," one classmate recalls. "Then you realized he was all wrapped up in himself and you thought, What a lonely person, what a queer fish. And then you didn't see much of him again." During his freshman year, Dale roomed alone in Stoughton Hall, one of the ancient dormitories in the Harvard Yard. He took up with a group of boys who were fond of bridge, as he was, and although they saw little of each other away from the card table, they spent as many as five nights a week at it. Early in May, Maple enjoyed a brief moment of fame when he was dealt a hand of thirteen hearts. The story got around, and a few days later the Boston *American* sent over a photographer for whom Maple and his fellow-sportsmen obligingly reconstructed the historic scene. The *American* published a picture of it next to one of a Harvard student who had attained passing glory by contriving to walk up a flight of stairs while balancing a broom on his chin. Maple's fame ultimately proved less legitimate than that of his acrobatic contemporary. It developed that a prankster had stacked the cards as a joke.

In his sophomore and junior years, Maple occupied a single room in Dunster House. He had an upright piano, a radio-phonograph, and an extensive collection of records. He got to be on fairly good terms with a number of men in the house whose tastes, like his, were aesthetic and who preferred each other's company to that of girls. Maple occasionally double-dated Wellesley girls with a classmate, but he didn't care much for young ladies, and he never showed up at the house dances, except for one costume party, for which he got himself up as Hitler. (There could hardly be a costume party then without *somebody* in that role, so nobody gave Maple's impersonation a second thought.) From time to time, he presided at informal musicales in his quarters, and after dinner he frequently played the piano in one of the house common rooms, where, according to a classmate, he would "run through Grieg and Chopin in a casual, offhand way, while he gazed trancelike through a window at the traffic moving along outside." In his sophomore year, Maple switched from history to chemistry, abandoning diplomacy in favor of chemical engineering, a field his father had hoped he would go into. In his junior year, having briefly raised the hopes of both his parents, Dale switched once more, this time to comparative philology, with emphasis on German. He had long been attracted to languages, even though, curiously, for a winner of the Wayne Gridley Simmons Scholarship Prize, his spelling was atrocious — "apparantly," "conceed," "drousy," "seperate," "tournement," "occassion," "occured," "resistent," "champaign," "salomi," and "psyciatric" being a few examples. Comparative philology turned out to be his academic dish. "Maple was a born philologist, one of the most brilliant Harvard students I have ever known," a professor of his in that field recalls today. "He was particularly interested in Germanic languages and explored such recondite corners as Old Danish with remarkable diligence. He also devoted much study to entirely unrelated languages, widening his linguistic horizon to an extraordinary degree. He studied Assyrian, or Akkadian, for two years, and became quite proficient in reading ancient Babylonian cuneiform texts, even unpublished tablets. He asked to be allowed to study Maltese, which is a mixture of Arabic and Italian. He did some excellent research on the history of Malta and on the background of the Maltese language, and read Maltese texts quite well. I think I am right in saying that he is the only student who ever studied Maltese at Harvard." Among the other languages, recondite or commonplace, that Maple explored were French, Spanish, Portuguese, Dutch, Swedish, Icelandic, Latin, Greek, Japanese, Sanskrit, Hebrew, Persian, Hittite, and Old Church Slavonic.

In the fall of 1940, at the start of Maple's senior year and on the eve of his dissonant departure from the Verein Turmwächter, Harvard was, like the rest of the country, much concerned with the war in Europe and the relation of the United States to it. Selective Service legislation had just been passed, President Roosevelt was trying almost daily to amplify the lend-lease program, interventionists and isolationists were having a rhetorical field day. President Conant of Harvard was one of the country's most ardent interventionists; many of his students, including the editorial writers of the *Crimson,* were isolationists. New campus organizations favoring one point of view or the other sprang up in abundance — the Committee for Militant Aid to Britain, the Harvard Anti-War League, the Harvard Pacifist League, and the Harvard Committee Against Military Intervention, to name a few. Maple had a roommate that year, and the roommate was the president of the Harvard chapter of the American Student Defense League, an outfit advocating voluntary military drill by students, but Maple wasn't tied up with any of these groups, or, as far as is known, for that matter, any off-campus groups. He was not a joiner. He did participate, though, in some impromptu discussions of the world situation, many of which had to do with how much, or how little, aid the United States ought to give the British. Despite his previous interest in the Court of St. James, Maple didn't have much use for the British. Furthermore, he was opposed to the policies of President Roosevelt, he thought the war in Europe was none of this country's business, and he felt that if we had to aid anybody, the Nazis were the more deserving of help. As early as 1938, during the Munich Conference, he had indicated sympathy toward Hitler's conduct of foreign affairs. He had invited a classmate to his room to listen to his radio, and had tuned in on a policy statement Hitler was making. Maple interpreted for his visitor whenever the speaker paused to bask in a flurry of *"Sieg"s* and *"Heil"s.* "My recollection is that Dale not only was amused but was quite pleased with the bombastic utterances of the Führer," Maple's guest remembers.

Maple's study of the German language and German literature now caused him to identify himself closely with Germany. As he had done in high school, he let the idea get around that he had been there. One of his classmates, a student of social psychology who was studying propaganda techniques, asked Maple for some first-hand observations on contemporary ones in Germany. "I thought Dale was extremely vague about them," the man has since said, "but it never occurred to me then that he hadn't been any nearer to Germany than the Lowell House tower." Actually, Maple's knowledge of Nazi propaganda and Nazi political theory was unimpressive. He had dipped into

Spengler and Nietzsche, but he had never read "Mein Kampf."
He had a pretty clear notion of the kind of government he fancied,
though, and once he outlined to a college acquaintance his concept of the ideal political state. It was a pyramidal structure,
with one man at the top, the intellectuals directly beneath him,
and the ignorant masses subserviently at the bottom. "'Of course,
bright men like us,'" the acquaintance recalls Maple as saying,
"'would be in the upper regions of the pyramid.' I remember
asking Dale where he would place those who fitted in this category but happened to be Jews or Negroes. I don't recall exactly
what his answer was, but I do recall that he sort of brushed
the question aside as being a brutal and unpleasant nonessential
of his ideal Fascism." Maple's visionary state was not unlike the
ideal of Lawrence Dennis, a Harvard man himself and the author
of "The Coming American Fascism," who favored the rule of the
gentlemanly elite and who during Maple's senior year bought
several full pages of advertising space in the *Crimson* to expound
his views. Dennis's sort of Fascism was ostensibly a tidy, efficient, well-mannered, indigenously American variety, devoid of the
nastier characteristics of the foreign species and not overtly
anti-Semitic. There is little evidence that Maple was anti-Semitic.
His love for German cultural accomplishments was expansive
enough to embrace Heine and Mendelssohn, and although he had
few friends, some of his best acquaintances, including most of the
fellows he played bridge with, were Jews.

A lot of the members of the class of '41 had no definite
postgraduation plans, being edgily aware of the possibility that
their country would soon be at war and they would be in the
armed forces. Maple, though, wanted to go to Germany. His
family couldn't pay his way, so he decided to try to get the
German government to. Not long after the unpleasantness at the
Verein Turmwächter, he called on Dr. Scholz, the consul in
Boston. Scholz received him cordially and took the trouble to
introduce him to several young men who were eager to improve
Maple's knowledge and understanding of modern Germany.
Among them was an American studying at Harvard whose background had included enthusiastic membership, while he was living
in the Reich, in the Hitler Jugend, a well-disciplined and specialized variation of the Boy Scouts. Scholz suggested that Maple
help defray his expenses abroad by lining up a part-time job as

a newspaper correspondent. Maple wangled a letter from the International News Service expressing polite but noncommittal interest in anything he might write while overseas, and applied for a passport. The State Department turned him down, undoubtedly after checking with the F.B.I., which had heard about his declaration of political sympathies and had kept tabs on him from then on. Scholz must have felt that a serious-minded and cultured American boy like Maple was worth some special pains, for he proposed looking into the matter of furnishing Maple with an alias, a fake passport, and passage on a Spanish steamship line with which he had connections. Nothing came of this scheme, because Scholz soon was in so much hot water that the Germans closed down their Boston office and transferred him to their Embassy, in Washington. Scholz's eagerness to help Maple was probably motivated by the hope that he could be transformed into a Nazi agent of usefulness in the event of war between Germany and the United States. Maple's motives for visiting Germany may possibly have been less sinister. He has since said on one occasion that he wanted to attend a school at Hamburg that specialized in sabotage, but he has said on another that he wished to attend the University of Berlin and specialize in Hittite. It would seem an odd time to study philology there, however. The attitude of the Nazis toward education must have been obvious to everybody at Harvard, because a number of eminent refugee scholars had joined its faculty. What may have been less generally obvious was the attitude of the Nazis toward the department of comparative philology in the University of Berlin, but any student in that field could have found out without too much effort that a distinguished authority on Celtic had been dismissed from his post there because he happened to be one-quarter Jewish, and that the successor to another scholar in linguistics was a young Nazi who, aside from his fervent political convictions, had no discernible qualifications for the job. Such considerations, as he himself has said, were irrelevant to Maple; he may have been influenced in taking the view he did by a member of the comparative-philology department at Harvard who kept a swastika over his mantelpiece, was in amicable correspondence with German propaganda agents in this country, and at one lively Cambridge cocktail party was thrown down a flight of stairs by a fellow-guest who objected to his espousal of Hitlerism.

About the time that his negotiations with Dr. Scholz fell through, Maple graduated from Harvard. His consistently high grades — all A's, except for a scattering of B's — earned him a *magna cum laude* citation and a Phi Beta Kappa key. He went to San Diego to visit his father and spent the summer in California, where he applied for work in an aircraft plant but was rejected, presumably because some government intelligence agency considered him a poor security risk. In the fall, he returned to Harvard to do graduate work in Polish, Hungarian, and Russian, languages he had somehow overlooked. He helped support himself, briefly, by working for the physics department on a national-defense research project, but he was soon removed from the job, again apparently on a suggestion from higher up. All that term, he secretly took instruction in Catholicism from a priest in Cambridge, and one day he surprised a Catholic teacher of his by asking him to serve as godfather at his baptism into that church, an event that dismayed Maple's father, who was not only a Baptist but a Mason, and who some years before had approvingly seen his unpredictable son enroll in the De Molays, the junior auxiliary of the Masonic Order.

After the United States went to war that December, Maple felt more out of things than ever. Many of his classmates were already in the armed services; most of the men with whom he had taken R.O.T.C. were now commissioned officers. Several of the men he had associated with were to be killed in the war. The fellow he roomed with his senior year died during a bombing raid over Yugoslavia; another young man with whom he had gone around some died at Pearl Harbor aboard the Arizona, on December 7, 1941. That same day, Maple put in a phone call to the German Embassy, in Washington. He wanted to let the Embassy know that if the United States and Germany went to war and the German diplomatic staff in this country returned to the Reich, he would like to go along.

A STATE OF AGITATION

On December 24, 1943, three dozen G.I.s assigned to the 620th Engineer General Service Company, a tiny unit of the Army of the United States stationed at Camp Hale, Colorado, held a Christmas Eve party in a barracks. They bought an evergreen tree, put on their dressiest uniforms, shined their shoes, combed their hair, trimmed the tree with ornaments and tinsel, and had a gay and sentimental time, with plenty of wine and song. Their celebration was like thousands of other stag affairs thrown by American soldiers who were unable to spend Christmas with their families, except that most of the conversation was in German, and that of all the carols that were sung the two that had the greatest emotional impact on the participants were "Deutschland Uber Alles" and the Horst Wessel Song.

Soldiers have always liked having group pictures taken of themselves, and before dark that evening the merry-makers posed self-consciously on the barracks steps for a holiday snapshot. One of the men, a naturalized American citizen who speaks and writes excellent English, kept a print of it for his scrapbook. *"Weihnachtstag 1943,"* he wrote on the back, and on the front he put down the names of his buddies — Wilhelm, Paul, Theo, Richard, Bill, Ernst, Franz, Rudi, Karl, Kurt, Bob, Walter, Otto, Putsi, Dale, and all the others. The 620th contained a singular lot of American soldiers. Two of them — one before the war was a brewery worker in Newark, and the other was in the importing business in New York — were members of the Nazi Party. Karl had served in the German Army in 1939, during the Polish campaign. Richard had four brothers in the German Army. Rudi had a female relative who had shaken hands with *der Führer* and had not washed the sanctified palm for three weeks. Bob had not merely belonged to the German-American Bund — so many members of the company had belonged that *that* was scarcely noteworthy — but had been on the staff of Camp Siegfried, a Bund *Festung* on Long Island. Some of these American soldiers hoped devoutly that Germany would win the war. Others had less resolute war aims; they simply hoped that Germany would not lose it.

Perhaps the most unusual member of the convivial group was Dale — Private First Class Dale Maple, Army Serial No. 11048476 — who, though he was not German by either birth or heritage, had become intensely interested in all things German while studying languages at Harvard and was thought by a couple of awe-struck Bund men in the 620th to hold the honor of himself having once shaken hands with Hitler, during a prewar visit to Nuremberg. The Bund men had picked up this notion in conversation with Maple, who, as it happened, had never seen Hitler except in newsreels. Private Maple admired German military discipline, thought Germany had been treated poorly after the First World War and was justified in seeking territorial expansion, and knew the Horst Wessel Song as well as anyone in the 620th, but he was cut from different cloth. He was a quiet, standoffish fellow — nearly six feet tall and well built but with an odd air of delicacy — who was exceptionally finicky about his appearance and, although his family was by no means well-to-do, had a tailor-made uniform for dress occasions, a rarity among enlisted men. Forgoing the lieder-singing and beer-drinking that most of the other men in the company enjoyed in their off-hours, he preferred to spend his leisure time listening to classical music, poring over Sanskrit dictionaries and Slavonic grammars, playing bridge, or making crêpes Suzette.

All in all, Maple gave little evidence of being a man of action. Seven weeks after *Weihnachtstag,* however, he was to earn himself a special place in the memories of the men of the 620th — not to mention the annals of American military history — by setting forth on a strange expedition that led to his becoming the first United States soldier ever to be convicted by a court-martial of a crime equivalent to treason. He won this distinction by deserting the Army, taking with him two former members of the Afrika Korps who had been interned in a prisoner-of-war stockade at Camp Hale, and escorting them more than six hundred miles. They were apprehended three miles south of the Mexican border, on their way to Germany. Maple was sentenced to death, but the sentence was commuted to life imprisonment, and ultimately to ten years. He is now in Leavenworth.

Maple was only twenty-three that winter, but he was fond of thinking of himself as, to use his own phrase, "a soldier of the old Army." The basis for this doughty self-characterization was that he had taken R.O.T.C. courses in high school, in San Diego, where he was born and raised, and at Harvard, where he received a Bachelor of Arts degree in 1941. He had not got a Reserve commission, because during his senior year at college he was dismissed from the R.O.T.C. after he publicly expressed the opinion that dictatorship was a form of government inexpressibly better than democracy. In the fall of 1941, when many soldiers of the old Army were girding themselves for action, he had returned to Harvard as a graduate student of comparative philology. On December 7th, when the Japanese attacked Pearl Harbor, he was diligently studying several Slavic languages. That day, he put in a call to the German Embassy, at Washington. The circuits to the capital were very busy, and it was not until the following day that he got through. On being connected with the Embassy, he identified himself to the attaché who took the call by mentioning that he was acquainted with Dr. Herbert Scholz, a high-ranking member of the Embassy staff — as well as of the Gestapo — whom he had met the year before while trying, unsuccessfully, to get to Germany. Maple explained that he wanted to find out what the chances were of his accompanying the German diplomatic corps back to the Reich if, as seemed almost certain, the United States and Germany went to war. Maple said he would like, on completing the trip to Germany, to join the German Army. He was informed that the time was inauspicious for considering his proposal, and that concluded the conversation.

Like most other young men on college campuses, Maple found it difficult in the following weeks to concentrate on his studies, but he decided to finish out the term, which ended in late January, and then, for what he has claimed were patriotic reasons, go into the American armed forces. On learning that a college friend had been killed at Pearl Harbor while on naval duty, he tried to get a commission in the Navy, but he was turned down because of ear trouble, which he had had since boyhood. On February 27th, without waiting to be drafted, he enlisted in the Army. He was sent for three months of basic training to the Field Artillery Replacement Training Center at Fort Bragg, North Carolina. The Center had five units for the reception of new soldiers — four gunnery regiments, for cannoneers, and a signal-training outfit, for cryptographers and radio operators. The brightest of the trainees were customarily assigned to this last unit, and Maple, who was a Harvard *magna cum laude,* was put there. Military Intelligence at Fort Bragg was aware of his political views — the Army and the F.B.I. had kept dossiers on him ever since his dismissal from the R.O.T.C. — but that didn't bar him from this important line of work. The mere learning of cryptographic techniques didn't mean, of course, that he would have access to confidential information, and, besides, his commanding officer, a lieutenant, happened to have been a classmate and a fellow-R.O.T.C. man at Harvard. He was inclined to the view that Maple had said the things he had up there largely in jest.

Maple proved to be an excellent soldier during his basic training, and he stayed at the Center afterward as an instructor, with the rating of corporal. He was impressed with the importance of his new responsibilities. "We have been out in the field almost every day for the last few weeks," he wrote in a letter soon after getting the job, "and I have to organize all the details of the trip, make out all the assignments, get all the equipment together, and do just about everything. I am not supposed to be the big boss, but I am the only one who knows the men well and knows what they can do. As a matter of fact, I have invitations from about half the men to come home with them at one time or another; I just wish I could get enough time off to take up all the offers." If this estimate of his popularity was accurate, the men in his outfit must have been unusual, for Maple had always been the antithesis of a social lion. In the same letter, he indicated that he was not exactly the comradely type of non-commissioned officer. "I am charge of quarters," he wrote. "That is, I have complete charge of everybody and everything for today. All I have to do is sit in the office all day and sleep there all night, give out passes (or refuse to give them out and make people mad), dig up trucks to haul people swimming, make sure that everybody is in bed and all the lights are out when they should be, see that the grounds are in order at all times as well as the barracks, make sure that none of the people confined to quarters escape, etc. I had the pleasure of putting under arrest this morning one boy just returning from a 17-day vacation without leave."

Late in September, 1942, Maple wearied of such pleasures and applied for transfer to a combat outfit, offering to take a demotion to private to accomplish this end. His wish was granted and he was presently shipped, stripeless, to the 76th Infantry Division, then stationed at Fort George G. Meade, in Maryland, where he was made an instructor in a divisional school for radio operators. "The radio sergeant went on furlough and I had to take over in his place," Maple wrote. "Since he had let the radios all run down, I had to spend a week getting them into shape. I even had to spend all day one Saturday and Sunday working. But the sets all work now." He dwelt on his skill as an operator. "I had thirty messages piled up before I even started. I didn't mind, but I wore out about four men who turned the generator for me. I transmitted for three hours without stopping! I got all the traffic cleared through and could have been through in one-third the time if I had had any decent operators on the other sets. I can send 20 and receive 25 words per minute, but they couldn't go faster than 5, so what could I do?"

Maple stayed at the school for five months. Early in March, 1943, he was summoned for an interview with a couple of representatives of Counter Intelligence. They revealed that they already knew a good deal about him, including, to his surprise, the gist of his conversation with the German Embassy fifteen months before. Two weeks after his session with Counter Intelligence, Maple was shipped to a camp at Indiantown Gap, Pennsylvania, and, after a short stopover there, on to another Fort Meade, in the Black Hills of South Dakota, where, in compliance with his orders, he reported for duty with the 620th Engineer General Service Company.

The 620th, which then occupied some old C.C.C. barracks at one edge of the fort, was, in an Army of specialists, special to a high degree. The soldiers in it received hardly any military training and were not issued arms. On the rare occasions when they had guard duties, they were given only flashlights and clubs. Except for a dozen or so individuals — the officers, some of the noncommissioned officers, and perhaps a Counter Intelligence operative or two — the members of the company had been hand-picked for assignment to it; most of them were men who were considered conspicuously poor loyalty risks or men who had refused to fight against one or more of the nations at war with the United States. The question of what to do with such soldiers during a war is not a simple one. There were in the United States, when hostilities began, not a few young men of military age who had records indicating a profound lack of sympathy with the Allied cause. Many of them were inducted into the Army by draft boards that were trying to meet their quotas and that were not equipped or disposed to concern themselves with security matters. Other such young men enlisted voluntarily, for one reason or another. If the Army had permitted them to serve anywhere, they might have attempted to infect their comrades with their virus. If it had discharged them because of their political views, potential draft dodgers might have claimed that they, too, held such views and have demanded exemption from service. In most cases, the Army didn't have enough evidence to prefer charges that might have tucked them safely away in jail. It was in the fall of 1942, after the United States had been at war for nearly a year, that the Army arrived at a solution of the problem. It decided to segregate these soldiers. This was not a solution peculiar to the American Army. The German Army did almost precisely the same thing with some of *its* nonconformist soldiers. The American version of the scheme involved the establishment of units with such elegant, if hardly pertinent, designations as the 620th and 525th Engineer General Service Companies and the 358th Quartermaster General Service Company. Up to V-J Day, between twelve and fifteen hundred soldiers served, all told, in these three outfits. The 525th was composed mainly of men of Japanese extraction. The two others were made up principally of men of German or Italian extraction.

When Maple arrived at Fort Meade (the sergeant to whom he reported asked him whether he was German or Italian), there were close to two hundred men in the 620th, not counting the supervisory officers and noncommissioned officers. The company was really an international outfit. There were, for example, besides the Germans and Italians, a Finn, a Dane, a Hungarian, a Yugoslav, and a White Russian. The makeup of the 620th varied considerably from one time to another; soldiers were constantly being assigned to it and soon thereafter being assigned elsewhere. Presumably, further investigation of their cases had convinced the Army that they either had never or no longer required special handling. A substantial majority of the men in the 620th were of extreme Right Wing persuasion; the minority were just as far to the Left, and one of this category, a German-born Communist, spent much of his time trying, with notable lack of success, to proselyte for his Party. Some of the Germans and Italians were aliens and complained that they were being held in the Army illegally. They wanted to be discharged and placed in one of the civilian internment camps run by the Department of Justice. These complaints were not entirely without merit, for under international law citizens of a nation at war may not be compelled to join the armed forces of the enemy. Several of the Germans in the 620th were seamen. They told their buddies that they had been practically shanghaied into the Army while awaiting deportation hearings. One maintained that he hadn't taken the oath of allegiance when he was inducted and that he had been told by some official or other of the United States government that if he went into the Army, his wife, who was also an alien, would not be put in an internment camp. When she was put in one, he took the position that the Army had welshed on a deal, and on being ordered by an officer to report for work he sat on his bunk and refused to budge. He was court-martialled for disobedience and given a three-year sentence in Leavenworth, but when his case reached the War Department for review, the verdict was reversed, on the ground that he hadn't been properly inducted, after all, and that the Army had no jurisdiction over him. He was then turned over to the Department of Justice and interned in a civilian camp.

Maple declared after his arrest that it was outrageous that the Army should have placed him in the 620th, but he didn't seem unduly distressed when he first joined it, even though he was almost instantly aware of the kind of outfit it was. "I'd like to be sure of staying here," he said in a letter, and remarked that the food was first-rate. One of the company cooks had been a chef on the Europa, and the like of his *Apfelstrudel* had probably never been tasted in the Black Hills before. Maple was further pleased when, after less than two months, he was promoted to private first class. "The addition of Pfc. to my name isn't much," he wrote, "but more will follow in due course. To be advanced too rapidly would not look or be good." Aside from weaving camouflage nets and grading a landing area for Army gliders, the 620th was assigned few duties that appeared to be directly related to the Allied war effort. The company's other work consisted of such estimable but hardly essential tasks as transplanting trees, pulling weeds, digging ditches, and rehabilitating a tennis court. Though the labor was far from stimulating intellectually, the hours were agreeable. Most of the men were free every weekend, and on weekdays from retreat to reveille. Quite a few lived off the post, and Maple and two other members of the company took a four-room furnished apartment in the town of

Deadwood, fifteen miles away. The rent came to only seven dollars a month apiece. Deadwood was a rip-roaring old-style Western community, where the silver dollar was abundant and there were plenty of opportunities to fling it around. The main street was liberally embellished with saloons, most of which had roulette tables, and equally prominent were two other hospitable places, with red neon signs identifying them as "Virginia's Rooms" and "Rose's Rooms." Maple had never given any evidence of caring much for girls, with or without their names in red lights, but he was fond of gambling. He was even fonder of reading, though, and the relaxed tempo of military life at Fort Meade gave him a lot of time for that. Inspired by his new associations, he sent home for a German-Italian dictionary and for a two-volume edition he owned (but had never thoroughly examined) of Spengler's "Der Untergang des Abendlandes." After looking into it, he gave a couple of lectures on the subject in a Service Club library.

Early in December, while the disgruntled men in the 620th were still much more preoccupied with covert agitation than with overt action, the Army closed down Fort Meade and shipped the company to Camp Hale. The 620th's last assignment in South Dakota was to raze a crude replica of a German village that had been built to train other units in street-fighting tactics. The demolition job was not without its rewards; it gave Maple and some of his friends a chance to have snapshots taken of themselves lounging in front of edifices that bore such heartwarming signs as "Biergarten" and "Bürgermeisters Heimat." Camp Hale, situated deep in the Rockies, a hundred and twenty miles west of Denver, housed around ten thousand American soldiers when the 620th marched in, and around two hundred German soldiers, who lived in a prisoner-of-war enclosure surrounded by a barbed-wire fence and did menial chores around the post. The 620th was billeted in some buildings only three hundred yards from the prisoners' stockade. The prisoners were a sturdy, brawny lot, and they liked to show off their manliness. Every Sunday, their day off, they played soccer inside their compound, and they played it shirtless and in shorts even when the temperature was below freezing. The proximity of these rugged representatives of the Reich had a profound effect on some of the men of the 620th. The one who had four brothers in the German Army was emotionally disturbed to the point of storming through his barracks and, using alternately his fists and a fire extinguisher, breaking most of the windows. Fraternization between the prisoners of war and the American soldiers was, as was customary, forbidden. To some of the men in the 620th, this was an arbitrary and capricious regulation, and soon they had established warm, although clandestine, relations with the prisoners.

Almost as soon as they became acquainted with the prisoners at Camp Hale, Maple and his associates began revising the plans they had discussed in South Dakota, in order to make provision for new allies. The man who had conceived the idea of the guerrilla army, for instance, was overjoyed at the idea of swelling his insurrectionist ranks with two hundred hardened veterans of the Afrika Korps. Moreover, there were other potential recruits not far away. The 358th Quartermaster General Service Company was stationed at Camp Carson, less than a hundred and fifty miles distant. There were men in the 620th who had known men in the 358th, through the German-American Bund or other social groups, before the war, and the two outfits had already been in communication. A delegation from the 620th arranged to meet a delegation from the 358th in Denver one weekend. They held some informal staff talks in a hotel room — one man unfurled a swastika for appropriate décor, and then bought some champagne, in which Hitler was gravely toasted — and discussed joint action, but they didn't decide on anything. Meanwhile, the 620th men continued to mull over unilateral action. By now most of the plans had to do with deserting and simultaneously assisting a few of the prisoners toward freedom. But, for all the blustering and fuming, nobody except Dale Maple — with some aid from Kissman, Leonhard, and a couple of others — proved resolute enough to do anything. Maple had been preparing to make a move for quite a while (in December, he had guardedly written in a letter, "There is some reason for believing that I won't be here long"), and on February 15th he made it. He departed from camp without bidding many goodbyes, got behind the wheel of a battered old Reo sedan he had bought a couple of days earlier, took the two prisoners aboard just outside the camp, and set out for the Mexican border.

WHO WANTS TO GO TO GERMANY IN WARTIME?

The members of the 620th, many of whom thought that Roosevelt had dragged the United States into a war that was none of its business and that he was therefore a traitor, never organized themselves into a rebellious unit called, say, the Company of Horst Wessel, but, disturbed by the fact that the Army had segregated them in a special unit, a few of them had dwelt at length on the possibility of becoming civil warriors, and they might have taken steps in that direction if it had not been for Maple, who, a couple of weeks after the debate in the service club, drew the Army's attention to their formidable discontent by engaging in unilateral un-American activity. He was a singular member of a singular company. For one thing, although he could speak German fluently, he didn't have a drop of German blood in him and had never been to Germany. He was a nice-looking, soft-spoken, intense boy of twenty-three, and an honor graduate of Harvard, where he had majored in comparative philology. (One of his professors once said that "he seemed to find relaxation only in the study of recondite languages and abstruse philological problems," and in his leisure hours in the Army he was wont to leaf through a Pali reader for pleasure.) He was an accomplished pianist. (His notion of a good time while on furlough was to spend an afternoon playing, at sight, accompaniments to Bach compositions for the recorder.) He was asocial and humorless.

After Maple was arrested, over six hundred miles away from Camp Hale, he was arraigned in a federal court in New Mexico on the charge of treason, which, as defined in the Constitution, "shall consist only in levying war against them [the United States], or in adhering to their enemies, giving them aid and comfort." "No person," the Constitution adds, "shall be convicted of treason unless on the testimony of two witnesses to the same overt act, or on confession in open court." Since Maple did adhere to and simultaneously give aid and comfort to the enemy, and since more than enough witnesses to his acts were available, he undoubtedly could have been convicted of treason, a capital offense. (A civilian in Detroit was pronounced guilty of treason in 1942 and sentenced to life imprisonment for harboring and protecting only one escaped prisoner of war in his home for two days, certainly a lesser offense than furnishing two prisoners with things of value for three days while automotively transporting them out of the country.) But because Maple was a soldier, the Army was entitled to try him, and it did.

Just how far Maple intended to go, literally and figuratively, is a question that was subsequently brought up by the accused himself, and his answer to it, or one of his answers to it, was his principal argument in his own behalf.

"He wanted to go to Germany," said the witness, "and, of course, I thought it was a joke. Who wants to go to Germany in wartime?"

Maple was under no compulsion to take an active role in the trial; he could have kept mum; but he chose to take an extremely active and articulate role. During the presentation of the case against him, he personally cross-examined most of the prosecution's important witnesses. He did this with uncommon detachment; nor did he seem unduly ruffled when the prosecution introduced a confession he had written voluntarily within a week after his arrest, while he was being interrogated by the F.B.I. In that statement, he had said that his object was to get to Germany and to establish liaison between the Nazi government and his pro-German cronies in the 620th, who were anxious to do their bit for the Reich but couldn't decide whether to try their hand at sabotage, espionage, or insurrection. He had said, furthermore, that when the Army indicated, by assigning him to an outfit like the 620th, that he was under special surveillance, he had considered himself no longer bound by the oath of allegiance he had taken at induction to serve his country loyally; in fact, he had felt justified in disserving it. However, when Maple took the stand, as the first defense witness, he said that the statement he had given the F.B.I. was not to be taken seriously. He had written it with his tongue in his cheek, he claimed, more or less as a publicity release calculated to call wide attention to the treason trial in a civil court that he then anticipated facing. Now, he explained, he had prepared a new statement, showing that he had never intended to go to Germany — or, for that matter, to Mexico — and that he had always been a patriotic citizen and soldier. And, if it pleased the court, he would read the second statement, which would clear everything up, and the court had his word for it that this time he wasn't spoofing.

To set the stage, Maple had his civilian counsel ask him a few biographical questions. He said, in response to them, that he had been born in San Diego on September 10, 1920; had concentrated on sciences and languages — Latin and German — in high school; and had been "regarded as one of the better student pianists" of that city. He liked horseback riding, surfboarding, and swimming, and one of his eardrums had had to be pierced nine times because of an infection he had picked up, it was thought, in a Y.M.C.A. pool. After he had graduated, first in his class, from high school, he had gone on to Harvard, where he had got a B.A., *magna cum laude*. The counsel, who was less of a linguist than his client, asked, "*Magna cum laude* means, of course, 'with the highest praise'?"

"'With high praise,'" said the witness, thereby undoubtedly dimming the splendor of the impression the lawyer had hoped to create.

They moved along hastily to a catalogue of the subjects Maple had pursued at college — engineering, mechanical engineering, history, chemistry, physics, mathematics, literature, and languages.

"How many languages have you studied?" asked the counsel. "English, of course — we know that."

"I am familiar with practically any European language except the Balkan languages," said Maple.

"Name what languages you are familiar with."

"With varying degrees of proficiency — Russian, Polish, German, Hungarian, Italian, Spanish, Portuguese, Danish, Swedish, Icelandic, and Dutch."

"French also?"

"French also."

"Any of the so-called classical languages?"

"I was also familiar with Latin, Greek, and Sanskrit. That is the ancient language of India. Also some Semitic languages — Babylonian, Assyrian, Hebrew to a slight extent, and Arabic. I was also engaged in the study of Maltese."

Then, while the court was probably still blinking, Maple launched into his prepared *apologia pro vita sua,* a speech more than seven thousand words long.

While it is not my intention in the course of this statement [he began] to deny my part in the events of February 15th, 16th, 17th, and 18th, it is my intent to define more clearly the role which I played in those events and to give meaning to that role. *Acta exteriora indicant interiora secreta* — acts indicate intentions — the learned trial judge advocate will probably affirm, and with that resounding phrase invoke the whole doctrine of constructive intent, but the court will, I am sure, not follow him in his folly. Treason is, in the United States, an extraordinarily rare crime — an almost unknown crime, and the court will rightly feel that, although an American may under certain circumstances associate himself with the enemy, his intent will probably — almost must — be other than treasonable. I am an American, with family firmly rooted in the Revolution. Some English and Irish infusion you will find four generations back. German stock you will seek in vain. My preparatory education was in the public schools of California. I have never travelled abroad. If then, as an American, I find it necessary to associate myself, under certain circumstances, with the enemy of America, my intent can hardly be dismissed as obviously treasonable. On the contrary, both those circumstances and my intent must be examined closely. This statement will serve as a guide to the examination of those circumstances and to the understanding of my intent. To obtain a proper perspective on the events immediately involved in this case, it is necessary to go back to the fall of 1940 . . .

Going back, Maple said that he had studied German in high school, and that in college, being obliged, in his pursuit of comparative philology, to specialize in one language, he had naturally picked that one. By studying German at Harvard, and associating with others who were doing so, he had acquired the reputation of being a "cultural German sympathizer." "No one had any illusion, however, that this sympathy extended to the political sphere," he added. In the fall of 1940, his senior year, he had begun to think about a postgraduate career. He had decided in favor of teaching comparative philology, and a logical step toward that was a Doctor's degree in the subject. "The University of Berlin is usually regarded as the outstanding institution for the study of philology," he said. So he had resolved to go there and, unable to figure out any other way of financing the venture, had hit upon the notion of getting the German government to foot the bill. He had felt that the Nazis would not consider his reputation as a cultural German sympathizer adequate warranty of getting a decent return on such an investment, so he had decided to try to dupe them into thinking he was one of their kind by acquiring the reputation of being a German political sympathizer. To accomplish this, he had taken advantage of his membership in the Verein Turmwächter, the Harvard German club, a cultural organization devoted in part to the singing of non-political songs. At one of its meetings, he had pretended to show where he stood politically by singing "Die Wacht am Rhein" and the Horst Wessel Song, and then he had resigned, maintaining that the club's pussyfooting attitude toward National Socialism was irreconcilable with his own forthright espousal of it. The idea, he said, had been to impress Herr Doktor Herbert Scholz, the German consul in Boston. The story had got into the campus daily, and the Boston papers had followed it up. He went on:

> Whereas I had intended only to convince certain German officials that my attitude toward Nazi Germany was sympathetic, I had ended by convincing the whole press that I was the recognized Nazi leader of Boston. My discomfort was only increased by the fact that any statement which I might make to refute these charges would also be my farewell statement to the University of Berlin. . . . At the present time, in the midst of a war against Germany, it seems incredible that I should have allowed such statements to go unchallenged — that I should indeed have been the somewhat unwitting instigator of these statements. In October of 1940, however, the necessity for a complete refutation of the charges was not so evident. . . . According to the public opinion poll of *Fortune* magazine — noted for its accuracy — approximately seventy-three per cent of the American public disfavored becoming involved in the war even if Germany should be victorious, and Germany seemed well on the road to victory. It was no more un-American to be pro-German than it was to be pro-British. This was not our war.

The only other witnesses for the defense were Maple's parents. They had no direct knowledge of his alleged crimes and could testify only as to his character. His mother said that he had always been a sensitive, nervous, highly emotional boy, who found association with older people more agreeable than association with his contemporaries, and that he had never expressed any Nazi-like opinions to her. His father said that Dale had an "invincible mind" but had always been deficient in judgment, which very likely accounted for the unconventionality of his actions. "There is before you a most unusual man," he told the court. "I say man because he is twenty-three years old, while on the other hand he is just a boy, with all the fanciful dreams and ideals and imaginations of a boy. A man with the mind of almost a genius, a mind that grasps the knowledge of the deepest science almost with the reading of the printed word, a brain capable of absorbing knowledge at a rate almost unbelievable."

Then came doctors, physical and psychiatric. Inevitably, Maple's counsel brought up the question of his sanity. He had been hit by an automobile at the age of nine, and his parents had testified, without going into clinical details, that his "brain jelly" had been "scattered" in the accident, but two doctors who had given him physical examinations at the Disciplinary Barracks told the court that they could find no trace of damage to his skull or his brain. Four Army doctors with psychiatric training then took the stand. Two of them had examined Maple before the trial, and the others had done so during a ten-day recess ordered by the court for that purpose. The first psychiatrist said that Maple had an I.Q. of 152, denoting "very superior intelligence," and a mental age of twenty-two years and ten months. He said that the accused was conspicuous for a "bland smile — even when discussing things of utmost gravity to him," and for "poverty of emotional tone." Maple, he testified, seemed to have no remorse and no awareness of the seriousness of the offense with which he was charged; indeed, so prodigious was his composure that, instead of brooding about his fate, he had been diverting himself while in custody by solving problems in higher mathematics. "His mood is not in keeping with the situation," the psychiatrist went on. "Thus he talks with a smile about the possibility of being sentenced to hanging for his offense and at the same time volunteers to be restored to the service, providing he is not returned to a unit composed of subversive elements." The psychiatrist continued:

He shows no understanding for the discrepancy between his intellectual reasoning and the emotional poverty and lack of identification with his native country and to that extent he shows impaired insight. There is also lack of judgment in his reasoning of the causes for the present offense. He considers himself a "professional soldier," but he does not appreciate the inconsistency in violating his oath by escaping in the company of German prisoners of war.... It is a pathetic indictment of the parental and educational influences to which he was exposed that this "intellectual genius" could proceed through life and graduate from a university without absorbing any emotional warmth or developing any lasting attachments and criteria of adult behavior beyond the philosophical rationalizations which singled him out for outbursts of publicity and notoriety.

The second psychiatrist echoed the first and added that, in his opinion, many of Maple's actions were attributable to latent hatred of his father and an Oedipus complex. He then said:

He has been thinking so much and fighting within himself at all times that being ready to be a traitor didn't mean anything. He wasn't doing this in a sense of probably hurting his country. He didn't care whom he hurt, as long as he secured his own benefit. He is in a way like a youngster who has been given a spanking from father and cries in the corner and thinks he would rather be dead and wouldn't everybody be sorry they were so mean to me.

The defense, undoubtedly anticipating a negative reply, asked this psychiatrist if he would call Maple "vicious." The doctor answered that Maple was "a very vicious type" and explained what he meant:

Ability to say things without feeling them is very much vicious, if it is combined with a person who has the kind of intellect the accused has. The leaders of the Nazi party have the same kind of ability. They are the kind of people who will rationalize things but not feel them, aren't they?

The psychiatrist might have made an even more pointed historical analogy by referring to the case of Major General Benedict Arnold, who, not long after he tried to sell out West Point to the British and then fled to England, said of his detractors, "Conscious of the rectitude of my intentions, I shall treat their malice and calumnies with contempt and neglect," and of whom General George Washington said succinctly, "He wants feeling." The third psychiatrist didn't hold with the "poverty of emotional tone" theory. He said that a person of Maple's background could quite easily have believed that he was doing right in doing what he did. "He doesn't actually feel that he has committed a military offense," this witness said. "He thinks he has done the government of the United States a good turn in exposing this situation." The final psychiatrist didn't say much, but, like his three colleagues, he stated that he had arrived at a firm conclusion: the accused was sane.

Maple was thereupon sentenced to life imprisonment and moved from the Disciplinary Barracks to the Federal Penitentiary at Leavenworth, six miles from the scene of his trial. After he had been there seventeen months, the Army reduced his sentence to ten years. If he is credited with the maximum time off for good behavior, he will be released not later than February, 1951.

As the months have passed in Leavenworth, Maple has taught classes in trigonometry, geometry, algebra, shorthand, statistics, public speaking, French, and English. His pupils in the last course were a group of Spanish-speaking prisoners of Mexican extraction, and, taking advantage of an opportunity to do some field work in the interrelation of languages, he addressed them every so often in Latin, noting with pleasure that they seemed to comprehend him. Maple has also been a clerk in the office of the prison supervisor of education and has worked in the prison bakery; has been a trainer for a prizefighter; has played the organ and led the church choir; has done some philological research in Old Bulgarian; has written a psychological monograph on the identification and analysis of reading difficulties in adults; has contributed to the *New Era,* a magazine published quarterly by and for the inmates; and has helped a couple of fellow-prisoners get reestablished in civilian life after being let out by giving them letters to people he thought might be able to find them jobs. Of one of them, a fellow who he heard was nonetheless having a tough time becoming readjusted, Maple wrote, not long ago, "I have found that the best way to help people who are impatient is to have all the more patience myself. I know, too, how difficult it can be sometimes, but I have never found it to fail in the end."

Let us return quickly to the psychiatrists' reports on Dale Maple's sanity. Yes, certainly he was sane, they all agreed. They also found that he had an IQ of 152, denoting superior intelligence. Dale's father characterized his son's mind as "invincible" but highly deficient in judgment. Dale, he noted, is a man capable of absorbing knowledge at unbelievable rates, of grasping complex scientific concepts and facts at first reading; yet, he is still a small child in his dreams, behavior, and goals.

Dale's bland smile and poverty of emotion were noted by one of the psychiatrists. In that vein, Dale talked about the possibility of being sentenced to hanging for his offense and at the same time volunteered to be restored to the armed service. There are no connections between Dale's heart and mind — between his bright mind and retarded emotions. ("It is a pathetic indictment of the parental and educational influences to which he was exposed that this intellectual genius could proceed through life and graduate from a university without absorbing any emotional warmth or developing any lasting attachments and criteria of adult behavior.")

The defense attorney (expecting a negative reply) asked a psychiatrist if he would call Maple "vicious." Yes, replied the doctor, and went on to spell out the danger of societies developing persons of high intellect with deficient feelings. Interestingly enough, even George Washington had recognized this problem in his assessment of Benedict Arnold, of whom the general said, "He wants feeling."

In thinking about Dale Maple and other highly gifted individuals, one might differentiate between the competent gifted and the creative gifted person. Competent gifted persons are clearly in a class by themselves developmentally and academically. Creatively gifted individuals may or may not be academically successful, but they attempt metaphorical and conceptual leaps. The creative person, as Albert Szent-Gygorgy (Nobel prize winner) put it, sees what everyone has seen and thinks what no one has thought.

Terman's long-term follow-up of gifted children found them at mid-life to be successful, competent personally and financially, somewhat conservative, and unaesthetic in their tastes.[3] On the other hand, the Goertzels' study of eminent persons describes a different group — individuals who were troubled by broken homes, poverty, and physical handicaps, and who were unpopular with

---

[3] L. M. Terman and M. H. Oden, "The Gifted Group at Mid-life: Thirty-five Years' Follow-up of the Superior Child" in *Genetic Studies of Genius,* vol. 5 (Stanford, CA: Stanford University Press, 1959).

peers. More than sixty percent disliked their teachers, and a still larger majority disliked school.[4] One might describe this group of creative persons as inventive, determined, individualistic, enthusiastic, and intuitive. The competent group might be contrasted as responsible, sincere, dependable, clear thinking, logical, and socially minded. The creative gifted person is not fearful of standing alone but more often does so in good cause. Dale Maple selected an area of aloneness that was rebellious. One wonders where he would have chosen to stand alone had there been no Hitler and no World War II.

People in the so-called "genius" category — as contrasted to the "gifted" — are conceivably subjected to greater inner and outer emotional stress. Nevertheless, this should not suggest that Dale Maple and his experiences are typical or even representative of the very bright or very creative person. Frank Barron, reporting on the findings of the Institute of Personality Assessment and Research at Berkeley, suggested that rebellion — an adamant insistence on one's own perception of knowledge and self — can be a sign of psychological health. "We should not be too hasty in giving a bad name to what gives us a bad time," he cautioned (p. 144).[5] Barron also noted that psychologically healthy persons have a tendency to do what they think is right irrespective of social convention or desirability. The contributing geniuses of our species may not have been actualized if they had been overly concerned about the impact of their actions.

Unlike Dale Maple, though, a healthy genius has a good sense of the real world and rarely jumps off the deep end without judging the distance. As Barron noted, the effectively original person does regress into primitive and fantastic modes of thought, but without wandering off and getting lost in this state of mind. If the ego is strong and healthy, it encourages and supports this kind of regression because the individual has confidence in his or her ability to differentiate what is inside from what is without. In other words, when these persons can clearly define, differentiate, and connect imaginative creations and rational thinking, they can actualize both processes more effectively.

Apparently the highly creative person — as contrasted with the bright, competent person — places great emphasis on intuitive

---

[4] Victor and Mildred Goertzel, *Cradles of Eminence* (Boston: Little, Brown, 1962).

[5] Frank Barron, *Creativity and Psychological Health* (Princeton, NJ: D. Van Nostrand Co., 1963).

or primary process thinking. Einstein, in his reply to Jacques Hadamard — who was attempting to discover how creative mathematicians thought — described his own methods: "Words or language . . . do not seem to play any role in my mechanism of thought. The psychical entities which seem to serve as elements in thought are certain signs and more or less clear images which can be voluntarily reproduced and combined. . . . It is also clear that the desire to arrive finally at logically connected concepts is the emotional basis of this rather vague play with the above-mentioned elements. But taken from a psychological viewpoint, this combinatory play seems to be the essential feature in productive thought" (p. 142).[6]

In a sense, Einstein in his early school life could have been a Dale Maple. When Einstein's father asked the principal what profession Albert should be trained for, the answer was, "It doesn't matter; he'll never make a success of anything." (p. 10). Einstein was slow and spoke haltingly, often hesitating for embarrassing lengths of time before answering simple questions. But it didn't seem to bother him. In fact, he pointed out in his serious, playful manner how it helped him: "I sometimes ask myself how did it come that I was the one to develop the theory of relativity. The reason, I think, is that a normal adult never stops to think about problems of space and time. These are things which he has thought of as a child. But my intellectual development was retarded, as a result of which I began to wonder about space and time only when I had already grown up. Naturally I could go deeper into the problem than a child with normal abilities" (p. 11). I don't suppose that the average person, including myself, really thought much about space and time as a child either, but somehow the payoff was not the same!

Notwithstanding thoughts on space and time, one can detect in Einstein and other creative persons a healthy attachment to reality, a feeling of comfort in encouraging images to play around inside them and then having the competence to direct such images toward real goals. What went wrong with Dale's brilliance? (Or did it?) If credited with good behavior at Leavenworth, he would have been released in February, 1951, and, perhaps with a little psychotherapy, could be doing all sorts of creative things in philology or psychology. He seemed to be gaining some maturational momentum at Leavenworth as a teacher, clerk, baker, prize

---

[6] Jacques Hadamard, *The Psychology of Invention in the Mathematical Field* (New York: Princeton University Press, Dover Publications, 1945).

fight trainer, organist, researcher on reading problems, writer, and good samaritan. The best way to help people who need help, he said, is to be patient. Things can be difficult but, he felt, with patience change is possible.

> *How poor are they that have not patience*
> *What wound did ever heal but by degrees?*
> *(Othello, Act II).*[7]

---

[7] William Shakespeare, "Othello," *Shakespeare's Complete Works* (Boston: Houghton Mifflin. Cambridge: Riverside Press, 1920).

QUESTIONS FOR DISCUSSION

1. Considering the realities of Dale Maple's early home and school life, what would you consider in retrospect to be some possible effective interventions that might have helped Dale become more effectively creative?

2. How would you visualize Maple's life after his release from Leavenworth?

3. School programs for the gifted and creative, when available, are sometimes classified as (a) acceleration, (b) enrichment, and (c) special classes or tracks. What do these terms mean as programs? Which one(s), if any, would have been most appropriate for Dale Maple?

4. "All geniuses are a little crazy" has been a popular belief. Do you agree with this? How would you convince someone who doesn't believe as you do?

5. Some societies identify highly gifted children early in their life and send them to separate schools, often away from their families. How do you feel about this? What are possible payoffs and dangers in this kind of program?

6. Would you consider eminent people in areas like politics, statesmanship, commerce, and labor unions to be as gifted and creative as those in the arts, music, science, and invention? If yes, what would be some major differences? If no, why not?

7. If creative people think intuitively and playfully, should that sort of "curricula" be instituted in public schools? If yes, where and how? If no, why not?

8. What are your own creative characteristics? How might these have been more effectively enhanced in your home and school life?
9. One of the psychiatrists who examined Dale Maple reflected on the fact that Dale could graduate from a first-rate university without developing any emotional warmth or lasting attachments. Is this common or uncommon? If the criticism is justified, what do you suggest be done about it?
10. Consider how the story of Dale Maple was shaped by world events. How might the story have changed if Maple had been born in 1940 instead of 1920?
11. What are Maple's explanations for his "treasonous" behavior? Can you think of other possibilities?

ADDITIONAL READINGS

- Barron, Frank, *Creativity and Psychological Health*. Princeton, NJ: D. Van Nostrand Co., 1963.
- Clark, R. W. *Einstein, The Life and Times*. New York: World Publishing, 1971.
- Goertzel, Victor, and Goertzel, Mildred. *Cradles of Eminence*. Boston: Little, Brown. 1962.
- Hadamard, Jacques. *The Psychology of Invention in the Mathematical Field*. New York: Princeton University Press, Dover Publications, 1945.
- Koestler, Arthur. *The Act of Creation*. New York: Macmillan, 1964.
- Levitt, M. *Freud and Dewey on the Nature of Man*. New York: Philosophical Library, 1960.
- Singer, J. L. *The Child's World of Make-Believe. Experimental Studies of Imaginative Play*. New York: Academic Press, 1973.
- Wallach, M., and Kogan, N. *Modes of Thinking in Young Children*. New York: Holt, Rinehart and Winston, 1965.

"The year was 2081, and everybody was finally equal"

10

Harrison Bergeron

Kurt Vonnegut, Jr.

10

We come again to a story much like H. G. Wells' "Country of the Blind," which presents the relationship of a person to a handicapped culture. In that story, the "country of the blind" is the "country of all equality." On the basis of the "211th, 212th, and 213th Amendments to the Constitution," Vonnegut has set up a Bureau of the Handicapper General, headed by Diana Moon Glampers, whose vigilant agents are out in the field enforcing the law — *everyone must be equal every which way with everyone else.*

As Conrad Festa noted, Vonnegut writes satire that often comes out as black humor. It is a kind of fiction that "has none of the scorn, resignation or hope of reform that accompanies satire. It is amoral and resists moral abstractions although it exercises our consciences" (p. 136).[1] Above all, one sees Vonnegut through his fiction as a fierce fighter for freedom — to reduce our imprisonment by our own constraints and the constraints of institutions, corporations, and government to an absolute minimum.

Many of his readers think of Vonnegut as European born and reared. Actually, he was born in middle America — Indianapolis, Indiana — in 1922, and went to Cornell, where he majored in chemistry and biology. He was captured by the Germans during the Battle of the Bulge and lived through the Allied firebombing of Dresden. "When people ask me who my culture heroes are," Vonnegut wrote in the preface to *Between Time and Timbuktu,* "I express pious gratitude for Mark Twain and James Joyce and so on. But the truth is that I am a barbarian whose deepest cultural debts are to Laurel and Hardy, Stoopnagel and Bud, Buster Keaton, Fred Allen, Jack Benny, Charlie Chaplin, Easy Aces,

---

[1] Conrad Festa, "Vonnegut's Satire," in *Vonnegut in America,* ed. J. Klinkowitz and D. Lawler (New York: Dell, 1977), pp. 133-149.

Henry Morgan and so on. They made me hilarious during the Great Depression and all the lesser depressions after that."[2]

At one point in his career, Vonnegut worked for General Electric in Schenectady, where he became convinced that corporations and government were destined to defeat the individual. If Vonnegut's writings emit a sense of the absurd, he would be the first to say that it isn't he who is absurd. In a preface to a book by Bob Elliot and Ray Goulding (Bob and Ray), he wrote, "Man is not evil . . . He is simply too hilariously stupid to survive."[3]

"Harrison Bergeron" made his first appearance in the *Magazine of Fantasy and Science Fiction* in October, 1961, and was incorporated into a volume of Vonnegut's short stories called *Welcome to the Monkey House,* published in 1968.

---

[2] Kurt Vonnegut, Jr., *Between Time and Timbuktu or Prometheus 5* (New York: Delacorte Press, 1972), p. iv.

[3] Kurt Vonnegut, Jr., "Foreword" in Bob Elliott and Ray Goulding, *Write If You Get Work: The Best of Bob and Ray* (New York: Random House, 1975), p. vii.

HARRISON BERGERON

Kurt Vonnegut, Jr.

The year was 2081, and everybody was finally equal. They weren't only equal before God and the law. They were equal every which way. Nobody was smarter than anybody else. Nobody was better looking than anybody else. Nobody was stronger or quicker than anybody else. All this equality was due to the 211th, 212th, and 213th Amendments to the Constitution, and to the unceasing vigilance of agents of the United States Handicapper General.

Some things about living still weren't quite right, though. April, for instance, still drove people crazy by not being springtime. And it was in that clammy month that the H-G men took George and Hazel Bergeron's fourteen-year-old son, Harrison, away.

It was tragic, all right, but George and Hazel couldn't think about it very hard. Hazel had a perfectly average intelligence, which meant she couldn't think about anything except in short bursts. And George, while his intelligence was way above normal, had a little mental handicap radio in his ear. He was required by law to wear it at all times. It was tuned to a government transmitter. Every twenty seconds or so, the transmitter would send out some sharp noise to keep people like George from taking unfair advantage of their brains.

George and Hazel were watching television. There were tears on Hazel's cheeks, but she'd forgotten for the moment what they were about.

"Harrison Bergeron" excerpted from the book *Welcome to the Monkey House* by Kurt Vonnegut, Jr. Copyright © 1961 by Kurt Vonnegut, Jr. Originally published in *Fantasy and Science Fiction*. Reprinted by permission of Delacorte Press/Seymour Lawrence.

On the television screen were ballerinas.

A buzzer sounded in George's head. His thoughts fled in panic, like bandits from a burglar alarm.

"That was a real pretty dance, that dance they just did," said Hazel.

"Huh?" said George.

"That dance — it was nice," said Hazel.

"Yup," said George. He tried to think a little about the ballerinas. They weren't really very good — no better than anybody else would have been, anyway. They were burdened with sash-weights and bags of birdshot, and their faces were masked, so that no one, seeing a free and graceful gesture or a pretty face, would feel like something the cat drug in. George was toying with the vague notion that maybe dancers shouldn't be handicapped. But he didn't get very far with it before another noise in his ear radio scattered his thoughts.

George winced. So did two out of the eight ballerinas.

Hazel saw him wince. Having no mental handicap herself, she had to ask George what the latest sound had been.

"Sounded like somebody hitting a milk bottle with a ball peen hammer," said George.

"I'd think it would be real interesting, hearing all the different sounds," said Hazel, a little envious. "All the things they think up."

"Um," said George.

"Only, if I was Handicapper General, you know what I would do?" said Hazel. Hazel, as a matter of fact, bore a strong resemblance to the Handicapper General, a woman named Diana Moon Glampers. "If I was Diana Moon Glampers," said Hazel, "I'd have chimes on Sunday — just chimes. Kind of in honor of religion."

"I could think, if it was just chimes," said George.

"Well — maybe make 'em real loud," said Hazel. "I think I'd make a good Handicapper General."

"Good as anybody else," said George.

"Who knows better'n I do what normal is?" said Hazel.

"Right," said George. He began to think glimmeringly about his abnormal son who was now in jail, about Harrison, but a twenty-one-gun salute in his head stopped that.

"Boy!" said Hazel, "that was a doozy, wasn't it?"

It was such a doozy that George was white and trembling, and tears stood on the rims of his red eyes. Two of the eight ballerinas had collapsed to the studio floor, were holding their temples.

"All of a sudden you look so tired," said Hazel. "Why don't you stretch out on the sofa, so's you can rest your handicap bag on the pillows, honeybunch." She was referring to the forty-seven pounds of birdshot in a canvas bag, which was padlocked around George's neck. "Go on and rest the bag for a little while," she said. "I don't care if you're not equal to me for a while."

George weighed the bag with his hands. "I don't mind it," he said. "I don't notice it any more. It's just a part of me."

"You been so tired lately — kind of wore out," said Hazel. "If there was just some way we could make a little hole in the bottom of the bag, and just take out a few of them lead balls. Just a few."

"Two years in prison and two thousand dollars fine for every ball I took out," said George. "I don't call that a bargain."

"If you could just take a few out when you came home from work," said Hazel. "I mean — you don't compete with anybody around here. You just set around."

"If I tried to get away with it," said George, "then other people'd get away with it — and pretty soon we'd be right back to the dark ages again, with everybody competing against everybody else. You wouldn't like that, would you?"

"I'd hate it," said Hazel.

"There you are," said George. "The minute people start cheating on laws, what do you think happens to society?"

If Hazel hadn't been able to come up with an answer to this question, George couldn't have supplied one. A siren was going off in his head.

"Reckon it'd fall all apart," said Hazel.

"What would?" said George blankly.

"Society," said Hazel uncertainly. "Wasn't that what you just said?"

"Who knows?" said George.

The television program was suddenly interrupted for a news bulletin. It wasn't clear at first as to what the bulletin was about, since the announcer, like all announcers, had a serious speech impediment. For about half a minute, and in a state of high excitement, the announcer tried to say, "Ladies and gentlemen —"

He finally gave up, handed the bulletin to a ballerina to read.

"That's all right —" Hazel said of the announcer, "he tried. That's the big thing. He tried to do the best he could with what God gave him. He should get a nice raise for trying so hard."

"Ladies and gentlemen —" said the ballerina, reading the bulletin. She must have been extraordinarily beautiful, because the mask she wore was hideous. And it was easy to see that she was the strongest and most graceful of all the dancers, for her handicap bags were as big as those worn by two-hundred-pound men.

And she had to apologize at once for her voice, which was a very unfair voice for a woman to use. Her voice was a warm, luminous, timeless melody. "Excuse me —" she said and she began again, making her voice absolutely uncompetitive.

"Harrison Bergeron, age fourteen," she said in a grackle squawk, "has just escaped from jail, where he was held on suspicion of plotting to overthrow the government. He is a genius and an athlete, is under-handicapped, and should be regarded as extremely dangerous."

A police photograph of Harrison Bergeron was flashed on the screen — upside down, then sideways, upside down again, then right side up. The picture showed the full length of Harrison against a background calibrated in feet and inches. He was exactly seven feet tall.

The rest of Harrison's appearance was Halloween and hardware. Nobody had ever born heavier handicaps. He had outgrown hindrances faster than the H-G men could think them up. Instead of a little ear radio for a mental handicap, he wore a tremendous pair of earphones, and spectacles with thick wavy lenses. The spectacles were intended to make him not only half blind, but to give him whanging headaches besides.

Scrap metal was hung all over him. Ordinarily, there was a certain symmetry, a military neatness to the handicaps issued to strong people, but Harrison looked like a walking junkyard. In the race of life, Harrison carried three hundred pounds.

And to offset his good looks, the H-G men required that ne wear at all times a red rubber ball for a nose, keep his eyebrows shaved off, and cover his even white teeth with black caps at snaggle-tooth random.

"If you see this boy," said the ballerina, "do not — I repeat, do not — try to reason with him."

There was the shriek of a door being torn from its hinges.

Screams and barking cries of consternation came from the television set. The photograph of Harrison Bergeron on the screen jumped again and again, as though dancing to the tune of an earthquake.

George Bergeron correctly identified the earthquake, and well he might have — for many was the time his own home had danced to the same crashing tune. "My God —" said George, "that must be Harrison!"

The realization was blasted from his mind instantly by the sound of an automobile collision in his head.

When George could open his eyes again, the photograph of Harrison was gone. A living, breathing Harrison filled the screen.

Clanking, clownish, and huge, Harrison stood in the center of the studio. The knob of the uprooted studio door was still in his hand. Ballerinas, technicians, musicians, and announcers cowered on their knees before him, expecting to die.

"I am the Emperor!" cried Harrison. "Do you hear? I am the Emperor! Everybody must do what I say at once!" He stamped his foot and the studio shook.

"Even as I stand here —" he bellowed, "crippled, hobbled, sickened — I am a greater ruler than any man who ever lived! Now watch me become what I *can* become!"

Harrison tore the straps of his handicap harness like wet tissue paper, tore straps guaranteed to support five thousand pounds.

Harrison's scrap-iron handicaps crashed to the floor.

Harrison thrust his thumbs under the bar of the padlock that secured his head harness. The bar snapped like celery. Harrison smashed his headphones and spectacles against the wall.

He flung away his rubber-ball nose, revealed a man that would have awed Thor, the god of thunder.

"I shall now select my Empress!" he said, looking down on the cowering people. "Let the first woman who dares rise to her feet claim her mate and her throne!"

A moment passed, and then a ballerina arose, swaying like a willow.

Harrison plucked the mental handicap from her ear, snapped off her physical handicaps with marvellous delicacy. Last of all, he removed her mask.

She was blindingly beautiful.

"Now —" said Harrison, taking her hand, "shall we show the people the meaning of the word dance? Music!" he commanded.

The musicians scrambled back into their chairs, and Harrison stripped them of their handicaps, too. "Play your best," he told them, "and I'll make you barons and dukes and earls."

The music began. It was normal at first — cheap, silly, false. But Harrison snatched two musicians from their chairs, waved them like batons as he sang the music as he wanted it played. He slammed them back into their chairs.

The music began again and was much improved.

Harrison and his Empress merely listened to the music for a while — listened gravely, as though synchronizing their heartbeats with it.

They shifted their weights to their toes.

Harrison placed his big hands on the girl's tiny waist, letting her sense the weightlessness that would soon be hers.

And then, in an explosion of joy and grace, into the air they sprang!

Not only were the laws of the land abandoned, but the law of gravity and the laws of motion as well.

They reeled, whirled, swiveled, flounced, capered, gamboled, and spun.

They leaped like deer on the moon.

The studio ceiling was thirty feet high, but each leap brought the dancers nearer to it.

It became their obvious intention to kiss the ceiling.

They kissed it.

And then, neutralizing gravity with love and pure will, they remained suspended in air inches below the ceiling, and they kissed each other for a long, long time.

It was then that Diana Moon Glampers, the Handicapper General, came into the studio with a double-barreled ten-gauge shotgun. She fired twice, and the Emperor and the Empress were dead before they hit the floor.

Diana Moon Glampers loaded the gun again. She aimed it at the musicians and told them they had ten seconds to get their handicaps back on.

It was then that the Bergerons' television tube burned out.

Hazel turned to comment about the blackout to George. But George had gone out into the kitchen for a can of beer.

George came back in with the beer, paused while a handicap signal shook him up. And then he sat down again. "You been crying?" he said to Hazel.

"Yup," she said.

"What about?" he said.

"I forget," she said. "Something real sad on television."

"What was it?" he said.

"It's all kind of mixed up in my mind," said Hazel.

"Forget sad things," said George.

"I always do," said Hazel.

"That's my girl," said George. He winced. There was the sound of a rivetting gun in his head.

"Gee — I could tell that one was a doozy," said Hazel.

"You can say that again," said George.

"Gee —" said Hazel, "I could tell that one was a doozy."

Harrison Bergeron is the last of our handicapped protagonists — except in this case the protagonist may well be the United States Handicapper General. As you were reading the story, you may have found yourself thinking about Nunez and his problems in *The Country of the Blind.*

Cultural characteristics, like personality characteristics, are not always clear, consistent, and understandable. Historically, American culture, born out of making one's way on the frontier, subscribes to the notion of individuality. One gets ahead in our society by doing something, by achievement and accomplishment. Inheriting wealth may be an excellent start, but it's what you do with it that counts. The accompanying concepts of freedom and equality of opportunity have been activated in stressful times in the form of social programs like Franklin Roosevelt's New Deal, Lyndon Johnson's War on Poverty, programs on civil rights for minorities and women, and such legislation as PL 94-142.

Above all, our cultural values support the doctrine of fairness. During the New Deal days, which came during an economic depression, this notion implied that the people who wanted to work ought not to be deprived of the opportunity to do so. New arrangements between concepts of individualism and government came into being, including agencies to provide more opportunities for those disenfranchised by the depression. In time, these agencies became the alphabet soup of Washington — NRA, NYA, WPA, SEC, NLRB, and SSA. Some remain to this day; others are forgotten ancestors to present-day programs. The thinking during the New Deal days was that it wasn't fair or equitable for people who wanted to work, to achieve, to succeed, not to have an opportunity to do so.

Lyndon Johnson, in his war on poverty, took another giant step toward fairness. Not only must we help those who are handicapped by a lack of jobs and work opportunities, he said, but we must extend a helping hand to *all* citizens, especially those who are handicapped economically, ethnically, and culturally. The concept of fairness as applied to blacks, Mexican-Americans, poor Appalachians, American-Indians, and others produced a host of legislation, Supreme Court decisions, and popular acceptance, representing another stride on the road to equal opportunity for all.

Fairness as a philosophy, however, is a long way from fairness in practice. If one is to have equal opportunity to succeed and achieve, one needs to be close enough to the starting line to get into the race. Affirmative Action may raise the numbers of disadvantaged who can take advantage of higher education, but it cannot guarantee the necessary skills and experiences required by institutions of higher education to be successful in such achievement. Our society becomes somewhat anxious when equal opportunity to *try* comes out as equal achievement whether or not one tries. J. R. Poole, an English political scientist, pursued this conflict in an interesting fashion. Should equal opportunity be simply a *carte blanche* to get in the "game?" Doesn't the term "handicap" as applied, for example, to horse racing (and other fair-minded sporting events) imply lessening the weight on some horses to give them an equal chance to win? Also, must we all run on the same track? Must success be defined by a "melting pot" philosophy or can diversity in achievement goals and processes be incorporated as an acceptable cultural value?[3]

The equal opportunity/equal achievement controversy becomes most visible and relevant to handicapped children who are retarded, as well as those with highly creative skills and talents. Should retarded children who conscientiously try to do their best in school be denied graduation because they cannot pass state level basic skill examinations? When standards are set beyond the capacities of the handicapped, should they be doubly penalized? Conversely, should the merits of the gifted be discounted and reduced in value? Realistically, we don't expect blind people to drive or deaf people to conduct orchestras. Being deaf, nevertheless, didn't stop Beethoven from conducting his Ninth Symphony.

We are not so distant from 1984 or 2081 to treat Vonnegut's fable as nonsense. During certain periods in our history, budding Diana Moon Glamperses have prospered. Societies that pride themselves on individuality and diversity must also pride themselves on their diligence and vigilance in protecting and enhancing these rights. Equal opportunity for all must never drift into sameness for each.

One of our society's major conceptual difficulties in this regard is our widespread belief that bright and creative children are already better equipped to achieve and learn than others. Why help the winners? When these children grow up, they will naturally become the most effective and competent adults in our society. Do such children really need a boost? Indeed, the gifted

---

[3] J. R. Poole, *The Pursuit of Equality in American History* (Berkeley: University of California Press, 1978).

and creative group that Terman and his colleagues followed into adulthood were found to have these virtues in addition to being nonaesthetic and politically conservative.[4] Most were bright and middle class — the kind of "good" student that any overwrought teachers drool over.

In contrast, the Goertzels, who studied the childhood of 400 gifted and creative persons, retrospectively, found that future eminent and creative adults were not exactly good or highly cherished students in school. Most had little patience for or interest in routine or drill; a majority of them were less than popular with their classmates. Over sixty percent disliked school with more than moderate intensity.[5]

Schools serve parents and society as well as children. Often, educational goals include other necessary outcomes like socialization, disciplined behavior, and learning to manage rules. The gifted and creative child may be less able to see these goals as important or relevant. Most punishing to them are images held by many teachers, parents, and other loving adults that these children have larger and more easily filled brains; it follows, then, that they should learn more, achieve more, do more, score more, and work more — in short, do what such children find most repugnant — more of the same. Perhaps this is what Vonnegut had in mind when he has Harrison proclaim, "Even as I stand here — crippled, hobbled, sickened — I am a greater ruler than any man who ever lived! Now watch me become what I *can* become," as he tears off his handicapping harness.

Gifted and talented children tend to be, by their very nature, disturbing youngsters. They are not afraid to play leap frog with metaphors and to seek the snarks and platypuses of our universe. Can they survive our coercive institutions and our distrust of the unknown? Where are the Diana Moon Glamperses in our minds and values? Can Harrison survive in the world of tomorrow?

---

[4] L. M. Termen and M. H. Oden, "The Gifted Group at Mid-Life: Thirty-five Years' Follow-up of the Superior Child," in *Genetic Studies of Genius*, Vol. 5 (Stanford, CA: Stanford University Press, 1959).

[5] Victor and Mildred Goertzel, *Cradles of Eminence* (Boston: Little, Brown & Co., 1962).

QUESTIONS FOR DISCUSSION

1. Is there any reality to the story, or is it a piece of science fiction? On balance, what can you see as real and what as sheer fantasy?

2. In "Harrison Bergeron" Vonnegut seems to warn us that by 2081 bureaucratic government may completely control individual behavior and outlaw any deviations from the norm. What factors appear to confirm this trend? Do you see any possibilities for changing or reversing it?

3. Consider the relationship between the number and complexity of societal rules or laws and individual freedoms. Must an increase in rules necessarily reduce individual degrees of freedom?

4. Professor J. R. Poole, a Cambridge University professor, has suggested that the United States is in a continuing dilemma about its commitment to equality. Equal access to the resources, or equal opportunity, is seesawing with equality of results, or equitable distribution of resources. To a great extent, this is the dilemma that the Supreme Court attempted to resolve in the recent Bakke case. What implication does this seesaw have for handicapped persons?

5. "Harrison Bergeron" relates readily to the problems of the gifted and talented and society's inability to enhance and support such far-out individuals. What other kinds of handicapping conditions would also be relevant to the theme of the story?

6. What does the name "Diana Moon Glampers" do to your emotional and cognitive perception of the Handicapper General? Who do you suggest on stage or screen, past or present, might best play her role? Why?

7. Could you outline or write an anti-"Harrison Bergeron" story suggesting other relationships, values, and outcomes? Could you make a heroine out of Ms. Glampers and semi-villains out of George, Hazel, and Harrison? Try it

ADDITIONAL READINGS

- Bertalanfly, Ludwig. *Robots, Men and Minds.* New York: Braziller, 1967.
- Crutchfield, Richard. "Conformity and Creative Thinking." In *Contemporary Approaches to Creative Thinking,* edited by H. Gruber, G. Terrill, and M. Wertheimer. New York: Atherton Press, 1962.
- Csikszentmihalyi, M. *Beyond Boredom and Anxiety.* San Francisco: Jossey-Bass, 1975.
- Freud, Sigmund. *On Creativity and the Unconscious.* New York: Harper and Row, 1958.
- Ghiselin, B., ed. *The Creative Process.* Berkeley: University of California Press, 1955. (also Mentor, 1964)
- Goertzel, Victor and Mildred. *Cradles of Eminence.* Boston: Little, Brown, 1962.
- Hampden-Turner, Charles. *Radical Man.* New York: Doubleday, 1971.
- Hersey, John. *The Child Buyer.* New York: Knopf (also Bantam) 1960.
- Hofstadter, Richard. *Anti-Intellectualism in American Life.* New York: Knopf, 1963.
- Jones, Richard M. *Fantasy and Feeling in Education.* New York: New York University Press, 1968.
- Klinkowitz, Jerome, and Lawler, Donald. *Vonnegut in America.* New York: Dell, 1977.
- Poole, J. R. *The Pursuit of Equality in American History.* Berkeley: University of California Press, 1978.
- Salk, Jonas. *The Survival of the Wisest.* New York: Harper and Row, 1973.
- Sanford, Nevitt. *Self and Society: Social Change and Individual Development.* New York: Atherton, 1966.
- Stewart, George. *The Year of the Oath.* New York: Doubleday, 1950.
- Whitehead, Alfred N. *The Aims of Education.* New York: Macmillan, 1929.

Epilogue

What can we say about our cast of people, experiences, and outcomes? On the one hand we have Nunez and Harrison Bergeron, with no apparent personal difficulties until entering an environment in which they do not fit. Nunez could possibly escape by scaling the Andes mountains. Harrison is not as fortunate. In a sense, Mr. Foreman, as verger at St. Peters, Neville Square was also personally and socially comfortable until the new vicar "with resolute benignity" decided to press the issue of his illiteracy.

On the other hand, we have Scott Moss and his family attempting to cope with aphasia and Johnny Bonham without limbs, taste, smell, hearing, or vision, seeking a way out. Then there are Algernon and his relationship to Eulalia; John Singer and Spiros Antonapoulis, two deaf friends in a small Southern town; Stevie Verloc, the unwitting pawn in an adult "game"; Brian Casey, a post polio politician and Sam Perkins, his alter ego; and our talented philologist, Dale Maple, as he relates to San Diego High, Harvard University, and the U.S. Army.

They are all a singular lot. Nothing in John Singer, a deaf person, sets him apart from other lonely persons. Brian Casey doesn't have to be a cripple to be a "bastard"; nor does Dale Maple have to be gifted to be devoid of feeling.

We live in biological and social systems. It helps when both systems are integral and healthy. It also helps to know that we are all alike and we are all different. Nothing in the human condition is alien to any one of us. Humankind has no grotesques — only persons seeking themselves.